SLAVES OF THE EMPEROR

Slaves of the Emperor

SERVICE, PRIVILEGE, AND STATUS
IN THE QING EIGHT BANNERS

David C. Porter

Columbia University Press
New York

Columbia University Press
Publishers Since 1893
New York   Chichester, West Sussex
cup.columbia.edu

Copyright © 2024 Columbia University Press
All rights reserved

Library of Congress Cataloging-in-Publication Data
Names: Porter, David C. (David Campbell), author.
Title: Slaves of the emperor : service, privilege, and status in the Qing Eight Banners / David C. Porter.
Other titles: Service, privilege, and status in the Qing Eight Banners
Description: New York : Columbia University Press, [2023] | Includes bibliographical references and index.
Identifiers: LCCN 2023025904 (print) | LCCN 2023025905 (ebook) | ISBN 9780231212762 (hardback) | ISBN 9780231212779 (trade paperback) | ISBN 9780231559553 (ebook)
Subjects: LCSH: Banner system. | China—History, Military—1644–1912. | China—Social life and customs—1644–1912.
Classification: LCC DS754.15 .P67 2023 (print) | LCC DS754.15 (ebook) | DDC 951.03—dc23/eng/20230620
LC record available at https://lccn.loc.gov/2023025904
LC ebook record available at https://lccn.loc.gov/2023025905

Cover design: Elliott S. Cairns
Cover image: Sodacan / Wikimedia Commons / CC BY-SA 4.0

Contents

Acknowledgments vii

Introduction 1

1 The Qing Status System 19

2 Who Belonged in the Banners? The Makeup of the Qing Service Elite 49

3 Duty, Service, and Status Performance 69

4 Privilege and State Support 96

5 A Female Service Elite: Status, Ethnicity, and Qing Bannerwomen 124

6 A Comparative History of Service Elites 147

7 Challenging the Service Elite Model 174

8 Expulsion, Resistance, and the Return of the Service Elite 200

Conclusion 227

Appendix: Reign Names, Dates, and Abbreviations 243
Source Abbreviations 245
Notes 249
Bibliography 309
Index 325

Acknowledgments

This book is the result of research and writing conducted at several institutions across more than a decade. I have been helped along the way by dozens of friends, teachers, colleagues, archivists, librarians, university staff, and family members in innumerable ways, and I will not manage to thank all of them here, nor to offer sufficient gratitude to those I do acknowledge. But without their assistance, friendship, and care, this book would never have come to be.

My advisor, Mark Elliott, certainly does not agree with everything that I argue in the pages that follow, in which I sometimes challenge ideas that he developed in his own work. And yet he has never ceased to support this project or my career, whether through explaining the finer points of Eight Banner administration when I was confused by an archival document, reading and commenting on numerous drafts of different stages of the project, or writing endless letters of support for fellowship and job applications. Moreover, although I have sought to advance a different understanding of the basis of the banner system than he did in *The Manchu Way*, my book would not have been possible had I not been able to rely on its findings.

The rest of my Harvard advisors also provided me with essential support. Michael Szonyi gave quick and straightforward feedback. David Howell and Kelly O'Neill provided me with both the training to enable the comparative work that I do in this book and the confidence to trust that those comparisons have value. My fellow PhD students, some of whom remain my closest friends, created the intellectual community in which I worked out many of my core ideas—Devin Fitzgerald, Billy French, Eric Schluessel, and Michael Thornton deserve particular thanks.

Although the COVID-19 pandemic interrupted my postdoc at the Council on East Asian Studies at Yale, I still benefited tremendously from the advice and support of Fabian Drixler, Valerie Hansen, and Peter Perdue. The Council funded a monthlong trip to the First Historical Archives in Beijing in 2019, which enabled me to complete the additional research necessary to transform my dissertation into what I think is a much more interesting book. It also put together a manuscript workshop for me, where I was lucky enough to receive substantial and valuable feedback from Pamela Crossley and Matthew Mosca, both of whom have continued to provide advice through the process of getting the manuscript accepted for publication.

At McGill, Gal Gvili, Jeehee Hong, Lorenz Lüthi, Griet Vankeerberghen, and Juan Wang have all welcomed me as a colleague despite the uncertainty of how long I would be able to remain. I am especially grateful for the two opportunities that I have had to present ideas from my book at the Yan P. Lin Centre and at the Department of East Asian Studies.

Much of the research for this book was conducted as a graduate student with the help of funding provided by the U.S. State Department, via the Fulbright U.S. Student Program, and by Harvard University's Frederick Sheldon Traveling Fellowship. I conducted that research at the First Historical Archives in Beijing and the National Palace Museum in Taipei, and I very much appreciate the assistance of archivists at both institutions. Oyunbilig Borjigitai helped me obtain affiliation at Renmin University during my stay in Beijing. Guan Xiaojing graciously included me in her regular Manchu reading workshop at the Beijing Academy of Social Sciences. Qiu Yuanyuan and Burged Kered always made me feel welcome in Beijing and have provided me with all sorts of academic and linguistic assistance. And my time in Beijing was improved both intellectually and socially by the companionship of other researchers, especially David Stroup and Jesse Watson.

None of my work would have been possible without the aid of staff members at several institutions who have solved countless problems for me, large and small. I owe particular thanks to Carolyn Choong and Jim Zigo in Harvard's Department of East Asian Languages and Civilizations; Julia Cai and Nick Drake at the Fairbank Center for Chinese Studies;

Serena Han at the Institute of International Education in Beijing; and Nick Disantis, Amy Greenberg, and Richard Sosa at the Council on East Asian Studies at Yale.

Caelyn Cobb at Columbia University Press has made it possible for this book to actually be published, taking a chance on my manuscript and sticking with it through two rounds of review. I owe her profound thanks. I am also very grateful to the two anonymous reviewers for the press; I think in the end that the book is stronger for their feedback.

Finally, I owe the greatest of all thanks to my family. The love and support of my parents, Diane Campbell and Ted Porter, have helped me through the ups and downs that come with trying to get an academic career off the ground. My father has been reading and giving me feedback on my historical writing for as long as I've been doing it, and this book is no exception; I recognize how lucky I am to have access to the advice of a great historian so close at hand.

My wife, Elissa Berwick, has had more influence on the shape of this book than anyone else. She has read more drafts than I can count. Conversations with her—pretty much the only ones that I had with a live person while drafting the first version of my manuscript during the height of COVID—were central to most of my major decisions about what to include in the book and how to structure it. And she even put her skills in R to use in making for me the map and figures that appear herein. But none of that is as important as her love, on which I am completely reliant and for which I am forever grateful.

Finally, though my son Isaac's appearance in the world scarcely predates this work's publication, I treasure nearly every effort he has made to prevent me from completing it. Thanks to him, seeing this book come out ranks a distant second place among the meaningful events of my life this year.

SLAVES OF THE EMPEROR

Introduction

There was, perhaps, no institution more essential to the Aisin Gioro family's rule over China and the other parts of the Qing empire than the Eight Banners (Ma. *jakūn gūsa*, Ch. 八旗 [*baqi*]). The banner armies formed by the founder of the Qing royal lineage and Jurchen leader, Nurhaci, helped him and his son Hong Taiji establish a powerful state in Manchuria, northeast of Ming China, and gain control over the region's diverse population, which included large numbers of Manchus, Mongols, and Han. Those same armies were the central force that, in 1644, brought Hong Taiji's brother Dorgon through the Great Wall and into Beijing, where he established the child Shunzhi emperor, Hong Taiji's son, as the first Qing emperor of China. Banner armies would then help to conquer the rest of China, before, over the remainder of the seventeenth century and first half of the eighteenth century, playing a crucial role in the Qing expansion into Mongolia, Qinghai, and Xinjiang as part of a series of wars with the Zunghar Khanate of the western Mongols. Banner garrisons were found in most of the empire's major cities, from the preconquest capital in Mukden (present-day Shenyang), to the new capital in Beijing, from Guangzhou and Fuzhou along the southeastern coast to Ili in the northwestern reaches of Xinjiang (figure 0.1). Even as the military importance of banner troops declined over the late eighteenth and nineteenth centuries, bannermen would continue to serve as an armed symbol of Qing rule across the empire, and also to defend the dynasty against attacks from both Taiping rebels and British invaders.

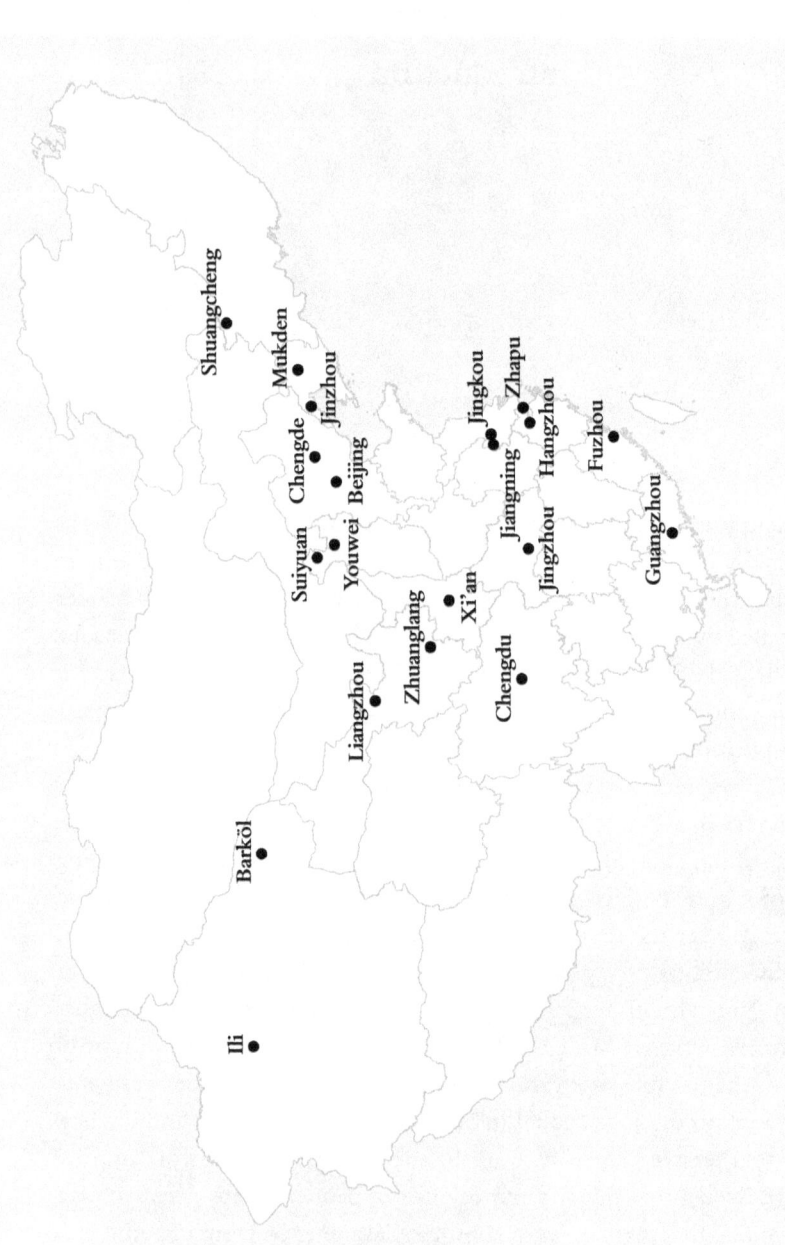

Figure 0.1 Map of the Qing empire c. 1820, with major banner garrisons and other important sites of administration and banner life marked.

Map produced by Elissa Berwick using a modified version of an open-access shape file created by Hu Shifang (available at https://worldmap.maps.arcgis.com/home/item.html?id=5612c062f3c64ade9656eee33598c71).

As rising nationalism among China's Han majority challenged Qing rule in the early twentieth century, Han revolutionaries pointed to the banners and banner people as symbols of Manchu oppression on account of both their perceived role as foreign military occupiers and the huge amount of government funds, mostly extracted from Han taxpayers, that went to their upkeep.[1]

The banners are usually understood as a quintessentially Manchu institution, tied to a political system dedicated to maintaining a privileged position for ethnic Manchus. They are thus often treated as existing outside of or in opposition to mainstream late imperial Chinese society.[2] And although there have been some important moves toward including the Qing in the global early modern history of empire, with a few scholars recognizing similarities between the banners and analogous institutions in other states, their apparent distinctiveness as a uniquely Manchu feature of the Qing order has consistently taken precedence over their potential as a subject of comparative history.[3]

This book makes three major interventions into the histories of the banner system and late imperial China and the comparative study of early modern empire. First, it demonstrates that the banner system is better understood not as an instrument for maintaining the power and position of Manchus, but rather as an institution designed to incentivize loyal service to the rulers of the Qing dynasty by a diverse group of imperial servants who acted as a multiethnic elite. Second, it shows that status, as both a legal category and a form of identity distinct from ethnicity, was fundamental to the social and political organization of the Qing empire, with banner people and commoners forming the two most prominent components of a complex status system. Finally, it connects the structure of the Qing elite to that of its early modern contemporaries in Japan, Russia, and the Ottoman Empire, arguing that the banners, like their analogs elsewhere, constituted a "service elite" that helped to meet dynastic demands for centralized bureaucratic power and reliable military service.

The Banner System

The Eight Banners were one of the earliest institutions of the state founded by the Jurchen chieftain Nurhaci, of the Aisin Gioro clan, whose descendants would go on to conquer China, around the turn of the seventeenth century.

Indeed, they predated Nurhaci's 1616 proclamation of himself as emperor of the (latter) Jin dynasty, which his son Hong Taiji would rename the Qing dynasty, by at least fifteen years. In 1601, in the middle of a series of successful wars with other Jurchen and Mongol groups that would make his confederation the dominant political power in the region northeast of Ming China, Nurhaci reorganized his army, previously based on hunting units organized by clan or village, into companies of three hundred men. From the beginning, these companies included not just soldiers but their entire families, who helped perform the auxiliary functions necessary to the support of a fighting man. Banner soldiers were granted land, meant to be the basis of their support and to be farmed by members of their household, including their agricultural serfs. Most company commanders obtained their position by bringing men with them when they joined up with Nurhaci and usually were granted the right to pass their posts to their heirs.

In the years after 1601, four military divisions called "banners" (Ma. *gūsa*, Ch. 旗 [*qí*]) were formed, each represented by a single color (yellow, white, red, or blue), commanded by a senior prince or official, and holding authority over many companies. In 1615, the number of banners was doubled by dividing each banner into two, one of which was represented with a plain colored flag, and one with a colored flag surrounded by a border in another color. As a result, there was both a Plain Yellow Banner and a Bordered Yellow Banner, and the same was true for each of the other three original colors. As the Jin state expanded, it defeated and absorbed neighboring Jurchen tribes and Mongol groups to the northwest and captured Ming territory in Liaodong, to the southwest. Many defeated or captured Jurchens, Mongols, and Han were incorporated into the Jin military, sometimes voluntarily and sometimes forcibly. Mongols were organized into their own banner companies, which were divided among the eight banners. In 1635, the same year that Hong Taiji invented the ethnonym "Manchu" and mandated its application to his Jurchen subjects, the Mongol companies were separated from the original eight banners, now the Manchu banners, and formed into their own set of eight Mongol banners.[4]

The Jin state began using Han soldiers in large numbers in 1621, when it conscripted 5 percent of its adult male Han population. This first Han army was disbanded in 1625 after a Chinese revolt killed many Jurchens.[5] By 1631, Hong Taiji formed a new Han army, which appears in later historical documents under the name "Old Han Army" (Ch. 舊漢軍 [*jiu Han jun*]) or "Old Han Troops" (Ma. *fe Nikan i cooha*, Ch. 舊漢兵 [*jiu Han bing*]).[6]

In 1634, this army was renamed the Hanjun 漢軍 (Ma. *Ujen Cooha*).⁷ The Chinese term "Hanjun" literally means "Han troops" and is not a direct translation of the Manchu term *Ujen Cooha*, which means "heavy troops" and is likely derived from the most important early function of this group, which was to haul and operate cannons. Hanjun soldiers carried out this task in numerous battles, including the siege of the Ming fortress of Dalinghe in 1631 and the invasion of Chosŏn Korea in 1636.⁸ In 1637, the Hanjun were divided into two banners, under the command of Shi Tingzhu 石廷柱 and Ma Guangyuan 馬光遠, and, according to the *Veritable Records*, their soldiers were organized into banner companies.⁹ Two years later, in part to punish Shi and Ma for their role in a failed attempt to take the Ming city of Songshan in Liaodong (the eastern part of present-day Liaoning province) by reducing the scope of their authority, the two Hanjun banners were divided into four, each consisting of eighteen companies and having its own commander.¹⁰ In 1642, the Hanjun were divided a second time, and ninety-nine companies of Han soldiers in the Manchu banners were incorporated within them. The Hanjun finally had their own, fully separate set of eight banners.¹¹

Although all Jurchens/Manchus who were defeated by the Qing had been incorporated into the banner system, many Mongol and Han subjects of the empire remained outside it. Thus, although the banner system was decidedly multiethnic, only Manchu ethnicity necessarily carried banner membership with it. Mongols and Han could be banner people, but the system covered only a portion of the subjects of the Jin/Qing state. However, even though most Han were outside the banner system, by the middle of the seventeenth century the banner population was mostly Han. As of 1654, ignoring Han household slaves of banner families (Ma. *booi aha Nikan*), Han made up approximately 50 percent of the total number of adult men (Ma. *haha*) in the banners, with Manchu making up just over 33 percent of the population and Mongols just under 17 percent.¹² The banners that conquered China were not only a multiethnic group, but one in which Han outnumbered Manchus. This would remain true until the middle of the eighteenth century.

In the wake of the 1644 Qing conquest of China, the Eight Banners became the dynasty's main garrison force. Commoners were expelled from the Inner City of Beijing, which was given over to the banners, and Beijing became the center of banner life, the place where by far the largest number of banner people lived, with a population of perhaps 500,000.¹³ Smaller garrisons were created in other cities across the empire over the course of the first century or so of Qing rule. In each of them, banner people lived separately from commoners. Some garrisons had soldiers from only some of the banners or banner ethnicities. For instance, although Manchus, Mongols, and Hanjun from all eight banners were represented in Xi'an, until the 1750s Fuzhou had only Hanjun from four banners, with no Manchus or Mongols present.

Following the conquest, the lives of banner people were defined by two key factors. First, they were forbidden employment outside state auspices. Most able-bodied adult bannermen were expected to serve as soldiers or officers in the banners. Although this did not always involve much actual fighting, they were expected to participate in regular training and to demonstrate competence in military skills. In addition, some bannermen served as officials in the civilian bureaucracy, which was the only legal form of employment outside the banners. The most common sort of administrative work done by banner people was translation, especially between Manchu and Chinese to enable the functioning of the Qing's bilingual bureaucracy. Bannermen also specialized in the administration of the empire's Inner Asian possessions in Tibet, Xinjiang, Mongolia, and Manchuria, through both appointments to the frontier and service in central government agencies dedicated to the management of these areas. In addition, they could serve in nearly any post in the rest of the Qing bureaucracy. In general, both the rules banning outside employment and the preferential access that bannermen had to government jobs meant that military and administrative service were central to banner life.

Second, banner people relied on the support of the state. In the first years of the postconquest period, banner families in Beijing and a handful of garrisons were granted land around the capital to generate income for their support, with the actual farming done by Han commoner tenants. In most cases, this land soon fell out of banner control and did not provide much of the basis of banner support from the late seventeenth century on.[14] However, banner soldiers also received salaries in both grain and silver, and those who had not been granted land received additional grain stipends on the basis of household size. Moreover, widows, disabled soldiers, and the like were paid pensions and soldiers received allotments to feed their horses that outstripped the actual costs of doing so. The court frequently offered banner people debt relief, and beginning in the eighteenth century, banner families also received payments to cover weddings and funerals, while unemployed bannermen often received supernumerary stipends.[15] Although the average bannerman was certainly not rich and, particularly toward the end of the dynasty, many banner people found themselves in difficult financial straits, they could expect the state to help them to meet their basic needs.

Bannermen as the Imperial Elite

The idea that the people of the banners constituted a status-based imperial elite may appear to conflict with long-standing ideas about Chinese politics and society in the late imperial period. Unless further specified, a reference to the "elite" of early modern China probably points to the group usually called the "gentry," "literati," or even "gentry-literati." This group, understood to be Han, or at least nearly exclusively Han, held wealth in land and, particularly by the Qing period, commercial enterprises. It used this wealth to access intensive education in a set of classical texts and commentaries that formed the basis of the imperial civil examination system, the graduates of which dominated the ranks of the civil service. This gentry-literati elite is treated as having controlled most of the empire's wealth, cultural prestige, and political power. It used its ability to make exchanges, mediated by institutions like the exam system, among economic, educational, cultural, and political capital to dominate late imperial Chinese society.[16] Revisionist work focusing on the role of tactics like purchasing degrees or government appointments, in contrast to the idealized exam-focused model, also deals with the same type of elites, who used a variety of methods to maintain their social position.[17]

Scholars focused on the Manchus and on the Inner Asian territories of the empire have drawn attention to the importance of power holders who stand outside the literati-focused account of the Qing elite. Local elites in Xinjiang, Mongolia, Tibet, and even parts of southwestern provinces like Yunnan and Guizhou held power that was mediated through institutions that differed from those in the Han-majority regions of the empire. In place of civil examinations and the study of texts in the Confucian tradition, their authority might spring from Gelug or Islamic religious lineages or hereditary princedoms and chieftainships. But the geographic scope of influence for these Inner Asian and Southeast Asian elites was limited and rarely extended into the empire's central provinces.[18]

It was the men of the banners who served as the only empire-wide elite. Even in the regional-level administration of the Han-dominated provinces of Ming China, banner people played a role at least as large as that of literati. Over the course of the dynasty, 53 percent of provincial governors and their superiors, the governors-general who handled the affairs of one or two provinces, were bannermen.[19] At the central government level, their dominance was more total. The presidencies of each of the Six Boards, the basic agencies of central imperial governance, were held jointly by a bannerman and a Han commoner official.[20] At lower levels within the central administration, a much higher percentage of positions were reserved for bannermen. For instance, 83 percent of the midlevel posts within the Grand Secretariat were held by men of the banners.[21] And the ambans who served as the only centrally appointed officials in most of the Inner Asian territories of Tibet, Mongolia, and Xinjiang were chosen exclusively from among bannermen.

Treating the people of the banners as an elite that stood above all the others, including Han examination graduates, Tibetan lamas, Mongol *jasagh* princes, and Dai *tusi* headmen, is not a new idea. However, most work that takes this perspective has focused on banner people as an elite whose power and influence were based on who they were, not what they did. That is, just as membership in the banners has been treated as more an ethnic category than a status one, its role in defining an elite has usually been viewed in connection with ideas of ethnic privilege and ethnic sovereignty. In discussing the Qing as a Manchu dynasty or the Qing period as one of Manchu rule, scholars suggest that banner people held power far out of proportion to their numbers because they were Manchu or Manchu-adjacent, just like the imperial family. The Qing in this vision becomes almost like apartheid-era South Africa, with the minority Manchu population ruling over a Han majority for the purpose of benefiting the Manchus as a group. This was the explicit position of early twentieth-century anti-Manchu nationalist polemicists like Zou Rong 鄒容.[22] The current scholarly position is certainly far more nuanced than that of Zou, but the idea that the Qing conquest was a "Manchu conquest," Qing rule constituted "Manchu rule," and the government of the empire constituted "Manchu sovereignty" has become a commonplace.[23]

But for the actual rulers of the empire—the emperors of the Aisin Gioro lineage, and, at times, some of their close relatives by blood or marriage—the empire was their property, not that of the Manchu people as a whole. They found it useful for other Manchus to identify with the empire in this way, as many clearly did.[24] The Qing court empowered Manchus as a group because it believed that their position as an alien people outnumbered by clearly distinct local populations, most notably the Han of the densely populated Chinese core, would enhance their loyalty to a ruling house that shared their identity. But once we recognize that Manchus outside the court were privileged not because the empire was the property of the Manchu people as a group, but because the actual rulers saw advantages to themselves in elevating Manchus, it becomes possible to look for other explanations of banner privilege in addition to ethnicity.

The Hanjun: Moving beyond Ethnicity in Studying the Banners

Much of the source material for this book, including Qing archival documents and banner garrison gazetteers, is focused on one portion of the banner system: the Hanjun. Ethnic Han banner people made up the overwhelming majority of the Hanjun banners, and policies directed at the Hanjun banners collectively were generally based on the idea that "Hanjun" and "Han banner person" were synonymous.[25] The Hanjun often seem to be a series of contradictions. Although not Manchu themselves, they were supposed to learn the Manchu language and the martial skills associated with Manchu ethnicity. Even though they were usually discriminated against relative to their Manchu colleagues, they were institutionally privileged relative to the bulk of the Qing empire's ethnically Han population. And though they included many of the most powerful officials of the empire during the late seventeenth and early eighteenth centuries, by the mid-eighteenth century, many Hanjun, though far from the entirety of the group, were forcibly removed from the banner system.

The fact that the Hanjun made up a substantial component of the banner system, with most of the same duties and privileges of Manchus, is well known to those who study the Eight Banners. But scholars have seen their position in the banners as tenuous. Mark Elliott argues that the failure of the Hanjun to uphold "the old 'Manchu' way of life" led the Qing court to see them as dispensable. That is, for him, it was Manchuness that defined the banner system, and the very existence of the Hanjun was problematic because they were in the banners without being Manchu.[26] Pamela Crossley has paid a great deal of attention to the Hanjun as a lens for understanding Qing ideology, but she suggests that already by the late seventeenth century, their loyalty had become suspect in the eyes of the court, and as a result, their role and their relationship to the emperor were redefined to be more like that of nonbanner Han.[27] Edward Rhoads, studying the very late Qing, treats "Manchu" and "banner people" as synonymous categories in this period, though he acknowledges the separate existence of the Hanjun.[28] These approaches, though not identical to one another, share a common feature: Manchuness and banner membership are not treated as analytically distinct.

My approach, which examines the banners primarily through the lens of the Hanjun, has certain advantages over the dominant framework, which treats the banners as a basically Manchu organization with little attention paid to the other peoples included in the system. First, at the most basic level, it recognizes the fundamental importance that this group had within the banner system and to Qing rule more generally. From a purely quantitative perspective, Han banner people outnumbered their Manchu counterparts until the 1750s. Even during the nineteenth century, after their numbers had been greatly reduced by the mid-eighteenth-century expulsions, the Hanjun banners had a population between three-fifths and two-thirds the size of the Manchu banners. One cannot expect to understand the banners while downplaying the importance of such a large portion of them.

At a more analytical level, close consideration of the Hanjun enables me to clearly distinguish status from ethnicity in understanding the Qing banners. By "ethnicity," I refer to the axis of difference that separated Manchu from Han, as well as from other categories like Mongol. As Crossley has pointed out, the sorts of considerations important to people in the Qing do not line up precisely with current social scientific definitions of ethnicity. And, moreover, Qing ideas about categories like Manchu and Han were not static; they changed over the course of the dynasty.[29] This book is not an attempt to resolve the long-running debate on the appropriateness of the term "ethnicity" as a lens for understanding the Qing.[30] The distinction between Manchus and Han was complicated and based in ideas about culture, environment, and, as a supposed result of environmental factors, inborn moral and physiological differences.[31] But what is important for my purposes is that Qing officials recognized the existence of Manchus, Mongols, and Han as distinct categories, and these distinctions had administrative and ideological significance for the entirety of Qing rule. I call this type of distinction "ethnic" as a generic term, to distinguish it from a different kind of identity category that, I argue, was far more important to Qing social and political organization than has been previously recognized: status.

By "status," I refer to a set of heritable identities, defined in law, that divide a population into categories, each with a different relationship to the state, reflected in how and by whom it is governed, what sort of responsibilities it has in terms of taxes and service obligations, and what sorts of rights and privileges it possesses. Although Manchuness was certainly of great importance to Qing rulers during most of the dynasty's history, much of what has been identified as "ethnic solidarity" in explaining the banners aligns better with status boundaries than with ethnic ones.[32] Looking at the banners as a status group, one whose status position and identity is not reducible to being Manchu, enables productive comparison to other elite status groups elsewhere in the early modern world. Studying the banners as a Manchu group has enabled important advances in our understanding of the Qing, demolishing the long-standing Sinicization paradigm that treated the supposed assimilation of Manchus by the Han whom they had conquered as the product of Chinese cultural superiority, and thus as an essential prerequisite for the maintenance of "foreign" rule. Unfortunately, in recent years, debates over Sinicization have become sites of tired ideological battles tied to contemporary worries about ethnic difference in the People's Republic of China, which do little to help us make sense of the Qing.[33] A study of the banners less tied to Manchu ethnicity presents the opportunity to distinguish the evolution of Qing institutions from the question of cultural change among the Manchu population. Moreover, it recognizes that it is not necessary to treat the banners as an inherently Manchu institution to see them as an important and distinctive component of Qing rule.

Chronology

This book offers an analytical treatment of the banner system across the entire period of Qing rule following the installation of the Shunzhi emperor on the throne in Beijing in 1644. Except for chapters 7 and 8, which focus on a temporally limited challenge to the system described in the rest of the book, I take a thematic approach rather than a chronological one. This form of organization is essential to providing a clear and coherent explanation of each of the elements that I see as important to understanding the banner status group. It allows me to discuss topics like Qing ideas about status or the role of banner women in one place, rather than spread across a chronological narrative. But an unfortunate side effect of this structure is to obscure the trajectory of the banner system over time. So I will briefly lay out the main stages of banner development here, as a useful reference point for understanding the context of any incident, decision, or source described later in the book.

By the time of the conquest, the banners had already evolved into complex bureaucratically administered units. But the bureaucratization of the banners and the imposition of direct imperial control over them, both processes that led to the diminution of hereditary authority within the banner system, progressed even further over the next eighty to ninety years, culminating in the 1720s during the reign of the Yongzheng emperor. This period of bureaucratization, the "consolidation era," resulted in the emperor gaining direct control over all the banners, some of which had originally been controlled by imperial relatives, as well as the development of many of the administrative forms and much of the specialized vocabulary used to govern the system. Thus, by the 1720s, the banners had reached their ultimate institutional form, in the "mature era."

The mature era, lasting from the 1720s to about 1750 was one of relative stability, despite difficulties related to financing the livelihoods of an ever-growing banner population. But beginning in the late 1740s and early 1750s, the Qianlong emperor launched an attack on the ideological system that underpinned the banners, attempting to replace the idea that banner membership was based on status with the claim that the Han in the banners did not really belong there and could be expelled for the benefit of Manchus. This period, which I call the "expulsion era," lasted from the 1750s until the early 1780s and is the focus of chapters 7 and 8.

The "postexpulsion era," which made up the remainder of the Qing, from the late eighteenth century until the dynasty's demise in 1912, can be characterized in two ways. It is most common to see this as a period of decline for the banners—one in which the political power of bannermen diminished even as they were replaced in their military function by new units of Han soldiers from outside the banner system. This narrative is true to a certain extent, but it is also often exaggerated—the banners remained of great importance to the Qing state even in its final years, as has been made clear by Edward Rhoads.[34] In this book, I provide a different characterization of this period, demonstrating that it featured a reassertion of much of the approach to the banners that had characterized the first century of Qing rule, as most of the changes pushed by the Qianlong emperor in the expulsion era were rolled back. The Han bannermen who had avoided expulsion, still at least three-fifths as numerous as Manchu bannermen, regained a secure hold on their status.

Many of the chapters that follow discuss both the consolidation era and the mature era alongside the postexpulsion era. This juxtaposition allows me to make clear the continuities that persisted across the expulsion era and thus supports my contention that an ethnically inclusive approach based on hereditary legal status, rather than an exclusivist approach based on Manchuness, characterized the overall Qing approach to the banner system across time. Because the expulsion era featured such a substantial challenge to the previous (and subsequent) systems, it generated an extensive discourse about how the banners should operate. This volume of bureaucratic correspondence directly addressing the question of who belonged in the banners and what role they should play is likely responsible for previous historians' focus on Manchu identity, as well as the Qing state's efforts to create and define that identity, as the key to understanding the banners. This book, though certainly not ignoring the drama of the expulsion era, takes our understanding of the banners in a new direction by excavating the ideology implicit in more routine bureaucratic documents and everyday administrative practices and using that to explain how the banners worked in ordinary times.

Service Elites

The final goal of this book is to develop a rich comparative framework for understanding the role of the Eight Banners in the Qing political and administrative system and how they contributed to the expansion and maintenance of dynastic power. The relationship between the banners and the Qing court and their place in imperial governance bear striking similarities to groups from elsewhere in Eurasia, most notably the samurai (Ja. 侍) of Edo/Tokugawa Japan, the service nobility (Ru. *dvorianstvo*) of imperial Russia, and the governing *askeri* elite of the Ottoman Empire, a group that included, most famously, the janissaries. Although there were certainly significant differences among these groups, from how individuals entered them to what sort of privileges their members possessed, all can be described as examples of a single broad framework of social organization: the service elite.

The term "service elite" is not in widespread use among historians, whether they study China or the other states of interest here. But the term, or one with clear similarities to it, has been used in a few relevant contexts, which are worth distinguishing from my use of it. As the name might suggest, I use the term "service elite" to describe groups that provided military and administrative *service* to a ruling dynasty and received in exchange institutionalized legal privileges, making them *elite*.[35] But unlike Brenda Meehan-Waters's use of "service elite" to describe the very upper echelon of the imperial Russian state, I use the term far more broadly.[36] Service elites did not consist solely of wealthy men or those who exercised substantial political power. Rather, they were broad social formations, whose members had certain guaranteed privileges, but the vast majority of whom were not individually notable. Their value to rulers came both from the role of soldier that most male members shared and from their collective value as a large reservoir of potential administrators, from whom officers and bureaucrats could be selected, often in meritocratic fashion, to fill ranks both high and low and carry out a variety of important functions.

In this sense, my understanding of the service elite differs from Pamela Crossley's description of the Qing "conquest elite." She emphasizes the hereditary division of the banners into a core of titled elites with real power, intended to receive broad educations that would enable them to become omnicompetent administrators, and a much larger group of common banner people with little access to power.[37] For her, the eighteenth-century displacement of the "hereditary conquest elite . . . by bannermen of lowly origin" who had risen into the upper ranks via service in the frontier wars of that period constituted a diminishment of the conquest elite ideal.[38] She analyzes in the same fashion the "abandonment of the liberal plan for development of a consolidated imperial elite" in favor of "more specialized programs for the cultural and professional preparation of the new segments of the elite."[39] This book, in contrast, sees the bureaucratization of the banners, its members' development into specialists, and the increased use of meritocratic promotion over hereditary position as a means of selecting officials from it, as all fundamental to the service elite as a social form and political structure. However, like Crossley, I argue for the importance of the service elite's joining of proximity to the ruling house with a political function that extended to all corners of the empire.[40]

In writing a book that, although focused on the Qing, is far more devoted to comparison than most historical monographs, I build on past work in comparative imperial history that has emphasized the use of analogous strategies of rule by different empires to gain and maintain control over diverse domains.[41] As Peter Perdue argues, the history of Western Europe has served as a normative source for the study of state development during the early modern period. Yet, he notes, the large agrarian empires of Eastern Europe and Asia—he points specifically to the Ottoman and Qing empires, but it seems clear that Russia and the Mughal Empire fit within similar paradigms—shared certain patterns of rule different from those seen on the western fringes of the Eurasian continent. Perdue looked specifically at frontier administration.[42] I argue that elite groups like the banners represent another example of states in Eastern Eurasia developing analogous strategies to deal with common challenges.

In this way, I extend a suggestion made by Sudipta Sen, a historian of India, in a 2002 review essay discussing some of the comparative implications of then-novel developments in the study of Qing institutions. Sen, using the term "service elite," compares the banners to the core elites of Safavid Iran, Mughal India, and the Ottoman Empire. Sen recognizes that these elite groups cannot really be described as constituting a "nobility" or "aristocracy," despite past scholarly tendencies to apply such terms to the elite of some Islamic empires. And perhaps most important, he argues, as I will, that the banners, like similar groups elsewhere in early modern Eurasia, enabled the Qing dynasty to bring multiple competing ethnic and tribal groups together in an elite that owed allegiance to the ruling dynasty and was dedicated to supporting that dynasty's interests.[43]

However, unlike either Sen or most previous scholarship on the banners, I do not see the management of ethnic or cultural difference or the maintenance of the superior position of a single ruling ethnic or racial group as the single most important function of service elites, common to all of them. Rather, although service elites could and did enable the incorporation of culturally distinct elements within a single loyal elite, the benefits of this type of institution to both rulers and members of such elites were far broader. Therefore, my comparative frame extends even to societies where ethnic diversity was not a central political concern.

My use of the word "elite" to describe these groups may invite some criticism. After all, can groups whose members numbered in the hundreds of thousands, or even millions in the case of the Qing banners, most of whom neither held positions of substantial political influence nor possessed large fortunes, really be thought of as elites? However, the degree of legal privilege enjoyed by these groups, all of whom were clearly elevated above the broader population, was essential to defining their role and should be recognized by the term used to describe them. And even though most members of service elites were not rich, they were protected against starvation, a real and ever-present risk for members of less favored groups. Although, from a contemporary perspective, a guarantee that one would have enough to eat, even in the face of drought or natural disaster, does not seem like a marker of extreme privilege, it constituted an unusual degree of economic security for people of early modern agrarian societies. Moreover, members of these groups, even those of relatively humble position and limited financial means, saw themselves as possessing greater dignity due to their special relationship to the emperor; that is, they believed themselves to be elites. Finally, as collective entities, these groups dominated political institutions. Although individual power was unequally distributed within it, membership in a service elite was necessary to reach many positions of substantial power, including nearly all such posts in the case of Russia, Japan, and the Ottoman Empire. Thus, while I recognize that some might prefer a different word, I hope that readers will understand my use of the term "elite" in the sense that I intend it.

Why did a similar approach to the organization of elites and the relationship between elites and ruling dynasties emerge in multiple early modern Eurasian societies? There were, to be sure, certain shared political and institutional legacies in what Pamela Crossley calls the "postnomadic world," tied to the great empires, especially that of the Mongols, that emerged from the Eurasian steppe earlier in the second millennium.[44] But each of the four service elites that I discuss developed out of culturally distinct institutions: the Ottoman janissaries from an Islamic tradition of using non-Muslim slaves as imperial agents, the Russian *dvorianstvo* from landholding cavalry, the banners from village-based hunting parties, and the samurai from warrior bands in the employment of noble clans. Japan, for its part, probably cannot even be considered to belong to the postnomadic world, as the only attempts to conquer it made by an empire from the continental steppe ended in complete failure. So rather than arguing for a common set of origins, I see the development of service elites as the result of a kind of convergent evolution.

Each of the four states in question experienced rapid growth in either territory, administrative ambition, or both. They were confronted simultaneously by the need to develop greater state capacity to carry out more complex tasks of government over larger numbers of people, and by the risk that reducing the influence of a well-armed elite essential to the state's creation and expansion would be met with dangerous resistance. The development of highly bureaucratized service elites helped solve this dilemma, enabling centralization of control and meritocratic recruitment without challenging the position of the elite at the top of the social and political hierarchy. Service elite systems incentivized the loyalty of a warrior class, made it dependent on the ruler, and aligned its interests with those of the dynasty.

Structure of the Book

Chapter 1 of the book lays out an argument for understanding hereditary legal status as an essential element of the Qing social order. It begins by defining status as a general cross-cultural category through an examination of the historiography of Tokugawa Japan, in which scholars have developed a robust theoretical framework for the concept. It then proceeds to suggest that a Tokugawa-style idea of status can also help explain the social structure of imperial Russia, another of the book's important comparative cases. The remainder of the chapter applies the concept of status to the Qing social order generally. It describes some of the types of status identity that existed in the empire, with a particular focus on the division between commoners and banner people. It ends by exploring the complexities of banner status in particular, including the several types of subcategories that helped create social differentiation within the banner population.

The heart of the book is in chapters 2 through 5, which show how the Qing banners functioned as a status-based service elite. These chapters explore how people acquired banner status, the nature of banner service and banner privilege, and the role that banner women played in serving the dynasty and maintaining the cohesion of the banners as a social group. Collectively, these chapters demonstrate that the idea of the banners as a multiethnic service elite was central to how the Qing state managed them across nearly the entirety of the dynasty's time in power. They show that the relationship between the Qing court and the banners was one of reciprocal obligations and mutual dependance. The court supported the banners despite the immense cost of doing so because it needed their loyalty, while banner people remained consistently loyal to the court because their privilege depended on the Aisin Gioro house remaining on the throne. The book's main comparative section follows in chapter 6, where I show that many of the features of the banner system described in the preceding four chapters were shared by analogous institutions in three other early modern Eurasian states: imperial Russia, Tokugawa Japan, and the Ottoman Empire.

The final section of the book examines a major challenge to the Qing service elite system: the expulsion of many Hanjun from the banners between the 1750s and 1780s. Chapter 7 describes the process leading to expulsion, arguing that it was a clear departure from previous understandings of how banner people could be managed. Chapter 8 explains how key participants in the banner system reacted to the expulsion project, showing how members of the banner bureaucracy adjusted to a radical shift in approach to the institution and how ordinary Han bannermen attempted to resist and evade expulsion until the end of the expulsion era, after which the court returned to its earlier approach to the banners. The chapter concludes by looking at analogous ideological challenges to the service elite model in other early modern states at around the same time. In the Ottoman case, the challenge would prove strong enough to destroy the janissaries entirely, but in Russia and Japan, like the Qing, service elites survived until the political system that sustained them had itself collapsed. The first section of the book's conclusion is a postscript exploring the ultimate demise of these three service elites in the wake of the Meiji Restoration and the Xinhai and October Revolutions. I end by considering the importance of service elite systems in early modern history and explaining how the role of the banners as a service elite should be understood in relation to that of other components of the Qing ruling class, especially the degree-holding gentry, who have traditionally been seen as the governing class of late imperial China.

CHAPTER 1

The Qing Status System

In late 1781, the case of a bannerman named Lin Xiang 林祥, a resident of the Jinzhou 錦州 garrison in southern Manchuria, appeared before the Board of Revenue (Ma. *boigon i jurgan*, Ch. 戶部 [*Hubu*]).[1] According to Lin, in 1759, Shi'er 十兒, aged 4 *sui*,[2] the son of Xiang's elder brother Lin Yu 林玉, had contracted smallpox and become critically ill to the point where he appeared to stop breathing. Lin Yu had Lin Xiang wrap Shi'er's body in straw and abandon it on the outskirts of the city. The next day, the boy's body was gone. After Lin Yu's death, Lin Xiang heard rumors that his nephew had in fact survived and been taken in by someone, but although he tried to investigate the matter, he couldn't come up with any real evidence.

In early 1781, however, concerned that Lin Yu's aging widow lacked an heir, Lin Xiang decided to renew his efforts to look for his nephew. On April 13 of that year, he visited the village of Shenjiatun 沈家屯. That evening, he happened to meet a commoner (Ma. *irgen*, Ch. 民人 [*minren*]) named Zhang Lin 張麟, who put him up as a guest for the night. When Lin told Zhang the story of his nephew and his search, Zhang responded that he was the adoptive father of a boy named Zhang Jiwu 張繼武, whom he had found covered in smallpox pustules on the side of the road in 1759, resuscitated, and carried home, where the boy had grown to manhood. The details of date and place all matched and, what was more, Zhang Lin was willing to return the boy to the Lin family! Lin Xiang told his widowed sister-in-law the news, confirming that the boy was his missing nephew on account of a distinguishing mark and the similarity of the boy's appearance to that of the boy's supposed father, Lin Yu.

Why had this heartwarming, if perhaps too-good-to-be-true, story garnered the attention of the highest levels of the Qing imperial government, with a memorial on the case authored by the imperial favorite Hešen 和珅, the most powerful official in the late Qianlong-era Qing state? The initial appraisal of the matter by the Jinzhou lieutenant general (Ma. *meiren i janggin*, Ch. 副都統 [*fudutong*]) made the stakes clear: "This case is related to banner and commoner status (Ch. 旗民名分 [*qi min mingfen*]); it may be some sort of fraudulent collusion involving the use of impersonation to enter the banners (Ch. 假冒入旗 [*jiamao ru qi*])."[3] The Qing government paid great attention to the boundary between commoners and banner people and to the analogous boundaries that differentiated other categories of dynastic subjects, like non-Han people under the administration of *tusi* (土司; "native chieftains" or "native officials"), or Mongols under the authority of hereditary rulers known as *jasagh*s (Ma. *jasak*, Ch. 扎薩克 [*zhasake*]). Critically, these distinctions were not ethnic.[4] Both the Lin family, who were in the banners, and Zhang Lin, who was a commoner, were officially considered Han. Similarly, there were people recognized as Mongols in both the Eight Banners and under *jasagh* rule. Even among Manchus, for whom banner membership is normally treated as universal, certain "new Manchu" groups were not included in the banner system.[5] The boundaries at issue in the Lin family case were tied to the Qing empire's status system.

Status is not central to most recent scholarly analysis of Qing society. The commercial expansion of the previous Ming dynasty led to "the emergence of a fluid and flexible status system, largely free of effective legal barriers to status mobility."[6] The Qing, it is generally agreed, surpassed even the Ming in its rejection of hereditary status boundaries, as membership in occupational groups like artisans and military colonists ceased to be inherited.[7] One of the major exceptions to this rule, the continued legal marginalization of people of hereditary servile or mean status (Ch. 賤民 [*jianmin*]), was formally abolished by the Yongzheng emperor in the 1720s for most such groups. Whether this reform was meant to emancipate the people in question or impose more rigorous control on their sexual morality, it certainly continued an apparent trend under which hereditary status was becoming less and less important.[8] Although a few scholars argue for the importance of the traditional division of Chinese society into four ranked classes—scholars, peasants, artisans, and merchants—the broad consensus is that this categorization was mostly an ideological conceit and did not reflect real legal boundaries.[9] The banner system is generally acknowledged to depart from this general principle and to have constituted a real and important hereditary status group.[10] Yet this recognition has not meant that status has been treated as a fundamental aspect of Qing social organization, but rather as an exception, something relevant to only a small percentage of Qing society.

In sharp contrast to this common consensus on the limited role of status, Qing historians have come to recognize the great importance that ethnic and cultural difference played in the organization of the empire. It is now widely accepted that categories like race or ethnicity were central to Qing governance, with the Qing empire ruling over groups like the Manchus, Mongols, Tibetans, Muslims, and Han through parallel but distinct institutional structures.[11] Although the overwhelming majority of the empire's population was Han, even the standard accounts of Qing society in textbooks treat ethnic difference as a basic and essential feature of the empire.[12] This book does not challenge the idea that ethnic and cultural difference were highly significant to Qing rulers; indeed, I will pay a great deal of attention to the interactions and intersections of ethnicity and status. Rather, I propose that the Qing state's governance of its subjects was based on the division of the population into a set of distinct status categories, which constituted an essential feature of the Qing social order. That the vast majority of the Qing population was officially subsumed under the single status category of "commoner" does not undermine the importance of status, just as the numerical dominance of the empire's Han population does not mean that ethnic categories had little importance.

This chapter begins with a comparative analysis of the workings of status systems in early modern Japan and Russia to develop a theoretical understanding of status as a type of identity and form of social organization different from categories like ethnicity, class, and caste. It then proceeds to analyze the commoner/banner divide in Qing law and society in terms of status, while also identifying other sorts of status categories that may be useful for describing the structure of society in the Qing empire. Finally, the chapter dives further into the banner status category to explain the complex status divisions within the overarching label "banner" and the intersections and overlaps between banner status, its various subgroupings, and the analytically separate category of ethnicity.

What Is Status? A Comparative Perspective

Although status currently receives little attention from historians of late imperial China, it has become one of the most important lenses through which to analyze the society of one of the Qing empire's contemporaries: Edo Japan. Status (Ja. 身分 [*mibun*]) was an essential feature of the "Tokugawa Peace," sorting people into fixed categories that carried particular duties and privileges and determined how they would be governed. It was once common among Japanese historians to associate status with a division of society into the four major categories of warrior, peasant, artisan, and merchant (Ja. 士農工商 [*shi-nō-kō-shō*]), derived from Confucian precepts and thus neatly analogous to traditional accounts of social division in China. In this telling, status was a reactionary and anachronistic institution imposed by the Tokugawa state to maintain a static feudal system, or even to take Japan backward toward an idealized Chinese past.[13]

This is no longer how most historians of the Edo period view the status system. Rather, they recognize that the institutionalization of status in the early years of Tokugawa rule was an important part of Japan's early modern state building, one that created a new form of social order whose resemblance to the imagined Confucian four-class society was more an ideological construct than a depiction of reality. Instead, the status system is best understood, at a basic level, through the framework of a "container society," the term applied to early modern Japan by the historian John W. Hall. By "container society," Hall meant that all Tokugawa subjects were divided into a set of nested boxes that defined who would have authority over them, what sort of laws would apply to them, and what sort of occupations they would take up. Early modern Japan did not provide its subjects with equality under the law, but, Hall argues, it did administer members of the same containers uniformly. The creation of these legally defined containers allowed the state to break the power of local personal rule by warriors and village headmen, and to create instead more impersonal and neutral rule, with authority centralized to a much greater degree and local authority tied more to appointment by central or domain-level authorities than to hereditary right.[14] The Tokugawa version of status thus was not a feudal institution, but part of a move, in Weberian terms, away from traditional authority and toward rational-legal authority.[15]

The four traditional Confucian divisions were not the "containers" that possessed actual legal relevance. While warriors did indeed constitute a status category, peasants, artisans, and merchants were not legally distinguished; they made up a single commoner group, which, as with the Qing, was the numerically dominant status grouping. But other categories did exist, including clergy, various types of outcastes, and members of the imperial court.

Membership in most status categories was inherited.[16] Thus, the child of a warrior would be a warrior, the child of a commoner would be a commoner, the child of an outcaste an outcaste. It was not impossible to move among these broad status divisions, but it was rare and difficult, particularly to move upward in the hierarchy. When economically successful members of a hereditary outcaste group in Ōno domain attempted to join commoner society in the mid-nineteenth century, they were refused by the town elders. On the other hand, commoners who absconded from their place of registration and became beggars could be stripped from the commoner rolls, effectively making them outcastes. Yet the importance of heredity to status was such that most people stricken from the commoner rolls could be readmitted if they returned to their proper place, even as financially self-sufficient members of the hereditary beggar status group were denied admission to commoner status, including in a case where one was adopted by a commoner.[17]

Members of different status groups fell under different forms of administration and were subject to different laws. In the city of Edo, for instance, commoners came under the authority of the two city magistrates, priests under a temple magistrate, and samurai under the direct authority of the domain lord to whose household they officially belonged, with those subject to the Tokugawa house itself falling under a variety of possible types of administration depending on their rank. Most castle towns emulated this arrangement.[18] Outcastes in Edo and its vicinity fell under the authority of a hereditary leader who took on the name Danzaemon 弾左衛門. Although outcaste administration was more fragmented in other parts of the archipelago, outcaste groups governed themselves separately from commoner villages and towns, with whom they frequently negotiated over the provision of services in areas like policing, executions, and beggar management.[19] When a man was arrested for a crime, he would be subject to different conditions of imprisonment, different forms of trial, and different punishments depending on his status. Only commoners could be fined, for instance, while priests were subject to unique forms of public humiliation and samurai, famously, were the only group who could be ordered to commit ritual suicide.[20] Adultery was subject to different penalties depending on the status of the individuals involved; samurai men had more leeway to use violence to punish their wives' adultery than did commoner men, and a relationship between a man of lower status and a woman of higher status was subject to harsher penalties than other types of adulterous liaisons.[21] Warriors even had the legal right to immediately kill a commoner who did not behave respectfully toward them; although the use of this power was subject to substantial limitations, it still clearly reflected the legal differences among status groups.[22]

Status in early modern Japan was not merely an administrative category that shaped how Tokugawa subjects related to the state, but also one of the most important types of identity, defining how Japanese perceived themselves and each other. Status was marked in sumptuary and tonsorial practice. All warrior and commoner men, for instance, were ordered to shave off their facial hair, but the regulation did not apply to some groups of outcastes, who were also frequently required to leave their hair untied, in contrast to the top-knot that was standard among other men, creating an obvious visual marker of their legal inferiority.[23] Clergy also sported noticeably different hairstyles, as Buddhist priests shaved their heads.[24] Perhaps the most important visible markers of status difference were the pair of swords worn by samurai and forbidden to most commoners. Moving beyond the physical level, warriors held the exclusive right to use surnames publicly and engage in martial activities like horseback riding.[25]

Perhaps the most important role of status in the lives of most early modern Japanese was in defining occupation. Occupation (Ja. 職分 [shokubun]) refers to the economic activity that was tied to one's status position; that is, the work that constituted one's officially defined contribution to the social order. Occupational subcategories existed beneath the level of the broad status divisions, like those of commoner or warrior, discussed previously. Movement between occupational subcategories, particularly those associated with commoner status, was thus much easier than movement between higher-order status divisions, which was usually subject to significant restrictions. Some scholars treat these occupational groups, which usually had a substantial degree of self-governance tied to village or city block associations and trade and craft guilds, as "status groups," noting that in most cases, they were the level at which status was managed.[26]

The importance of occupational groups is undeniable, but so is their link to higher-level conceptions of status. Outcastes and samurai alike did not appear on the registers of occupational groups or those of local residential units designated for commoners. Movement between occupational groups was possible in part because such movement did not require giving up one's membership in, say, a block association (Ja. 町 [*chō*]). Indeed, although different neighborhoods of Japanese towns and cities often had different occupational characters, most *chō* included residents of a variety of occupational backgrounds. Groups like samurai, clerics, and outcastes, in contrast, lived in separate zones, with separate registrations associated with their more fully distinct status identities.[27]

Thus, although one's membership in a particular trade or craft guild could change without a change in one's basic status, one needed to possess the proper status identity to belong to any given occupational category.[28] For instance, only a commoner could be recognized as a peasant (Ja. 百姓 [*hyakushō*]), even though others also supported themselves through agriculture. Indeed, rules around status were one of the reasons that, as David Howell has argued, many Japanese had an official "occupation" that was different from their livelihood—the way that they supported themselves in practice. This was particularly true for noncommoners, whose range of possible official occupations was often quite narrow.[29] Many outcastes engaged in agricultural pursuits instead of or in addition to their official occupations as prison guards or disposing of animal carcasses. In addition, there were many samurai without official employment who took up work as artisans or wage-laborers to provide for themselves, even as they retained their samurai status and thus their official occupation as warriors, a pattern that is quite familiar to scholars of the Qing banner system.[30]

Thus, the Tokugawa status system consisted of the division of the population into a number of mostly hereditary, legally distinct groups, with one of those groups, commoners, making up the vast majority of the population. Membership in a particular status group defined the range of occupations available to a given person, with much stricter occupational limits on noncommoners. Within the commoner population, there were a variety of partly self-governing social groups, including both geographic divisions like urban city blocks and rural villages, as well as occupational guilds based on collective monopolies on particular sorts of artisanal production or commerce in a given region. These monopolies on specific, geographically delimited economic activities, like begging or leatherworking, were also a feature of outcaste social organization.[31]

Members of different status groups had different obligations to the state and possessed different legal rights. These differences existed both at the level of broad status groupings and at narrower sublevels, as between occupational groups within the commoner population or between samurai of different levels of hereditary rank. But within each grouping, there was a legal expectation of uniform treatment at the level of the household head.[32] Boundaries between broad status categories, though not impossible to breach, particularly for movement downward, were fairly rigid; one could not change one's status simply through economic success or literary or scholastic achievement. Marriage across status lines was generally legally forbidden, although adoption could sometimes help circumvent these restrictions, particularly for commoners marrying samurai.[33] In sum, status was the defining institution of early modern Japanese society.

Although scholars of the Tokugawa have developed a detailed and compelling analysis of early modern Japanese society in terms of status, the possible comparative and theoretical uses of *mibun* outside Japan have attracted little interest. It is true, of course, that no two social systems are perfectly identical and so status in the Edo period is unique. But it does seem that there are other societies for which status, in something like the early modern Japanese sense, would provide a useful vocabulary and set of analytical tools. This book will make much use of status to talk about Qing society. But before turning to China, I will discuss the Russian empire to show how status-based analysis can help illuminate social history outside the Japanese context in which it was developed.

At least since the middle of the nineteenth century, historians have described the social organization of imperial Russia in terms of a division into four "estates" (Ru. *soslovie/sosloviia*): nobility, clergy, townspeople, and peasants. Despite the use of the term "estate," Russian historians have generally seen Russian estates as different from those of Western Europe, having developed later and lacking the power to restrain autocratic royal authority.[34] Some go further to suggest that the *soslovie* paradigm, in its standard form, does not adequately convey the real nature of imperial Russian society. Groups like trading peasants, and later the industrial proletariat, did not actually fulfill the social and legal functions that were expected of the *soslovie* category to which they belonged. Moreover, *soslovie* categories were nonuniform; the nobility, for instance, consisted of groups with widely varying wealth, social position, and origin of their membership in the *soslovie*. The peasant *soslovie*, meanwhile, included both serfs and state peasants, a distinction of essential importance to everyday life despite not being reflected in the quadripartite *soslovie* system. The best reason to use *soslovie* to describe Russian society, suggests Michael Confino, is that nothing else works any better and the term is of such long standing that it can no longer be abandoned.[35]

Other scholars view the use of *soslovie* more favorably, recognizing it as an essential category in law, administration, and how ordinary people publicly represented themselves.[36] Yet the only comparative framework remains that of Western Europe, even as Russian historians have come to realize that an idealized image of, say, the estate system of *ancien régime* France is a far cry from a more complex reality.[37] A Europe-focused comparison is not an arbitrary choice; it was on the minds of the rulers and administrators of imperial Russia themselves, with monarchs like Peter I and Catherine II (the two "Greats") making conscious attempts to imitate European institutions in reshaping Russian society. But analytically, it has become a dead end. Indeed, the most original and exciting recent English-language work on Russian estates moves past the issue of comparison in a single paragraph, thereby implying that *soslovie* was a category particular to Russia, best understood within the Russian context and without reference to larger theoretical models.[38]

The classic European model of estates, based on the idea that a handful of distinct social groups with clearly differentiated social functions each constituted a single political constituency represented separately in a parliamentary assembly, works poorly as a descriptor of imperial Russia, but the early modern Russian social order lends itself to productive comparison.[39] Indeed, not only does the Japanese model of status describe many aspects of the Russian system quite well, it also provides good solutions to some of the problems with relying on *soslovie* as the basic descriptor of Russian society that scholars like Confino have identified.

At the most basic level, *soslovie*, like *mibun*, was hereditary. As in Japan, one's ability to move between the top-level *soslovie* categories was limited, although to different degrees depending on which group was under discussion. For instance, while in Japan, it was extremely difficult to enter the warrior *mibun*, but relatively easy to enter the clergy, in Russia, it was basically impossible to enter the clergy, but, at least after Peter the Great's creation of the Table of Ranks (Ru. *Tabel' o rangakh*), it was possible to enter the nobility if one achieved a sufficiently elevated position in the officer corps or the bureaucracy.[40]

As in Japan, one's obligations to the state and one's legal rights both depended on one's status. In Russia, a major issue was the capitation, or "soul tax," from which higher-ranked groups were exempt but which lower-ranked ones were obliged to pay.[41] But one's *soslovie* membership extended beyond the soul tax issue to determine whether one was subject to military service, to rent payments and labor obligations to a serf-owning noble, and to a variety of other taxes.[42] Members of the clerical *soslovie* monopolized control of the priesthood and the incomes that accompanied it, but they also were responsible for a variety of religious and state functions, not only performing the liturgy but also assisting in the collection of statistics and the public reading of secular laws.[43] They were also exempt from taxation, military service, and corporal punishment, rights that extended even to the non-Orthodox clergy.[44] The nobility held the exclusive right to own serfs, while the right to pursue various forms of trade and nonagricultural production required membership in the townsperson *soslovie*.[45]

As in Japan, status determined how one was governed. Membership in a particular *soslovie* was also tied to registration in a particular locality, with subjects lacking the right to change the locality to which they were bound without permission.[46] What sort of locality one could belong to, and how that locality was administered, depended on status. Serfs were subject to the authority of landholders, who held a substantial degree of judicial power over them, including the right to sentence them to detention, beatings, and exile, although these powers were gradually restricted over time.[47] Belonging to a particular village or town society entailed participation in the collective responsibilities of the *soslovie* associated with that society and shared at the level of the locality. Yet, as with the overlapping geographical jurisdictions that existed in Japan, membership in a particular society was not tied to mere residence. Societies of townspeople were often reluctant to admit new residents whom they believed would be a burden on the town. This led many urban residents to fall outside the authority and protection of the official local institutions in their place of residence.[48] Similarly, although clergy lived in urban and rural communities, they were subject to the independent authority of the church, not to local town or village society. People of the merchant *soslovie* lived in the same places as townspeople but did not share in their responsibilities.[49] Nobles, meanwhile, frequently held administrative offices that gave them power over members of lower-status groups but were not themselves subject to the authority of villages and towns.

Not only is it reasonable to analyze both early modern Japanese and imperial Russian society within the same conceptual framework of status, but insights about the Japanese status system developed by scholars of Edo Japan also help to resolve some of the problems with the *soslovie* framework that have been identified by Russianists. I have identified two major criticisms of the *soslovie* paradigm. First, there is the idea that many people did not fill the economic role expected of people of their status. This is the same issue that David Howell has explained by contrasting occupation with livelihood. He argues that the distinction between formal occupation and actual livelihood did not render status-associated occupation unimportant; even peasants were very committed to defining themselves in terms of their legal status. But permitting a degree of flexibility helped encourage social stability.[50] The idea that occupation still mattered in a Russia where its link to livelihood was imperfect is confirmed by the work of Alison Smith. She shows that many Russians who sought a formal change in their *soslovie* affiliation were already engaged, as a matter of livelihood, in the work associated with the occupation of the status category that they sought to enter.[51] So although it was possible, perhaps even common, for occupation and livelihood to differ, the idea that they should align was important enough that many people went to a fair amount of expense and bureaucratic effort to bring their status in line with the way they made a living.

The other major criticism of *soslovie* is that individual *soslovie*, perhaps particularly the *dvorianstvo* (noble) status group, contained so much variation in wealth, power, social position, and way of life that these broad categories do not serve as helpful ways to understand the actual division existing in society. The same sorts of divisions existed within Japanese *mibun* categories, and, analogously to Russia, perhaps most particularly within the samurai group. Yet, as scholars of Japan have shown, the existence of subgroups within broader status categories did not obviate the importance of those more capacious main groupings. This mattered at the level of identity. A samurai like Katsu Kokichi 勝子吉, ranked among the unemployed *kobushingumi* 小普請組 and frequently facing severe financial difficulty, still described himself as "an honorable bannerman of the shogun" to elevate himself above the commoners he interacted with.[52] But it also mattered in practical terms. Katsu's son Kaishū 海舟 would become a leading official of the shogunate (Ja. 幕府 [*bakufu*]) in the final years of Tokugawa rule, despite his father's relative poverty. This trajectory would have been unthinkable had he not been born a samurai.[53]

Similarly, in Russia, it was true that nobles of high rank and wealth lived very different lives from the 44 percent of serf-owning nobles in 1857 with fewer than twenty-one serfs under their control, or the 61 percent of nobles who were landless as of 1907. But all members of the noble stratum retained privileged access to bureaucratic posts.[54] And a noble, regardless of wealth or rank, who sought to have a bureaucratic or professional career that required education beyond the basic level had a great advantage over a peasant who might need to secure a change in status to even be allowed to attend secondary school.[55] Although status groups could be internally fractured by class, the legal barriers separating members of the same status group from one another were far more surmountable than those separating them from members of other groups.

Status and Its Alternatives

Using the examples of Edo Japan and the Russian empire as a guide, we can identify some of the defining characteristics of status as a form of social organization and compare it to other possible means of dividing a society. Status has five principal characteristics.

First, it is defined in law; status categories are necessarily legal categories, and do not exist simply in the realm of social convention or cultural practice. This was the case in both Japan and Russia, with each state registering each of its subjects within a particular status group.

Second, status categories have implications for how people are administered, what legal rights they possess, and to what obligations they are subject. The legal existence of status is not merely as a set of census categories. Rather, status systems are based on a principle of nonuniform governance. A Japanese samurai was subject to different structures of authority and different laws than was a Japanese commoner; the same was true for a Russian priest and a Russian peasant.

Third, status is linked in law to occupation. Certain areas of economic activity and certain social functions are limited to members of particular status groups; conversely, members of certain status groups are expected to engage in certain types of work. These restrictions need not operate at an extremely detailed level, and they are often flexible to a degree, permitting individuals to fill their occupational role even while engaged in a livelihood apparently at odds with it. But they exist in more than name, hence the desire of many Russians to change their status category when entering new types of work.

Fourth, status is heritable and boundaries between status groups cannot be crossed freely. This is not to say that movement across status lines is impossible, but it is subject to regulation and approval by political authorities and, in some cases, the status-based community that one wishes to enter or leave.

Finally, status is not understood as natural, but rather as tied to one's relationship to the particular legal and governmental system in place. When the regime maintaining a particular status system collapses, the status categories that it maintained are likely to disappear, as happened in both Japan and Russia after the Meiji Restoration and 1917 Revolution, respectively.

These essential characteristics of status produce common features in status-based societies. First, because status systems rely on the nonuniform administration of people living in the same space, they produce multiple overlapping local administrative and social geographies. The relevant geographical boundaries were not necessarily the same for members of different status groups. Japanese outcastes were sometimes subject to outcaste headmen whose zone of control extended across the boundaries between domains, while Russian priests were subject to a church administration and legal apparatus whose diocesan boundaries were different from those of the empire's provinces.[56] Second, in part due to the legal barriers between status categories, as well as their principally hereditary nature, there were cultural differences among status groups. At times, these were legally enforced through sumptuary law and the like, but differences in cultural norms and practices could certainly arise organically as well. I emphasize this point because, in the case of the Qing, it is tempting to treat cultural differences between bannermen and commoners as reflecting an ethnic division between the two groups. Yet, in the Tokugawa, there was a particular culture of honor associated with samurai status, while in eighteenth- and nineteenth-century Russia, the use of the French language was a marker of membership in the noble *soslovie*.[57] Finally, status often operates at multiple levels, with harder boundaries between higher-level groupings and easier movement between status subgroups.

Status can be distinguished from other modes of social organization. Although the hierarchical nature of status systems, as well as their ability to create clear divisions within ethnic, national, or linguistic groups, give status some resemblance to class, status is embedded in law to a much greater extent than class. Class, of course, is highly heritable, largely because of the heritability of capital, whether financial, cultural, or social. Status, in contrast, is inherited in law; the child of a samurai was a samurai, regardless of their parents' ability to pass on capital.

Status is also different from race or ethnicity. Although racial and ethnic categories, in addition to being hierarchical and hereditary, have frequently been defined in law, they are less commonly associated with occupation than is status. More important, race and ethnicity, though social constructs, are often perceived as natural and persist across borders and major changes in political systems. An ethnically Georgian noble who emigrated to the United States in the late nineteenth century could retain Georgian ethnicity but would no longer possess noble status. Similarly, a Tatar peasant would continue to be Tatar after the 1917 Revolution but no longer possess an imperial-style status identity.[58]

Finally, status is different from caste. Although caste has a strong occupational component in addition to being based in heredity and defined in law, it, like ethnicity or race, is perceived as natural and not tied to one's position vis-à-vis a particular political regime. Although ideas about caste and political approaches to it have certainly changed over time, just as with race or ethnicity, caste has persisted through large amounts of political change in South Asia. As will prove to be the case with ethnicity and status in the Qing, caste can intersect with, overlap with, and help to define status identities. Indeed, the use of the term "outcaste" for the most marginalized status groups in Edo Japan reflects certain caste-like features of the identity of groups like *hinin* 非人 and *eta* 穢多 in the Edo period, as well as the contemporary *burakumin* 部落民 who identify as their descendants—particularly perceptions of pollution that contributed to the continuing existence of communities identified as outcaste even after the Meiji government legislated the relevant status categories out of existence.[59] It is the political contingency of status, including the ability of the state to change someone's status unilaterally, that marks a clear difference with caste, which can persist even through the overturning of a previous political order.

The Qing Status System

As in early modern Japan and Russia, status in the Qing empire was a fundamental principle of social organization and of how individuals related to the state. Although the documents dealing with Lin Xiang and his putative nephew, introduced at the start of this chapter, used the term *mingfen* to refer to status, this was not the most common way to talk about the concept in Qing law. Rather, official documents make frequent reference to the register (Ma. *dangse*, Ch. 籍 [*ji*]) in which someone was listed. Commoners were enrolled in the commoner registers (Ma. *irgen i dangse*, Ch. 民籍 [*minji*]), banner people in the banner registers (Ma. *gūsai dangse*, Ch. 旗籍 [*qiji*]). The use of the language of registration to define status reflects the role of status as, first and foremost, an administrative category. It shows as well that status was defined in terms of who kept track of a particular person and was a category with material consequences. To be a banner person meant to be someone about whom records were kept in an administrative office within the banner bureaucracy, as opposed to a commoner, about whom information was stored in an office within the civil bureaucracy. As such, status in the Qing empire was not just a piece of information attached to one's name or a box ticked off on a census. Rather, status determined which list one belonged on in the first place and where that list would be located.

Status in the Qing operated at the level of the household, with all members of a household included in the same register. This was a practice shared with Edo Japan, but not with imperial Russia, where status was an individual attribute. It was also inherited from earlier Chinese regimes; the Ming state, too, had registered households according to hereditary occupational categories. In the Qing legal code, many new substatutes dealing with matters of banner and commoner registration were included within a Ming-era statute titled "Households Should Be Established According to the Registers," which, in its original Ming text declared:

> In all cases [of household registration], the various households of military people, civilians, post couriers, salt workers, physicians, diviners, artisans, and musicians shall be established according to their [original] registers. For those who falsely or deceitfully claim (Ch. 詐冒 [*zhamao*]) [to be another sort of household] so as to escape [from their own household registers] and to avoid their heavier obligation and assume others' lighter obligation, they shall be punished by 80 strokes of beating with the heavy stick. If authorities casually permit households to escape, or to alter registers, the punishment shall be the same.[60]

Many Qing legal documents use this same language, especially the terms *zha* and *mao*, the latter of which appears in the Lin family case with which this chapter began, in describing and assigning punishment to crimes involving status transgression. Although the household as legal unit and the household as family unit were not necessarily identical, such distinctions usually involved a legal household that was larger than the family in which people lived.[61] The principle that status registration operated on a household scale rather than at the individual level was clear and consistent, with the Qing adapting Ming laws on status to suit its own purposes and its own, quite different, status system.

As the principal method of categorizing subjects of the Qing empire, status was a basic identifying feature included in official documents, like those related to criminal cases, in which Qing subjects dealt with the state. Such documents also show that, as in Japan and Russia, status identity not only existed in general terms but also was localized to a particular place. Take, for instance, a 1738 case of a bannerman murdering the husband of his commoner lover. At the beginning of its description of the facts of the case, a routine memorial (Ma. *wesimbure bithe*, Ch. 題本 [*tiben*]) from the Board of Punishment introduced the matter as follows: "A case of Xi'an garrison Plain White Banner Hanjun soldier Cai Youfu 蔡有福 and his wife, née Bai 白, strangling to death Xianning County commoner Li Fengxiang 李鳳翔."[62] Cai's and Bai's banner identity was tied not just to the broad category of banner membership but to more specific identifiers: a garrison, Xi'an, and a specific banner, the Plain White Hanjun banner. Similarly, Li was not just a commoner, but a commoner of a particular county, Xianning. These geographic identifiers serve both to tie the people involved to a particular community consisting exclusively of people who shared their status, and to make clear which officials were responsible for them. In addition, we can see a feature familiar from the study of the early modern Japanese system: overlapping and distinct geographies tied to various status categories. Xianning County was the location of the city of Xi'an. The Xi'an garrison was thus located inside Xianning County. Xianning County and the Xi'an garrison were divided less by physical location than by the sort of people, defined by status, that they were responsible for.[63]

The specific location of status identity for banner people was defined more narrowly than the level of the garrison, as all banner people were enrolled in a particular company (Ma. *niru*, Ch. 佐領 [*zuoling*]). Companies were themselves affiliated with a particular banner and were based in a particular geographical location, whether Beijing or one of the provincial garrisons. So, for instance, in a 1793 case of a bannerman in Guangzhou killing a commoner couple in a dispute over money, the protagonists were identified as follows: "The unemployed bannerman (Ma. *sula*, Ch. 閒散 [*xiansan*]) of Zhao Yuheng's 趙玉衡 company of the Plain Yellow Hanjun Banner, Zhao Xinglu 招興祿 . . . stabbed to death Panyu County commoner Ling Maokui 凌茂魁 and his wife, née Shang 尚."[64] Where the commoners are identified with their county of residence, the bannerman is identified by the company to which he belonged, which was itself subordinate to a particular banner.

The use of the company as the standard form of identification for banner people was not limited to legal and administrative contexts. At the very beginning of a notebook produced by a ten-year-old boy of the Manchu banners named Leping as part of his Manchu-language education, the student recorded a basic dialogue that served as a self-introduction:

A: Sir, which banner are you?
B: I am [of] the Bordered Red Manchu Banner.
A: Which division?
B: The first division.
A: Whose company?
B: Xuqing['s] (Ma. *Sioiking*) company.
A: What clan?
B: Tatara clan.
A: What name?
B: The name Leping.[65]

The company was thus not merely a structure of military organization. It was the basis of social organization for banner people and formed the structure through which even a ten-year-old boy might understand his identity and his place in society, ranking in importance alongside his membership in a family or clan and his own name. The company captain in this framework took on a role analogous to that of the county magistrate for commoners, the "father and mother official" (Ch. 父母官 [*fumu guan*]) responsible for the well-being of the people he administered.[66] In practice, in part because he administered a population that was a tiny fraction of that in an average county, a company captain's involvement in the lives of the people whom he oversaw was much greater than his commoner counterpart. Indeed, his pseudo-parental role even extended to a requirement that banner people receive the permission of their company captain before they could be legally married.[67]

Banner registers also kept much more careful track of the people included in them than did records of commoners, paying close attention to births, deaths, marriages, and employment.[68] The vast population difference between companies and counties helped enable this detailed record keeping, but so did the employment of many subcompany officials, including lieutenants (Ma. *funde bošokū*, Ch. 驍騎校 [*xiaoqixiao*]) and corporals (Ma. *bošokū*, Ch. 領催 [*lingcui*]). These men could accomplish far more than could the *baojia* 保甲 (Ma. *gašan falga*) mutual surveillance system under which commoners were assigned to groups of ten households (*jia*) and one hundred households (*bao*) responsible for one another's behavior.[69] Banner corporals were treated like *baojia* headmen in situations where someone under their authority misbehaved, as in one 1737 case in a rural area outside Beijing in which a bannerman unlawfully produced a set of playing cards and sold them to a commoner who was arrested for hosting an illegal gambling party on his birthday. In addition to the punishment meted out to the principals, the commoner's *baojia* headman and the bannerman's supervising corporal were each sentenced to a beating of eighty strokes, commuted to a whipping for the corporal in line with standard reductions in punishment for bannermen.[70] By having paid state functionaries take the roles otherwise assigned to mutual surveillance units, the banner bureaucracy was able to produce a complete census of the entire banner population every three years, while the commoner population was never surveyed in such detail.[71]

The principle that different status groups should be administered differently created problems when the governmental structures in a particular region were not set up to accommodate people of a particular status group, a situation frequently created by the migration of Han commoners into frontier regions. For instance, as commoners poured into Fengtian, in Manchuria, in the latter half of the eighteenth century, one official noted that certain "degenerate commoners" living in "banner zones" (Ma. *gūsai hešen*, Ch. 旗界 [*qijie*]) frequently refused to obey the banner officials who came to their villages because, as commoners, "they were administered by department and county magistrates."[72] The banner officials, for their part, had negligently left these commoners alone for years. Commoner officials at the county level were, however, too few in number for the large area in question, one in which many places now had substantial commoner populations that had not been foreseen when the administrative system was set up. This meant that sometimes commoner criminals fell through the cracks.[73]

This concern for proper status-specific administrative forms appeared elsewhere in the empire as well. As commoner settlers moved into Xinjiang in the wake of the mid-eighteenth-century conquest, the Qing state created appropriate jurisdictions to manage them, including prefectures and counties. These commoner administrative units, like those near banner garrisons in China proper, sometimes overlapped geographically with other types of administrative geographies, like that of the Turkic Muslim princes of Turfan. Despite their ethnic background, the Turfan rulers held their authority under the *jasagh* system, most commonly associated with the Qing empire's use of hereditary Mongol princes to oversee the empire's nonbanner Mongol population. Moreover, although located in a territory in which the highest-ranking official was the Ili general, who held a banner post, magistrates responsible for the Han commoners of Xinjiang reported not to him, but to the governor-general of Shaanxi and Gansu, whose post was within the administrative hierarchy responsible for commoners.[74]

People of different status groups were subject not only to different forms of bureaucracy and geographies of administration but to different laws. Perhaps the most visible example of this difference comes from comparing the treatment of banner people to that of commoners in criminal matters.[75] Banner people accused of crimes were judged outside the ordinary legal system that applied to commoners—they were spared torture during interrogation and held in separate jails while awaiting trial to avoid the foul smells and evil character of commoner criminals. Even after being convicted, banner people received automatic commutations of certain punishments, from flogging with a bamboo stave to whipping, and from long-term penal servitude or permanent exile to wearing the cangue for a much shorter period of time.[76] But, in addition, some laws applied specifically to members of just one status group. For instance, the Qing Code's statute on gambling included several substatutes with specific application only to either banner people or commoners.[77]

In practice, the combination of status-specific laws and automatic commutations could combine in surprising ways. For instance, although the substatute on banner people who produced gambling implements like cards and dice specified that they should be sentenced to exile to a malarial region, a Board of Punishments official in Manchuria complained in 1762 that he encountered many repeat offenders among the banner population because the criminals in question knew that their penalty would be commuted to wearing the cangue. Apparently, even a substatute that applied only to banner people and that prescribed a sentence of exile was automatically commuted under Qing legal logic.[78] The basic principle underlying the legal system was that banner people should not be treated like commoners, even in those rare instances when the law specifically demanded otherwise.

Differences in the legal treatment of status groups were not limited to those between banner people and commoners. Mongolia was subject to a separate legal system, with its own legal code, although the influence of Chinese law on Mongol law did increase during the Qing. The increasing importance of Chinese law, however, did not mean the elimination of differences between the Mongol legal codes and those for commoners or bannermen. Even in the late Qing, different laws applied to Mongols in Mongolia than to commoners in the provinces of the former Ming dynasty. Although it is easy to treat this difference as based in territoriality, with the Mongol Code applying in a certain space, Mongolia, and not to a certain group, this was not the case. Chinese settlers who lived in Mongolia were not generally subject to Mongol law, although for some crimes, like livestock theft, the marked discrepancy in the punishments prescribed by each code was a source of conflict.[79] In cases involving both Mongols and commoners, officials from both groups were required to collaborate.[80] In general, despite occasional moves to make territoriality, rather than identity, the principle governing choice of legal code, Qing officials looked at who was involved in a crime, rather than where it took place, when making judgments.[81] Similarly, in Qing Xinjiang, Chinese merchants who committed crimes were subject to Chinese law rather than the Muslim law that applied to locals, with identity again trumping territoriality in most cases.[82]

It is tempting to describe these identity differences as based on ethnicity rather than status, and, indeed, this has been the practice of most historians. But Mongols in the Eight Banner System were not subject to the Mongol Code that applied to Mongols under *jasagh* rule. Rather, they faced the same legal system and legal code as did the Manchus and Hanjun who were their fellow bannermen. There was no legal system for Mongols or Han as groups; laws were instead applied to bannermen, *jasagh* subjects, and commoners.[83]

The legal and administrative separation between banner people and commoners was tied to a notion of legally defined occupation, akin to that in Russia and Japan. To be a bannerman was to be a warrior or a bureaucrat;

indeed, bannermen who lived in urban garrisons were legally forbidden from taking up most ordinary employment. The range of occupations designated for commoners under Qing rule was much larger due to the breakdown of hereditary social divisions within the commoner population during the preceding Ming period. Commoners were farmers, craftsmen, and businessmen, as one mid-eighteenth-century official suggested when arguing for allowing Han bannermen to give up their banner status.[84] This occupational divide can also be expressed in terms of duties: commoners were taxpayers, while bannermen provided service.[85] This split is clearly analogous to that of the Russian status system, under which certain status groups paid the poll tax while others, most notably the nobility and the clergy, performed service.

Occupational restrictions associated with banner status had important effects. For instance, positions as translators in the Qing bureaucracy, as well as the right to take the official examinations in translation, were restricted to bannermen. In 1822, Qing officials discovered that a handful of translation examination graduates and translation clerks were the children of commoners who had been illegally adopted by banner people. As such, they were not entitled to banner status and were returned to the commoner registers. But, in addition, their loss of banner status meant that they could no longer legitimately hold translation degrees. So, in response to a proposal of the Board of Rites, these men's translation degrees were converted to the equivalent civil examination degrees.[86]

Yet, as in other status systems, the Qing also featured a distinction between occupation and livelihood. Many bannermen made a living doing something other than their legally prescribed occupation. Often, this was not state-sanctioned. For instance, the bannermen of Beijing who worked as professional theatrical performers were subject to frequent denunciation by the court, and occasionally even prosecuted.[87] But many people registered in the banners lived lives much like those of commoners in perfect compliance with the law, with agricultural work being common among ordinary bannermen in Manchuria and Imperial Household Department bondservants in rural estates outside Beijing. At times, as with the creation of the Manchurian settlement of Shuangcheng 双城 in the early nineteenth century, the Qing state even pushed banner people to take up agricultural life as a means to support themselves.[88] Yet making a livelihood as a farmer did not fully separate rural bannermen from their occupation as soldiers. Indeed, banner people in such situations remained organized in the same bureaucratic-military structures as banner people living in urban garrisons and could be called upon to serve when deemed necessary.[89] So, as in Japan and Russia, the divergence of livelihood from occupation did not obviate the importance of occupation.

As in other status systems, individuals could not freely cross the barriers between Qing status groups. The case of Lin Xiang, described in the opening of this chapter, was a product of the careful attention paid by the Qing state to the maintenance of status boundaries. Adoption across status lines was a particular concern to Qing authorities, in contrast to Tokugawa Japan, where it served as a workaround to avoid limits on cross-status marriage. The Qing court viewed the adoption of commoners by banner people as a means to illegally redirect funds intended for the support of the banner population. The court made repeated efforts to undo cross-status adoptions that had already occurred by offering time-limited amnesties to those who confessed and gave up their falsely obtained status.[90] Yet illegal adoptions still sometimes came to light, as in a 1737 case in which Piantu 偏圖, a commoner illegally adopted by a bannerman, had his real status origins revealed when he assisted his birth mother in reporting the drunken misbehavior of her other son to the Wanping County authorities. The prescribed punishment was severe: for the adoptee, exile to a miasmatic frontier to be a military slave if he was judged complicit in the matter, and for those banner officials who covered the matter up, a beating. Although the men involved ended up avoiding punishment on account of a general amnesty, there is no question that this was considered a serious transgression.[91]

The strength of the legal barrier between banner people and commoners was such that the state would undo status changes resulting from an adoption even after all of the people originally involved had died. In 1787, officials discovered that a Manchu bannerman named Kuicūn 奎春 was the grandson of a man named Totoho 托托和, who was actually the son of a commoner named Liu Jinyi 劉進義, who had been adopted by a bannerman named Silantai 希蘭泰 during the Kangxi period, which had ended sixty-five years earlier.[92] All of Totoho's descendants were ordered to be removed from the banner registers and redesignated as commoners, although they were not subject to criminal punishment, likely in recognition of their lack of culpability in the original illegal adoption.[93] But the banner official responsible for supervising the family at the time the case came to light was demoted one level and fined a year's salary.[94]

The same stringent conventions governing banner adoption ultimately decided the case of Lin Xiang that began this chapter. Not only was the request to restore the supposed Lin Shi'er to the Lin lineage rejected, but the officials who had let matters get this far were to be investigated for failing to stop the problem of "commoners pretending to be of banner registration" (Ch. 民冒旗籍 [*min mao qiji*]). Lin Xiang, Zhang Lin, and some neighbors who testified in support of the story were reported to the Board of Punishments for possible criminal sanctions. The boy, Zhang Jiwu, was returned to Zhang Lin's family. Hešen interpreted the case in light of a law prohibiting a banner family from sending their son to be fostered by a commoner and then returning him to the family and to banner status. Practices of this sort created status confusion, and it was the duty of banner officials to prevent them from occurring. In Hešen's view, Lin Xiang was clearly aware of the rules governing the inheritance of status. He had concocted a claim that the young man in question was his brother's lost son in order to be permitted to bring in a commoner as his brother's heir, despite the lack of a genuine blood relationship.

Although status was based on descent and claims of descent were essential to claims of status, status was not understood as a natural category. Rather, status was a political category tied to a particular regime, the Qing. This meant, first, that nothing about one's family background prior to the formation of the Qing (or, at least, the Latter Jin) state was relevant to whether one would be a banner person or a commoner. Second, the court itself had the right to change someone's status without having to justify the change in genealogy. This politically constructed nature of status differentiated it from ethnicity, which was perceived as a natural and objective fact, grounded in environment and culture, that existed outside the particular administrative policies of the Qing regime.[95]

There are many examples of the Qing court granting banner status to those who had not previously possessed it, decades after the dynasty's founding. One of the most prominent examples is that of Shi Lang 施琅, the admiral who defected from the Zheng family to the Qing in 1646 and played a major role in the conquest of Taiwan. Shi and his family were granted banner status in 1669 when they were entered into the Bordered Yellow Hanjun Banner.[96] The same conflict produced other elevations into the banners, including many members of the Zheng family themselves, after the third and final Zheng ruler, Zheng Keshuang 鄭克塽, surrendered to Shi Lang and the Qing in 1683. Zheng and two of his top subordinates who had advocated for surrender, Liu Guoxuan 劉國軒 and Feng Xifan 馮錫范, were all entered into the banners the following year.[97] They and their families would continue to serve as bannermen through the fall of the dynasty.[98] The Zheng family controlled one company, and for a brief period, a second company, under the Hanjun Plain Red Banner, based in Beijing. They would take full advantage of their banner status, holding numerous official posts, sending sons to study in banner schools, and, reflecting official expectations of all banner people, even producing Manchu-language documentation of their banner company.[99]

The elevation of surrendered opponents to the banners might, perhaps, be seen not as a change in status but as the assignment of status to someone who, as a new subject of the Qing state, previously lacked it. Shi Lang was, however, only elevated in status more than twenty years after he joined the Qing cause. And there are other examples of status change that demonstrate more clearly its potential malleability in accord with the court's desires. On his deathbed in 1796, the Han commoner and Sichuan governor-general Sun Shiyi 孫士毅 requested that his grandson, Sun Jun 孫均, be allowed to enter the banners. Sun Shiyi had a long record of distinguished military command, particularly in the Gurkha wars and the suppression of a Miao rebellion, although he had a more mixed record in the disastrous Vietnam campaigns of 1788–1789. His request was granted, and Sun Jun entered the Plain White Hanjun Banner the following year.[100] A decade later, the Jiaqing emperor stripped Sun Jun of his banner membership and returned him to the commoner registers, likely due at least in part to Sun Shiyi's close connections to Hešen, the now-disgraced confidant of the Qianlong emperor who was ordered to commit suicide after his patron's death, and to whom Sun had addressed his original appeal for banner status.[101] But neither the elevation nor the lowering of Sun Jun's status had been based on any claims about a right to banner status that the court was required to recognize; the court could decide that someone had earned a status change without any hereditary claim to that status.

The Organization of the Banner Status Group

As with all broad status groupings, in the Qing just as in Japan and Russia, banner status was not a uniform, undifferentiated category. Rather, it was divided into numerous status subgroups, featuring differences in social position and degree of privilege. Banner people included multiple ethnic groups, most notably Manchus, Mongols, and Han, although smaller groups, including Chahars, Russians, and various groups of "New Manchus" like the Sibe and the Orochen, also had a place in the banner system. In addition, banner people were differentiated by where they were assigned to live, from the capital to urban garrisons in the provinces to rural zones, mostly in Manchuria and the region around Beijing. Finally, many people administered within the banner system were in fact slaves or bondservants of banner households. Such individuals sometimes obtained their release from slavery, whether by purchasing their freedom, by providing military service, or simply because their masters could no longer afford to support them. Although they did not possess banner status in their own right, they had been registered within banner households while in bondage, so they generally remained in the banner registers after being freed. Their treatment in banner registers, where they were generally differentiated from other banner people, marked an additional form of status difference internal to the broader banner status category.

One obvious division within the broader banner status group was between the different banners. It is common to speak of eight banners; indeed, both Qing officials and contemporary historians refer to the banners, taken as a whole, as the "Eight Banners." But the division of the banner system into eight parts, though having substantial administrative importance, did not produce particularly important differences in status, with one exception. In the earliest years of the banners, from prior to the conquest of China through the early years of Qing rule, different banners were under the control of different members of the imperial family. Initially, the emperor had personally controlled two of those banners, the Plain and Bordered Yellow, and in 1650, a third, the Plain White, was officially added to his possessions.[102] These three banners would become known as the Upper Three Banners, in contrast to the Lower Five Banners, and would receive a disproportionate share of resources, leading them to become larger than the rest. By the late seventeenth century, the Kangxi emperor had taken for himself the power to appoint commanders for the Lower Five Banners as well. The hereditary banner princes lost their last practical role in managing these five banners during the Yongzheng emperor's reign (1722–1735), when they were stripped of power over the individual banner companies that they still controlled.[103] The symbolic distinction between the two categories would remain, and the Upper Three Banners remained larger and better funded, but many of the practical distinctions ceased to be of much import to the banner social order.

Despite the ubiquitous use of the term "Eight Banners," there were in reality at least twenty-four administratively distinct banners, as eight separate banners existed for each of three categories: Manchu, Mongol, and Hanjun.[104] There were, for instance, a Bordered Yellow Manchu Banner, a Bordered Yellow Mongol Banner, and a Bordered Yellow Hanjun Banner, each administratively distinct. The boundaries between each set of banners did not align precisely with ethnicity. But, by and large, members of the Manchu banners were perceived to be Manchu, members of the Mongol banners to be Mongol, and members of the Hanjun banners to be Han.[105] This meant that ethnicity became an axis of status difference, not in the high-level context of the banner/commoner divide, but at a lower level, internal to the banner system.

The commonly recognized ethnic hierarchy within the banners, with Manchus and Mongols ranked above Hanjun, had its legal basis in banner affiliation. That is, the mechanism by which Manchu bannermen received greater privilege than did the Hanjun was that people registered in the Manchu banners were treated differently from those registered in the Hanjun banners. This hierarchy played out in differences in the number of salaried administrative posts available to members of each ethnic category, in the exclusion of Hanjun bannermen from various prestigious military ranks, and in the mid-eighteenth-century policies that resulted in many Hanjun being expelled from the banner system.[106] In each case, the target of the discriminatory policies were people of the Hanjun banners, identified by their membership in that status subgroup.

A final major status grouping tied to membership in the banners consisted of the bondservant banner people under the administration of the Imperial Household Department (Ma. *dorgi baita be uheri kadalara yamun*, Ch. 內務府 [*neiwufu*]). Although bondservants and other people of hereditary servile status were owned by many banner households, those of the Imperial Household Department were, as reflected in their affiliation with the Upper Three Banners, bondservants of the emperor himself. They were organized into separate companies in the late 1610s.[107] These bannermen took on many of the functions that had been associated with eunuchs in earlier Chinese states, handling the management of the imperial household, including the personal finances of the imperial family and the manufacture and supply of goods used by palace residents.[108]

Although their identification as bondservants might suggest that bannermen of the Imperial Household Department were of relatively low status, their close links to the inner court allowed some such individuals to develop personal ties to the emperor and to rise to positions of great power and prominence. Most famous, perhaps, is the case of Cao Yin 曹寅, a friend of the Kangxi emperor from childhood due to his mother's service as the emperor's wet nurse, who rose to the position of textile commissioner in Nanjing. In that role, he served as a secret informant to the emperor, helping to keep tabs on high-ranking local officials in the empire's wealthiest region.[109] Other Imperial Household Department bannermen became crucial intermediaries between the wealthy salt merchants of Jiangnan and Zhejiang and the court through their role in managing the imperial salt monopoly, a task frequently delegated to bondservants.[110] But the majority of these bondservant bannermen, like the rest of the banner population, did not reach such lofty heights. Their status was clearly differentiated from other banner people, both because of their administrative separation and because they took on a different occupational role by working in large numbers for agencies of the imperial household, rather than the army or the state.

Banner people who shared a particular banner affiliation were not identical in terms of status. One of the most important distinctions among banner people was geography: to what sort of place a given banner household was assigned. Bannermen based in the capital held substantial advantages over those in urban garrisons in the provinces, who in turn were preferred over rural banner people. To start at the bottom, rural banner people, the largest number of whom were in Manchuria (although many others were based in the vicinity of Beijing), were expected to support themselves via agricultural work and in some cases to supply rural Manchurian garrisons with grain. These banner people were bound to the land, forbidden from leaving their villages by the same laws that banned garrison banner people from deserting. And yet they clearly fit within the banner status category, remaining differentiated from commoner peasants by their administration within the banner system, which entailed far closer supervision than that experienced by commoners. Moreover, they retained some of the privileges of banner status by being exempted from paying rent and subjected to far lower rates of taxation than were commoners doing similar work.[111]

They retained the right to the privileges of banner people in criminal cases as well, receiving the same sort of mitigation of punishment applied to their garrison-based brethren. For instance, in an 1805 case of a wine shop owner in the Heilongjiang banner village of Ulan Noor (Ch. 烏蘭諾爾 [*Wulan Nuo'er*]) murdering a customer in a dispute, two other rural bannermen present at the time of the killing were deemed criminally responsible for failing to stop it. Their statutory penalty of a beating with a bamboo rod was commuted to a whipping because of their banner status; that they were rural villagers and not salaried soldiers made no difference.[112] And, as might be expected of people of banner status, rural bannermen often remained potentially liable for military service, as illustrated in a 1732 report by the Heilongjiang censor Jangge 章格 that dealt in part with accommodating spring and autumn musketry training to rural bannermen's need to work in the fields.[113]

Urban banner people in both Beijing and other cities had lifestyles that were much more similar to one another than either was to those of rural bannermen. But bannermen in provincial garrisons received lower cash salaries, and, in many garrisons, they never received the land grants that had been provided to banner people in the capital as a source of additional income. To make up for this, they received an additional grain stipend, but capital bannermen remained better off, a difference reinforced by their receipt of larger sums as special stipends to pay for weddings and funerals than were awarded to those in the provinces.[114] The assignment to a provincial garrison was hereditary, and thus, as with other types of status, banner identity was often geographically localized.[115] Sometimes one's geographical identity and the advantages that came from assignment to the capital could persist even if one left Beijing. For instance, as part of a nineteenth-century resettlement scheme that sent banner people to rural Manchuria, those who moved from Beijing were granted more land than those who came from elsewhere in the empire.[116]

The final axis of status difference within the banners did not depend on the bureaucratic and administrative divisions that structured banner organization. This was the difference between regular banner people and "secondary status" banner people, who were officially recognized as having a lesser right to the privileges of banner status on account of the way they acquired that status. By and large, this group consisted of former slaves and their descendants.[117] Banner people were allowed to own slaves and did so in large numbers in the early years of the dynasty, although few slaves remained by the late nineteenth century.[118] Slaves entered the banners in a number of ways: capture during the conquest period; purchase; imperial gifts; criminal exiles sentenced to slavery; and when desperately poor, commoners attached themselves to banner households as a means to stay alive.[119]

Although banner slaves lacked the privileges of banner status, they were still subject to the authority of the banner bureaucracy, and counted in banner censuses, because they were part of banner households. This fact of administration also meant that banner slaves were treated like banner people for the purpose of status mobility, so banner slaves could not easily become commoners, even if they were freed from slavery. There was one 1725 precedent that permitted freed slaves who had been entered in the commoner registers for more than ten years and whose masters had voluntarily freed them in recognition of their "hard work" over "multiple generations" to retain the commoner status they had illegally acquired. But this exception existed mostly to prevent unscrupulous owners from trying to regain control over freed slaves who had managed to have a bit of economic success after obtaining their freedom.[120]

In general, freed slaves remained in the banners, but with a type of status, as recorded in the banner registers, that ranked them below ordinary banner people. There were two main legal terms used by the Qing state for people in this position, depending on when and how they had left slavery and entered the banner registers in their own right: "entailed householders" (Ma. *dangse faksalaha urse*, Ch. 開戶者 [*kaihu zhe*]) and "people separately recorded in the registers" (Ma. *encu dangsede ejebuhe urse*, Ch. 另記檔案人 [*ling ji dang'an ren*]).[121] As with slaves themselves, these people were denied many of the regular privileges of banner status, yet, as we will see in chapter 2, their marginal position within the banner system gave some slaves and secondary-status bannermen the ability to attain regular banner status, a possibility not available to commoners except in very exceptional cases. Similarly, adoptions of both children of household slaves and secondary-status banner people by regular banner people were sometimes tolerated, even as adoptions of ordinary commoners were treated as wholly illegal.[122] Moreover, although the Lin Xiang case suggested that it was illegal to send a banner boy to be fostered by a commoner and then return him to the banners, it was permissible to have a son be fostered by a banner slave family and then returned to the banners, assuming that the whole matter was properly documented.[123] It follows that the boundaries between commoners and banner people were more impermeable than were those within the banner status category, even for those banner people who had entered the banner registers as slaves.

Conclusion

The wide variety of types of people in the banner system raises the question of whether all people who held banner status should be treated as part of the Qing service elite. It is probably necessary to exclude slaves of ordinary bannermen from the service elite; although included in the banner registers, and, as we have just seen, permitted easier access to regular banner status than commoners, they clearly lacked the privileged position associated with other banner people. A more complicated case is that of rural bannermen, who did possess some of the privileges of banner status, especially those related to the adjudication of criminal cases. But they did not receive the same sort of economic privilege accorded to their urban counterparts; indeed, they generally supplied the state with agricultural products rather than receiving stipends from it. With this complexity in mind, the rest of this book will focus on garrison-based bannermen who, regardless of their ethnic background or whether they resided in Beijing, Manchuria, Chinese provincial cities, or later-conquered Inner Asian territories, should be understood as part of the service elite. The question of whether to extend this framework to rural bannermen must await further study.

Analyzing Qing society in terms of status does not mean abandoning the idea that the difference between Manchus and Han was of great importance to Qing rulers. Ethnicity and status were deeply intertwined, with the entire Manchu population included in the banner status group. Many of the duties and expectations of banner people were based on ideas about Manchu identity promoted by the Qing court. But treating the banners as an ethnic institution, rather than a status-based one, neglects the ethnic Han who made up a large portion (and even a majority for the first century of Qing rule) of the banner population. Only by incorporating status can we make sense of the actual dynamics and divisions that characterized Qing society, in which members of different ethnic groups were often treated as legally similar, while members of the same ethnic category could be divided into multiple, very different legal categories. Moreover, the lens of status enables new and productive comparisons between the Qing and other early modern states that are not possible to make through an ethnic frame. The remainder of this book will show how the banners took on the role of a multiethnic service elite whose members had their privileged position defined more in terms of status than of ethnicity.

CHAPTER 2

Who Belonged in the Banners? The Makeup of the Qing Service Elite

The origins of the Qing service elite lie in the preconquest period, at a time when many of the features that characterized the mature banner system of the eighteenth century did not yet exist. Indeed, the banners were not really a service elite at the time of their formation because they were subject not to institutionalized bureaucratic management, but instead to systems of hereditary governance often tied to preexisting social and political structures. As a result, to understand Qing ideas about who belonged in the service elite, it is perhaps less useful to study the initial formation of the banners than to look at questions of banner status and the inclusion of new groups in the service elite in the postconquest period. This includes the consolidation era, but especially the mature era and later, after the bureaucratization of the banners was complete.[1]

Most banner people in the high Qing were descended from bannermen who had served the dynasty in the first half of the seventeenth century. Yet there are enough cases of newcomers entering the banners, banner slaves being granted full banner status, and people defending their right to full membership in the banners against accusations that they did not belong that we can get a sense of how the Qing court and Qing officialdom thought about who was entitled to banner status. A few of these cases, of men raised from the ranks of commoners to those of the banners as a reward for exemplary service, and, in the case of the high official and military commander Sun Shiyi, for good connections to the imperial favorite

[49]

Hešen, were introduced in chapter 1. Such cases, including that of Shi Lang, the admiral who defected from the Zheng Chenggong organization to lead the Qing conquest of Taiwan, suggest that distinguished military service in major frontier campaigns could mark exceptional individuals as worthy of admission to the service elite. However, as suggested in the introduction to this book, one crucial feature of a service elite is that membership not be based on individual power or direct personal connections between particular high-ranking individuals and the ruler. Rather, it is defined by the creation of a relationship between the ruler and a large group of elites, most of whom have never met or corresponded directly with him, much less won his regard for themselves as individuals. With this in mind, it is not great men like Sun and Shi whose entry into the banners best helps us understand the institution, but cases involving whole groups of people, most of them of much more ordinary backgrounds.

This chapter explores a few distinct types of acquisition of banner status. Earliest in time are instances from the immediate postconquest period of commoner relatives of banner people being enrolled in the banners. Next are cases of members of distinct ethnic populations, sometimes newly conquered and sometimes linked to foreign states, being enrolled in banner companies. Related to this are cases of defeated rebels, perhaps most notably soldiers of the armies of the Three Feudatories, receiving entry into the banner ranks. Finally, we have cases of banner slaves being freed from slavery and made into regular banner people as a reward for military service. The best documented large-scale case of the elevation of slaves is that of a group called the Household Selected Soldiers, released from slavery in 1731, whose story will both be at the core of this chapter and make a return in chapter 7 as part of an examination of the fragility of banner status during the expulsion era, under the reign of the Qianlong emperor. Linked to the stories of slaves being granted banner status are cases of banner people asserting a right to full banner status in the face of claims that they should be treated as banner slaves.

These cases lead to a few important conclusions about banner status, introducing features that will be explored further in subsequent chapters. First, they suggest that banner status was designed to incentivize and reward loyalty to the ruling house. Moreover, in cases where loyalty was questionable, banner membership could provide an opportunity for the supervision and oversight of potentially troublesome groups. For this reason, the banners could be used as a tool to successfully manage difference, especially ethnic difference, in a large and diverse empire. They also show how close the ties were between banner status and service to the dynasty, with military service in wars of expansion and the suppression of rebellions having particular importance. That is, although the ordinary duties of banner people consisted of a mix of administrative service and routine military service, which included garrisoning major cities, drilling, and maintaining certain military skills, it was a direct role in the active conquest or defense of imperial territory that could create a new entitlement to banner membership. Nevertheless, these cases also reinforce the importance to banner membership of administrative boundaries based in status, as well as the significance of heredity, with elevation into the ranks of the service elite far more easily accessible to banner slaves and relatives of banner people than to ordinary commoners who served in military campaigns.

Banner Status and Family Ties in the Early Qing

In the years immediately following the Qing conquest of Ming China in 1644, some Han commoners believed that they would be better off as banner people. The Qing court was thus faced with many claims from Han who lacked banner status that they should be enrolled in the banners. The logic used by these claimants, and accepted by the court, shows that banner status was already seen as a hereditary category even at this early date. The court implicitly assumed the right of family members of banner people to hold the same status as their relatives, treating the banners as a space for the creation of a cohesive and loyal military elite.

A few examples will help illustrate the court's approach. In 1653, Gadahūn 噶達洪, the president (Ma. *aliha amban*, Ch. 尚書 [*shangshu*]) of the Board of Revenue, reported a petition from a man named Li Guangzu 李光祖. Li was originally from the Liaodong town of Tieling 鐵嶺, captured from the Ming by the first Aisin Gioro emperor, Nurhaci, in 1619.[2] Li had fled the city at the time of the battle and accompanied his father-in-law to Lu'an 潞安 prefecture, in the province of Shanxi. Li's father's younger brother had just been enrolled in the Plain Yellow Banner, joining up with a more distant male relative named Li Sizhong 李思忠. Now Li Guangzu sought to be enrolled in the banners himself, along with all his dependents, with Li Sizhong's banner status serving as the basis for his claim.

Li Sizhong was admittedly not an ordinary Hanjun bannerman. He had been captured in Nurhaci's 1618 assault on Fushun 撫順, although his father, uncle, and brothers had escaped to Tieling, where they died in the attack of the following year.³ Beginning in 1621, Li Sizhong had served as an officer in the Manchu army, where his performance led to repeated promotions, the receipt of a fox fur robe from Emperor Hong Taiji, and the eventual bestowal of the hereditary noble rank of baron (Ma. *ashan i hafan*, Ch. 男爵 [*nan jue*]). His son, Li Yinzu 李蔭祖, also had a successful career, serving as vice president of the Censorate (Ch. 副都御史 [*fu du yushi*]) at the time of Li Guangzu's appeal, for which he acted as guarantor (Ma. *akdulara niyalma*).⁴ The Board of Revenue's investigation of Li Guangzu's request consisted of an inquiry to a banner officer named Yang Shangju 楊尙舉, who confirmed Li Guangzu's familial connection to Li Sizhong—the former was the son of the latter's first cousin. Li Guangzu thereupon received approval to be registered in the banners, along with eleven other adult men, twelve adult women, and four boys, who presumably comprised his household and perhaps those of his own descendants.⁵

A connection to a powerful official like Li Yinzu was not essential to claiming banner status. Later that same year, a memorial from Ceke 車克, the new president of the Board of Revenue, presented a similar case involving men of lower rank. Li Ruilong 李瑞龍, a native of Jinzhou in Liaodong, claimed that in 1627, he had gone south of the Great Wall with his father to engage in trade. According to Li, they heard about the coming of the Manchu army, which unsuccessfully laid siege to Jinzhou in the fifth month of that year, and so decided not to return to Liaodong.⁶ Instead, they took up residence in Xiayi 夏邑 County, Henan. Now he had learned that his cousin, Liu Wenjin 劉文進, was a captain (Ma. *nirui janggin*, Ch. 佐領 [*zuoling*]) in the Plain Yellow Banner, and he asked to be permitted to join Liu's company.⁷ His three guarantors, who included Liu Wenjin, verified their relationship—one of their fathers was the brother of the other's mother—and Li Ruilong's family of six was registered in Liu Wenjin's company.⁸

Cases like those of the two Li men suggest that the Qing court saw expanding the banners and incorporating family members of existing banner people as means of consolidating its authority. Neither man seeking banner enrollment had a claim to that status on the basis of his own service to the dynasty—indeed, both had fled Qing advances. Nor were their descent-based claims particularly compelling. Neither was the patrilineal descendant of a participant in the conquest; rather, both relied on the service of collateral relatives as justification for their own banner enrollment. In Li Ruilong's case, his relative in the banners was not even of the same patriline, but a cousin through the female line. So, if neither had earned banner status himself, and neither had inherited it, at least according to conventional rules of inheritance, why let either one in? It seems likely that in the seventeenth century, the Qing state still sought to expand the banner system, in contrast to the eighteenth century, when it worried about the burden created for state finances by a large banner population. Thus, it was advantageous to incorporate the men and their families—in Li Guangzu's case, quite a large family—into the banner system. Yet the familial connections that these men had to the banners were treated as important enough that they had to be verified before registering the two applicants as banner people.

One possible explanation for this is that banner status, in addition to being a reward for loyal service, was itself a means of inculcating and guaranteeing loyalty. By bringing the extended families of men who were already enrolled as Hanjun into the banners, the Qing court was helping to define the banners as a group apart from the commoner population. Combined with official disapproval of intermarriage between banner people and commoners, the incorporation into the banners of agnates and cognates of banner people would ensure the full commitment of Hanjun to the banner system, and through the banners, to the court itself.[9] Even as the Hanjun came to play an important role as intermediaries between the Manchu court and the overwhelmingly Han population of the empire, they were to be kept distinct from their fellow Han, socially as well as legally. Thus, the court could create a loyal group of Han servitors as part of a service elite whose members were bound to each other by family ties that separated them from the commoner population.

Although only a few specific instances of Han being incorporated into the banners in the Shunzhi period survive in the archives, population records suggest that the practice of allowing certain Han commoners to enroll in the banners was probably more widespread. For instance, over the three years from 1651 to 1654, a time when both the Manchu and Mongol banner populations underwent slight decreases, the number of military-age males in the Hanjun population increased by 2,702, or 3.7 percent.[10] The contrast between a rising Hanjun population and a static or falling Manchu and Mongol banner population implies that Hanjun growth was not simply due to natural population increase, but rather reflects the inclusion of additional Han commoners in the ranks of the Hanjun banners.

Managing Ethnic Difference Through Banner Membership

Bringing certain members of non-Manchu populations into the banners was a technique applied to more than just new Han subjects of the dynasty. In the early years of the Aisin Gioro dynasty, under the rule of Nurhaci, banner membership had been a means to organize the entirety of society, with the banners including the entire population under Nurhaci's rule, at least in his core Manchurian territories.[11] All Han were under banner administration in the early period of Nurhaci's state-building, though many were held as slaves, as were some Jurchens.[12] This system changed as the banners transformed from the governing institution of the entire latter Jin state into an institution administering only the service elite of the Qing state. With only a fraction of the subject population enrolled in the banners, the state had to determine which newly submitted subjects would be included in the banner rolls and which would remain in other status categories.

Who was brought into the banner system and how they were brought in when new people or territories came under Qing control depended on the political circumstances of their submission. One complex example is that of the Chahars, a Mongol subgroup whose subjugation by the Qing is traditionally linked to the surrender of Ejei (Ch. 額哲 [*Ezhe*]) Khan, the final ruler of the Northern Yuan dynasty, in 1635. At the time of Ejei's submission, he and the Chahars subordinate to him were not entered into the banners. Instead, Ejei was made into a *jasagh* Mongol prince, retaining political control of his Chahar followers outside the hierarchy of the banner system. He was subject to the oversight of the Lifan yuan 理藩院 (Ma. *tulergi golo be dasara jurgan*), the agency responsible for managing the Qing state's Inner Asian territories and relations with continental neighbors like Russia, after its creation in 1636.[13] But even as Ejei Khan was handled under the framework of the *jasagh* system, other Chahars who came under Qing control at around the same time were enrolled in the banners, forming separate Chahar companies, who would soon come to form a separate ethnic subdivision of the banner system from the three main categories: Manchus, Mongols, and Hanjun. In 1675, Ejei's nephew Burni (Ch. 布爾尼 [*Bu'erni*]), now the holder of Ejei's *jasagh* post, attempted an anti-Qing uprising that was quickly put down. Burni was executed, and his *jasagh* title, rather than being passed to an heir, was abolished. The Chahars who had been subject to *jasagh* rule were entered into the Eight Banners. But rather than being added to the Chahar banners, they were distributed among Manchu and Mongol Eight Banner companies. In subsequent decades, a number of non-Chahar Mongols, including some Oirat and Khalka Mongols, were entered into the Chahar Eight Banners when they submitted to Qing rule during the Qing-Zunghar wars.[14]

This brief overview of Chahars and the banner system reveals a variety of approaches to banner incorporation. Some Chahars were brought into the banners, while others were not. Later, some Chahars were put into non-Chahar banners, while some non-Chahars were put into Chahar banners. So, how best to make sense of these decisions by the Qing state? First, it is clear that incorporation into the banners would have been a diminution of the standing of people who had previously held powerful political positions independently, as Ejei had through his leadership of the remnants of the Northern Yuan dynasty. The Qing state was apparently willing to forgo this sort of demotion in the hopes of winning the voluntary submission of politically powerful allies. As I will discuss shortly, a similar logic may explain why Ming generals like Wu Sangui 吳三桂, Geng Zhongming 耿仲明, and Shang Kexi 尚可喜 were not fully incorporated into the banner system upon submitting to Qing rule.

Second, people who had participated in a rebellion could be entered into the banners, as were the Chahars previously subject to Burni after his failed uprising. But this did not mean that the Qing treated those who had submitted voluntarily or been conquered identically to those who had been rebels. The original Chahar bannermen were included in Chahar companies, and thus they were permitted to retain their previously existing social ties. Similarly, the Oirats and Khalkas who were entered into the Chahar banners were generally allowed to remain in their own companies, perhaps combined with members of another group if there were not enough fighting-age men to make up a full company. But Burni's former subjects were divided among many non-Chahar companies, presumably in the hopes of breaking the social ties and political structures that might facilitate further disobedience. This formed an additional sort of social control beyond the level of supervision that came from banner membership.

Another example of how the Qing state used the banners to manage a potentially troublesome population of former rebels comes from the aftermath of the 1673–1681 Revolt of the Three Feudatories, the most serious threat to Qing rule between the conquest and the mid-nineteenth century. The Three Feudatories were Wu Sangui, Shang Zhixin 尚之信, and Geng

Jingzhong 耿精忠, all either Ming generals, or descendants thereof, whose defection to the Qing had been important to its conquest of China and who had been given territories in the southern part of the empire to govern, which they treated as their personal fiefdoms.[15] Their revolt, intended to prevent the Qing state from abolishing these fiefdoms and putting them under central control, was defeated and the principal leaders executed or forced to commit suicide. But many of the soldiers who followed the feudatories were dealt with in a very different way—they were integrated into banner garrisons in the cities where their masters had previously held sway. In Fuzhou, 1,000 of the 2,050 banner soldiers and officers assigned to the newly created garrison in 1680 were former members of Geng Jingzhong's cavalry.[16] In Guangzhou, whose garrison was established the same year, 1,125 of the initial 3,000 banner households were selected from the troops of Shang Zhixin.[17] Other feudatory troops were recalled to Beijing to be integrated into the banners there.[18]

Whether the inclusion of these troops into newly created garrisons constituted a change in status is a complicated question. In a certain sense, the armies commanded by Geng Jingzhong and Shang Zhixin were already banner armies. Geng's and Shang's soldiers, as well of those of Kong Youde 孔有德, who joined the Qing at the same time but died without an heir soon after the conquest and is not considered one of the Three Feudatories, were officially designated as Hanjun in 1642.[19] The official posts held by their subordinates carried banner-type titles rather than titles associated with officers in the commoner Green Standard (Ma. *niowanggiyan turun*, Ch. 綠營 [*luying*]) army, and their armies were officially divided into *niru*, banner companies, a term not used outside the banner context.[20] It was these armies, not that of Wu Sangui, that were permitted to join banner garrisons—although whether this was because they were considered bannermen or because Geng and Shang had given up their rebellion prior to the final defeat of Wu is unclear. Indeed, Wu's troops, though never officially designated as bannermen, had also been divided into *niru* and assigned officers of banner rank in the years prior to the revolt.[21]

Yet, in certain important ways, Geng's, Shang's, and Kong's troops were not really part of the banner system. They were not incorporated into the larger banner hierarchy, and the three generals were consistently treated separately from banner commanders in imperial edicts, while their troops were listed separately from banner troops when describing military deployments.[22] Indeed, in 1683, a few years after the end of their participation in the revolt, the Geng family petitioned the emperor to be recalled to Beijing and treated like regular Hanjun by being assigned military work and stipends to support the large number of lineage members who could no longer provide for themselves.[23] Therefore we can infer that prior to 1683, they had not been treated like ordinary banner people, who would have relied on state employment, which indeed was a key feature of banner status. After being entered into their new garrisons, the former feudatory soldiers in Guangzhou and Fuzhou continued to be marked as a distinct population from the other Han bannermen in their garrisons. They were designated as "feudatory" (Ch. 藩下 [fanxia]) soldiers and denied the right to audiences in Beijing, which was necessary for promotion into the officer ranks, until the Kangxi emperor eliminated the designation in 1710, declaring that "the feudatory people are equally my people and included among the Hanjun."[24]

There are two ways to interpret the treatment of the former feudatory soldiers. The first is that these men had not really been part of the banner system before the revolt, and their integration into the banners was a way to manage a group of former rebels and avoid the problems that might come with demobilizing a large number of armed and trained soldiers. In this interpretation, Shang's and Geng's former troops were treated differently from Wu's because their act of rebellion was considered less severe, either because Shang and Geng returned to the Qing fold and assisted in the defeat of Wu or because other prominent members of the Geng and Shang families had remained loyal and the troops could be associated with their loyalty rather than Shang Zhixin's and Geng Jingzhong's treachery.[25]

The second possible interpretation is that the Qing banners of the early consolidation era lacked the cohesion and uniformity associated with the banner system in the mature era, and although the feudatory troops had always been bannermen, their integration into the Guangzhou and Fuzhou garrisons was part of a process of consolidating the banner system under imperial control. In this sense, it would have been part and parcel with consolidation-era policies that stripped personal control of banners from relatives of the emperor to tie the entire system to the emperor himself, and assigned an imperially appointed bureaucracy to manage them. Both interpretations lead to similar conclusions about the purpose of the banner system: it was being used to forge a loyal population of military men who could be counted on to support the emperor rather than serving his rivals or becoming rivals themselves.

The use of the banner system to control potentially problematic subjects continued in the mature era. After the defeat of the Zunghar Khanate and the conquest of Xinjiang in the late 1750s, the Turkic-speaking Muslim populations of the Tarim Basin (the southern portion of present-day Xinjiang Uyghur Autonomous Region) came under Qing rule. The population of the Tarim basin was largely left to the rule of local hereditary rulers called *begs*, who were themselves subject to the Lifan yuan. But a small number of Turkic Muslims from the newly conquered region were brought to Beijing. A few of these, due to the particular noble titles that they had been granted by the Qing state, remained under Lifan yuan authority. A much larger group, numbering more than two hundred individuals, were enrolled in their own newly established company of the Plain White Mongol Banner and given their own residence zone within the Inner City of Beijing, the area designated officially as the nearly exclusive residence of banner people.[26]

As Onuma Takahiro has detailed, many of the people enrolled in this banner company, including those made officers within it, were not men with unblemished records of service to the Qing. The first company commander, Bay Khwāja (Ch. 白和卓 [*Bai Hezhuo*]), was the son of Manggalik, who joined an Oirat rebellion against the Qing. Bābāq (Ch. 巴巴克 [*Babake*]) and Pulat (Ch. 頗拉特 [*Polate*]), two begs from Aksu, were sent to Beijing after embezzling government property. Chalama (Ch. 察拉瑪 [*Chalama*]), who had briefly served as a high-ranking official near Kashgar, was sent to Beijing after his younger brother supported the Afaqi Khwājas in their anti-Qing uprising.[27] The inclusion of men like this in the banners suggests that banner membership could be used to supervise potential troublemakers to ensure their loyalty, not just as a reward for past loyalty for those who had participated in Qing imperial expansion and state-making. Another major group of banner Muslims were an array of artistic professionals, including musicians, acrobats, and craftsmen, who were managed under the Imperial Household Department and provided entertainment in court, including performances of ropewalking that were noted in a quadrilingual imperial stele, authored by the Qianlong emperor and erected in the official zone of residence for the Turkic Muslims of Qing Beijing.[28] The use of the banners to supply specialist professionals to the court was not unique to this group, but it was one of the important functions of the banners, which will be discussed at greater length in chapter 3.

Just like potentially rebellious new subjects, troublesome foreigners could be put into the banners to keep them under the eye of the Qing military bureaucracy. Following the collapse of the Vietnamese Lê dynasty and the defeat of Qing forces who invaded Vietnam on its behalf in 1788–1789, the final Lê ruler, Lê Duy Kỳ 黎維祁, was invited to Beijing to be entered into the Hanjun banners, along with around one hundred of his followers, with Lê himself receiving a hereditary banner captaincy. The Qianlong emperor's motive for extending this invitation was not any particular respect for Lê Duy Kỳ, whom he called "cowardly and incompetent" (Ch. 怯懦無能 [qienuo wuneng]), but rather the hope that it would prevent Lê, his followers, and his half-brother, Lê Duy Chi 黎維祗, who was still fighting in Cao Bằng province in northern Vietnam, from continuing to stir up trouble for the new ruler, Nguyễn Quang Bình 阮光平, who had already been officially recognized by the Qing. Moreover, the emperor refused to let all of Lê's 376 men who had accompanied him to Guilin become bannermen, instead ordering that fewer than two hundred be sent to the capital to enter the banners, while the remainder went to Jiangnan, Zhejiang, or Sichuan to join the Green Standard army, whose soldiers were commoners. Those who were dissatisfied with their position and tried to flee back to Vietnam to make trouble there would be captured and executed.

The Lê followers remained in the banners for only fifteen years, as in 1804, the Jiaqing emperor permitted them to return to Vietnam, which was now under the control of Nguyễn Phúc Ánh 阮福暎 and the new Nguyễn dynasty, who had been enemies of the ruler who had forced Lê into exile. Banner commanders were ordered to strike the Vietnamese population from the banner rolls.[29] The case of the Lê king, like that of the Turkic Muslim banner company, is evidence of the Qing court using admission into the banners to grant continued privilege to ethnically distinct elites without permitting them to hold independent authority.

It is telling that the same solution was used for all sorts of potentially dangerous populations, from the subjects of former Mongol khans to the political elite of newly conquered Muslim oases to the former soldiers of rebellious Han generals.[30] The Qing court saw banner status as a way to manage a diverse population, helping to ensure that diversity would not simply mean a multiplicity of reasons to rebel. Membership in the banners created both incentives for loyalty and opportunities for close supervision by imperial authorities. It was thus a crucial tool for an expanding empire dealing with a wide variety of subject populations.

Raising Banner Slaves to Regular Banner Status: The Rewards of Loyalty

In the previous section, we saw that the Qing court used banner status to try to win the loyalty, or at least supervise the behavior, of populations with a history of rebellion or that the court believed might become disloyal. In these cases, banner status became a form of control, of both newly incorporated elites and previously militarized populations. But banner status did not maintain the loyalty of key groups simply through heightened supervision, as it also incentivized and rewarded loyalty. As will be discussed at length in chapter 4, banner status provided privileged access to political power and material resources to those who held it. This fact meant that providing banner status to the groups discussed here could help to mollify as well as supervise them. But it also meant that banner status could become a reward for loyal service. The logic of status registration, discussed in chapter 1, meant that commoners were not the usual recipients of this sort of reward for loyalty, even though commoner soldiers in the Green Standards played an integral part in expanding the empire and defending Qing control. Rather, it was people who were already included in the banner registers as slaves who had the best chance to be promoted into the ranks of ordinary banner people following military service. Although I will discuss a number of instances of such elevations in status, perhaps the most notable was the case of a group called the Household Selected Soldiers, whose 1732 elevation to banner status constituted one of the largest additions to banner ranks in the postconquest period.[31]

The origins of the Household Selected Soldiers (Ma. *booi sonjoho cooha*, Ch. 家選兵 [*jiaxuan bing*]) lie in a 1731 edict from the Yongzheng emperor. In it, the emperor ordered all banner companies, whether Manchu, Mongol, Hanjun, or bondservant, to "choose from among their household slaves (Ma. *booi ahasi*, Ch. 家僕 [*jiapu*]) 2,000 talented and sturdy men, with prior experience, who are accustomed to bearing up to suffering and hardship and are capable of either doing their duty in battle, caring for horses, or construction." Each man and his master would be asked whether they were willing to allow him to be selected, and the final group would be sent to the "western region" (Ch. 西路 [*xilu*]) to participate in the Qing campaign there. Their masters would receive compensation of 100 taels of silver per soldier, and the men would be made into detached households (Ma. *encu boigon*, Ch. 另戶 [*linghu*]), which is to say that they would enter the regular banner ranks, upon their "triumphant return." At that time, their families would also be bought out of slavery, also at a rate of 100 taels per person. They would be supplied and paid in the same manner as ordinary banner cavalry (Ma. *moringga cooha*, Ch. 馬家 [*majia*]).[32]

An edict from a few months later reiterated the decision and explained that the actual process of changing the status of these men and compensating their masters would be handled "in accordance with previously selected slave soldiers" (Ma. *kutule cooha*).[33] This nonspecific reference to precedent suggests that the Household Selected Soldiers were not the first group to be chosen in this matter. Another example of the practice from around the same time is a group called the "Retribution-Bringing Soldiers" (Ma. *karu gaire cooha*), who had been slaves of Qing officials before entering military service, and who occasionally appear in the same documents and context as the Household Selected Soldiers.[34] But it may also have been intended to evoke a related, but smaller-scale, practice dating to the early years of the dynasty, in which household slaves who received official recognition of military merit, particularly for leading the way in scaling walls of enemy cities, were granted the right to "form households" (Ch. 開戶 [*kai hu*]) and be entered into the registers of detached householders. That is, they and their families would leave the households of their masters to form their own households as ordinary banner people rather than banner slaves.[35]

The men selected in response to this order must have been chosen and mobilized quickly, because before the end of the year, a group of 2,000 "slave soldiers" had left Hohhot under the command of an officer named Acengga 阿成阿, setting off for Barköl (Ch. 巴里坤 [*Balikun*], in what is now eastern Xinjiang) to reinforce the Qing garrison there following a resumption of Zunghar raids.[36] After a series of misadventures, including having to change their route on account of the lack of fodder on their originally planned path, the loss of their guide, and an inability to resupply at Qing garrisons north of the Gurvan Saikhan mountains due to Zunghar attacks, Qing commanders briefly lost track of the army's whereabouts and began asking merchants returning to Hohhot from Barköl whether they had run into the army along the way.

Within a week of the initial reports that they had been lost, Acengga had been located, having taken his army to Jak Baidarik, a Qing encampment on the east side of Lake Böön Tsagaan, which had agricultural lands located nearby, perhaps along the river flowing into the lake. Jak Baidarik was regularly subject to Zunghar attacks, and was short of provisions for the army, leading Acengga to request a shipment of food and other supplies.³⁷ The final report to use the term "slave soldiers" to refer to this army shortly followed Acengga's request; in it, the Qing general Marsai 馬爾賽 informed the court that he would arrange for provisions to be sent to Jak Baidarik.³⁸ Shortly thereafter, the emperor granted the army the name "Household Selected Soldiers," supposedly to the great gratitude of the men, who, Acengga reported, professed their desire to "repay" (Ma. *karulara*) the emperor's generous "grace" (Ma. *kesi*).³⁹ The army's next appearance in Qing records occurred the following year, after the supply problems had been resolved by deliveries coordinated by the Qing state merchant Fan Yubin 范毓馪. The commander at Jak Baidarik, Sirin 西琳, reported that the "two thousand Household Selected Soldiers brought by Acengga" had left Jak Baidarik heading west toward Lake Beger.⁴⁰

In late 1732, while still on campaign, the Household Selected Soldiers received the reward promised them by the emperor when he had first called for their recruitment. As the imperial representative bringing this news told them: "Since coming from the capital last year to garrison Oden Cul, you all have carried everything out extremely well. In this instance of wiping out bandits, you all have put forth great effort." These actions in service of the dynasty were tied to a great act of imperial grace, through which they were freed from slavery and made into detached household banner people.⁴¹ According to their commander Acengga, when the edict announcing this decision reached their camp, the soldiers "leapt for joy," expressing particular happiness upon being told that their wives and children would also be allowed to join them in the banners.⁴² The Yongzheng emperor having made the Household Selected Soldiers into detached households benefited them greatly. As members of detached households, they could be employed equally with regular banner people.⁴³ So, following their return from campaign, the Household Selected Soldiers received salaried posts in the newly established Suiyuan 綏遠 (Ma. *goroki be elhe obuha hoton*) garrison (located in present-day Hohhot). Each of the 2,000 men employed there was to receive 2 taels per month in silver, as well as grain sufficient to feed five people, with half of this grain stipend commuted to cash.⁴⁴ These salaries were structured similarly to those paid to regular garrison bannermen, though the cash incomes of the new Suiyuan bannermen were somewhat lower, as ordinary banner soldiers in the provinces were paid 3 taels of silver per month.⁴⁵

The emancipation of the Household Selected Soldiers came with compensation for their previous owners in the capital, as had been specified in the Yongzheng emperor's original edict. The state paid their original masters a "body price" (Ma. *beyei hūda*, Ch. 身價 [*shenjia*]) for each of the newly manumitted slaves, "from unweaned babies on." The body prices of the soldiers themselves had been paid when they were initially sent out on campaign, at a total cost of 200,000 silver taels, a very substantial sum. A few years later, in 1736, when the Household Selected Soldiers finally returned from the frontier to take up their posts in Suiyuan, the court of the newly enthroned Qianlong emperor issued payments for the dependents of these soldiers, though at a much lower rate than had originally been promised, offering 10 taels of silver each for the soldiers' "fathers, mothers, wives, and children."[46]

The compensation issued by the Qing court clearly demonstrates the original status of the Household Selected Soldiers; they were not simply members of bondservant banners, but privately owned slaves. Moreover, it strongly suggests that the Qing state placed a great deal of value on being able to employ banner soldiers in its campaign against the Zunghars, as it was willing to spend a very considerable sum to increase the size of its banner armies in the west, though it would likely have been cheaper to expand the commoner Green Standard army. Even though the banner system was already facing substantial financial pressures, the court expanded the number of bannermen to whom it owed obligations of support. This allowed it to create and staff a new, strategically important, banner garrison in Suiyuan. And the cutback in spending at the time of their emancipation targeted not the new banner people themselves, but their previous owners. At least as of 1736, a promise to grant banner status and the pay that came with it to soldiers who served the dynasty was ironclad; the court saw its obligations to reward the loyal service of the Household Selected Soldiers as less subject to negotiation than its obligation to compensate their previous owners for the loss of their services.

Although the Household Selected Soldiers constitute a clear case of the Qing court rewarding military service with banner status, it is worth noting an important caveat—one that is suggestive of the multiple principles involved in Qing conceptions of who belonged in the banners. Even after their formal elevation to the banners and their inclusion among the three main ethnic divisions of the system of the basis of their ethnicity, the Household Selected Soldiers continued to be discussed as a separate and coherent group.[47] That is, there are no archival records referring to a member of the Household Selected Soldiers as being a "Bordered Yellow

Hanjun bannerman" or a "Plain Blue Manchu bannerman." Rather, they are, without exception, described as members of a single distinct institution: the Household Selected Soldiers.

The idea that this may have been a way of distancing them from bannermen with no origins in slavery is suggested by another practice: denying the privileges of rank to the low-level officers selected from among the broader group. Lieutenants, among the lowest-ranking of banner officers, who were selected from the ranks of the Household Selected Soldiers, as opposed to officers appointed from the regular banners to manage them, were referred to as receiving "empty epaulettes" (Ma. *untuhun jingse*). According to one 1736 memorial: "because they are not at all legitimate lieutenants, [they should] receive salaries and grain stipends just like those of the Household Selected Soldiers."[48] That is, though lieutenants needed to be appointed for practical military purposes, the Household Selected Soldiers lacked the right to hold officer posts, so even those appointed to posts as lieutenants would not receive higher salaries. Thus, though it had bought these people out of slavery and provided them the same support available to banner people who did not hold officer rank, the Qing state seems not to have forgotten their origins in slavery.

Yet denying the Household Selected Soldiers the full set of opportunities available to other bannermen did not reflect a retreat from the idea that banner slaves could earn banner status. Indeed, the case of the Household Selected Soldiers served as a precedent for granting regular banner status to others who fought in frontier military campaigns. In 1739, Plain Blue Mongol Banner colonel Sanjab 三扎布 requested that the descendants of those entailed householders—that is, former banner slaves who had obtained their freedom via self-purchase or adoption—who died in battle against the Zunghars at Lake Khoton and Usun Juil be elevated to detached household status and allowed to receive posts in the cavalry, not just the infantry posts to which they had previously been limited.[49] In support of his claim, he referred to the case of the Household Selected Soldiers, who for "having served vigorously" (Ma. *faššame yabufi*) had been made into detached householders, along with their families. Surely, he argued, if the men who had fought at Lake Khoton and Usun Juil had survived, they would have received the same favor, and their sons and grandsons would have been eligible for better-paying posts in the cavalry. Since their fathers and grandfathers had died for the dynasty, they deserved to receive the same favor as the Household Selected Soldiers.[50]

The idea that banner slaves could be raised to the status of banner people because of their military service remained important during the second half of the eighteenth century, even in the latter part of the expulsion era, when the Household Selected Soldiers themselves had been targeted for removal from the banners. During the second Jinchuan campaign of the early 1770s, the Qianlong emperor issued an edict declaring that men of various categories of slaves, "if they fight truly, persistently, and assiduously, should be made into detached households and enrolled in banner companies" as part of a policy of "encouraging (Turkic) Muslim and Oirat slaves [Ma. *Hoise Ūlet kutule*] who acted diligently." Following the victory in Jinchuan, one memorial by Agūi 阿桂, the commander of the Qing forces during the final years of the war, identified four men, Norbu, Batumungke, Bayarlahū, and Gumbu, each a slave of a banner soldier, as having "followed the official army for a long time, taken the lead in exerting themselves persistently, and killed bandits." Batumungke and Gumbu had even suffered wounds in battle. So, he suggested, they all should be made into detached householders and given posts as soldiers (Ma. *uksin*) of the banner companies with which their masters were associated.[51]

Thirteen years later, in the early postexpulsion era, the precedent of Jinchuan would reappear in the wake of the Taiwan campaign of 1787–1788, in which banner troops helped put down the rebellion of Lin Shuangwen 林爽文. After describing a heroic attack by banner soldiers to break the siege of Zhuluo 諸羅, the commander Fuk'anggan 福康安 emphasized the essential contributions of certain "Torghut, Oirat, (Turkic) Muslim, and Tibetan slaves" (Ma. *Turgūt. Ūlet. Hoise. Fandzi i kutule*) of his officers. He had selected these men on account of their prowess in mounted archery, spear wielding, and musketry and provided them with horses; and "in each attack, they were entered among the number of our brave men. They charged together and the bandits fled in terror. These men also performed assiduously, and each of them killed a certain number of bandits, seized flags and banners, and some even suffered wounds." Fuk'anggan noted that in the Jinchuan campaign, "this sort of people was enrolled in the banners," so he recommended that the Oirat slave Mamušan and the Torghut slaves Ūljei, Basang, Dacun, and Tahai receive the same reward. The emperor agreed, appending a rescript reading: "this is proper" (Ma. *giyan ningge*).[52]

Related to cases of slaves being elevated to banner status are cases of banner people arguing that they should not be treated as former slaves and thus denied some of the privileges of banner status. One such case comes from 1732, when a group of men at the Hangzhou garrison argued that they should be treated like regular Hanjun bannermen because of the service of some of their ancestors. The people in question were listed in the official registers under categories used for freed banner slaves, and thus were ineligible for many salaried posts. A group of eight of them, writing on behalf of more than 290 households, claimed that this was not appropriate to their history and situation:

> Our ancestors were originally all commoners from Mukden.[53] In the Tianming period [1616–1627], they became aware of the rise in fortune of our dynasty [the Qing], and accompanying the people of twenty-nine surnames, including Tong 佟, Shi 石, and Li 李, they came to surrender to our dynasty. They were divided among the companies of the people of the Tong, Shi, and Li clans, and after many years had passed, they made all of us people who had accompanied them in coming over [to the Qing] into their subordinates. If we truly are their slaves, how is it that our ancestors were not left behind in their ancestral villages to serve? How is it that in the fifth year of the Shunzhi period [1648], we were garrisoned in Hangzhou? We are clearly their subordinates (Ma. *hartungga niyalma*), and are absolutely not their slaves (Ma. *booi niyalma*). From the Tianming period on, our ancestors risked their lives in military service, expending their strength to the point of sacrificing their bodies.[54]

The petition from the men went on to list no fewer than fifty-eight battles and campaigns, ranging from the preconquest era to the rebellion of the Three Feudatories, in which their ancestors had fought, and noted that thirty-four of them had received official commendation for their service, while forty-five more had died in battle. The Hangzhou garrison general Arigūn, in relaying their petition, endorsed their logic, suggesting that this long history of family military service meant that they should not be compared to normal banner household slaves. The court accepted this argument, allowing those for whom evidence of their ancestors' service could be found to be treated like regular banner people.[55] Three years later, just weeks after the death of the Yongzheng emperor, this policy was modified by the Grand Council, requiring that the people included in the original petition be selected for promotion to posts as officers only when no qualified men who had always been listed as regular bannermen were available.[56]

Yet their position was still improved relative to before, when they had lacked any right to promotion.

The fact that these Hangzhou bannermen pointed to their ancestors' military service as a legitimation of their own position shows that the connection between service and status was a well-understood part of the Qing system. Grants of banner status to the Household Selected Soldiers and other banner slaves might be read simply as specific incentives offered to a particular group at a particular time. But the fact that bannermen themselves saw a past family history of fighting for the dynasty as justifying their status in the present makes clear that this was a general principle. Those who loyally served the dynasty at crucial moments, risking or sacrificing their lives, as the Hangzhou bannermen's petition pointed out, would see that loyalty rewarded. The hereditary nature of banner status had particular significance, as the expectation that banner people would put their lives on the line for the dynasty was justified by their descendants' continued enjoyment of the privileges of banner membership.

Principles of Service Elite Membership

The concern for managing a diverse population and for rewarding loyal service apparent in the Qing approach to entry into the banner system is emblematic of the role of the banners as a service elite. By early in the consolidation era, shortly after the Qing conquest, opportunities to join the banner system had become quite rare—the overwhelming majority of banner people in the mid- and late-Qing periods were descendants of people who had become followers of Nurhaci or Hong Taiji during the early development of the Aisin Gioro–ruled state. When new entrants were permitted, their selection was designed to ensure the continuation of the exchange of loyal service for institutionalized privilege that was the basis of service elite identity. For the Qing, as an expansive multiethnic empire, a willingness to incorporate people from a range of backgrounds into its service elite was a way to maintain stability and reduce the risk of rebellion. Banner membership was not the only way to manage newly incorporated elites, but the existence of the system gave the Qing more flexibility in how it dealt with truculent Chahars or recently conquered Turkic Muslims than would a more exclusive reliance on civil examinations to define an imperial elite.

The idea that some new banner people were granted banner status to permit their closer supervision by the Qing state does not run against the idea that the banners were an elite. Rather, the favorable treatment that came with banner membership worked in conjunction with the closer supervision that it entailed to both incentivize and enforce loyalty among populations that the dynasty did not think it could afford to alienate. Meanwhile, the state's willingness to elevate the position of banner slaves who served with distinction does not reflect any sense that banner people were themselves debased. Instead, it demonstrates the importance of the household-based logic of the Qing status system to determining who could be in the banners. Ordinarily, a banner slave was more likely to be raised to regular banner status than a high-ranking commoner official was. In many ways, the barriers between a high-ranking bannerman and his slave were more porous than those between two leading officials if one was in the banners and the other a commoner. It is only through recognizing the centrality of status to the Qing social order and to the Qing conception of the banners that we can understand why a slave might become a bannerman, but a member of the gentry would almost certainly not.

CHAPTER 3

Duty, Service, and Status Performance

Service elites were organized around the service that they provided to ruling dynasties. The Eight Banners were a key component of Qing dynastic rule, helping the Qing emperors to conquer, hold, and govern one of the early modern world's most extensive and populous states. Over the course of the banner system's existence, the Aisin Gioro–ruled state that it served grew from a small confederation, limited to part of southern Manchuria, to a large and diverse polity that ruled not just Manchuria and the former territory of the Chinese Ming dynasty, but large and culturally distinct swaths of Inner Asia, like Tibet, Mongolia, and the Turkic Muslim oases of southern Xinjiang. The deployment of bannermen in tasks and contexts very different from the ones in which they served Nurhaci in the early seventeenth century was essential to Qing control over these spaces. To direct bannermen into work that was useful to the court, the Qing state forbade them from taking on nonofficial employment.[1] This chapter will explore what bannermen actually did, and thus why the immense cost of their support was worthwhile for their lord, the Qing emperor.

In addition, this chapter explores a second dimension of banner service: the expectations of status performance that the court imposed on bannermen. The Qing rulers saw the propagation of a set of ethnically Manchu-inflected norms as key to maintaining the martial prowess of its ethnically diverse service elite. Moreover, demands that bannermen engage in certain sorts of behavior and develop particular skills were designed to maintain the separation between people of banner status and the rest of the dynasty's subjects. When bannermen, even those on nonmilitary career tracks, learned to shoot a bow from horseback, that training was itself a form of service to the emperor, just as actually fighting in a battle would have been. The distinctiveness of banner life bound banner people to the court, ensuring that it could make use of them in perpetuity.

While, in practice, the effectiveness of banner service in advancing dynastic interests may have declined over the years and adherence to the precepts defining banner status was uneven at best, the ideology of banner service remained powerful through the end of the Qing period. Even in the late nineteenth century, banner officials attempted to maintain the banners as a useful fighting force and deployed them to meet new challenges, like learning the languages of the European powers whose increasing presence in the empire posed one of the greatest threats to Qing power. Moreover, the provision of banner service was a genuinely multiethnic affair. Not only were Han bannermen, just like their Manchu and Mongol counterparts, expected to uphold the officially defined expectations of banner behavior, but they also performed the same categories of work for the ruler. There were, at times, ethnicized differences in the performance of particular types of service. Mongol bannermen did much more work in Inner Asian languages, especially Mongolian, while Han bannermen were the main component of banner artillery units. But all banner groups served.

Official discourse on banner service focused mostly on men, with the work of service coded as a masculine endeavor. This is not to say that women's service was irrelevant to the dynasty; its importance will be explored in chapter 5. But the specializations assigned to the banners, whether soldiery, translation, mapmaking, or the procurement of high-value manufactured goods for imperial use, were all treated as men's work. And, similarly, the expectations of banner people that appear with great frequency in official documents were directed at men. Although service elite women mattered, both to the Qing and to other early modern dynastic states, masculinity was central to how the banners and other service elites were defined and imagined.

In addition to describing the nature of banner service and official expectations of bannermen, this chapter briefly discusses the change in the nature of banner service during the consolidation era, following the Qing conquest and continuing until the early eighteenth century. Over this time, the banners were transformed from a feudal-like system, in which particular posts (and thus particular forms of authority) were passed from father to son, to a more bureaucratic and meritocratic system in which all men of banner status were, at least theoretically, eligible to hold most of the posts designated for members of their status group or subgroup.[2] Much of this transition, particularly the changes that took place in the Yongzheng era, has already been well covered in the work of Pei Huang.[3] But it is important to emphasize here to show how the banners fit into a broader comparative service elite paradigm, characterized by extensive bureaucratization. The conversion of a preexisting martial elite into a highly bureaucratized service class was not simply the result of the Manchu encounter with and emulation of the administrative institutions of Ming China.[4] Rather, the development of institutions for managing banner service was a solution to one of the challenges faced by many expanding early modern dynastic states: the need to increase state capacity while maintaining the loyalty of the dynasty's armed and powerful allies.

Official Service

The banners originated as a form of military organization, and banner people were and are understood, first and foremost, as soldiers in the service of the Qing dynasty. Banner armies carried out the conquest of Ming territory in 1644 and the years following; played crucial roles in Qing expansion into Inner Asia, including Mongolia, Amdo, and Xinjiang; and garrisoned major cities across the empire. But to reduce the role of banner people in the Qing system to that of soldiers would be an oversimplification. The banners supplied the Qing court with a range of crucial forms of service, from work as civil officials, especially in the administration of Inner Asia, to translation and interpretation between the empire's various languages, to scientific, technical, and artistic work in support of both imperial governance and the lifestyle of the dynastic house. It was this combination of various types of service, both military and administrative, that defined the role of the Qing service elite.

Because the military role of bannermen is so well known, I will give it less attention than it might otherwise merit.[5] But it was fundamental to the lives of men in the banners. In the dynasty's early years, spending large amounts of time on campaign was a common experience for bannermen. For instance, during the rebellion of the Three Feudatories, between 1673 and 1681, between 160,000 and 200,000 banner soldiers were sent south to fight the rebels, out of a banner population that, as of 1654, consisted of 387,274 men of fighting age.[6] Bannermen served in various military roles, with some specialization based on ethnic division. Manchus and Mongols controlled the units of imperial guards and were disproportionately represented in the cavalry, while infantry, firearms, and artillery were specialties of the Hanjun.[7] These areas of specialization were consistent for most of the dynasty's history. For instance, the creation of the earliest Hanjun banner companies was tied to Hong Taiji's efforts to acquire effective artillery, and two hundred years later, in the nineteenth century, the annual artillery drills in Beijing during the ninth lunar month were still conducted entirely by the Hanjun.[8] Similarly, the infantry of the Guangzhou garrison in 1884 still consisted exclusively of Hanjun, while the garrison's vanguard (Ma. *gabsihiyan*, Ch. 前鋒 [*qianfeng*]) included only Manchus.[9]

It is worth focusing at greater length on military service by banner people in the postexpulsion era to demonstrate the extensive continuities in the role of the banners across the two-and-a-half centuries of Aisin Gioro rule. Although campaign experience was no longer ubiquitous among bannermen in the dynasty's later years, particularly after the conquest of Xinjiang in the 1750s in the empire's final major act of expansion, the banners continued to be a major source of military power for the dynasty. Banner armies proved far less capable against the nineteenth-century challenges of European incursions and mass rebellions than they had against Russian, Ming, and Three Feudatory armies in the seventeenth century or Zunghar armies in the eighteenth. Yet the once commonly held notion that they were more-or-less worthless, still sometimes repeated in more general histories, has come under challenge.[10] British observers issued favorable reports of the bravery and discipline of the banner soldiers of the Jingkou 京口 garrison (located in present-day Zhenjiang) in the wake of an 1842 engagement in which British troops captured the city, suggesting that their defeat was due only to the massive technological gap between the sides.[11] Similarly, both the banner people of Zhapu 乍浦 and their British opponents insisted that the garrison's resistance had been heroic and ferocious, far exceeding the expectations of the European invaders.[12]

Regardless of how we assess their skill, it is clear that bannermen continued to be soldiers involved in every major military conflict of the nineteenth century. The Hangzhou garrison played a key role in defending the city against attack during the Taiping war, successfully against a first foray and then to the point of calamitous defeat and loss of life in what ended up being the second successful attack. And bannermen both participated in and helped to organize the famous midcentury armies of commanders like Zeng Guofan that eventually helped defeat the rebels.[13] The reconquest of Xinjiang, in the wake of another midcentury rebellion and invasion from the khanate of Kokand, was famously accomplished by the Hunan Army of Zuo Zongtang. But even here, the banner army led by the Manchu commander Ginšun, who commanded forces drawn in large part from the New Manchu populations of Jilin and Heilongjiang, was one of the main players.[14] The Daur writer Donjina, who served in that army, would later describe its role in heroic terms as having defended the empire and imperial rule, in the face of difficult conditions, against "base rebels." His work is evidence that in addition to their practical role as soldiers, military service to the dynasty remained essential to the self-conception of many bannermen.[15]

As a more comprehensive way of looking at the continued centrality of military service, including participation in battle, to the lives of bannermen in the postexpulsion era, consider the casualty records included in the late-nineteenth-century gazetteer of the Guangzhou garrison. The list of bannermen who lost their lives in battle shows that between 1787 and 1866, bannermen from that garrison alone participated in at least seven distinct wars or expeditions. These included the suppression of the Lin Shuangwen rebellion on Taiwan in 1787–1788, battles in Guangzhou as part of the First Opium War in 1841, a campaign in Guangxi against Taiping rebels in 1851, battles against Red Turban rebels around Guangzhou in 1854–1856, the Battle of Canton as part of the Second Opium War against both British and French troops in 1857, and two separate "bandit suppression" campaigns in rural Guangdong in 1858 and 1866.[16]

Moreover, Qing officials made some efforts to modernize banner armies and keep them relevant during the late Qing. For instance, beginning in 1875, the Guangzhou garrison general Cangšan worked to upgrade the firearms and artillery available to his men, to replace older types of cannons as well as flintlock and matchlock muskets with new "foreign guns" (Ma. *namu miyoocan*, Ch. 洋鎗 [*yangqiang*]) that were easier to use and could fire more rapidly and under adverse weather conditions because they used a caplock mechanism. Cangšan had 1,200 men trained on the new weapons, of whom 120 worked with artillery and the rest with the new, handheld guns. He described the training as successful, with the new weapons indeed proving far more workable than the older ones, and, declared that in light of the extreme importance of Guangzhou as a site of maritime defense, it would be best to "do away with old prejudices, and act according to the circumstances" in choosing military equipment. So, in 1880, he called for training an additional 800 men in their use, with the clear goal of eventually making the more modern weaponry ubiquitous at the garrison. Unfortunately, lack of funding impeded him in carrying out the desired expansion as quickly as he had hoped, but it was clear that Cangšan's plan was to maintain the military value of his garrison rather than let it decline into irrelevance. His proposal to this effect received the court's endorsement.[17]

By 1883, drills in the new weapons had become a standard part of garrison training, reported alongside local bannermen's abilities in the traditional military skills of mounted and standing archery.[18] Attention to maintaining an up-to-date garrison continued into the twentieth century. In 1902, the garrison general Shou-yin 壽蔭 discussed the garrison's adoption of Mauser rifles (Ch. 毛瑟洋槍 [Maose yangqiang]) and Krupp cannons (Ch. 克虜伯車礮 [Kelubo chepao]), while proposing a reorganization of the garrison that would include the creation of a new military academy.[19] Although banner armies indeed lost importance relative to various new army units, there is no question that military service remained a central function of bannermen, even in the final years of the dynasty. The Qing court, though impeded by financial difficulties, was not willing to give up on the idea of bannermen being central to its defense.

Second only to military service was the work that bannermen did as linguistic specialists, particularly as translators.[20] The Qing state operated multilingually. Within the imperial government, Manchu and literary Chinese were the most widely used written languages, but Mongolian was also of great importance and Tibetan and Chaghatay, though less ubiquitous, were crucial in certain administrative and religious contexts. Nearly all of the scribal and translation work needed to keep the polylingual state in operation was performed by bannermen.[21] Commoner officials, for the most part, were only capable of reading and writing Chinese, while banner officials were usually proficient in both written Chinese and written Manchu.[22] The expectation that bannermen in the bureaucracy would produce and consume communications in both languages, with the choice of language depending on what post a particular official held, what subject a document dealt with, and what type of document it was, meant not only that men with important posts would be bilingual, but their staffs would need to be as well. This need, combined with bureaucratic requirements that certain types of documents (most notably routine memorials) be bilingual, meant that large numbers of banner people were needed to carry out work in both Manchu and Chinese before even considering the empire's other languages.

In part to meet this need, the Qing court founded schools in both Beijing and provincial garrisons to teach bannermen to read and write Manchu and to translate between Manchu and Chinese. Although some such schools opened in the seventeenth century, their numbers grew most rapidly under the Yongzheng emperor in the years around 1730, when free Manchu-language schools for Han bannermen were founded for each banner in Beijing and for those provincial garrisons consisting exclusively of Hanjun.[23] The initial ethnic targeting appears to have sprung from a belief that Manchu and Mongol bannermen were likely to become sufficiently versed in Manchu without any special provisions. By 1760, though, that expectation no longer held, and similar schools were opened in Manchu-dominated garrisons.[24] These schools, as revealed by their standards for evaluating instructors, took training translators between Manchu and Chinese as their primary objective. Those instructors who trained a sufficient number of students capable of passing examinations in translation were eligible for promotion to higher-ranking posts in the bureaucracy.[25] Students themselves, if successful in their studies, were often employed as secretaries in local banner offices with the potential for further promotion.[26]

While Han and Manchu bannermen were trained in and relied on for work in translation between Manchu and Chinese, Mongol bannermen specialized in translation between Manchu and Mongolian, which was an important responsibility, particularly in the context of the Lifan yuan, the agency responsible for official oversight of Qing Mongolia. For instance, while Han and Manchu bannermen who wished to receive an official degree through the translation examination system, which existed in parallel to the regular civil service exams but was open only to bannermen, were tested in Chinese-Manchu translation, Mongol bannermen were tested in Manchu-Mongolian translation.[27]

Mongol bannermen's knowledge of Mongolian permitted them to take on work to which other bannermen were not suited. For instance, in 1739, the Mukden Board of Rites proposed appointing Mongol bannermen as officials to manage a nonbanner Mongol herding territory just outside the Willow Palisade, near Janggūtai (Ch. 彰武台 [Zhangwutai]). The proposal noted that their Mongolian-language abilities would make them much more suited to the task than the Manchu bannermen who were then being employed, who knew no Mongolian and, in part for that reason, were not able to avoid fraud and losses in the collection of revenue from the herders.[28] Their dominance of basic scribal and translation posts in the Lifan yuan similarly reflected the importance of their linguistic skills. Although full lists of low-level Lifan yuan officials are not available, of the forty-seven Lifan yuan translation clerks (Ma. *bithesi*, Ch. 筆帖式 [*bitieshi*]) who appear in a database of Qing officials on account of their later career success, thirty were Mongol bannermen, fifteen were Manchu bannermen, and one was a Hanjun bannerman.[29] Given that Mongols were by far the smallest of the three banner ethnic categories, these results suggest a strong preference for hiring Mongol bannermen to carry out basic documentary tasks in the Lifan yuan. The court relied on their linguistic skills to manage the non-Han portions of the empire.

Even when dealing with languages other than those that one might assume were naturally associated with banner people on account of their ethnic origins, the dynasty relied on bannermen. Over the course of the seventeenth and eighteenth centuries, the court established official schools for Tibetan, Oirat, Chaghatay, Burmese, Persian, and Russian in the capital. All such schools limited their enrollment to bannermen. Some were more specific in their choice of students, as with the Tibetan school, which enrolled only Mongol bannermen.[30] The need for this linguistic expertise was such that, at least in some cases, young bannermen received stipends for enrolling in the schools. In the 1790s, for instance, banner students at the Muslim School (Ma. *Hoise tacikū*, Ch. 回子官學 [*Huizi guanxue*]), where Chaghatay and Persian were taught, received monthly stipends of 2 taels of silver, in comparison to the 3 taels per month paid to ordinary soldiers in provincial garrisons.[31] As with Mongolian banner people, students from these schools could find employment in the Lifan yuan, which managed territories in which the relevant languages were used in official business. At other times, they could serve in the Imperial Household Department, helping to manage the production and supply of goods used in the court itself.[32]

Russian-language education for bannermen differed from education in many other languages in that it was not conducted exclusively in Beijing. Due to its proximity to the Russian empire, Xinjiang was faced with Russian border crossers from time to time, with whom local officials needed to be able to communicate. For much of the late eighteenth century, the office of the Ili general, the highest Qing authority in the region, relied on translators selected from among Oirats who had entered Qing territory from Kazakhstan and who could speak Russian.[33] But by 1792, such individuals were becoming scarce. So the Ili general Booning 保寧 proposed that a student from the Russian-language school in Beijing be sent to Ili to open a school there, where bannermen who were already competent in standard Mongolian and the Oirat clear script (Ma. *Tot bithe*) could study oral and written Russian. They would henceforth fill Xinjiang's need for Russian translators.[34] Initially, a dozen or so Ili bannermen were selected to study under an instructor named Mukdengge, and they saw good enough results, based on a review of their examination papers at the main Russian school in Beijing, that Mukdengge was permitted to return to Beijing and receive a promotion into the regular bureaucracy. Thereafter, a student in Ili who performed well would take over the job of instructor for a five-year term, with an opportunity for promotion into the local bureaucracy as a ninth-rank *bithesi* if his students learned the language well. This system was to continue in perpetuity.[35]

As it turned out, in the ensuing decades Russian arrivals in Xinjiang became infrequent. But after more than fifty years, when a group of Russian merchants arrived in Ili, the local banner translators proved incapable of translating fluently, understanding only the general gist of the documents that the merchants were carrying, and were completely incompetent at interpreting their speech. The Ili general at the time, Yishan 奕山, proposed having the local banner students study with visiting Russian merchants, who were now crossing into Ili more regularly, in the interest of restoring his office's linguistic capabilities.[36] The idea that bannermen were the proper source of linguistic expertise for the state remained strong even in the face of their discouraging performance.

The importance of languages, interpretation, and translation to the service provided by banner people continued even as new languages became significant to the Qing court. The official European-language schools, called Tongwen Guan 同文館, which were established in Beijing and Guangzhou in the early 1860s, initially enrolled student bodies made up exclusively of bannermen.[37] Although the Beijing school soon expanded to teach more subjects in addition to foreign languages, and, at the same time, to enroll commoners as well as bannermen, the Guangzhou school would remain focused on training bannermen in languages like English, Russian, Japanese, and French.[38] In keeping with the idea that translation was associated with the banners as a whole, not just one ethnic group within them, both Han and Manchu bannermen were enrolled in the school, though the former outnumbered the latter. The school in Guangzhou was clearly modeled on earlier Manchu-language schools for bannermen, reinforcing the sense of connection between training bannermen to use Manchu and training them to use other languages.[39] Students at the Guangzhou school were used to handle interpretation between foreigners and the Qing authorities, with the garrison general Cangšan explaining his preference for the school's students over hiring local commoners who knew languages like English on the grounds that the latter might translate "fraudulently" (Ch. 作弊 [*zuobi*]), either seeking to benefit themselves or working in cahoots with the foreigners.[40] Translation was a highly sensitive subject, and the Qing state saw translators as playing a crucial role in diplomacy.[41] The clear preference for assigning this task to bannermen reflected the court's trust in them, just as its reliance on them to garrison key cities did.[42] So translation and knowledge of multiple languages, like more martial activities, constituted a crucial part of how bannermen served the dynasty.

Although translation perhaps had a special importance due to the need for linguistic expertise in many areas of the Qing bureaucracy, it was not the only domain of technical expertise for which the court relied on banner people. Indeed, as Kaijun Chen has argued, bannermen served as "specialist technocrats" and as the key source of "technological expertise" for the Qing court, filling a role that has often been ignored in favor of a focus on generalist commoner officials. Chen's work focuses on bannermen in the Imperial Household Department and their role in the Imperial Porcelain Manufactory, where they oversaw the production of ceramic objects for use in the court. Bannermen who worked in this agency became experts on the technical aspects of porcelain manufacture, often bringing together knowledge from multiple regions or even continents. For instance, they recorded and disseminated learning from both artisans in the porcelain factories of Jingdezhen, in Jiangxi province, and from Jesuit missionaries in the court who shared their knowledge of European artistic and technical concepts, which could then be integrated into the manufacture of objects for the court.

Commoner officials were excluded from most aspects of technical work, as well as other specialized tasks like the oversight of customs houses. As Chen argues, this division of labor led to bannermen developing distinct ways of understanding, representing, and communicating knowledge, in part because their learning was often the result of hands-on training in particular physical techniques. Thus, in addition to written treatises, bannermen experts produced "preparatory sketches, drawings, and three-dimensional models" and developed specialized tools of experimentation, including "kiln furniture, test pieces, and specimen shards," which enabled the effective communication of "technical details between the court and the local manufactories." Bannermen were not just artisans—indeed, most of the actual production was done by commoner workers—but technocratic specialists in management, innovation, and design as well as intermediaries between the court and actual porcelain factories. They produced mock-ups of objects in accordance with direction from the court, even from the emperor himself, to communicate imperial desires in an effective manner to those who would produce the actual objects.[43]

As Chen notes, the use of bannermen of the Imperial Household Department as technocrats and technical experts extended far beyond the realm of porcelain production. In the first place, it extended to other domains of artistic production. The use of bannermen to oversee textile production is well known from Jonathan Spence's writing on Cao Yin, which observes that this work was officially put under the auspices of the Imperial Household Department in 1663.[44] Cao also was placed in charge of overseeing the imperial salt monopoly in the Lianghuai salt zone along the Yangtze River, a role that continued to be held almost exclusively by bannermen in subsequent years. These salt administrators, as part of their management of wealthy Jiangnan merchants, took responsibility for sourcing goods like jade objects, golden leaves, dishes, and furniture for the imperial court.[45] In addition to these manufactured goods, it was banner people who handled the production of wild products for the court. Pearl harvesting was not just overseen by the Imperial Household Department, but also carried out by a New Manchu group, the Ula, many of whom were officially enrolled in the banners of the department. Moreover, after an early attempt to directly assign bannermen to ginseng picking, a licensing system was used instead. But banner garrisons remained responsible for issuing permits to enter ginseng-producing mountains and preventing poaching.[46]

Bannermen also provided the dynasty with scientific and mathematical expertise. For a brief period in the 1730s, official instruction in mathematics was established for bannermen alone in the context of banner schools. Even when Han commoners were included in imperial mathematical initiatives, bannermen remained overrepresented, such as in the compilation of a set of official texts on mathematics completed in the early 1720s, for which more than half the contributors were bannermen. This included the vast majority of two types of technical experts involved: Observers, of whom 80 percent were bannermen, and Calculators, of whom 60 percent were bannermen.[47] The prominence of bannermen was even more pronounced in imperial cartography. During the grand imperial mapmaking projects of the late Kangxi period, teams consisting of European Jesuits, banner officials from the Imperial Household Department, banner military officers, and officials (nearly all of them of banner status) from the Board of Personnel, the Lifan yuan and the Directorate of Astronomy, carried out surveys across the empire.[48] Their work resulted in the largest mapping project seen anywhere in the world up to that date, a triumph of Qing-European scientific collaboration that relied, on the Qing side, on experts from within the banner system.[49]

In addition to their work as soldiers, linguists, and technocrats, bannermen served in a wide variety of administrative posts at all levels of the Qing government. For certain types of positions, particularly within local bureaucracies, there was only a weak association between banner status and government work. That is, bannermen could serve as county magistrates, for example, but were a distinct minority in such posts, with no sense that such employment was a function particular to their status. Rather, most local administrators in the provinces that had once belonged to the Ming dynasty came from the well-educated upper stratum of the commoner status group. But in other areas of the bureaucracy, bannermen played a disproportionate role in another form of specialist or technocratic work: namely, as specialists in particular types of administration. This included, of course, the administration of the banners themselves, which was the exclusive province of bannermen. While a bannerman could be a county magistrate or the commander of commoner soldiers in the Green Standard army, no commoner could ever be a banner garrison general or captain of a banner company. This was no minor point; the number of officials in the Eight Banner system likely exceeded that of the entire Qing civil administration.[50]

Bannermen also were specialists in frontier administration, especially in Inner Asia, where the work clearly related to their expertise in languages. The Lifan yuan was staffed entirely by bannermen at all levels, clearly differentiating it from the Six Boards, which employed both bannermen and commoners.[51] Similarly, the ambans who served as the dynasty's representatives in regions like Tibet, Xinjiang, and Mongolia were exclusively drawn from the ranks of bannermen, and it was only beginning in the late nineteenth century that commoner officials gained any power in these regions.[52]

It was not until about 1800 that Han commoner scholars even began to see the empire's Inner Asian possessions as falling within their area of concern—such was the degree to which bannermen monopolized the relevant expertise for the first century-and-a-half of Qing rule.[53]

The Bureaucratization of Service

A key feature of the Qing administrative system, and one that helps differentiate service elites like the banners from feudal aristocracies, was that even though there were many posts in the government open only to bannermen on account of their status, authority was, for the most part, not hereditary, but meritocratic. Bannermen were born into a privileged status group, but only those bannermen who distinguished themselves through their service would ever hold real power. This is not to say that all bannermen had equal access to rank or positions of authority. The Qing court issued noble titles, disproportionately to members of the ruling Aisin Gioro family, and such men had privileged access to the upper ranks of the banner bureaucracy.[54] But this sort of inheritance of privilege did not make the selection of bannermen for official posts any less meritocratic than the selection of commoners. For commoners, advancement through the examination system, though theoretically open to most of the male population, generally functioned as a form of social reproduction for a small portion of the population with family wealth and histories of educational achievement.[55] And, of course, contemporary societies with no legal form of hereditary social differentiation continue to replicate inequality across generations. So, in describing the banners as an internal meritocracy, I mean only that holders of particular positions of responsibility and power were selected via a competitive process, not a hereditary one. As a result, the general in charge of a particular garrison and the amban who oversaw a particular frontier territory would not be the sons of the previous incumbents, but rather bureaucrats who had been promoted through various lower-ranking posts in the government. There were certain exceptions to this general pattern, but they represented an ever-smaller portion of the positions available to bannermen as the Qing service elite developed into its mature form.

In the earliest years of their existence, the banners functioned more like a feudal aristocracy than as the bureaucratic meritocracy that they would become. As Nurhaci first began forming the banners, he incorporated preexisting social units like tribes, clans, and villages and left their leadership intact. But even under Nurhaci's leadership, there was a tendency toward bureaucratization, as in 1615, companies of approximately equal size were formed, which required the division and amalgamation of preexisting groups. A standardized set of officer posts was created for this more regimented banner organization, although ultimate control over the banners remained in the hands of princes from among Nurhaci's immediate family. For former local powerholders, these reforms began a process by which they lost their independent authority and, as Gertraude Roth-Li argues, "were transformed into military officers who drew their authority and prestige from their rank in the banner system." Beginning in the 1610s, Nurhaci also made successful efforts to reduce the power of the hereditary Jurchen elite, including many of his relatives, giving greater authority to ministers and advisors whom he had appointed. Yet his reliance on marriage ties to bind this new elite to him, with his five most important ministers all becoming his sons-in-law, gave a continued aristocratic flavor to state power in his fledgling empire.[56]

Under Hong Taiji, each of the eight banners remained a genuinely separate institution, and the upper ranks of each banner saw their interests as aligned with those of their banner as a whole. This was apparent in the succession dispute after Hong Taiji's death. Members of both yellow banners, for instance, lined up in favor of Hong Taiji's eldest son, Hooge, but they were resisted by the white banners, who followed the lead of Dorgon, Nurhaci's fourteenth son and lord of the Bordered White Banner. The leaders of the yellow banners, which were Hong Taiji's personal property, believed their interests rested in elevating one of his sons, who would maintain their superior position. White banner leaders, meanwhile, feared that they would see their position further diminished, as it had been when Hong Taiji had taken power in the first place. The ultimate decision was a compromise. Hong Taiji's five-year-old son Fulin, associated with the yellow banners like his father, took the throne as the Shunzhi emperor, and his uncle Dorgon served as his regent, assisted by Jirgalang, lord of the Bordered Blue Banner.[57] This sort of conflict among the banners suggests that, as of 1643, the banners were genuinely separate fiefdoms, although the fiefdoms consisted only of people, not of defined geographical territories.

Upon the fall of the Ming in 1644, the Qing banner system retained two major forms of hereditary, feudal authority. One was the ownership of banners by prominent members of the Aisin Gioro family, who owed their position to descent from sons of Nurhaci who had controlled the same banners. The other was the hereditary control of particular banner companies, which were eventually classified into two types. The first included those companies granted to men who, during the time of Nurhaci and Hong Taiji, either brought large numbers of followers with them to submit or had exemplary achievements in battle (Ma. *fujuri niru*, Ch. 勳舊佐領 [*xunjiu zuoling*]). The second comprised those given to capable men who served the dynasty faithfully in the conquest period and so were given the right to permanently pass on their posts (Ma. *jalan halame bošoro niru*, Ch. 世管佐領 [*shiguan zuoling*]). These were joined by a third type of company, the "public company" (Ma. *siden niru*, Ch. 公中佐領 [*gongzhong zuoling*]), whose captains were appointed.[58]

Under the reign of the Yongzheng emperor, both of these types of inherited power became less important. The power of banner lords was already in decline, in part because the Kangxi emperor had given control of the three Plain Blue Banners to his seventh son, Yunyou 胤祐, during the final years of his reign. Yongzheng went beyond his father's actions to appoint new commanders for several of the banners, and moreover to make the appointments temporary administrative posts rather than permanent hereditary ones.[59] Banner commanders were put under additional bureaucratic supervision, with censors and imperial bodyguards dispatched to oversee their work. That Yongzheng put an end to the banners' role as quasi-fiefdoms was perhaps best demonstrated by his firing of no fewer than twelve banner commanders (Ma. *gūsai ejen*, Ch. 都統 [*dutong*]) and seventeen lieutenant generals during the first three years of his reign alone.[60] In addition, he increased the number of public companies by removing many companies from the control of imperial princes.[61]

Although hereditary companies continued to exist for the entirety of the Qing period, even their commanders were subject to bureaucratic oversight. One form that this took was competition over promotion, where commanders of different types of companies were considered alongside one another. Take, for instance, the selection of a new colonel (Ma. *jalan i janggin*, Ch. 參領 [*canling*]) in the Bordered Yellow Hanjun Banner in 1759. The post of colonel was one step above that of company captain, and colonels commanded regiments, of which there were five in each of the metropolitan banners. As was standard for promotion decisions within the banners, the emperor was presented with multiple candidates of appropriate rank who had been judged qualified by their superiors.⁶² In this case, these were a "hereditary company captain" (Ma. *jalan halame bošoho nirui janggin*) named Ma Zhaogong, and two "public company captains" (Ma. *siden i nirui janggin*) named Hua Changyu and Zhou Dechang. All three men had their careers briefly described, including their age and length of service, their skill in standing and mounted archery, and their diligence in administrative work.⁶³ This entirely unexceptional promotion case, repeated with great frequency in the archives, suggests that all banner officers, even those who had inherited their posts, were to be treated as part of the regular bureaucracy and evaluated by the same standards as those applied to men who had reached their post via promotion.

Banner service was thus a highly bureaucratic and meritocratic affair, at least by the 1720s. The descendants of men who had held local power in their own right, in the context of village, clan, and tribal organizations in pre-1644 Manchuria, had, through their inclusion in the banner system, come to serve in ways controlled and directed by the Qing court. Moreover, they were evaluated side-by-side with, and on the same terms as, men of lesser pedigree who also held banner status. The Qing use of its service elite contributed to the centralization of power in the hands of the emperor and the inner court, with bannermen becoming agents of the dynasty and members of a ranked bureaucracy who were subject to a standardized set of rules and procedures.

Status Performance

Banner people did not just provide valuable practical services to the court. They were expected in addition, as part of demonstrating their fitness for banner status, to manifest certain virtues and develop certain skills. These expectations bore some relation to their actual duties but were not directly tied to those duties. The same standards of status performance generally applied to bannermen regardless of whether they were working as soldiers, scribes, or government officials. The norms in question were highly gendered, and the rules that were the subject of the greatest degree of official concern applied exclusively to men, although, as will be discussed in chapter 5, there were a few analogous status-based expectations for the women of the service elite. These expectations worked to create a shared banner identity, to differentiate banner people from commoners, and to tie banner people to the court.

The complex of skills and norms that I discuss in this section are well known to historians of the Qing, but they are usually explained using a different interpretative framework: that their purpose was to enable the Qing court to inculcate its version of Manchu identity in Manchus. In this telling, the banner system was an institutional vehicle to reach a goal that was mostly about ethnicity. The most important English-language work on the banner system, Mark Elliott's *The Manchu Way*, takes its title from the set of "what were held to be venerable [Manchu] customs and practices" that the court considered necessary for Manchus. Elliott argues that the Qing rulers saw the "Manchu way" (Ma. *Manjusai doro*), which included archery, horsemanship, the ability to speak and write the Manchu language, and frugality, as a means of maintaining Manchu ethnic sovereignty, group cohesion, and separateness from the Han population.[64] I agree with Elliott that the elements that he identifies held great importance in Qing policy toward the banners. However, the precepts of the Manchu way did not apply solely to Manchus.[65] Rather, all bannermen, regardless of their ethnic origin, were held to the same standard of performance. Although the elements that made up the Manchu way were certainly derived from the court's conception of "traditional" Manchu culture, in their application as a standard to uphold, they did not divide Manchus from Han, but rather people of banner status from commoners.

The expectation that ethnically Han bannermen would be proficient in the skills associated with the Manchu way appears repeatedly in evaluations of Hanjun. Recommendations for the promotion of Hanjun officers, like one for a Plain White Banner colonel in Fuzhou named Shi Ruxi 石如錫, frequently mentioned their skills in "horsemanship and archery" (Ch. 弓馬 [*gong ma*]).[66] Similarly, imperial instructions to banner commanders emphasized the need to ensure that their Hanjun soldiers be proficient in all aspects of the Manchu way. In 1745, for instance, the Qianlong emperor issued parting instructions to the new Guangzhou garrison general Sitku 錫特庫 before sending him to take up his post:

> The Eight Banner Hanjun garrisoned in Guangzhou are also banner people. The spoken Manchu of those among them who come to the capital to be received at court is entirely deficient. After you have taken up your post, make special efforts to instruct them. I have also heard that the skills in archery and horsemanship of soldiers in the provinces have degenerated into rustiness. During your term as

general, when you don't have much to do, you should focus entirely on training the officers and men.⁶⁷

After his arrival in Guangzhou, Sitku denied that his men were deficient in martial skills, pointing to their ability to pull bows of appropriate strength, and he argued that their Manchu problems were due mainly to the influence of the local accent and were easily correctible. But the emperor's concern about this issue, as well as his reference to the fact that the people in question "[were] also banner people" (Ch. 亦係旗人 [*yi xi qiren*]), clearly suggests that the skills under discussion were associated with banner status, even for Hanjun.

Maintaining one's martial skills was also a prerequisite for banner people to advance in their careers, even outside the context of the banners. This also applied to Hanjun, who in this context were treated like Manchus and Mongols if they sought to take the imperial civil service examinations. In 1746, Sitku worried that the martial skills of provincial bannermen who took the exams had become limited on account of their excessive studying, and he emphasized the importance of requiring prospective exam candidates from the banners to demonstrate their ability in mounted archery before being allowed to enter the exam hall. As the commander of a Hanjun-only garrison, his concerns necessarily applied the standards of the Manchu way even to Han bannermen.⁶⁸

For this reason, too, the annual garrison-wide drills held at the all-Hanjun Fuzhou garrison during the banner system's mature era required that the garrison general and lieutenant generals personally review the standing and mounted archery skills of the entire garrison. Although some banner soldiers in Fuzhou were members of companies that specialized in firearms rather than archery, they were still required to spend substantial portions of their training time on archery, a skill that mattered to their identity as banner people, not just to their military function.⁶⁹ Fuzhou's rules were not unique—Hanjun, as well as Manchus and Mongols, at other garrisons were subject to very similar requirements. Possession of martial skills associated with the Manchu way could even help justify claims to banner status. The bannermen from Hangzhou, who claimed the right to regular banner status on the basis of their ancestors' participation in battle, as discussed in chapter 2, had their case further bolstered by the garrison general Arigūn when he noted that many of them were skilled at standing and mounted archery.⁷⁰

This emphasis on martial skills for bannermen was tied to the court's gendered approach to understanding what was expected of those with banner status. As potential soldiers, there were practical reasons to demand proficiency in archery or horsemanship, of course, although the extension of the requirement even to civil examination candidates clearly shows that these rules went beyond practicality. And evaluations of such skills were a feature not only of banner garrisons, but also of soldiers in the Green Standard army, whose soldiers were commoners.[71] But in addition to these specific requirements, the court and banner officials frequently demanded that banner people demonstrate a more nebulous trait: "manly virtue" (Ma. *hahai erdemu*). This term might be translated instead as "martial skills," following its Chinese equivalent 技藝 (*jiyi*), which makes no specific reference to masculinity.[72]

But the Manchu term's explicit use of the word *haha*, meaning "man," was not simply a quirk of translation. The same word showed up in several descriptors of good bannermen, from the word "talent" (Ma. *haha sain*, Ch. 人才 [*rencai*]) to mentions of "manly appearance" (Ma. *haha fiyan*). Concern for the "manly virtue" of bannermen was more general than the specific question of ability in archery and horsemanship; indeed, the term often appeared as a separate item on lists of areas in which bannermen needed improvement, as in one Qianlong edict that ordered banner officers to instruct their men in "manly virtue, the Manchu language, and standing and mounted archery."[73] The combination of this language of manliness with the application of standards of martial ability even to bannermen who worked in nonmilitary official posts suggests that a sort of "martial masculinity," as Nicolas Schillinger puts it, was considered an essential attribute of bannermen.[74] When the Qing court conceptualized the banners, it was as a group of warrior men, their status tied to their martiality, that were distinguished from commoner elites whose masculinity focused on literary attainment. This distinction has often been framed in ethnic terms—Manchu masculinity as martial (Ch. 武 [*wu*]), Han as literary (Ch. 文 [*wen*]).[75] But the direct application of terms like "manly virtue" to Hanjun bannermen suggests that, as with the specific military skills of the Manchu way, martial masculinity was demanded of the entire service elite status group, regardless of ethnicity.[76]

In addition to Manchu-designated martial skills, in which they were regularly trained and examined, all bannermen (once again including Hanjun) were expected to be proficient in the Manchu language. The existence of this expectation appears in the archives mostly in the context of the failure of most Hanjun to live up to it. The Qianlong emperor's edict to Sitku, discussed previously, was just one instance of a common pattern. To deal with this problem, early in the mature era, the Qing state established special schools in both the Hanjun banners in Beijing and provincial garrisons with Hanjun populations, designed to teach Manchu to young men.[77] Not only were ordinary Hanjun usually deficient in Manchu, but even officers struggled, leading the Yongzheng emperor in 1733 to prohibit promotions for Hanjun officers who lacked the ability to converse fluently in Manchu, as well as to create a scheme to test and grade Hanjun officers according to their Manchu ability on a yearly basis.[78] But despite the extent to which Hanjun struggled with the language, the preoccupation of the court with ensuring their proficiency is clear evidence that Manchu knowledge was expected of all bannermen, on the basis of status, not Manchus alone on the basis of their ethnicity.

That said, language was not the only realm in which Manchus were perceived to be better at upholding the expectations of banner status than were Hanjun. Indeed, when Hanjun displayed martial prowess beyond that of Manchus, it was likely to be viewed as an anomaly. In 1735, for instance, the Yongzheng emperor simultaneously examined a group of candidates for promotion from Jingzhou, a Manchu garrison, and Fuzhou, a Hanjun garrison. The emperor declared:

> The people recommended by Jingzhou General Gun-tai 衮泰 used bows of very little force. Gun-tai previously was a man who could pull the strongest bow, but he only taught the soldiers the form of drawing the bow, and did not diligently teach them to draw bows of greater force, or to exercise to become strong. The men recommended by Fuzhou General Zhun-tai 準泰 seem to all use bows of acceptable force. When their bows were given to the Jingzhou men to draw, they could not pull them apart. This is a contrary case of Manchus being inferior to Hanjun; what sense does this make?![79]

The success of the men from Fuzhou was not treated as a great accomplishment on their part; rather, the Yongzheng emperor saw their superiority to the Manchus from Jingzhou as a sign of the Jingzhou general Gun-tai's laziness and incompetence and ordered that he receive administrative punishment. The idea here was not that the Hanjun were seen as incapable of meeting the standards for banner people set out by the court, or even that they were capable of meeting them only in rare cases or with great difficulty; if that had been the case, it would have been pointless for the court to set such requirements. Rather, because those standards were based on skills thought to be associated with Manchu identity, Manchus were expected to be better at them. Although the standards of performance were tied to status, there was still a powerful sense that the skills themselves had a close connection to ethnicity.

Given this discrepancy between the origins of the Manchu way, which lay in supposed Manchu ethnic traditions, and the applicability of it, which extended to all banner people, one might well wonder how Qing officials talked about the idea of the Manchu way in relation to the Hanjun. There is no single answer, and as was also the case with Manchus, the Manchu way was often no more than an implicit set of assumptions that lay behind rules mandating performance of some part of it, or edicts excoriating bannermen for failing at it, with the actual term "Manchu way" simply going unmentioned. When the idea was explicitly discussed, though, it appeared in two different ways.

The first possibility was to talk about the responsibility of the Hanjun to stick to the "Manchu" way. In 1735, for instance, the Plain Red Banner Hanjun general Baši 八十, worrying about the failure of Hanjun officials to use Manchu in their memorials, claimed that the emperor had repeatedly expressed the belief that "Hanjun banner people should study and imitate the Manchu way" (Ma. *Ujen Coohai urse be. Manjusai doro be tacikini. alhūdakini*).[80] Baši's memorial can be read to imply that the Manchu way was something somewhat foreign to the Hanjun—a property of the Manchus that they should imitate. But other documents use the term in ways that suggest that the "Manchu" way was integral to the Hanjun as well. In a 1738 discussion of the decline of Manchu ability in the Fengtian banners, the Mukden lieutenant general Jekune 哲庫訥 wrote that "because the Manchu language, archery, and mounted archery are extremely important customs of the Manchus . . . in regards to teaching [them] Manchu, for the Manchu and Mongol banners, let there be a one-year deadline, and as for the Hanjun, let there be a three-year deadline."[81] Although the extended deadline for Hanjun implied that Jekune thought that meeting the standard that he set would be harder for the Hanjun than for Manchus and Mongols, "Manchu customs" (Ma. *Manju i tacin*) were presented as something that belonged to all three banner groups, not a standard external to the Hanjun.

But there was another sort of official discourse about the Manchu way as it related to Hanjun: to refer to it as connected to the banners as a whole, not just to Manchus, deemphasizing its ethnic origins or even ignoring them entirely. One particularly common usage of this sort came in discussions of the Manchu language and translation. Numerous memorials from the first half of the eighteenth century declared that "the Manchu language is the root of the banner people" (Ch. 清話爲旗人之根本 [*Qinghua wei qiren zhi genben*]), that for the Hanjun not to know Manchu was to "obscure their root" (Ch. 昧根本 [*mei genben*]), or that translation work was "an essential duty of banner people" (Ch. 旗人之要務 [*qiren zhi yaowu*]). These phrases were clearly connected to the idea that "at root the Hanjun are originally of the banners" (Ch. 漢軍根本原是旗下 [*Hanjun genben yuan shi qixia*]).[82] Formulas of this sort suggested that the Manchu language, the Hanjun as a group, and the banners as a hereditary category made up a set of necessarily and inherently linked concepts, with no explicit reference to Manchu culture necessary.

In some instances, this idea was made more explicit. In a memorial justifying a plan to use some of the Hanjun soldiers under his command in local Green Standard garrisons, the Hangzhou general Arigūn wrote that his proposal contained safeguards ensuring that the men in question would continue their banner military training and instruction in Manchu. Thus, he argued, they would "not come to abandon the principles and ways of the banners (Ma. *gūsai doro ciktan*)."[83] *Gūsai doro* might reasonably be translated as "banner way," a direct parallel to the phrase *Manjusai doro*, "Manchu way." Arigūn thus was using a phrase that seemingly was identical to the idea of the "Manchu way," referring to the same set of skills but defined in terms of banner status rather than Manchu ethnicity.

Language like Arigūn's, though less common than references to the "Manchu way," recurs repeatedly in the Qing archives in multiple periods. For instance, in 1797, early in the postexpulsion era, a bannerman named Encungge, who was serving as a granary official in Manchuria and had previously worked as a *bithesi* in the Mukden branch of the Board of Punishments, was considered for a promotion to officer rank in the banners. When he was examined by the Board of War, though, his standing archery was mediocre and he was completely incapable of mounted archery. Linning 琳寧, the Mukden general who reported this case to the court, declared that his incompetence in these martial skills not only disqualified him to serve as an officer who would be responsible for training and drilling soldiers, but represented an abandonment of the "old way of the banner people" (Ma. *gūsai niyalmai fe doro*). "Standing and mounted archery," Linning declared, "are matters corresponding to banner people" (Ma. *gūsai niyalmai teisu baita*). Not only should Encungge be denied his new job as a military officer, the argument went, but he should be stripped of his previous post and his right to serve as a *bithesi* as well.[84] The Jiaqing emperor agreed, expressing concern that a bannerman with such deficiencies had received the post of *bithesi* in the first place.[85]

Just as with the "Manchu way" and its emphasis on frugality, discussions of the "banner way" reached beyond issues of military training and Manchu-language knowledge to encompass more general ideas about the proper behavior of banner people. In 1762, a banner official named Deboo 德保 equated banner people visiting venues where singing or opera were performed with the decline of the "old customs of the banner people" (Ma. *gūsai ursei fe tacin*) and suggested that such establishments should be required to post signs banning banner people from entering. He argued as well that there was a need to enforce regulations banning banner people from living outside the walls of Beijing's inner city; and he suggested that banner people should not be allowed to dress extravagantly, as young bannermen did in violation of the "old standards" (Ma. *fe kooli*).[86] Standards of dress and behavior, like rules requiring the mastery of certain skills, applied to the entire banner population and could be discussed in those terms. The banner way was fundamental to bannermen; when non-Manchus in the banners followed these expectations, they were not practicing a "Manchu way" that was foreign to them as non-Manchus, but rather a "banner way" that was directly linked to their status as bannermen.

This interpretation of the Manchu/banner way is one that still holds for the Hanjun when the idea of a "banner way" was not explicitly invoked, or even when they were discussed in terms of their relationship to the "Manchu way." Although the putative origins of this set of skills and practices lay in the Manchu past, its role in the Qing period was to bind all banner people to each other and divide them from the commoner population. Indeed, in 1738, the general Wang Yi 王釴 could write with no fear of contradiction that the reason why the Jingkou garrison, which consisted entirely of Hanjun, needed renewed attention to Manchu-language instruction was that "garrison Eight Banner people, dwelling close together with Han people, could not escape being infected by their local accent and coming to regard the Manchu language as superficial."[87] All banner people risked corruption from excessive contact and interaction with Han commoners, even those who were Han themselves. The term "Manchu way" described a code of behavior, but "banner way" explains who actually had to follow that code.

As a point of comparison, it is perhaps worth looking at the notion of a "Mongol way," which Qing officialdom did use on occasion in reference to the Mongol Eight Banners. Mark Elliott describes it as a "parallel" to the Manchu way, though he notes the relative infrequency of its appearance in Qing discourse.[88] Yet, at least in the early eighteenth century, the distinction between expectations for Mongols and Manchus (and Hanjun) in the banners appears to have been more limited than the existence of a genuinely separate "Mongol way" would imply. As we have seen in this chapter, generic discussions of the "Manchu way" often were meant to apply to Eight Banner Mongols and Hanjun as well. The only times that a "Mongol way" was discussed separately was in reference to Mongolian-language ability alone.[89] As one memorialist argued, "Mongol bannermen who can understand Mongol script and speech have become few. . . . The old way of the Mongols (Ma. *Monggosoi fe doro*) must not come to be abandoned."[90] The particularity of this concern is in keeping with the major contribution that Mongol bannermen specifically made to the Qing state—namely, working as clerks and translators in the Lifan yuan. That is to say, the Mongol way, in practice, seems not to have meant a wholly different set of cultural expectations for Mongols in the banners from that for Manchus, but simply referred to the court's requirement that they maintain proficiency in the Mongolian language in addition to meeting the general expectations of the "Manchu" or "banner" way.

In the years immediately preceding the start of formal Hanjun expulsion, a new kind of discourse began appearing in the official record, holding that the differences between Manchus and Hanjun did mean that the latter were incapable of fully participating in the Manchu way. For instance, in 1751, the new garrison general Sarhadai 薩爾哈岱 wrote of his Jingkou garrison that upon his arrival, they were poorly versed in archery, horsemanship, and musketry. He suggested that this problem lay in the fact that "though Hanjun and Manchus really belong to different categories, their training was originally supposed to be uniform."[91] Sarhadai emphasized that he would indeed stick to the same sort of training used for Manchu troops, suggesting that he still recognized that the standards of the Manchu way were meant to apply to Hanjun too, but his insistence on the basic difference between Manchus and Hanjun reflected ideas that had perhaps been gaining currency in the years since 1742, when an imperial edict permitting Hanjun to voluntarily give up their banner status had declared that the Hanjun were, at root, Han, and thus different from other banner people.[92] This new conception of a Manchu way that was less accessible, or perhaps even totally inaccessible, to Hanjun would prove part of a reconsideration of the meaning of banner status during the expulsion era. But the idea of the banner way as something relevant to all banner people never disappeared; it returned in the late eighteenth century, after expulsion policies came to an end. The continued use of the term in the postexpulsion era, as well as the return to expectations that Hanjun would live up to it, suggests that the status-based performance ideal was an important part of the Qing order across time.[93]

The notion that Qing expectations of who should follow the banner/Manchu way were based clearly in status, while imperial ideas about its content were derived from an official conception of Manchuness, may seem contradictory. What did it mean that Han bannermen were required to adopt ostensibly Manchu cultural norms?[94] One possibility is that the Qing court saw the Manjurization of the entire service elite as essential to dynastic security. That is, the Qing had come to power through the mobilization of a characteristically Inner Asian form of martial masculinity, the loss of which would endanger its hold on power. Even prior to the conquest, in 1637, the emperor Hong Taiji had commented on the history of the Jurchen-ruled Jin dynasty and declared that "the khans of later generations entered the Chinese way, putting aside shooting and riding. By the time of Aizong [1224–1233], the [Jurchen] Way was destroyed. The dynasty had been wiped out."[95] Although Qing official documents would not directly refer to the potential for their own dynasty to fall, worries about "abandoning" (Ma. *waliyambi*) or "forgetting" (Ma. *onggombi*) the Manchu way, or that it would "perish" (Ma. *ufarambi*) or "decline" (Ma. *eyembi*), were a frequent feature of memorials and edicts dealing with banner people. These phrases echoed Hong Taiji's concern, suggesting that the loss of Manchu practices among the banner population were a threat to the dynasty itself.

But the expectation that Han bannermen, as members of the service elite and a key force for maintaining dynastic rule, would take on standards of cultural performance tied to the Qing court's ideas of Manchu identity did not equate to a belief that Han bannermen would or could become Manchus. It is perhaps helpful to think of the situation of non-Manchus in the banners as being the inverse of that of Manchus as a people living in China. As many scholars of Qing history have pointed out, the fact that Manchus at the end of the Qing lived in garrisons in predominantly Han cities and had adopted many cultural practices coded as Han or had ceased to use Manchu as their primary language does not mean that they had ceased to be ethnic Manchus.[96] Rather, they identified themselves and were identified by others, particularly by Han nationalist anti-Manchu revolutionaries, as ethnically different from their Han neighbors. Similarly, although the Hanjun were required to take on Manchu cultural practices, the Qing court made it consistently clear that they remained Han.[97]

The sense of ethnic differences within the banners was not limited to the emperor and official policy. As chapter 5 will explore, the marriage patterns of banner people demonstrate that Han and Manchus within the banner system remained separate groups through the end of the dynasty, with Manchus holding a superior position. The imposition of the requirements of the banner/Manchu way on the Hanjun, including the cultural performance of service elite status, did not mean the elimination of ethnic difference within the banners. But it did contribute to the creation of a status-based banner identity distinct from Manchu ethnic identity.

Conclusion: Serving the Dynasty

The Qing banners began their history as a way of organizing the followers of Nurhaci so that they could be used effectively in his wars of expansion. As the needs and activities of the growing Aisin Gioro–ruled state became more complex, the range of tasks to which bannermen were assigned widened. Allowing bannermen simply to inherit important posts would not allow the dynasty to effectively carry out specialized tasks from translation to overseeing artisanal production to frontier governance to mapmaking. But filling the state apparatus only with commoner officials selected via the civil service examinations, and thereby sidelining the dynasty's oldest supporters, would have made the dynasty reliant on men of unproven loyalty and risked alienating the well-armed banner population. So the Qing court developed a compromise system. Much of the bureaucracy would be open exclusively to bannermen, but bannermen serving in government posts would be selected based on their records of achievement, whether in military service, scholarly study, or past administrative work. In the decades and centuries that followed the Qing conquest, bannermen would demonstrate their continued links to the Aisin Gioro house and distinctiveness from the commoner population through adherence to a set of standards of behavior and training associated with their status identity. Although this was not service in the same sense that being a soldier or bureaucrat was, the work of maintaining a separate banner identity was equally essential to guaranteeing the continuation of Qing rule.

The bureaucratization of service described in this chapter was enabled by a concomitant institutionalization of privilege, which incentivized Qing bannermen to maintain their commitment to dynastic service. Chapter 4 will take up the question of service elite privilege and how it helped create a new way of managing elites.

CHAPTER 4

Privilege and State Support

In late 1735, shortly after the death of the Yongzheng emperor, the Han bondservant bannerman and Lianghuai salt commissioner (Ch. 兩淮鹽政 [*Lianghuai yanzheng*]) Gao Bin 高斌 received an edict from the new Qianlong emperor, who had previously taken Gao's daughter as a secondary consort: "Your daughter has already been granted the title of Noble Consort (Ch. 貴妃 [*guifei*]) and I am ordering that you leave the banners."[1] As a bondservant of the Imperial Household Department, Gao Bin was legally a slave. His ancestors, if they had a history anything like that of other men in the same position, had been captured by the armies of Nurhaci or Hong Taiji prior to the Qing conquest and made the personal property of the emperor.[2] By releasing him from the banners, the emperor was declaring that Gao and his family would no longer be bondservants or slaves—they would be free people.

Gao responded to the emperor's edict as follows: "Your slave knelt, prostrated, and kowtowed, asking you to accept my humble thanks for your heavenly kindness. I then respectfully set up the incense burner table and led your slave's wife; your slave's son, your slave Gao Heng; and your slave's daughters, your slaves Sanjie and Sijie, in facing the palace and jointly performing the nine kowtows in humble thanks." But he would go on to say, "Your slave has received imperial grace for generations. My grandfather, father, sons, and grandsons, have been raised and nourished in the palace for five generations, and more than 100 years. . . . [I beg] that you continue to retain your slave's family in the bondservant companies." He added that the greatest honor would be for his family to be raised into the Manchu banners, a decision that would encourage the bondservants of the Upper Three Banners to exert themselves to loyally carry out their duties to the dynasty. The emperor granted this request, and Gao, his immediate family, and his descendants would remain in the Manchu banners thereafter.³

Gao Bin's insistence that even though he wished above all to be a bannerman of higher standing, he would rather remain a bondservant than leave the banners entirely was likely not an insincere expression of devotion designed to maximize his chances of being elevated to the Manchu banners. Nor was his use of the word "slave" (Ch. 奴才 [*nucai*]) to refer to himself and his family members, repeated six times in the span of just three lines in the first quotation given here, a reflection of genuinely abject status. Rather, as this chapter will show, the very real privileges of banner status, privileges that extended to all banner people (including those who were ethnically Han), were justified by an official conception of all banner people, not just bondservants, as slaves of the emperor. To be a slave of the emperor was not like being an ordinary slave; enslavement to the ruler both provided a claim on his resources and elevated those "slaves" above other subjects who lacked that personal connection to the throne (in theory, if not in fact). And, indeed, Gao Bin himself explained his request to remain a bannerman, even if that meant remaining a bondservant, by quoting a statement that the Yongzheng emperor had supposedly made to him during an imperial audience:

> Slaves within the palace are extremely intimate (Ch. 近 [*jin*]). If they depart from the banners, it seems they would become estranged (Ch. 疏遠 [*shuyuan*]). If there are any bondservants who should receive the grace of leaving the banners, it would be better to retain them as bondservants to serve as a model for those within the palace. Why must they leave the banners to have dignity (Ch. 體面 [*timian*])?⁴

The privileges of banner status are mostly quite well known and well studied, so this chapter will not focus on establishing their existence. But it is worth summarizing them here. Connected directly to the mandate that banner people serve the court was the privilege of vastly disproportionate representation among the prestigious and well-remunerated upper ranks of the bureaucracy. Not only did bannermen monopolize positions in the banners, the Imperial Household Department, the empire's Inner Asian territories, and the central bureaucracy that oversaw those territories, but they were guaranteed half the top positions within the Six Boards, the Grand Secretariat, and the Censorate. In lower, but still prestigious, central administrative positions, most slots were guaranteed to bannermen.[5] Even in the provincial administration, which in its lowest ranks consisted mostly but not entirely of commoners, the top positions of governor and governor-general saw bannermen wildly overrepresented, especially prior to the nineteenth century.[6]

In addition, while for commoners, receiving a post in the bureaucracy was an arduous and highly competitive process requiring success in multiple rounds of the civil service examinations, bannermen had a variety of entry paths into the bureaucracy, including examinations in translation and military promotion. Once there, rules requiring a shorter mourning period for banner officials who suffered the death of a parent than for commoner officials enabled bannermen to avoid resigning their positions, and thus interrupting their careers, in such circumstances.[7] Advantages like these meant that even a high official like Gao Bin was likely to care a great deal about his status, both for its impact on his career and for its potential impact on the careers of his sons.

Even within the banners, access to prestigious government posts and the treatment of those who held them were the concern of only a small minority. The privileges that mattered to most bannermen were more mundane, but certainly no less important. Banner people possessed special privileges in legal cases, particularly the commutation of penal sentences discussed in chapter 1, but also the existence of separate jail cells, exemption from judicial torture, and the right to stand before a magistrate (when a commoner was required to kneel).[8] But most important was the financial support that banner people received from the Qing court.

By the early eighteenth century, the banner system was at least as much a kind of welfare state as a military organization. In a parallel to the bureaucratization of banner service, incomes that, prior to the conquest, had come from war booty and landholding were transformed into salaries paid out of the state treasury during the consolidation era. In the first years after the conquest, bannermen were also provided with large tracts of land to be farmed by tenants or serfs, but most of this land was soon lost on account of the inability or unwillingness of banner soldiers, many of whom still spent much time on campaign, to manage it. So bannermen in fact relied on salaries of silver and grain. Those who had not been awarded land received additional allotments based on family size. Cavalrymen also received funds to provide for their horses. Ordinary salaries were at least double those of commoner soldiers in comparable positions. In addition, banner people received money from the court to pay for weddings and funerals. Widows, orphans, and those disabled in battle received stipends from the state. And, over time, the state developed ways to pay even many of those bannermen who did not have official employment on account of a dearth of available posts. On multiple occasions, the court even paid off large quantities of bannermen's debts.[9]

This chapter is concerned in large part with these economic privileges, which constituted the most valued advantage of banner status for most ordinary banner people. Indeed, it was the potential loss of stipends that provoked riots at the Chengdu garrison and worry among the older male relatives of the twentieth-century Manchu author Lao She 老舍 when the Qing court flirted with the elimination of the banner system in the final few years of the dynasty.[10] But rather than focusing on the core of this system of financing and how it worked in theory, or during the brief period when the Qing court was in a strong financial position and had little trouble providing for its banner people, I examine here the margins of the system and the lengths to which the court went to meet the needs of banner people even when it was not easy to do so. The responsibility of the Qing court to provide for the banner population came into frequent conflict with the financial burden that their growing population created for the state treasury.[11] With the exception of the expulsion era, the dynasty responded to this crisis of "banner livelihood" (Ma. *gūsai ursei banjire doro*, Ch. 八旗生計 [*baqi shengji*]) by seeking new ways to funnel money to banner people.[12] Moreover, it did not limit the scope of its obligations based on ethnicity, but rather developed a variety of schemes during both the eighteenth and nineteenth centuries, designed principally to support members of the Hanjun banners.

During the early eighteenth century, as it developed a policy allowing Hanjun men to receive employment in commoner-designated military posts in the Green Standard army, the court also took steps to ensure that those who took up this work would retain their full membership in the banners. This was not a policy designed to treat Han of banner status like Han commoners; instead, it was a chance to redirect state resources from commoners to banner people. In the nineteenth century, as the dynasty's financial situation weakened further, banner officials developed moneylending schemes to raise money to support additional banner people beyond those holding regular posts. These systems aimed to provide support to the maximum number of people, but at the expense of not providing very much to each recipient, again reflecting a dynastic commitment to ensuring the support of the entirety of the banner population. Support for ordinary banner people was justified by the same ideas that led Gao Bin to ask to remain a bannerman. All bannermen, not just bondservants, engaged with the court and were discussed by it in language that asserted that they were slaves of the emperor. It was as members of this enormous imagined imperial household that bannermen were owed support, and the work of the court over centuries of Qing rule suggests that, for the most part, the dynasty took this obligation seriously, despite its frequent struggles to live up to it.

Creating Jobs for Bannermen

One means of ensuring that all banner people continued to receive incomes, even as the banner population grew and the financial burden of supporting it increased accordingly, was to redirect state funds from less-favored populations of commoners to banner people. Probably the most extensive program of this sort was an initiative, beginning near the end of the Kangxi emperor's reign in 1718, under which Hanjun bannermen were permitted to hold salaried posts in the Green Standard army. This policy had the potential to undermine the status position of the bannermen who benefited from it, as Green Standard soldiers were normally commoners with no banner affiliation. Indeed, the Green Standards grew out of the Ming dynasty's garrison system, quite unlike the banners, which had been developed independently as the military force of the preconquest Manchu state.[13]

The implementation of this measure involved careful steps to ensure that the divisions between commoners and banner people remained intact, even as the decision to limit its scope to Han bannermen reflected the ethnic hierarchy within the banners. The use of Hanjun in Green Standard companies was directly motivated by a desire to secure employment for the growing Hanjun population. By increasing the number of ways to earn a living available to Hanjun while allowing them to retain banner status, the Qing court met its obligations to support a key banner population. Although the policy blurred the divide between Hanjun and Han commoners in terms of what livelihoods were open to each, it did not challenge the status distinction between them. Indeed, in a certain sense, it even reinforced the hierarchical system under which Hanjun, as banner people, were superior to commoners by asserting the right of unemployed Hanjun to take salaried jobs that otherwise would have provided income to commoner families. However, even as it maintained a status system that joined the Hanjun with their fellow banner people, the policy emphasized the ethnic division between Manchus and Han that operated within the banners. Hanjun, unlike Manchus, were suitable candidates for posts as Green Standard soldiers because of their Han ethnic background.

The first banner garrison to assign Hanjun bannermen to Green Standard companies was Fuzhou, whose entire garrison population was made up of Hanjun. This policy was initiated in response to a 1718 memorial to the Kangxi emperor by Mamboo 滿保, the governor-general of Fujian and Zhejiang, who wished to use Green Standard posts to provide salaries to otherwise unemployed bannermen. According to Mamboo, besides the two thousand Hanjun already holding banner posts, there were an additional two thousand men who would have been eligible for positions but were kept unemployed by a lack of vacancies. In his memorial, he wrote that "the livelihoods of those people without soldiers' salaries are somewhat arduous," but also noted that "observing the appearance of the men, they are far stronger than idle Green Standard men"—that is, the population from which new Green Standard soldiers otherwise would have been drawn. He proposed selecting two hundred men from the excess Hanjun population and assigning one hundred of them to the Green Standard units under the command of the garrison general, and the other one hundred to the battalions under the governor-general's own command. If a vacancy opened up within the garrison's banner units, those who had been transferred to Green Standard posts would remain eligible to fill it. The emperor approved the proposal, telling Mamboo that it was an extremely good idea.[14] Shortly thereafter, the policy was further refined, and an additional one hundred Hanjun men were granted posts in the Green Standard units commanded by the Fujian provincial governor.[15]

The use of Hanjun men in Green Standard posts soon expanded beyond Fuzhou. In 1727, the Yongzheng emperor endorsed this policy as a means of dealing with the excess number of unemployed Hanjun, noting that "each company has come to have some hundreds of excess [men] and there are even those who up to the end of their lives do not obtain a post."[16] Hanjun banner commanders (Ma. *gūsa be kadalara amban*,[17] Ch. 都統 [*dutong*]) were to either form new companies or assign Hanjun to Green Standard units to alleviate the employment problem. In 1729, the emperor further declared that the Green Standard companies in Jingkou, Fuzhou, and Guangzhou under the command of each city's garrison general had originally been created because the number of Hanjun in each place had been insufficient. In a sense, he was thus suggesting that the Green Standard posts in question were really supposed to have been within the banners to begin with. Now that the Hanjun had become so numerous, the number of excess men in these garrisons had expanded rapidly. Henceforth, the emperor decreed that whenever a post in these companies became available, it should be filled by an unemployed Hanjun man. To ensure that Green Standard families who had served for many generations were still provided for, their young men would be granted posts in other local Green Standard units, including those commanded by the provincial governor or governor-general.[18]

In 1733, the Hangzhou garrison general Arigūn asked to follow the precedent of what had been done in Fuzhou, as well as that of the 1727 edict discussed previously, and assign three hundred of his talented but unemployed men to Green Standard battalions in the city under the authority of the governor and governor-general, as the Hangzhou garrison general did not command any Green Standard troops himself. He emphasized that these men would be assigned to patrol Hangzhou's streets and guard its walls, gates, and granaries, and so would not be stationed far from the garrison. This would, he argued, allow them to continue to study spoken and written Manchu, ensuring that they would not abandon the "banner way," a term whose meaning and significance was discussed in chapter 3.

As his emphasis on maintaining instruction in Manchu and other elements of the banner way suggests, Arigūn's proposal would maintain the banner status of those Hanjun who were employed as Green Standard soldiers, just as in Fuzhou. Those who did not adhere to proper discipline would have their salaries stripped from them and then be returned to the banners to be punished—that is, they would remain subject to the legal authority of the banners. In addition, Arigūn held that the fundamental status difference between bannermen and commoners was part of why his plan made sense. While the family members of Green Standard soldiers could "still rely on farming the fields and engaging in trade in order to live," banner people "depend[ed] solely on official salaries."[19] As such, it was far more important to offer military employment to unemployed bannermen than to commoners, even those from families with a history of military service. Moreover, bannermen would happily take up such jobs, while the recruitment of commoners to join the army could be a hardship for them and hence was less likely to be welcomed.

In 1735, just two years later, Hangzhou officials reconsidered their policy. A memorial from the Zhejiang governor Cheng Yuanzhang 程元章 noted that because Zhejiang province no longer had a resident governor-general, the relevant Green Standard posts available in Hangzhou were limited to 646 men under the governor's command.[20] Moreover, troops under the governor's command were generally sent out of the city on assignment to root out salt smuggling, banditry, and the like. Because those Hanjun bannermen assigned to Hangzhou's Green Standard companies were forbidden from leaving the vicinity of the garrison as per Arigūn's original proposal, granting three hundred posts to them left the Zhejiang governor's forces substantially understaffed when carrying out many of their duties. In addition, Green Standard families had men awaiting posts—what would become of them if all the new vacancies went to Hanjun? This was a particular problem because he estimated that it would take more than ten years' worth of vacancies to bring the number of Hanjun up to their three-hundred-man quota. Instead of using Hanjun in his Green Standard forces, Cheng proposed creating three hundred stipends of 0.5 taels/month, substantially less than even a Green Standard salary, which would be given to unemployed Hanjun men who would be expected to train alongside regular banner soldiers.[21]

The Yongzheng emperor responded by noting that the excess population in the Hanjun banners had in recent years increased extremely rapidly and that, given the need to provide them with support, assigning Hanjun bannermen to posts in the Green Standard battalions under the authority of their own garrison's general was quite reasonable. However, the emperor agreed with Cheng's concern about what would happen to Green Standard families who had provided soldiers for many decades if more such posts were granted to Hanjun, and so forbade Hanjun in provincial garrisons from being assigned to any Green Standard battalion other than those commanded by the garrison general. He further ordered that those already assigned to such posts be required to give them up, declaring that "if excess Hanjun men are numerous, you must think of some other means to make provision for them." Whether this was meant as an endorsement of Cheng's specific proposal was left unclear.[22] Cheng had emphasized that the issues that he was describing were a result of the specific situation of

Hangzhou's garrison, which he explained was very different from that in Fuzhou. However, the emperor decided to apply this prohibition on the use of Hanjun in Green Standard companies run by governors and governors-general—in other words, by officials in the provincial bureaucracy—to Fuzhou, and presumably to the rest of the empire as well.²³

Although Hangzhou's lack of a garrison general–commanded Green Standard company meant that its Hanjun would indeed face a shortage of posts, the situation in other garrisons was not much changed by the new rule. The 1729 edict turning over all newly available posts in companies under the general's command to unemployed Hanjun was implemented in Guangzhou in 1733.²⁴ In Fuzhou, the garrison general Arsai 阿爾賽 declared in 1736 that the number of qualified Hanjun in the garrison was actually insufficient to fill all of the 2,042 posts in the main garrison, the 500 posts in the naval garrison, and the 1,860 total posts in the two Green Standard companies that he commanded. So he proposed that the number of Green Standard posts available to his garrison's Hanjun be decreased to 400, a suggestion that the new Qianlong emperor accepted.²⁵

The surplus of posts available in Fuzhou suggests that this policy was effective at relieving the pressure of population growth in Hanjun-dominated provincial garrisons. Perhaps for this reason, analogous policies were implemented elsewhere in the empire. Beginning in 1745, Hanjun from the capital were permitted to fill vacant Green Standard posts in the three police battalions in the capital (Ma. *siyūn bu ilan ing*, Ch. 巡捕三營 [*xunbu san ying*]) and in two garrisons in Zhili, the province surrounding Beijing. These latter two garrisons, at Malan 馬蘭 and Taining 泰寧, were responsible for guarding the Qing imperial tombs, causing the court to view them as more important, and more tied to the maintenance of the dynasty itself, than were most ordinary Green Standard companies.²⁶ The police units also had a closer connection to the banners than did other Green Standard units due to their responsibility for patrolling the capital, which served as the principal banner garrison in China proper, although the Green Standard police battalions were responsible only for the parts of the city outside the banner city walls.²⁷ Indeed, the memorial proposing this policy had also suggested assigning bannermen to other Green Standard forces in Zhili, including ones based in Tianjin, Xuanhua 宣化, and Yizhou 易州, but the emperor rejected this proposal on the grounds that these garrisons were widely dispersed. In the five battalions where the appointment of bannermen was approved, though, new vacancies were to be filled by Hanjun men, whether they were already eligible to serve as banner soldiers, male relatives of current soldiers, or men of secondary banner status. If a Hanjun man assigned to one of these posts retired, he would be replaced by another Hanjun.[28]

This new policy initially met resistance from Bulantai 布蘭泰, the commander of the Green Standard forces at Malan and Taining, who argued that his soldiers came from families that had moved to the tomb areas in the early Kangxi period, up to eighty or ninety years earlier, and had provided consistent military service over that time. They were, he said, "no different from banner people" (Ch. 與旗人無異 [yu qiren wu yi]), with entire families relying on military salaries and lacking any other source of income.[29] Bulantai's objections were dismissed by the grand councilor Zhang Tingyu, who, in addition to noting that various opportunities for service would remain for the commoner Green Standard troops at the two garrisons, emphasized the difference between them and genuine bannermen like the Hanjun of Beijing, writing that "the people of the Green Standard army, unlike the people of the Hanjun banners, aside from receiving salaries through government service, still [have] other means of livelihood."[30] The emperor agreed with Zhang, maintaining a firm sense of the difference between banner people, including the Hanjun, and commoners, even while sending banner people to serve in military units that normally were composed of commoners.

The ways in which Hanjun were used in Green Standard units offer compelling evidence for how the Qing state conceived of ethnic and status difference during the first half of the eighteenth century. At one level, the policy seemed to suggest that Hanjun were more like nonbanner Han than Manchus were. Although Manchus sometimes held positions as officers in the Green Standard army, Manchu bannermen were not assigned to regular Green Standard posts, nor have I found any indications that any Qing official ever proposed that Manchus of ordinary banner status should serve in them. As such, it seems that Hanjun service in the Green Standards was considered proper, while Manchu service in them, outside of officer posts, was not. This is a clear indication that the early-eighteenth-century Qing court saw less of a barrier between Hanjun and Han commoners than it did between Manchus and Han commoners.

However, even as Hanjun served in Green Standard companies, banner officials and the Qing court maintained very clear status divisions between Hanjun and commoners. One indication of this is the preference that Hanjun received in appointment to Green Standard units that would accommodate them; the livelihood of banner people always took precedence over that of commoners, and both officials and emperors emphasized the legal restrictions on nonofficial employment for banner people as a justification for this preference for Hanjun. Moreover, as seen in the temporary use of Hanjun in the Green Standards of Hangzhou, Hanjun who were sent to Green Standard units were still expected to uphold the standards of banner service and to study spoken and written Manchu. Service in the Green Standard army meant merely a change in *livelihood*, not *status*, and indeed Hanjun appointed to these units remained subject to the authority of banner officers and could return to their banner companies to fill newly opened vacancies in them.[31] Nor was granting posts in the Green Standards to Hanjun a means of marginalizing them relative to Manchus; rather, it was clearly designed to increase the amount of state support available for Hanjun families. This is made quite apparent in Cheng Yuanzhang's memorial ending this policy in Hangzhou and in the Yongzheng emperor's response. Since it was deemed impossible to employ Hanjun in the Green Standards at that garrison, both men agreed that it was necessary to find another means to increase the number of salaried posts available to them.

Although the ethnic similarity between Hanjun and commoners was the apparent basis for making regular Green Standard service acceptable for Hanjun but not Manchus, the policy certainly benefited the Hanjun who were included in it. To the extent that Manchus had access to Green Standard posts as officers, Qing officials saw that access as desirable for them, as shown by a 1738 memorial that sought successfully to give Mongol bannermen that same right, on the grounds that it was unfair to prefer Manchus over their Mongol colleagues.[32] Although there is no direct evidence that Manchus wished to have access to ordinary Green Standard posts, it seems likely that such posts would have been preferable to unemployment, a problem faced by bannermen of all ethnic backgrounds.

As we have seen, an additional consideration related to the employment of Hanjun in the Green Standard army was the nature of the specific Green Standard units in question. That is, though Hanjun were permitted to serve as soldiers in the Green Standards, even they were allowed access only to special sorts of Green Standard units. Apart from a brief period when they were permitted in units commanded by provincial governors and governors-general (a policy that the Yongzheng emperor quickly overturned), the units in which Hanjun could be enlisted were those guarding the two imperial tomb complexes in Zhili province, the police units of Beijing, and companies under the direct command of a banner garrison general. As argued previously, the first two of these types of Green Standard companies had clear connections to the maintenance of imperial rule, a strong reason for making them open to banner troops.[33] And the units commanded by the provincial garrison generals in Fuzhou, Guangzhou, and Jingkou, like the police units in Beijing, were located in the same physical place as banner garrisons, and remained under banner command, giving them a closer connection to the banners than most Green Standard units had. So rather than ignoring status difference, the employment of Hanjun as Green Standard soldiers ensured that they would continue to carry out duties for the imperial house and remain well integrated with other bannermen. Thus, the banner administration had managed to divert funds from the employment of commoners and toward the employment of thousands of previously unemployed bannermen without damaging the connections that bound banner people to one another and to the court. This choice to prioritize state support of banner people reflected the duty that the court had to provide for them.

Welfare for Banner People

The provision of state support to the banner population remained central to the management of the banners in the postexpulsion era, continuing until the fall of the dynasty. The difficulty of meeting this financial burden only increased over the course of the late eighteenth and nineteenth centuries as, though banner population growth slowed, the position of the dynastic treasury became weaker, in part on account of a series of ruinously expensive wars.[34] Valuable evidence for studying how the Qing state dealt with this problem comes from the Guangzhou garrison, which produced an extensive late-nineteenth-century gazetteer that documented its financial arrangements in detail, a source that supplements central archival records. In addition, Guangzhou was the only garrison outside of Manchuria and Beijing that continued to support a substantial population of Han bannermen in the postexpulsion era, making it an ideal site for determining how the Qing court dealt with ethnic difference in its support of banner people during this period.[35]

In spite of the state's financial difficulties, the Guangzhou garrison consistently expanded the numbers of jobs and stipends available to bannermen during the postexpulsion era and did so at a much faster rate for Hanjun bannermen than it did for Manchus. Both garrison officials and the Qing court were principally concerned with ensuring the livelihoods of the entire garrison population, whether Manchu or Han. Indeed, the changes made to the distribution of salaried jobs and income at the garrison over this time reflected a clear retreat from the policies of the expulsion period, which had relied on large preferences for Manchus over Han as recipients of state support within the banner system. Even so, as of the late nineteenth century, Manchu bannermen continued to receive higher rates of income than their Han counterparts. The garrison also developed new sources of revenue for supporting bannermen and created new types of salaried positions for them. Many of these new posts were supernumerary, carrying few or no requirements of actual service. In addition, they carried much lower rates of pay than did more ordinary posts as soldiers, creating a welfare state that may have met the court's basic obligation to support banner people, but that still left many impoverished. The late Qing court did not give up on its service elite, but the weakness of the system had become clear.

The initial postexpulsion composition of the Guangzhou garrison enforced rigid equality between Manchus and Hanjun in terms of available salaried posts, despite a much larger total Hanjun population. In 1756, the garrison was officially assigned 45 posts for Manchu officers and 45 for Hanjun officers, joined by 1,500 posts for soldiers of each category. The only difference was that the 1,500 Manchu-designated posts included 150 for members of the elite vanguard troops, a unit that was closed to Hanjun. The 600-strong naval garrison was also evenly divided.[36] The only extra consideration afforded to Hanjun was the continuation of the policy that allowed 400 of them to hold Green Standard posts in the detachment commanded by the garrison general, while still maintaining their banner status.[37] The total Manchu and Hanjun population figures for this period are unknown, but in the early nineteenth century, there were more than three times as many Hanjun in the garrison as Manchus.[38] Thus, it is likely that the percentage of Hanjun with salaried positions was perhaps one-third as large as the percentage of Manchus with such posts. The nominally equal division of the garrison had very unequal implications.

The even division of banner posts between Manchus and Hanjun was soon undermined by a serious logistical problem—namely, the shortage of Manchu men at the garrison. The basic problem, as explained by the garrison general Dzenghai 增海 in 1768, was that very few unemployed men had accompanied the Manchu troops transferred to Guangzhou only a short time before, and so almost all the male Manchus who lacked posts were children who had been born since Manchu bannermen had first arrived in the city in the late 1750s. Indeed, 229 of the posts for Manchu soldiers in the garrison were held by children under the age of 16 *sui*. Because there was no one else to fill posts vacated due to the death or retirement of a banner person, and because there were many widows and orphans who needed a source of support, garrison officials had for years been assigning military posts to boys as young as 6 or 7 *sui*.[39] Since these boys were incapable of fulfilling their duties, many spent half their salaries paying an adult bannerman to do their jobs. New soldiers were frequently selected solely based on the number of people in their household, with no attention to whether they actually could perform their duties, a situation that Dzenghai believed had greatly weakened the forces under his command. But, he noted, if all these boys were simply removed from their posts, it would mean the loss of the only means they had to support themselves and their families.[40] The state's duty to support the banner population had come into conflict with its need to get useful service from it.

Over the final four decades of the eighteenth century, the Guangzhou garrison resolved this tension by temporarily assigning unemployed Hanjun to work in posts designated for Manchus, while continuing to provide incomes, albeit smaller ones than those received by actual soldiers, to Manchu boys who were too young to serve. In 1761 and 1762, the garrison generals Fusengge 福增格 and Mingfu 明福 received permission to continue to exclusively employ Hanjun within the naval garrison, whose staffing was supposed to be evenly divided.[41] Dzenghai proposed in 1768 that all the Manchu boys who were employed as soldiers leave the military posts that they held. Those who had a father or elder brother who held a post that could support them were to enter the garrison school to study spoken Manchu, as well as both standing and mounted archery. The remaining ninety-three boys who lacked other means of support were to receive stipends of 1 tael of silver per month as supernumeraries (Ma. *hūwašabure cooha*, Ch. 養育兵 [*yangyu bing*]), a type of post usually granted to boys to enable them to receive an income prior to receiving an appointment to a regular post.[42]

In 1770, the new garrison general, Teksin 特克慎, noting that 376 of the 1,500 Manchu-designated posts at the main garrison were now vacant, decided to allow capable but unemployed Hanjun men to temporarily occupy vacant Manchu-designated posts, with the numbers of Hanjun in such posts to be reduced as more young Manchus came of age.⁴³ But at a time when the court was willing to ignore the needs of Han bannermen to improve its own fiscal position, with Hanjun expulsion still ongoing elsewhere in the empire, a dearth of Manchus did not always mean new jobs for Hanjun. In 1776, by which time there were only 1,074 active Manchu soldiers at the garrison, the garrison general Yongwei 永瑋 argued that 300 posts could simply be eliminated, pointing out that when sailors in the naval garrison and a newly established, 400-strong Hanjun infantry detachment were taken into account, the garrison had more than its requisite 3,000 soldiers and thus would not face any deficiencies in its overall military capability.⁴⁴

Toward the end of the Qianlong period, as the expulsion era wrapped up, the massive population discrepancy between Manchus and Hanjun continued to disadvantage the latter relative to the former. This was apparent in the aftermath of the Lin Shuangwen rebellion of 1787–1788, when banner troops from Guangzhou were sent to fight in Taiwan. Only a small number of soldiers from the garrison, among them both Manchus and Hanjun, died in the campaign, but the measures undertaken to provide for the families of the deceased differed between the two groups. In either case, a surviving son who had come of age was to be allowed to fill his father's newly vacant post. If a deceased soldier's sons were not old enough to take his place, however, Manchu sons would receive a supernumerary stipend. For Hanjun men, in contrast, a more distant male relative like a nephew would be found to take the deceased man's place, and no other accommodations would be made. As the garrison general Tsuntai 存泰 noted, the long history of Hanjun at Guangzhou meant that there were no instances in which an eligible male relative of a deceased Hanjun soldier could not be found.⁴⁵ In practice, this meant that Hanjun soldiers were expected to provide for a much larger number of people on a single salary than were Manchus. A Hanjun nephew who inherited his uncle's post, it seems, would be expected to provide for his aunt and young cousins, who would have no separate provision made for them. A deceased Manchu soldier's nuclear family, on the other hand, was guaranteed to receive direct support.

As the Qianlong period concluded, shortages of Manchus at the garrison ceased to serve as cost-cutting opportunities, with banner officials instead working to strengthen the financial position of the Hanjun under their command. In 1794—one year prior to the emperor's abdication—the garrison general Fucang informed the court that in the years since Yongwei's elimination of 300 Manchu-designated posts, the growth of the Manchu population had continued to be exceedingly slow, and once again there were not enough men to fill even the 1,200 available posts, with more than 200 remaining vacant. Fucang also noted the difficult situation of the Hanjun, pointing out that the additional posts created for them in the preceding decades, both in the infantry and the naval garrison, carried relatively small salaries and grain stipends, enough only to support a family of three or four, even though many Hanjun soldiers had eight or nine mouths to feed. Moreover, there were 1,512 Hanjun men between the ages of 16 and 40 *sui* who lacked employment entirely. To help deal with this problem, Fucang proposed taking 200 Manchu posts and dividing the salaries associated with them in half, creating 200 Manchu posts and 200 Hanjun posts for "auxiliaries" (Ma. *araha uksin*, Ch. 副甲 [*fujia*]). In the Manchu banners, these posts would be given to young men who had reached the age of military service but were deficient in some way, like being too small or too weak. If there were not enough such men, the posts would be left open. For Hanjun, in contrast, the posts would go to strong and capable adult men who lacked a salary.

Unlike the various schemes discussed previously, Fucang's plan focused on promoting the welfare of Hanjun, granting them salaries not merely intended to fill the garrison's military requirements, but aimed at supporting its large Hanjun population. The idea that the state had a responsibility to find ways to provide for all banner people, regardless of ethnicity, was perhaps regaining strength as the policy of Hanjun expulsion ceased to drive the official approach to the banners. The Qianlong emperor himself remained less than fully devoted to the well-being of Han bannermen as, although he approved Fucang's proposal, he decreed that it should be only a temporary measure, with the new Hanjun posts being taken away as soon as the Manchu population had grown sufficiently to fill them.[46] But after his abdication, the court began offering its full endorsement to initiatives that sought to secure livelihoods for as many bannermen as possible, regardless of ethnicity.

The first small move toward making policy designed principally for the benefit of the Hanjun occurred in the second year of the reign of the new Jiaqing emperor. A 1797 memorial from the top Guangzhou officials pointed out that, thanks to the establishment of supernumerary posts in 1768, Manchu widows and orphans were directly provided with state support. However, the same was not true for Hanjun, for whom no stipends existed other than those for actual soldiers. The 296 widows, orphans, disabled soldiers, and others who were incapable of providing for themselves among Guangzhou's Hanjun were supported through voluntary contributions from Hanjun soldiers. The officials noted that the local *Puji tang* 普濟堂, a Qing state–promoted charitable institution dedicated to poor relief, particularly for the sick and elderly, ran yearly surpluses.[47] These surpluses, they argued, could be given to those in the garrison who required similar support, at a rate of 1 tael per month per person.[48] By raiding general poor-relief funds to support Hanjun in need, the court demonstrated that the support of its service elite was a far greater priority than relief for poor commoners. But the unwillingness to use the banner treasury for this purpose perhaps reflected a continued reluctance to put the needs of Hanjun at the same level as those of Manchus as a garrison priority. That reluctance would soon disappear.

In 1810, garrison officials, led by General Qing-pu 慶溥, submitted a memorial that, like those from Fucang in 1794 and 1797, took explicit note of the difficult situation of the Hanjun in Guangzhou. Indeed, the memorial laid out in detail the extreme contrast in the situations of Manchus and Hanjun at the garrison, directly comparing the number of salaried posts (at this time, 1,613 for Manchus and, including naval positions, 2,504 for Hanjun); total population (then more than 4,500 Manchus and 14,300 Hanjun); unemployed adult men (72 Manchus and more than 1,800 Hanjun); and boys who had not yet reached the age of military service (650 Manchus and nearly 2,800 Hanjun). This situation, Qing-pu pointed out, meant an underutilization of the military potential of the Hanjun. Whenever a vacancy opened up in the Hanjun banners and officials examined unemployed men to find those men of talent capable of proficiency with both horse and bow, they did not lack for qualified candidates, but the relatively low quota for Hanjun troops prevented most from being selected. Perhaps even more important, though, it meant that "for unemployed adult men to obtain a position is extremely difficult, and with many mouths to feed in a family, their livelihoods are frequently impoverished."

Qing-pu then cited an edict from the Jiaqing emperor that ordered local officials to ensure that ordinary people could pursue legitimate livelihoods without resulting to "stirring up trouble as bandits" (Ch. 爲匪滋事 [*wei fei zishi*]).[49] This edict had nothing to do with the banners; the memorial that prompted it was about measures to deal with pirates and smugglers along the southeast coast.[50] However, Qing-pu interpreted the admonition as applying to him and his bannermen as well and informed the court that he had sought a means to alleviate the problem of a large Hanjun population combined with a small number of salaried posts. He noted that the dynastic treasury was already heavily burdened, and thus it would not be suitable to rely on drawing from it regularly. Yet he also rejected removing more Hanjun from the banner rolls; although he did not offer any reasons, he described such a policy as "rash" (Ch. 率 [shuai]).

Qing-pu then pointed out that the garrison treasury had two large funds, one for horse purchase and one for grain purchase, which were largely underutilized, to the point that a combined 46,200 taels of silver had accumulated. He proposed loaning this money to salt merchants and pawnshop owners at 1.2 percent monthly interest, which would bring in a little over 550 taels per month, enabling the garrison to support 1,100 Hanjun supernumeraries without rice stipends (Ch. 無米養育兵 [wumi yangyu bing]) at a rate of 0.5 taels per person per month. To prevent the bannermen receiving such stipends from becoming lazy or dissolute, and to maintain military readiness, the men in question would be expected to regularly participate in drills with the garrison's auxiliaries. When vacancies appeared in the auxiliaries, they would be filled from among those same supernumeraries.[51] The plan was approved without modification by the court in Beijing, who noted that it would benefit both banner livelihood and garrison defense.[52]

Although Qing-pu cited no precedent for his proposal, it was not in fact an entirely new idea. In fact, a very similar policy had been developed by the Yongzheng court in the mature era and implemented at garrisons across the empire. Between 1723 and 1746, 2.6 million taels of silver, mostly taken from provincial treasuries, were given to banner officials in both the capital and the provinces to be invested in business schemes that would produce returns capable of supporting a large portion of banner expenses. Pawnshops and salt merchants had been among the most common investment targets, although some garrisons opened retail shops or purchased land for rent. In most garrisons, these schemes were fairly successful for a time, but between the late 1740s and 1754, all of them were shut down by the Qianlong court. This was in part a response to corruption, as large portions of the proceeds were siphoned off to go into the pockets of the officials managing the programs, and in part due to concerns about the ethics of state-supported enterprises competing with private businesses.[53] The resurrection of a similar program by Qing-pu and the Jiaqing court, designed exclusively for the benefit of Hanjun, suggests a very real shift in thinking about the Hanjun following the death of the Qianlong emperor. Their welfare, like that of

Manchu and Mongol banner people, was now a state priority, worthy of substantial attention and important enough to justify reversing a major policy decision made by the previous emperor.

Similar schemes were adopted repeatedly over the course of the nineteenth century, using other funds held in Guangzhou treasuries. Beginning in 1829, an additional 80,000 taels from the provincial treasury were loaned to merchants, producing an annual profit of 5,000 taels to be used to support unemployed bannermen.[54] Because the garrison's more than 16,000 Hanjun far outnumbered its 5,000 Manchus, though the latter were finally beginning to experience shortages in the number of available posts, 4,000 taels annually were to be allocated to Hanjun and only 1,000 to Manchus. This did not produce per-capita fairness; 166 Manchus were to be supported at a rate of 0.5 taels/month, while 1,110 Hanjun were to be supported at a rate of only 0.3 taels/month.[55] In 1844, the number of Hanjun supported by this fund increased to 1,666 through a reduction in the monthly payment to 0.2 taels/month.[56] Yet even the smaller amount received by each Hanjun man, in comparison to Manchus, reflected the garrison's concern for Hanjun welfare; by deciding to allocate four times as much money in total to Hanjun as to Manchus, the garrison rejected an artificial equality between the two groups in favor of spending more on the more populous, and more disadvantaged, banner category.

The same 4:1 ratio would in fact recur in a later interest-based scheme for supporting bannermen. In 1836, 10,000 taels of silver from the provincial treasury were loaned out at 1 percent monthly interest for a monthly return of 100 taels, enabling the support of one hundred "supplementary soldiers" (Ch. 餘兵 [yubing]). Of these posts, eighty were to go to Hanjun and twenty to Manchus, meaning that in this case, there would be no difference in per-person income.[57] Beginning in 1855, an additional two hundred supplementary soldiers were created at the same 1 tael/month rate, using most of the 3,000 taels per year that had previously gone to repay the provincial treasury for the principal that financed the 1829 scheme just described. This time, though, all two hundred posts would be given to Hanjun.[58]

When a few other smaller similar investment projects are taken into account, the total scale of the Guangzhou garrison's plans to raise money to support its bannermen becomes quite impressive. These arrangements included an investment of 10,000 taels to support travel to the capital by metropolitan examination candidates from the garrison, two additional investments totaling 30,000 taels toward expanding the number of bannermen receiving small welfare payments of 0.5 taels/month or less, and 20,000 taels toward supporting funeral expenses for bannermen.[59] The total amount of funds invested over the course of the nineteenth century thus reaches at least 196,200 taels of silver, providing some support to over 3,000 bannermen and their families, almost all of whom were Hanjun. This represents a striking contrast from the second half of the Qianlong era, when active efforts were made to redirect funds from banner stipends to the garrison treasury, with additional support offered to Hanjun only as a result of military needs. Table 4.1 shows that the garrison had moved entirely in the direction of supporting the Hanjun in proportion to their numbers by the late

TABLE 4.1
The number of Manchus and Hanjun in each type of post in Guangzhou, 1884[a]

Position	Manchus	Hanjun
Total officers	46	46
Corporals 領催 (lingcui)	120	120
Vanguard 前鋒 (qianfeng)	150	0
Cavalry 馬甲 (majia)	730	1,180
Infantry 步甲 (bujia) (from the infantry unit that replaced the naval garrison, including officers and corporals)	0	1,015
Artillery 礮手 (paoshou)	120	304
Craftsmen 匠 (jiang)	13	13
Auxiliaries 副甲 (fujia)	200	200
Supernumeraries 養育兵 (yangyu bing)	400	1,111
Supplementary Soldiers 餘兵 (yubing)	60	440
Clerks 隨印外郎 (suiyin wailang)	0	4
Additional men (Manchus supported at a rate of 0.5 taels/month, Hanjun supported at a rate of 0.2 taels/month)[b]	166	1,666
Total	2,005	6,099

[a] Unless separately noted, data in this table comes from Cangšan 長善, ed., *Gazetteer for the Eight Banners Garrisoned in Canton* 駐粵八旗志 (Guangzhou, 1884; reprinted Taipei: Wenhai chubanshe, 1997), juan 1, 2a–5a.

[b] Cangšan, *Gazetteer for the Eight Banners Garrisoned in Canton*, juan 6, 13a–14a.

nineteenth century, in comparison to the initial plan from the 1750s, which ordered an even division between Manchus and Hanjun of the number of stipend-bearing posts. Although the small payments to holders of many posts reflected the limits of dynastic finances in this period, the total number of men supported by the garrison treasury had reached more than 8,000, in contrast to the 3,600 salaried posts that existed in Guangzhou in the 1750s. Even in its final decades, the dynasty was committed to the idea that it owed support to its service elite.

In addition to offering massively increased support to Hanjun through the creation of new banner posts, the mid-nineteenth-century Qing court resurrected the policy of allowing banner people to serve in the Green Standard army, which had been effectively abolished in provincial garrisons during the expulsion era. In the meantime, Hanjun in the capital had continued to be able to hold certain Green Standard posts in the gendarmerie—the units responsible for policing the capital (Ma. *baicara jafara kūwaran*, Ch. 巡捕營 [*xunbu ying*]). Indeed, beginning in 1805, even Manchu and Mongol bannermen were permitted to serve in the Beijing gendarmerie, out of concern for their overpopulation in the capital and the lack of available posts.[60] In 1826, Green Standard ranks were further opened to bannermen of all types, with the Daoguang emperor accepting a proposal by the Zhili governor-general Na-yan-cheng 那彥成 that called for Manchus and Mongols in provincial garrisons to be allowed to take Green Standard posts, following the precedent of the Beijing gendarmerie. This would, the edict said, constitute equal treatment for Manchu, Mongol, and Hanjun bannermen.[61] These decisions reflected a changing view of the differences between Manchus and Hanjun. The mature era policy of allowing Hanjun, but not other bannermen, to serve in the Green Standards had suggested that it was their ethnic background that made them suitable for what was otherwise a post for commoners; that is, it was fine for Hanjun to do the jobs of Han commoners, but not for Manchus to do the same. This was apparently no longer the case by the middle of the postexpulsion era. Rather, the need to expand employment opportunities and find new forms of support for all banner people—Manchus and Mongols as well as Han—trumped the maintenance of clear ethnic divides within the banner system.

In the Guangzhou garrison, officials took advantage of the new policy to benefit the garrison's Hanjun population, not just its Manchus. Shortly after the edict permitting provincial Manchus and Mongols to take up Green Standard posts was issued, the garrison general Kingboo implemented the new regulation in Guangzhou. Ten years later, a new general, Sulfangga, noting that the Manchu population remained quite low but many Hanjun remained unemployed, received permission to apply the procedures that Kingboo had designed to Hanjun as well. Sulfangga proposed that two of every three Green Standard positions opened to bannermen in Guangzhou should go to Hanjun, but also that if there were no Manchus to fill the third post, that could go to a Hanjun man as well. However, Sulfangga worried that Hanjun entering Green Standard posts would be treated like those who had been expelled from the banners and forced to give up their banner registry. He strongly urged that they be allowed to retain their banner status, writing:

> The Hanjun Eight Banners have been garrisoned in the province for a long time. Dwelling in this tiny plot of land [the garrison], they have come to depend on it as if it were their native land, and they have bonds of friendship and mutual protection with all their clansmen, relatives, and friends. Moreover, the men of the Eight Banners make mounted archery and military drills their daily focus, but are not accustomed to practicing agriculture, trade, industry, or commerce. If they are immediately stricken from the banner rolls upon entering the Green Standards, then if in the future they must give up their posts due to old age or illness, they will not be able to remain in the Green Standard camp and it will be extremely difficult for them to return to the banners. This will certainly lead to them becoming homeless and destitute.[62]

Sulfangga's memorial and its imperial endorsement demonstrate the nineteenth-century Qing state's commitment to providing for all banner people within the framework of the banner system.[63] Even when outside sources of financing and employment in nonbanner-affiliated jobs were used to pay bannermen, these measures were used to ensure that income was distributed broadly within the banner population, not to divide the service elite between core members and marginal ones. Although the dynasty's ability to provide sufficient support to banner people may have declined, its commitment to doing so had not.

Bannermen and the Emperor's Metaphorical Household

Understanding the privileged position of banner people as members of the service elite requires looking not just at their special access to public resources, but also at their relationship with the ruling family and how that relationship provided ideological justification for their receipt of state support. Banner people were not just employees of the Qing state, but metaphorical members of the emperor's household. This was not true at a literal level, of course; most banner people were unlikely to so much as lay eyes on the emperor or set foot in the palace. But it was true in a symbolic sense; one might even say at a ritual level. Banner people were understood to be slaves of the emperor. What was meant by this idea, embedded in memorials from banner officials to the imperial court, in which bannermen used the term "slave" (Ma. *aha*, Ch. 奴才 [*nucai*]) as a first-person pronoun, was something quite different from slavery as it existed in the Americas at the same time, the context with which most contemporary readers may be more familiar. The emperor did not buy and sell banner people as slaves, nor were they a debased group of people, denied legal personhood. Slavery in something like this more traditional sense did exist in the Qing empire, although the specific cultural and legal context of course was different from, say, the antebellum United States.[64] Indeed, as has already been discussed, banner people themselves often owned slaves.[65] But the employment of the term "slave" in reference to ordinary banner people was used not to deny them rights, but rather to elevate them. Slaves, in a legal sense, were part of the households of their masters. This is why, as we have seen, banner slaves appeared in the banner registers; they were part of the households of bannermen.[66] They owed service to their masters but were also entitled to their material support.[67] When one's master was the emperor himself, as was the case for all banner people, being a slave thus became the basis of a secure claim to privileged access to the resources of the state.

The role of the slave-master relationship as the defining feature of the relationship between banner people and the emperor had its origins, Pamela Crossley argues, in pre-Qing ideas of governance in both Manchuria and Mongolia. As she explains it, "in his relationship with his slaves the owner gives protection and sustenance. In return, the slave gives loyalty and obedience." Moreover, the service of the slave won him a sort of symbolic intimacy with his ruler/master, although that symbolic intimacy could become real for certain high-ranking bannermen.⁶⁸ But, she suggests that by the late seventeenth century, this relationship had ceased to be the province of all bannermen and had become ethnically limited to Manchus and Mongols, with Han bannermen who were still included within this framework transferred to the Manchu banners and reimagined as Manchus.⁶⁹

Yet the idea persisted that all banner people, Han as well as Manchu and Mongol, belonged to the emperor, symbolically at least, as slaves of his household. At the most basic level, the usage of "slave" as a first-person pronoun continued among Hanjun until the very end of the dynasty. A 1910 memorial by the imperial prince Zaixun 載洵 on the elimination of the term "slave" as a term of self-address in official documents, framed as part of a broader move toward constitutional government and the "mixing together" (Ch. 融合 [*ronghe*]) of Manchu and Han under equal terms of honor, observed that the word was still used by Manchus, Mongols, and Han "military officials" (Ch. 武官 [*wuguan*]). This was in contrast to the practice of Han "civil officials" (Ch. 文官 [*wenguan*]) who all referred to themselves by the term "minister" (Ma. *amban*, Ch. 臣 [*chen*]), the standard form that he wished all officials to adopt.⁷⁰ Zaixun's reference to Han military officials must mean Hanjun bannermen, as there is no precedent for Han commoners, even those with military posts, using the term "slave" in reference to themselves. Moreover, there are late-Qing examples of memorials in which Hanjun officials still call themselves "slaves."⁷¹ So, though discussing the problem in ethnic terms, the practical import of Zaixun's memorial seems to be that "slave" was considered a normal term of self-reference for all banner people, regardless of ethnicity. And although his memorial might appear to have been the end of the practice, as on the following day the regent Zaifeng 載灃 banned the use of "slave" by banner officials, one day later, Zaifeng clarified that when writing in Manchu rather than Chinese, the use of "aha" remained acceptable.⁷²

Perhaps, by the early twentieth century, the use of the term "slave" by bannermen had become an empty gesture devoid of any real ideological significance—simply the legacy of an earlier time in which the term did mean something. Yet its meaningfulness had certainly extended past the seventeenth century. In a 1758 edict in response to a Manchu official misusing the terms *aha* and *amban* in his memorials, the Qianlong emperor insisted that there was no real difference between the two words. His claim was undermined, however, by the distinction that he drew between when it was necessary to use one and when the other, as well as by the mere fact that he was denouncing an official for getting it wrong. The emperor explained that for official business (Ma. *siden i baita*), an official should use *amban* because such memorials were widely distributed. But in the case of greeting memorials (Ma. *elhe be baire*, literally "asking after health") and memorials for "kowtowing to imperial grace" (Ma. *kesi de hengkilere*), it was necessary to use *aha*.[73] In practice, bannermen holding posts in the banners or as frontier officials in positions restricted to bannermen would also often use *aha* in their memorials on official business.[74] Taken as a whole, these rules meant that bannermen would refer to themselves as "slaves" precisely in the contexts most closely connected to their roles as part of the symbolic imperial household and as service elites. That is, the term "slave" was used in personal communications with the emperor, as well as when carrying out duties that were assigned only to bannermen, but not when working in posts that were also open to commoners, even extremely high-ranking ones like grand councilor, president of a board, or governor-general.[75] Its usage thus reinforced the relationship between emperor and service elite.

The term "slave" was not the only word used to describe banner people as members of the emperor's household. Qing official documents made frequent use of terms with meanings like "nourish" and "nurture," which can also be used to refer to child-rearing or the support of dependents in one's family, to describe the support provided by the court to members of the banners.[76] Memorials and edicts make reference to banner people receiving the "divine lord's [i.e., the emperor's] nourishing, nurturing grace" (Ma. *enduringge ejen i hūwašabume ujihe kesi*).[77] Similar expressions could be combined with references to the slave-master relationship.[78] One 1766 document reported that the bannermen of Mukden had, in response to an imperial decision to provide them with rents from a certain set of lands as additional income, knelt, kowtowed repeatedly, and declared: "We slaves have generation after generation received the lord's (Ma. *ejen*; i.e., the emperor's) nourishing, nurturing, great, and generous grace; there is no effort we could make that would repay it."[79] Another from 1802 described the "lord's grace that nourishes and nurtures slaves of the banners."[80] This language, like the use of "slave" as a first-person descriptor in memorials, did not peter out in the later years of the dynasty. An 1830 memorial thanking the Daoguang emperor for approving one of the Guangzhou garrison's schemes to loan out government funds at interest to provide support for bannermen includes a line in which the Manchu colonel Ulangga and the Hanjun colonel Dong Chaochen are reported to have said that "the people of our official troops have generation after generation received boundless nourishing and nurturing [imperial] grace."[81] Taken together, the frequent repetition of this kind of language suggests a view of the banners according to which the Qing service elite were slaves of the emperor, nourished both literally and figuratively by his "grace," a benefit that they repaid through their loyal service. This language and this interpretation of the banner-emperor relationship were directly associated with the deployment of state resources to provide income to banner people, and indeed they formed the ideological basis that both justified and required the continued use of vast sums for their support.

Moreover, the relationship was understood as continuing indefinitely through time, as exemplified in the recurrence of phrases like "generation after generation" (Ma. *jalan halame*) in the documents cited here. The idea that the emperor's responsibility for providing for banner people was not only part of the enduring history of their relationship, but also a requirement for the future was also sometimes made explicit. In 1742, for instance, the Qianlong emperor issued an edict that spoke of the need "to repair and rectify the customs that eternally (Ma. *enteheme*) benefit the livelihoods of the people of the banners."[82] The obligation of support that the court owed its service elite would never end, and policies needed to be established to ensure the dynasty's continued ability to fulfill its obligations.[83]

One practice that helped bind banner people, and particularly those within the upper strata of banner society, to the court was the imperial hunt. Although largely discontinued in the nineteenth century, the regular assemblies during the eighteenth century at the imperial hunting grounds at Mulan 木蘭, north of the imperial lodge and complex at Chengde, brought together a cross-section of the imperial elite, extending beyond the banners but not, notably, to Han commoners, even those of high official rank. Across Eurasia, the opportunity to participate in a royal hunt was "a gesture of approval and trust, an overture, a recognition of one's utility and a call upon one's loyalty."[84] The Qing was no exception. The imperial hunt, particularly as it was conducted during the reign of the Qianlong emperor, represented an institutionalization "of the old Mongol and Manchu rule according to which the chief exercises his power by the means of the hunt and the vassal fulfills his duty by participating in it."[85]

The imperial hunt, like so much else related to the banners, has been discussed largely in relation to ethnicity and to solidarity among ethnically Inner Asian elites, from the imperial court itself to Manchu and Mongol bannermen, to Mongol *jasagh* princes, to Tibetan lamas and Turkic Muslim leaders.⁸⁶ Indeed, it is widely believed that Hanjun bannermen were excluded from the hunt entirely.⁸⁷ And yet, although it is true that participation in the hunt was a privilege that Hanjun bannermen were far less likely to enjoy than were their Manchu and Mongol counterparts, Hanjun did sometimes participate, and banner officials occasionally offered a conception of the hunt that was based on status, not ethnicity.⁸⁸ In 1738, for instance, the Hangzhou garrison general Fusen argued that when the garrison next sent soldiers to the capital to join in the hunt, Hanjun should be included alongside Manchus and Mongols. He pointed to their assiduousness in the emperor's service and in performance of the Manchu/banner way, as well as the fact that "as for the official troops of the Manchus, Mongols, and Hanjun, they all are slaves who have generation after generation received the nurturing, nourishing, and valued grace of the divine lord."⁸⁹ There was, Fusen suggested, no real difference in the relationship that Manchu bannermen and Han bannermen each had with the emperor, whether in terms of their service or their membership in his household, so all should be eligible to participate.

The imperial rescript does not make it clear whether Fusen's argument convinced the emperor, who referred it elsewhere in the bureaucracy for further discussion. But another set of sources demonstrates conclusively that some Hanjun did get the opportunity to join the hunt. The personnel records associated with promotion decisions for banner officers often included a mention of how many times they had participated in hunts. Many Hanjun officials had only a few experiences. The Bordered Yellow Banner corporal Tang Xie had joined the hunt two times as of 1744, while the Plain Red Banner captain Wang Huailiang had hunted once as of 1751.⁹⁰ But a few must have been regular participants, like the Bordered Blue Banner captain Pan Shiliang, who had participated an impressive twenty-five times when he was considered for promotion in 1741, at the age of 62 *sui*.⁹¹ It is reasonable, therefore, to treat banner status, not just Manchu/Mongol ethnicity, as one of the qualifying factors for participation in this form of solidarity-building between emperor and elites.⁹²

Conclusion: Bureaucratizing Loyalty

That banner people were imagined as part of the ruler's household does not mean that the Qing political system should be understood as a simple example of patrimonial rule. Michael Chang is certainly right that the Qing state was patrimonial in conception, given the insistence of its dynastic rulers on making officials dependent on the emperor and loyal to him as an individual and on treating that loyalty as a qualification that was at least as important as any sort of knowledge or skill.[93] Yet the service elite system that characterized the banners overcame many of the supposed limitations of patrimonialism, or even patrimonial bureaucracy, as identified by Max Weber. As the last two chapters have shown, both service and privilege in the banner system were subject to substantial rationalization, and the development of the banners as a service elite was based to a great degree on the bureaucratization of feudal powerholders. Moreover, though the relationship between bannerman and emperor had the ritual forms of a patrimonial relationship, with members of the service elite presenting themselves as their ruler's slaves, in practice most officials of banner status had very little personal connection to the man they served.

Unlike the administrators in the governmental form that Weber calls "patrimonial officialdom," bannermen did not treat the offices that they held "as a personal right," nor was their selection, except at the highest levels of administration, "based on personal trust." The purpose of banner status was to create a relationship of institutionalized, pseudo-personal trust between the ruler and a group of potential servitors far too large to know the ruler personally. Thus, bannermen could be subjected to bureaucratic management and form a genuine civil service even as their loyalty to the throne remained secure. In contrast to Weber's idea that patrimonial rulers attempted to circumvent potential monopolies on power by particular status groups through appointing personal dependents to office, the Aisin Gioro house used the concentration of political authority in the hands of the service elite as a way to secure their loyalty.[94] The Qing state had managed to bureaucratize loyalty—to make the personal virtue of loyalty into a collective one, mediated by the institutions that relied on banner service and guaranteed banner privilege.

CHAPTER 5

A Female Service Elite

Status, Ethnicity, and Qing Bannerwomen

The role of banner people as service elites was highly gendered. Only men could serve as soldiers or in government office. Although some widows might receive direct access to government stipends, the vast majority of official financial support for the banner population was directed at men. As discussed in chapter 3, the martial practices associated with banner status, foremost among them archery and horsemanship, were understood as masculine attributes; indeed, the phrase "manly virtue" was used routinely in reference to these skills in the abstract, as well as to individual men who demonstrated their prowess in them. Perhaps unsurprisingly, given that state-funded education in the Manchu language was designed to ensure an adequate supply of competent translators and officers in the banner bureaucracy and the administration of Inner Asia, there is no archival evidence that the court took any interest in whether bannerwomen could speak Manchu. Although women were certainly part of the banner system, most of the meaning commonly ascribed to banner status applied to only half the banner population.

And yet, despite this exclusion from the central narratives of banner status identity, there were attributes of bannerwomanhood of interest to the court. Indeed, bannerwomen themselves played a part in defining the banner population as a service elite, making their own essential contribution to the maintenance of the dynasty. This chapter examines two areas in which women were central to maintaining the banners as a distinct status category that served as the bulwark of Aisin Gioro rule: the selection of palace women and marriage. The selection of palace women gave bannerwomen a formal role in the Qing service elite. Through the triennial reviews in which teenage girls of banner status were selected to work in the palace or marry a member of the imperial family, bannerwomen took on the service elite role themselves, becoming more than just the wives and daughters of a service elite status group. Participation in the selection of palace women was a duty to the court that bannerwomen performed on account of their status. Performance of this duty was understood to be an essential part of the relationship between banner people and the ruling dynasty, in exchange for which banner people received legal, economic, and political privileges.

The idea that female service was important to the Qing court is not wholly new. Shuo Wang has argued that bannerwomen served the dynasty by helping maintain the ethnic purity of the court and avoiding Chinese cultural influence.[1] However, the requirements of female service, like those of male service, were defined by status, not ethnicity, and the women who entered the Qing court through marriage were ethnically mixed, though dominated by members of a single status category. As such, unlike Wang, I see neither ethnic purity nor the "ethnic security" of the ruling family and its fellow Manchus as the principal goal of Qing policies surrounding marriage and female service.[2] Rather, marriage and female service helped maintain a cohesive service elite that was linked to the ruling family and separated from the commoner population.

Another account of female service to the Qing dynasty comes from Yue Du, who argues that women of the Qing imperial family worked on behalf of the emperor in the course of their marriages to Mongol nobles. Du shows that princesses sent to Mongolia served as imperial agents, reporting to the court on the activities of their husbands and in-laws via informal channels that operated outside the formal bureaucratic reporting structures that were usually controlled by those same men.[3] This chapter will show that expectations of female service extended beyond the Aisin Gioro line itself to encompass much of the broader banner population. Although the amount of service required of ordinary bannerwomen, limited for most to a single instance of participation in the process of selecting women for the palace, was far less burdensome than that of close relations of the emperor, the importance of this service to the dynasty was probably just as great.

The role of bannerwomen in the service elite did not come just from their formal role as potential brides of the ruling family, but also from their participation in more ordinary marriages. Both official regulations on marriage and the marriage arrangements that banner people made in practice helped to define the shape of banner identity and the boundaries of the Qing service elite, contributing to the separation of banner people and commoners while simultaneously reinforcing ethnic hierarchies internal to the banners. Ideas of ethnicity, status, and gender all intersected to structure marriage practice; the Qing court frowned on marriage between bannerwomen and commoner men, even as it often tolerated marriage between bannermen and commoner women, especially in cases where a commoner woman was to become a concubine rather than a wife. Similarly, marriage between Manchu or Mongol bannermen and Han bannerwomen was fairly common, while marriage between Han bannermen and Manchu or Mongol bannerwomen was quite rare.

This chapter consists of two parts. In the first, I analyze the Qing selection of banner girls to serve in the palace and act as potential marriage partners for male members of the imperial line as a gendered form of service. In addition, I show that many of the features of banner status that defined banner people as a service elite applied to bannerwomen along gendered lines. The court supervised status performance through attention to female compliance with status-based sumptuary regulations and articulated a claim that girls' participation in the selection of palace women was related to the special relationship that banner people had with the emperor, their lord. Service and privilege were tied together for bannerwomen in ways related to, but distinct from, the ways that they were tied together for bannermen. In the second part of the chapter, I move to an examination of marriage in the banners. I show that official regulation of banner marriage, especially restrictions on the ability of bannerwomen to marry commoner men, helped define the people of the banners as a coherent and distinct group. But I also demonstrate that actual marriage patterns within the banners reflected an ethnic hierarchy internal to the banners, in which Manchu and Mongol banner people ranked higher than their Han counterparts. Marriage was a place where gender, ethnicity, and status came together to define the nature of the Qing service elite.

The Selection of Palace Women and Female Service

Every three years, banner girls between the ages of 13 and 16 *sui* were subject to selection to enter the palace. Girls so selected were known in Chinese as *xiunü* (秀女, "elegant women"), the term most commonly applied to them in English-language scholarship as well.[4] Only banner girls participated in the *xiunü* selection process, which was one of the main means through which brides were found for the emperor and his close male relatives. Girls selected as *xiunü* could either be immediately married to the emperor or an imperial prince or be required to serve as ladies-in-waiting for five years, during which time they might be selected for marriage. Those ladies-in-waiting who were not married after five years were dismissed from the palace with a grant of 20 taels of silver.[5] Of the 155 official consorts of the postconquest Qing emperors, 76 percent entered the palace as *xiunü*. Most of the remainder became imperial consorts after another banner-exclusive process, the annual selection of palace maids (Ch. 宮女 [*gongnü*]) from among girls in the three bondservant banners of the Imperial Household Department, who made up 16 percent of imperial concubines over the course of the Qing. Although palace maids, unlike *xiunü*, were brought into the palace as servants rather than to marry imperial relatives, they could become low-ranking consorts if they caught the eye of an emperor or prince.[6] The only other group to produce a substantial number of imperial brides was the Mongol aristocracy, who regularly intermarried with the Aisin Gioro lineage for the entirety of the Qing period.[7]

Participation in the *xiunü* draft, and, for girls of the Imperial Household Department's bondservant banners, the palace maid draft, was mandatory. Bannerwomen could not receive official permission to marry—and all banner marriages needed to be approved by the company commanders of the people involved—unless they had participated in the system.[8] Participation in these selection drafts, and marriage into the imperial family if selected, can thus be seen as the female analog to male military and administrative service. Moreover, just as bannermen were responsible for maintaining the political authority of the dynasty through their contributions to imperial security and governance, bannerwomen, given their dominance of the ranks of imperial consorts, were responsible for dynastic reproduction. Bannerwomen were the mothers of future emperors; their service therefore was as integral to the continuance of Aisin Gioro rule as that of their fathers and brothers. And this service was not without its own hardships. Although a woman selected as an imperial consort would lead a life of immense material privilege, regulations designed to prevent imperial in-laws from gaining influence meant that her contact with her natal family would be heavily restricted. A palace woman could not so much as receive a gift from her parents, nor could she send a servant to convey a message to them, without special permission.[9] What most differentiated the nature of female banner service from male service was less the depth of commitment required and more the number of people that it applied to. Only a small fraction of women would be selected as *xiunü*, and an even smaller number would enter a marital relationship with a member of the imperial house, while all men, even those without official employment, were expected to maintain their martial abilities.

As with male military service, female participation in the *xiunü* selection process helped mark the banners as a distinct status category. And as with military service, although status identity and ethnic identity interacted with each other in the *xiunü* selection process, the status division between commoners and banner people was of greater significance than the ethnic distinction between Manchus and Han. Members of the imperial family married Hanjun women with some frequency, while marriage between Aisin Gioro men and commoner women was strictly prohibited.[10] Indeed, this rule extended beyond the imperial lineage (Ma. *uksun*, Ch. 宗室 [*zongshi*]), to encompass more distant imperial relatives registered as Gioro (Ch. 覺羅 [*Jueluo*]). As of the late eighteenth century, this prohibition was enforced strictly enough that when a Gioro man named Sengbooju married the daughter of a Chengde County commoner named Yu Xiangxian in the summer of 1779, he claimed that the girl was in fact the daughter of a Plain Blue Hanjun Banner man named Yang Yong. An investigation, prompted by Sengbooju's request for the imperial gift of silver granted to bannermen upon marriage, determined that Yang Yong's two daughters were both married to other men. Sengbooju's father, Giyahūn, thereupon falsely claimed that the Yu family had told him that Yu Xiangxian's daughter was adopted as an infant after being born to Yang Yong.[11] The case made clear the important distinction between marriage to a Hanjun woman, which would have been entirely legitimate, and to a Han commoner, which was not. Sengbooju was not only denied the marriage money that he had sought, but he, his father, and the local banner village headman were all punished for their respective roles in the unlawful marriage. The clan officials responsible for managing them, who had permitted the marriage to go forward, were referred to the Imperial Clan Court (Ma. *uksun be kadalara yamun*, Ch. 宗人府 [*zongren fu*]) for reprimand.[12]

Prior to 1806, all banner girls were subject to participation in *xiunü* selection regardless of ethnic affiliation, making the link between banner status and the potential to be chosen for palace service clear.[13] That year, the Jiaqing emperor issued an edict stating that, for Hanjun, only daughters of civil officials of the rank of *bithesi* or higher and military officials of the rank of lieutenant or higher would be required to participate. The selection of the daughters of ordinary Hanjun soldiers would cease.[14] Yet we should not make too much of the distinction between Hanjun women, on the one hand, and Manchu and Mongol women, on the other, that this edict created. In practice, during the nineteenth century, ordinary banner girls of all ethnic backgrounds frequently avoided participation in *xiunü* selection. During the latter part of the Jiaqing period, the daughters of Manchu and Mongol soldiers with monthly salaries of 3 taels of silver or less, as well as the daughters of men subsisting on supernumerary stipends, were exempted from participation in selection. This exemption would have encompassed a large number of ordinary banner girls, including the daughters of virtually all nonofficers serving outside the capital, as the standard monthly salary for a provincial bannerman was 3 taels of silver.[15] In the Daoguang era, a rule was put in place that prior to each triennial selection of *xiunü*, the court would determine whether any daughters of soldiers would participate or if that year's selection would be limited to the daughters of military officers and civil officials. In 1854, for instance, the court of the Xianfeng emperor decided that in the 1855 *xiunü* selection, soldiers' daughters would be exempted. This meant that a total of 446 daughters of Manchu and Mongol officials and 131 daughters of Hanjun officials were required to participate.[16]

It is true that these numbers reflect diminished Hanjun participation compared to that of the other two major ethnic constituencies, and that daughters of Hanjun soldiers were not even potentially considered for inclusion, unlike those of Manchu and Mongol soldiers. Yet more than 20 percent of candidate girls in 1854 would have been Hanjun, meaning that ethnically Han bannerwomen remained an important component of the women of the court. In the postexpulsion era, this was lower than, but not wildly different from, the percentage of Hanjun in the total banner population, which stood at about 27 percent as of 1812.[17] As with so much else in the banner system, an ethnic hierarchy that subordinated Hanjun banner people was apparent, but Hanjun membership in the service elite remained intact. While Hanjun women made it to court at lower rates than other bannerwomen in the postexpulsion era, no woman of commoner status, no matter how highly placed her father was, would ever be eligible to be selected as a *xiunü*. Even in the very late Qing, as the court began to reduce the salience of banner status, *xiunü* selection was not extended to include commoners; a 1902 edict from the Guangxu court declared that to do so would be to risk "following in the misrule of the former Ming dynasty" (Ch. 蹈前明弊政 [*dao qian Ming bizheng*]).[18]

The selection of *xiunü* to enter the palace not only supplied the ruling family with brides but provided an opportunity to assess bannerwomen's compliance with a set of norms associated with banner status. Unlike bannermen, who were subject to routine oversight through their attendance at banner schools, their participation in examinations, and their military and administrative service, most bannerwomen came under the gaze of the state only through the *xiunü* selection process. Yet bannerwomen, like bannermen, were subject to rules that differentiated them from the broader commoner population.

Where requirements for bannermen focused on martial and linguistic skills as well as personal conduct, those for bannerwomen were primarily sumptuary and tonsorial. In 1759, the Qianlong emperor complained that among the girls presented for selection that year, there were many who "imitated Han adornment" (Ma. *Nikan i miyamigan be alhūdame*) by wearing their hair in a bun. This was in contrast to the Manchu style, in which a woman's hair was twisted around a piece of wood, ivory, or metal into a narrow, elongated shape that sat above the head and extended beyond it on both sides so it sat in the air at about shoulder width, a hairstyle often called *liangbatou* (兩把頭)—"two fistfuls of hair"—in Chinese.[19] Qianlong described this departure from proper hairstyle as an "extremely evil custom" (Ma. *umesi ehe tacin*) and declared that "the old way of the Manchus (Ma. *Manjusai fe doro*) is originally very plain and simple and not at all like this. Although this is merely women's adornment, if we do not instruct that it be prohibited . . . it will have significant implications for Manchu customs."[20] As was frequently done in the case of requirements for bannermen, such as proficiency in archery and the Manchu language, the emperor here associated a requirement of bannerwomen with specifically Manchu practices. Yet, as with the martial skills required of bannermen, the sumptuary demands made of bannerwomen were not ethnically limited but rather applied to all women of the banners.

The applicability of supposedly Manchu standards of appearance to all bannerwomen is made clear in an 1804 edict of the Jiaqing emperor. In it, he complained that in that year's *xiunü* selection, nineteen girls of the Hanjun Bordered Yellow Banner were found to have bound feet, which were prohibited to bannerwomen. The emperor described this transgression as a violation of the "fixed standard" (Ma. *toktobuha durun*) of the "attire of our dynasty" (Ma. *musei gurun i mahala etuku*) and declared it "extremely wrong" (Ma. *fikatala waka*). Although the girls in question were Hanjun, the emperor also tied this sumptuary regulation to an ethnic standard, declaring that if this misbehavior were not corrected, it would lead to "becoming just like Han" (Ma. *šuwe Nikan gese ombi*). The emperor coupled his complaints about Hanjun *xiunü* candidates with one about Manchu and Mongol girls presented that year, noting that many among them wore "sleeves [that were] overly wide and large," which he described as a "completely Han style" (Ma. *fuhali Nikan durun*) and one that, as with Hanjun foot-binding, would "gradually lead to the adoption of Han customs" (Ma. *ulhiyen i Nikan tacin de dosinara*).[21] Manchu apparel, as standardized by the Qing court, featured close-fitting sleeves, reflecting traditions of Inner Asian dress in which free movement was prized and arms needed to be protected from the cold wind while on horseback. This contrasted with Han Chinese styles, in which extremely wide sleeves served both as a display of wealth and status, due to the amount of fabric required, and, on formal occasions, as a means of creating slow and stately movements.[22] Although the emperor complained at much greater length about foot-binding than about sleeve style, perhaps because the former was permanent and thus was harder to correct, the juxtaposition of the two issues demonstrates that the sumptuary regulation of women of banner status cut across ethnic lines. Hanjun women, just like Manchus, were required to maintain their distinctiveness from the bulk of the commoner population.

Concern about the sumptuary performance of bannerwomen was not tied solely to their potential entrance into the court. Shortly after excusing the daughters of ordinary Hanjun soldiers from participation in the *xiunü* selection process, the Jiaqing emperor issued another edict emphasizing that these girls were still expected to abide by the same sumptuary regulations that applied to all bannerwomen. These women had been exempted from participation, the emperor explained, out of compassionate concern for their poverty; if they then "came to wantonly change their adornment, bind their feet, or make the sleeves of their clothes wide and large," it served to "turn their backs on" (Ma. *jurcehebi*) the emperor's benevolence. In the edict, sumptuary rules were framed not just in ethnic terms, but also in terms of loyalty to the dynasty, the fundamental basis of the privileged status of the service elite. The emperor declared:

> Our dynasty's sumptuary standards (Ma. *mahala etukui durun*) were laid down by our ancestors at the time of the establishment of the dynastic enterprise. Moreover, previously the enlightened and cultured emperor Taizong [Hong Taiji] issued an edict proclaiming: "let the children and grandchildren of future generations eternally follow the sumptuary standards. On no account may they be changed." My khan father, the perfected emperor Gaozong [Qianlong], in admiration of this edict, further expounded on the edict's intentions and had it engraved on a horizontal stele in the Archery Pavilion [of the palace].[23]

Although violations of sumptuary rules for bannerwomen were framed in terms of succumbing to Han customs, here as elsewhere in the Jiaqing emperor's edicts, those rules themselves were described not in ethnic terms, as Manchu customs, but in political terms, as the fundamental regulations of the ruling house. Han attire was wrong for bannerwomen not because they were Manchus—indeed, Hanjun women, for their part, were Han—but because adopting such attire meant choosing the dominant fashions over obligations to the ruling house. The emperor's primary concern was not avoiding ethnic acculturation or Sinicization, but rather maintaining visible signs of loyalty, both to the Jiaqing emperor himself and to his dynastic predecessors.[24]

The emperor went on to note the difficulty of enforcing such rules on women because, unlike men, they remained largely confined to the household, outside the official gaze. So banner officials were ordered to strictly investigate female attire and to hold the fathers and elder brothers of women who violated it criminally responsible. Officials themselves were, for the time being, absolved of any responsibility for violations. If, however, there were repeated instances of sumptuary infractions, the emperor threatened possible impeachment for officials who, at the next *xiunü* selection, were discovered to have let standards slip.[25]

Yet, just as with state expectations of martial performance for men, the Qing court recognized that Hanjun women were less likely than their Manchu and Mongol banner counterparts to adhere to official expectations for their behavior. So, in the wake of the initial discovery of widespread foot-binding, it suggested leniency for their male relatives. Although banner foot-binding was clearly illegal, the emperor declared that "because all of these are Hanjun banner people and have lived in villages since they were small, and only thus were corrupted by Han customs," it would be best to pardon the fathers and brothers of the women with bound feet and instead focus on making the prohibition better known. Future violators would be punished, but this first group could be excused.[26] This edict made clear that two factors justified leniency. Residence in villages meant living outside garrison communities, which presumably meant greater exposure to commoner populations. As such, it would be natural, the emperor seems to have thought, for people living in such circumstances to pick up cultural practices that were common to Han commoners but forbidden to banner people.[27] But, even aside from the issue of residence, the Hanjun identity of these villagers was assumed to make them susceptible to corruption by "Han customs." Status determined the rules and cultural practices according to which a Qing banner person was expected to structure his or her life, but the court still recognized that ethnic difference among banner people was, in practice, likely to affect their behavior.

The link between participation in *xiunü* selection and the role of banner people as service elites was always implicit in the structure and function of the process. *Xiunü* selection marked the special relationship between banner people and their ruler, enabled the reproduction of the dynasty, and provided an opportunity to enforce cultural norms that distinguished banner people from commoners. But on at least one occasion, this link was also made explicit in Qing court discourse. In early 1747, the Qianlong emperor noted that many banner people were evading *xiunü* selection and arranging engagements for their daughters without submitting them to the process, while others were openly complaining about the requirement to participate and describing it as an unwanted burden. He then proclaimed:

> This is all born of not clearly knowing the great principle of loyalty between lord and slave (Ma. *ejen aha i jurgan i amba giyan*). The people of the banners (Ma. *gūsai urse*) are all my longtime slaves (Ma. *fe ahasi*). One must not still speak of them as akin to ordinary commoners

(Ma. *an i irgese*), who have but the correspondence of lord and official (Ma. *ejen amban i teisu*). That on account of the matter of exhibiting daughters [that is, selecting *xiunü*] they have all harbored thoughts of concealment means they do not think at all of anything like the ideas of the prior time of their elders, which were of honoring the lord and loving the superior. Upon seeing this, I worry a great deal that the old ways of Manchu slaves are slowly slipping away.[28]

The emperor's edict made clear that the relationship between the emperor and banner people was fundamentally different from that between the emperor and commoner officials. Indeed, it is striking that he directly connects "officials" (Ma. *amban*, the equivalent of Ch. 臣 [*chen*]) to "commoners" (Ma. *irgese*, the equivalent of Ch. 民 [*min*]), reflecting the fact that the nature of the basic status division in the Qing was not between ordinary people and degree-holding officials, but rather between banner people and commoners, with most degree-holding officials included in the latter group. Participation in *xiunü* selection, the emperor declared, fit neatly into the relationship between slave and master, which defined both the connection of the emperor to banner people specifically and, as will be discussed in chapter 6, of rulers to service elites more generally. Indeed, to avoid participation was to violate the principles of that relationship.

The language of the edict offers a partial challenge to my portrayal of *xiunü* selection as a form of gendered service performed by women. The emperor focused not on women themselves as participants or nonparticipants, but on their male relatives hiding them and refusing to submit them for inspection. That is, the service demanded by the emperor was the presentation of girls by their fathers, not the participation of girls as autonomous individuals. This distinction is probably not tied to anything specific about the banners, but rather to the broader gender and household ideology of late imperial China. The state dealt with people as members of a household, not as individuals, and women were subordinate to male heads of household. The assumption that the emperor made in treating a girl's participation in *xiunü* selection as her father's service, not hers, was that women were not independent actors with their own agency, but simply objects of their fathers' will. From a contemporary perspective, this idea seems unreasonable, and indeed we know that even in the Qing era, women often acted in opposition to their parents in matters of marriage.[29] As such, although I acknowledge that the Qing court viewed the service of banner people as an exclusively male endeavor, it remains important to recognize that most of the actual burden of *xiunü* selection, as well as the sumptuary regulations attached to it, fell on women, and thus female service was a real and important part of the obligations of banner people as members of the Qing service elite.

Marriage, Ethnicity, and Banner Status

The selection of women for the imperial court was not the only arena in which marriage ties and gendered expectations of women helped shape membership in the Qing service elite. All marriages of banner people were subject to state oversight, with company captains required to approve the marriages of all individuals in their companies.[30] Marriage reinforced the status boundary between banner people and commoners, as intermarriage across status lines was illegal. However, enforcement of the prohibition varied along ethnic lines, with marriages between Hanjun banner people and Han commoners frequently tolerated. Ethnicity also intersected with gender to influence marriage patterns within the banners. Manchu, Mongol, and Hanjun banner people frequently married across ethnic lines, but although marriages between Manchu or Mongol bannermen and Hanjun bannerwomen were common, those between Hanjun bannermen and Manchu or Mongol bannerwomen were exceedingly rare. So, for banner people, marriage was an institution that both maintained their status distinctions from commoners and reinforced the system's internal ethnic hierarchy. For a simple schematic overview of the sorts of marriage rules and practices that existed for most of the Qing period and will be the focus of the analysis that follows, refer to table 5.1.

Perhaps the best-known evidence of the prohibition of banner-commoner intermarriage is the edict that repealed it, issued by the empress dowager Cixi in early 1902.[31] The empress dowager proclaimed that banner-commoner intermarriage had been prohibited after the conquest because of the differences in language and customs between the two groups. After more than 200 years of Qing rule, she went on to say, customs had become unified, so the court should "defer to popular sentiment" and eliminate the prohibition.[32] Cixi's edict did not provide any indication of the actual content of the intermarriage ban, and, indeed, by referring to the ban as applied to "Manchu–Han" intermarriage, she suggested the existence of an ethnicity-based rule that never actually existed.

TABLE 5.1
Legal status of various types of intermarriage in the eighteenth and nineteenth centuries

	Imperial lineage man	Manchu/ Mongol bannerman	Hanjun bannerman	Han commoner man
Imperial lineage woman	Incestuous (so presumed illegal)	Legal	Legal	Illegal
Manchu/Mongol bannerwoman	Legal	Legal	Legal but uncommon	Illegal
Hanjun bannerwoman	Legal	Legal	Legal	Officially illegal, but sometimes tolerated
Han commoner woman	Illegal	Usually legal, but with possible exceptions	Usually legal, but with possible exceptions	Legal

Qing law codes mention no prohibition of intermarriage prior to 1822, when the *Regulations of the Board of Revenue* (Ch. 戶部則例 [*Hubu zeli*]) recorded:

> Daughters of banner people are not permitted to become the wives of commoners. If there is a case of a daughter of a commoner forming a marriage with a banner person, and the respective lineage head and company captain investigate in detail and submit a report, they will identically [to banner people marrying other banner people] be given an imperial gift.[33]

Based on a comparison of different editions of the regulations, Ding Yizhuang argues that this rule likely first appeared in the Jiaqing period (1796–1820). From the regulation, we learn that the Qing state clearly differentiated marriages between banner people and commoners on the basis of gender. Bannerwomen could not marry outside the banners, but commoner women could marry into them.

The existence of both these rules predates their appearance in the statute books. That marriages between banner people and commoners were not freely permitted in the eighteenth century is made clear in documents related to Hanjun expulsion. Multiple memorials about expulsion, from several garrisons, note that after expulsion, former Hanjun "will be permitted to take exams and marry just like commoners."[34] Clearly, then, prior to expulsion, marriage rules for Hanjun banner people must have been different from those for commoners; there could not have been free intermarriage between the two groups. Indeed, a shift in who expelled banner people could marry was understood to be one of the fundamental changes that accompanied their loss of banner status. It is not clear from these memorials exactly what the previous restrictions on intermarriage had been, although they do suggest that intermarriage had not been freely permitted, regardless of whether the banner person involved was male or female; several mentioned specifically that both men and women of the banners (Ch. 子弟男女 [*zidi nannü*]) would be affected by the changes.

Yet, that bannermen could (at least in some circumstances) marry commoner women is suggested by a substatute dealing with adoption that was added to the Qing code in 1740. This rule permitted a commoner child (Ch. 民間子弟 [*minjian zidi*]) of a widow who remarried into a "detached household" banner family to be treated as a person of "unclear registration" (Ch. 戶口不清 [*hukou bu qing*]) and to be "recorded separately in the registers" (Ch. 另行記檔 [*lingxing ji dang*]).[35] The regulation presumes that a woman who had been married to a commoner could marry a bannerman. For this to be the case, either it had to be legally possible for a woman originally from a commoner family to marry a bannerman, or it had to be possible for a bannerwoman to marry a commoner man but then return to the banners after his death. It seems quite unlikely, however, that the latter case was permitted but the former was not. As was true in cases of adoption, someone who lost banner status was usually not allowed to take it up again; if bannerwomen were allowed to marry commoners, it follows that they would have been treated as commoners thereafter.[36] Hence this regulation makes clear that there were circumstances under which bannermen could legally marry commoner women. As confirmation of the greater ability of bannermen to marry commoner women than of bannerwomen to marry commoner men, many more instances of the former than of the latter appear in both private and public Qing records.³⁷

But certain sorts of intermarriage were forbidden to bannermen. The case of Sengbooju, discussed in the preceding section, demonstrates that members of the imperial lineage and its collateral branches were forbidden from marrying commoner women. In late Qianlong-era Mukden, a Bordered Yellow Banner Hanjun lieutenant named Jiang Xingzhou 姜興舟 married a Muslim commoner (Ch. 回民 [*huimin*]). When this became a matter of discussion in his community, Jiang "feared punishment" and so decided to desert. Although he soon returned to his post of his own accord, he was arrested by local banner officials and in early 1787 was "sentenced to delayed strangulation in accordance with the statute on military or civil officials who, feeling the weight of their guilt, flee their posts."³⁸ Jiang's death sentence was eventually commuted, as was common for those given delayed death sentences.³⁹ Although Jiang was not punished directly on account of his marriage, his fear of punishment and the fact that the statute under which he was punished referred explicitly to deserting a post on account of criminal guilt suggest that officials did consider his marriage to be legally problematic. It is difficult to say for sure what sort of rule Jiang's marriage had violated. His wife was a Muslim commoner, but the brief surviving discussion of his case does not clearly indicate whether it was her ethnoreligious background or her commoner status that was problematic.⁴⁰

A late Yongzheng-era case offers another example of restrictions on extrabanner marriages. A Plain Blue Banner Hanjun man named Tong Guozhong 佟國忠 married the daughter of Yang Changlang 楊長朗, a member of a *tusi* native official lineage near Chongqing, becoming an adopted-in son-in-law (Ch. 入贅 [*ruzhui*]).⁴¹ Tong had come to live in the southwest of the empire on account of the fact that his elder clansman of the same generation, Tong Guorang 佟國勷, was serving as Yunnan financial commissioner (Ma. *dasan be selgiyere hafan*, Ch. 布政使 [*buzhengshi*]). Following his marriage around 1705, the younger Tong spent three decades moving across the empire, engaged in trade as a member of the Yang household, before finally coming to official attention in 1735. A Board of Rites official discussing the case expressed outrage that no one, from local officials in Sichuan, to the banner administrators overseeing the units to which the Tong family belonged, to Tong's own family members, among whom were included officials of fairly high standing like Tong Guorang, had reported the matter sooner.⁴²

The key problem with the marriage did not appear to be the specific identity of the bride as the daughter of a native official. Indeed, during the Qing, intermarriage was quite frequently permitted between Han commoners and indigenous peoples of the southwest, despite some attempts to stop it.[43] Rather, as one official put it, the nature of the marriage meant that Tuo Guozhong had "shed his banner registry" (Ch. 漏脫旗籍 [loutuo qiji]).[44] As an adopted-in son-in-law, he became part of his wife's nonbanner household. He thereby was abandoning his responsibilities as a bannerman, in clear violation of the principles of banner status. Marriage of this sort, to a nonbannerwoman, was a sort of desertion. A standard marriage between a bannerman and a woman outside the banners, in which the woman entered the bannerman's family, might be accepted, but a bannerman could not shed his status through marriage.[45]

Restrictions on intermarriage between bannerwomen and commoner men were softened at times by the court's attitude toward ethnic differences among banner people. Late in the reign of the Yongzheng emperor, the acting Fuzhou garrison general Zhun-tai informed the court about a Plain White Banner man named Hou Hongzuo 候弘祚 selling his daughter to be the concubine of an expectant magistrate in Fujian named Leng Qihui 冷岐暉. He also noted that similarly, while in Beijing, the Zhejiang provincial judge Yang Hongxu 楊弘緒 had illicitly bought a banner girl as his concubine, for which he had been impeached by the Fujian-Zhejiang governor-general Hao Yulin 郝玉麟 and dismissed from office.[46] Moreover, he reported that he had heard that in many provincial garrisons, there were cases of Hanjun betrothing their daughters to commoners. A failure to establish a specific precedent prohibiting this behavior had led, he argued, to it "becoming well-established practice" (Ch. 相沿成習 [xiangyan chengxi]). Zhun-tai clearly believed that these marriages were out of keeping with the institutional framework of the banners, under which the "distinguishing" (Ch. 區別 [qubie]) of "banner and Han" (Ch. 旗漢 [qi Han]) had great importance. Moreover, he described Leng and Yang as "entirely unscrupulous" (Ch. 尚無顧忌 [shang wu guji]). He asked that the emperor bring regulations on Hanjun marriages into line with those on Manchu and Mongol marriages by prohibiting the sale of Hanjun girls to Han commoner men and banning the illicit drawing-up of marriage contracts between Hanjun women and Han commoner men.[47]

The emperor took no interest in Zhun-tai's memorial, writing a rescript saying that "this is not an important matter at present." Ding Yizhuang convincingly argues that this document shows that a general prohibition on banner-commoner intermarriage, which itself did not actually appear in the Qing Code until the nineteenth century and which likely applied only to bannerwomen marrying commoner men, was never really enforced against Hanjun women marrying Han commoner men.[48] Zhun-tai's attitude suggests that all marriages between bannerwomen and commoner men were considered improper, and quite possibly illegal, thus supporting the idea that the prohibition of such marriages predated the appearance of such a rule in the Qing Code. Moreover, it is further evidence that even commoners who became officials, like both grooms mentioned by name, still possessed commoner status and thus were legally forbidden from marrying bannerwomen. However, the shared ethnicity of Hanjun and Han commoners meant that the court saw their intermarriage, though illegal, as a matter of relatively little concern, perhaps because that shared ethnicity made maintaining clear divisions between the two groups seem less important, or perhaps simply because it made such prohibitions more difficult to enforce.

The role of ethnicity in shaping marriage practice was not confined to intermarriage between members of different status categories. Marriages within the banners provide clear evidence for the existence of an ethnic hierarchy between Manchu and Mongol banner people on the one hand and Hanjun on the other. As there were no apparent legal restrictions on interethnic marriage, as opposed to interstatus marriage, the ethnically inflected nature of banner marriage demonstrates that the banner ethnic hierarchy extended beyond any actual rules imposed by the Qing court to shape the daily life of banner people. An analysis of banner marriages shows that Manchu and Mongol bannermen and bannerwomen intermarried in large numbers. Yet, though many Manchu and Mongol bannermen were married to Han—most of whom were presumably Hanjun—women, marriage between Hanjun bannermen and Manchu or Mongol women was quite rare. In a society in which marriage patterns tended strongly toward female hypergamy—that is, where women often married men of higher social position but very rarely men of lower social position—marriage rates within the banners are clear evidence of an ethnic hierarchy that placed Manchus and Mongols above Hanjun.[49]

The most comprehensive data on banner marriage patterns comes from the "chaste women" (Ch. 列女 [*lienü*]) section of the *Imperially Commissioned Comprehensive History of the Eight Banners* (Ch. 欽定八旗通志 [*Qinding baqi tongzhi*]).[50] This section consists of a list of every single bannerwoman between 1653 and 1795 who was granted an honorific tablet (Ch. 旌表 [*jingbiao*]) for maintaining her chastity by refusing remarriage following the death of her husband, as well as a small number of women honored for other behaviors seen as particularly virtuous.[51] The total number of bannerwomen so honored during the years covered by the *History of the Eight Banners* was 15,436.[52]

Although this data is extremely valuable to the study of the "late imperial chastity cult"[53] and has been used for those purposes, particularly in Mark Elliott's work on the extension of the chastity cult to bannerwomen, it has another sort of value. In the *History of the Eight Banners*, lists of chaste women specified the name, banner affiliation, and position of the widow's deceased husband, followed by the family (or clan) name of the widow herself. Since the family or clan name can usually be identified as either Manchu, Mongol, or Han, the data thus suggests the frequency with which the three groups of banner people intermarried.[54] Unfortunately, no indication of the woman's original banner affiliation is given, so some women with Han surnames may have been from commoner families. However, marriages of bannermen to Han commoner women seem to have been uncommon compared to those of bannermen, even Manchu bannermen, and Hanjun women. In an examination of a variety of sources spanning most of the Qing, Ding Yizhuang uncovered forty-six examples of Manchu men marrying Han commoner women, in comparison to seventy examples of Manchu men in a single branch of the Niohuru clan—the family of the early Qing aristocrat Eidu 額亦都—who married Hanjun women over the course of six generations.[55] Most bannermen, it seems, limited their marriage pool to bannerwomen.

Because of the large volume of data—more than 15,000 names—I decided to look only at every fifth year. I began not in 1653, when the first names are listed, but in 1672 because prior to this date, many women were listed by something other than their family name, either by a given name or by some sort of nickname. The names, like Xinjie 辛姐 ("hardworking elder sister") or Siji 四姬 ("fourth woman/fourth concubine"), are nearly impossible to identify as belonging to a particular ethnic category. Therefore, my data set includes women honored in 1672, 1677, 1682, and so on through 1792. In addition, because I was interested in ordinary banner people rather than the imperial family, I ignored wives of members of the imperial clan (Ch. 宗室 [*zongshi*]) and of their collateral Gioro relatives, although I did count women from these groups as Manchus when they appeared as chaste widows. Overall, this left a sample of 3,067 names, which is sufficient to establish the trends that I will discuss here.

The most noticeable trend, as well as the most important, is that Hanjun men almost never married non-Han women. Out of 663 Hanjun men in my data set, only six were married to non-Han (five Manchus and one indeterminate), a rate of endogamy of over 99 percent. At the same time, Manchu and Mongol men frequently married Hanjun women—approximately 44 percent of Manchu banner male marriages and 50 percent of Mongol banner male marriages were to Han women (see figure 5.1), most of whom were likely Hanjun. The fact that Hanjun women were sexually available to Manchu and Mongol men, but Manchu and Mongol women were not sexually available to Hanjun men, is clear evidence of a social hierarchy in which the Hanjun were ranked below their fellow banner people. This was not the result of any legal prohibition, as intermarriage among banner people of different categories was permitted by the central Qing state, a situation confirmed by the fact that a handful of Hanjun men did marry Manchu women and their wives were able to receive chastity awards.

At least on the basis of marriage patterns, Manchus and Mongols seem to have been almost equal in the ethnic hierarchy. Nearly 22 percent of Mongol men married Manchu women, and although only 3 percent of Manchu men married Mongol women, this is likely due to the much smaller

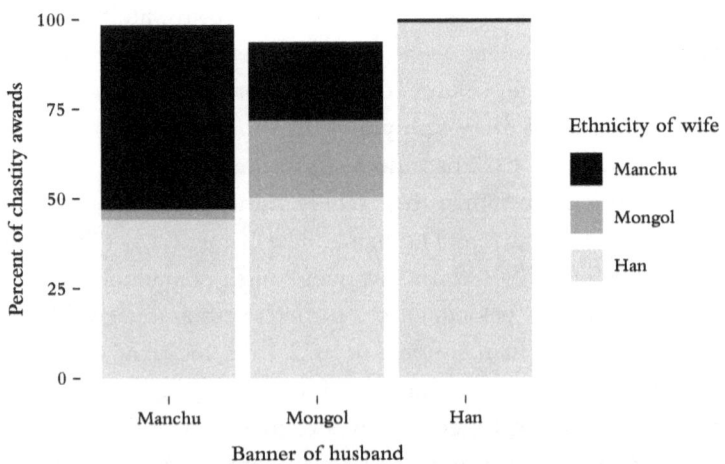

Figure 5.1 Widow chastity awards in the banners by ethnicity, 1672–1792.

[142] A FEMALE SERVICE ELITE

Mongol banner population, combined with a tendency toward endogamy in all three banner groups.[56] The standard explanation of banner hierarchy, with Manchus outranking Mongols, who in turn outranked Hanjun, is thus perhaps a bit misleading, as the gap between Manchus and Mongols was far smaller than that between Mongols and Hanjun.[57] Socially, Manchus and Mongols jointly formed the upper portion of the banner hierarchy, far ahead of the Hanjun.

In general, the banners appear to have become more socially integrated during the seventeenth and eighteenth centuries. Between 1672 and 1722, the final fifty years of the reign of the Kangxi emperor, among those listed in chaste widow records, 66 percent of Manchu men were married to Manchu women, 50 percent of Mongol men were married to Mongol women, and 100 percent of Hanjun men were married to Han women. In contrast, from 1737 to 1792, under the reign of the Qianlong emperor, only 52 percent of Manchu men, 13 percent of Mongol men, and 99 percent of Hanjun men were married to women of their same background. Figure 5.2 shows that during the eighteenth century, as compared to the seventeenth century, Mongol men became more likely to marry Manchus and Hanjun, while Manchu men became more likely to marry Mongols and Hanjun and less likely to marry Manchus.[58] However, in the wake of the expulsion of the Hanjun, which began in the 1750s, Manchu marriages to Hanjun women

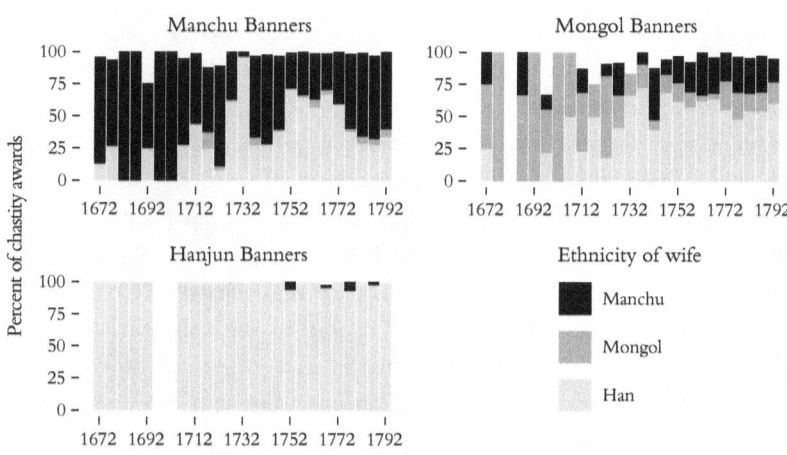

Figure 5.2 Widow chastity awards by banner and ethnicity over time. Note that bars may not sum to 100 due to indeterminate ethnicity of wives' names.

declined sharply, a trend that becomes particularly clear in the late 1770s, about twenty years after the beginning of expulsion.[59] Whether this was the result simply of a reduction in the number of Hanjun women available to Manchus or of increasing social segregation between the two groups as Hanjun were judged less deserving of banner status cannot be determined.

A final feature of the ethnic hierarchy within the banners apparent in this data, unrelated to marriage patterns, is that women who married into Manchu banner families were overrepresented among recipients of *jingbiao* tablets. A total of 62 percent of the chastity awards in my data set went to Manchu banner families, although the combined population of Mongol banner people and Hanjun was at least as high as that of Manchu banner people over the entire period in question, and substantially higher prior to Hanjun expulsion. Yet this did not mean, *pace* Elliott, that Manchu women were far more likely to receive chastity awards than their Hanjun counterparts.[60] Rather, wives of Manchu men were much more likely to be awarded than wives of Hanjun men. Indeed, although 62 percent of chastity award recipients had been married to Manchu men, only 35 percent of recipients had Manchu clan names, while 57 percent had Han surnames. This suggests that, for official purposes, ethnicity was a characteristic that existed at the level of the household (or, alternatively, was attached only to men)—a Hanjun woman who married a Manchu man would receive the preferential treatment that the court offered to Manchus. This further implies that the official policies that preferred Manchus and Mongols over Hanjun within the banners were directly linked to the social hierarchy revealed in marriage patterns. For a bannerwoman, marriage into a Manchu family meant gaining official privilege, while marriage out of one, into a Hanjun family, meant losing it.

Similar records from the Guangzhou garrison show that many of the same social distinctions described here continued into the second half of the nineteenth century, with Manchus holding a social position substantially superior to that of Hanjun. The 1884 Guangzhou garrison gazetteer includes a list of women awarded honors for their chastity (Ch. 貞節年表 [*zhenjie nianbiao*]) in each year from 1783 on. As with the earlier, empire-wide data, the list in the gazetteer is useful as a source of information on marriage practices in the garrison. Each entry lists the banner affiliation and name of the woman's deceased husband, as well as her surname or clan name. Although surnames cannot necessarily be perfectly mapped onto ethnic background—some Manchu clan names may have been reported using a one-character abbreviation—it is highly suggestive. In general, it is possible to get a good sense of whether a given chaste widow was Manchu or Han, and with 899 women listed, the gazetteer forms a very substantial and extremely valuable source of marriage data.

From 1809, Manchu clan names began to be fairly consistently reported in full transcription, whereas before they seem to have generally been shortened, with the frequent appearance of surnames like Guan 關 (likely short for Gūwalgiya) and Yi 伊 (presumably short for Irgen Gioro). Beginning with the entries from this date still leaves a sample of 746. Of these, 189 of the men were Manchu, of whom thirty-seven were married to women whose surnames clearly marked them as Han, in addition to two women with ambiguous surnames; while 150 were married to Manchus or Mongols.[61] This suggests that approximately 20 percent of the Manchus in Guangzhou were married to Han women. Of the 557 Han men in the sample, however, 552 were married to women with obviously Han surnames and five to women with ambiguous surnames (Guan or Tong 佟), while not one was married to a clearly Manchu woman.[62] As I argued in relation to the eighteenth-century data, the fact that Hanjun women sometimes married Manchu men, while Manchu women never married Hanjun men, is likely indicative of an ethnic hierarchy in the Guangzhou garrison in which Manchus were clearly superior to Hanjun. So, despite official policies, discussed in chapter 4, that increasingly treated Manchus and Hanjun as status equals over the course of the postexpulsion era, the garrison remained internally divided at least as late as the middle of the nineteenth century.[63] Indeed, these results hardly differ from those for the banner system at large in the pre-expulsion period.

In addition to the apparent continuation of a Manchu/Hanjun hierarchy within the garrison, the nineteenth-century reduction of discrepancies in the state's treatment of the two groups did not lead to a lowering of social barriers. During the first thirty years (1809–1838) of the data set, 27 percent of the listed Manchu men were married to Han women. From 1839 through the end of the data set in 1883, however, only 14 percent of the Manchu men listed were married to Han women. That is, not only did a hierarchical arrangement that made it virtually impossible for a Hanjun man to marry a Manchu woman persist, but any intermarriage between the two groups became less common even as their status in the eyes of garrison and dynastic officials became more equal. Why Manchu men in Guangzhou became less likely to marry Han women over the course of the nineteenth century is not certain, although one possibility is that the relatively small total Manchu population in the decades after Manchus first came to Guangzhou initially limited the ethnically endogamous marriage prospects of Manchu men, who increasingly chose to marry Manchu women as the number of them who were available grew. Regardless, it is difficult to escape the conclusion that ethnic differences between Manchus and Hanjun persisted, even in the face of declining differences in status.[64]

Conclusion

The Qing state understood the banner system as a fundamentally masculine enterprise, based around manly virtue and requirements of military and administrative service from which women were excluded. Yet at the same time, women's banner status was not merely the technical legal consequence of living in households headed by bannermen. By submitting to *xiunü* selection, following imperially defined sumptuary codes, and marrying appropriate partners chosen from among their fellow banner people, bannerwomen maintained the integrity of the banners as a status group and reinforced the links between the banners and their imperial master. The combination of legal restrictions and social practices that kept most banner people marrying other banner people helped ensure that banner garrisons remained distinct from the commoner-filled cities that surrounded them. The use of bannerwomen as imperial wives and servants meant that the banners provided the throne not just with the military force and administrative talent that it required, but with the reproductive labor that ensured the dynasty's continuation. By following requirements to keep their feet unbound and dress in particular styles different from those adopted by commoner women, bannerwomen demonstrated their loyalty to the dynasty, a loyalty bound up with following dynastic traditions, just as it was for their husbands, brothers, and sons when they learned to shoot an arrow from horseback. The Qing service elite was not only a group of male household heads who served in banner armies, but rather the entire banner population, its women as well as its men.

CHAPTER 6

A Comparative History of Service Elites

The Qing Eight Banners were not unique in their role as a service elite. In other early modern states across the Eurasian continent, ruling dynasties developed analogous methods for cultivating an elite that was both loyal to the ruler and useful for enhancing the power of the state. Exploring these comparable systems serves three purposes. First, it helps clarify what about the Qing banner system was unique to the particular context of Qing rule, including the role played by Manchu identity, and what was a response to needs and challenges faced by many contemporaneous states, not just the Qing. Second, it permits the development of a theory of service elites as an ideal institutional form, one that has not previously been recognized as a distinct mode of social and political organization. Finally, it offers a new way to think about the history of states other than the Qing—one that I hope may provoke new approaches and insights from scholars of other parts of the early modern world.

Social categories that can be productively analyzed as service elites may have existed in a wide range of places and times, but I focus here on three examples contemporaneous to the Qing. In imperial Russia, Tokugawa Japan, and the Ottoman Empire, newly powerful states developed mechanisms for managing their militaries, selecting their bureaucrats, and maintaining the loyalty of their political elites that bore a striking resemblance to those of the Qing. These service elite systems were certainly not identical, but they shared a common set of essential features. In each case, a large and distinct population with a primarily military function received guarantees of legal, economic, and political privilege in exchange for an obligation to provide service to their rulers. Entry into these groups and exit from them were limited; a nonmember could not simply choose to join, nor could a member freely depart. Members of these groups played a leading role in each state's bureaucracy; indeed, the Qing was the only case in which they did not have nearly exclusive control of political institutions.

These core elements of service elite institutions were accompanied by certain common patterns that characterized most of or all the groups in question. Service elites were generally inclusive institutions, rather than the exclusive domain of a dominant cultural or ethnic group. Members of service elites were conceptualized as metaphorical slaves of their ruler, or at least as members of his household. Service elite populations were much more urbanized than the rest of the societies that surrounded them. Official conceptions of service elites were highly focused on maintaining certain ideals of masculinity, and yet women were part of these groups alongside their husbands, brothers, fathers, and sons, and they sometimes provided certain forms of service to their dynastic rulers. Service elites frequently had reputations for idleness as a result of the economic privileges that usually freed them from the kinds of work done by the bulk of early modern Eurasians. Despite their economic privileges, they also often had reputations for indebtedness, although their access to credit is perhaps better understood as a product of privilege, enabled by the promise of future income that was guaranteed by their special relationship to the state. And service elites had distinctive cultures, tied to their social status rather than their ethnic origins, that marked them as different from the broader population.

Comparing the three service elites described in this chapter to each other and to the Qing banners provides a sense of the range of circumstances in which service elites could exist and the range of techniques that could be used to link them to their rulers. Each service elite system had certain key differences from the others. Unlike their Ottoman, Russian, and Qing counterparts, the rulers of Tokugawa Japan were not particularly concerned with the management of ethnic diversity. And the early modern Japanese state was not a unitary one; rather, it had two layers of hereditary administration: the shogunate in Edo and the daimyo (Ja. 大名 [*daimyō*]), who ruled subordinate domains across the archipelago. The Ottoman Empire did not have a status system analogous to those of Russia, Japan, and the Qing, and the best-known members of its service elite, the janissaries, were not supposed to inherit their posts but rather to be selected as slaves from among the empire's Christian subjects. Russian service elites were unique in not primarily relying on state stipends for their economic privilege, which was instead maintained through their right to own serfs. But despite these major differences in organization, elite groups in each of these states can be productively understood as service elites.

The Russian Service Nobility

The service elite of imperial Russia consisted of the *dvorianstvo*, the service nobility. Like the Qing banners, they were a hereditary status group, constituting one of the major categories of the Russian *soslovie* system. However, from the early eighteenth century on, their rolls were open to members of other status groups who managed to acquire sufficient rank in the officer corps or civil service. Like other service elites, Russian service nobles worked as both soldiers and administrators, but unlike their counterparts elsewhere, who filled all ranks of their respective militaries, they were far more likely to be officers than ordinary soldiers, most of whom were recruited from among the peasantry. Beginning with Peter the Great's creation of the Table of Ranks in 1722, *dvorianstvo* service became highly bureaucratized, similar to the banners, as both systems employed a highly systematized set of ranks within which members could be promoted and demoted. Unlike other service elites, the principal reward of *dvorianstvo* membership was not a guarantee of income from the state (although all those who served received one), but rather the right of serf ownership. Members of the Russian nobility, or at least its more well-to-do segments, were thus less reliant on the state for their day-to-day economic well-being than were Qing banner people, though as with all service elites, their long-term position depended on the maintenance of the existing political system, which kept serfs bound to their estates.

Russian inclusion of non-Russians in the imperial service elite bore many similarities to the Qing approach. Indeed, the Russian state practiced elite inclusion to an even greater extent than did the Qing. The nobility or other wealthy or landed elites of conquered territories were frequently granted entry into the Russian noble class, such that the imperial elite included Tatars, Baltic Germans, Finns, Poles, and others alongside Russians.[1] For instance, during the sixteenth century, numerous Muslim Nogai Tatar aristocrats were brought into imperial service and some were granted large estates.[2] By the early eighteenth century, many of their descendants had become Russified, and they included a substantial portion of the most powerful members of the imperial nobility.[3] In the Baltic provinces of Estonia and Livonia after the 1710 Russian conquest, the local German elite had their privileges not only preserved, but extended, and this population both helped rule this newly acquired territory and made substantial contributions to the empire's central administration.[4] The annexation manifesto issued by Catherine the Great on the occasion of the conquest of Crimea in the late eighteenth century explicitly promised the Crimean Tatar *murza* elite the "rights and privileges enjoyed by a Russian of [their] status" in exchange for their loyalty.[5]

Perhaps the most notable example of elite incorporation in the Russian empire was that of the Polish nobility after the partition of Poland, accomplished in three stages between 1772 and 1795. In some ways, bringing Polish nobles into the imperial service nobility was easy, as the social function of the Polish *szlachta* bore a great degree of resemblance to that of the Russian *dvorianstvo*. Polish nobles took on most of the administrative posts in Russian-controlled Poland, and their right to own land and serfs, the same privilege extended to the Russian nobility, was maintained. But the Polish *szlachta* far outnumbered the Russian *dvorianstvo*, and a much larger proportion of the Polish group were entirely landless and owned no serfs. Hoping to avoid the empire's service nobility becoming dominated by impoverished Poles, the Russian state required Polish nobles to provide proof of their status, resulting in a large reduction in the postpartition size of the Polish nobility. Even so, as of 1850, Poles made up 55 percent of the Russian hereditary nobility.[6] In general, in the Russian empire, the inclusion of conquered elites in the ranks of the nobility was seen as a way to incorporate new territory and gain those elites' loyalty to the tsar. The case of Poland shows that the Romanov dynasty was flexible, at least to a substantial degree, about accepting preexisting definitions of non-Russian elites to minimize social disruption and resistance to imperial expansion. This policy went far beyond that of the Qing state, which permitted many non-Manchu elites to remain in place without incorporation into the banners, using banner membership only selectively to deal with specific problems. But in both cases, service elites became a tool to manage new territories and peoples and to handle problems arising from ethnic and religious difference.

As with its use of grants of service elite status to manage newly incorporated territories and elites, Russia applied a policy of promoting men who served the state into the service elite more widely and consistently than did the Qing. Following Peter the Great's creation of the Table of Ranks in 1722, those commoners who reached rank 14, the lowest in the officer corps, as well as those who reached rank 8 in the civil service, received hereditary noble rank, thus becoming full members of the service elite. Those members of the bureaucracy who did not reach a high enough rank to enter the hereditary nobility gained nonhereditary noble status and so they received the honor due to members of the service elite even if they did not enter the actual status group. As Lindsey Hughes has noted, the development of the Table of Ranks and the right of promotion into the nobility existed not for the benefit of individual subjects, but for that of the state. The goal was to ensure that the hereditary elite would consist of people who provided useful service to the dynasty. The Table of Ranks was an inducement to serve and serve well, not an attempt to create social mobility for ordinary Russians. And it was one that worked on those who already held noble status, who, although they could not lose that status, could see their relative position in society fall if they did not continue to reach the upper ranks of state service.[7] This principle, that the ruling dynasty conceived of its service elite institutions as a vehicle for securing valuable contributions from the upper echelons of society, applied both in the Qing and in Russia.

The service performed by the Russian service elite shared much in common with that performed by Qing bannermen. In both cases, we see the development of specialized administrative responsibilities and the imposition of bureaucratic control over the exercise of state power by elites. Service for Russian nobles was clearly divided into two main categories, military and administrative, reflected in two separate tracks within the Table of Ranks. As with the Eight Banners, the origins of the *dvorianstvo* were military, deriving principally from the cavalry of the sixteenth- and seventeenth-century Muscovite state.[8] Unlike the banners, however, Russian nobles did not dominate the ranks of ordinary soldiers, who were usually commoner recruits. Instead, although some nobles served in the ranks alongside commoners, members of the Russian service elite monopolized only positions in the officer corps.[9]

The rationalization of noble service mirrored that of the banners. As previously noted, the seminal event in the bureaucratization of the Russian nobility was the creation of the Table of Ranks. Its introduction meant that nobles in imperial service were treated as members of a ranked bureaucracy in which one's position, at least theoretically, was to be based on merit, not hereditary right.[10] In addition to the Table of Ranks, Peter created a new bureaucratic structure for the Russian state based on a set of "colleges" (Ru. *kolegii*) with particular domains of responsibility, which was modeled after the Swedish system.[11] These colleges would enable increasing bureaucratic oversight of nobles who performed administrative work, while also permitting the first steps toward specialization among these servitors.

Although officially freed from service obligations in the second half of the eighteenth century, most nobles continued to serve, whether in the army or the bureaucracy.[12] Positions ranging from the highest ranks, like those of generals and government ministers, through midranking men like colonels, governors, and midlevel central bureaucrats, down to relatively low-level posts in battalion staffs or police administration, were filled by members of the service nobility.[13] And the rule that reaching a sufficient rank in the military or civil hierarchy could earn a man entry into the nobility further solidified the link between service and status. But as the Romanov dynasty's ideas about proper forms of administration changed, the forms of service undertaken by the nobility did as well. For instance, the creation of noble assemblies under Catherine the Great introduced a new role for Russian nobles.[14] This work was tied to the idea, as expressed in a law issued by Catherine's government in 1790, that the purpose of the nobility lay in "military service, in peacetime in administering civil justice, for which they should from youth prepare themselves in such and other knowledge."[15]

After gradual growth in the eighteenth century, including the creation of a new provincial administrative structure during the reign of Catherine the Great, the size of the Russian bureaucracy exploded in the nineteenth century, with the number of ranked posts in the administration growing from 16,000 in 1796 to 75,201 in 1850. Noblemen with poor backgrounds filled many of these posts, and the competition for promotion encouraged such men to seek higher levels of formal education and to develop specialized expertise. By the 1840s, crucial government departments like the Ministry of Internal Affairs relied on a cadre of highly educated nobles from families of relatively little means, with specialized ability in relevant fields like statistics.[16] Thus, like the Qing, the early modern Russian empire had developed many of the features associated with modern states, including specialized officials in a ranked bureaucracy. And, like the Qing, but unlike most modern states, it did so by relying on meritocratic recruitment within a service elite whose position was based on hereditary legal status.

Although the types of state service performed by the two groups were similar, there was far less consistency in attempts to regulate the lives and comportment of Russian nobles than there was for Qing bannermen. Perhaps the clearest example of dynastic interest in creating a distinct elite culture and set of norms came during the reign of Peter the Great. Peter demanded that young members of the nobility receive formal education, although he focused his attention on those from relatively wealthy backgrounds rather than the service elite as a whole.[17] As with the Qing rulers, Peter's requirements for his service elite were tied to his vision of ideal masculinity, which for him was based around education and literacy, European forms of sociability and attire, and the idea that public service was fundamental to the role of elite men.[18]

The specific economic privileges of the Russian service nobility took a quite different form from those of Qing banner people and other service elites. Although actively serving nobles were paid salaries, there was no sense in which the state, at any level, was directly responsible for the maintenance of all the members of the *dvorianstvo soslovie*. But despite this reduced reliance on salaries, the Russian service nobility possessed an institutionalized economic privilege that was ideologically linked to the service they provided. Most important, in response to the petitions of members of the service nobility, the Ulozhenie, a new legal code instituted in 1649, provided that serfs would be firmly bound to the land under the ownership of nobles.[19] This right, as initially envisioned, was itself tied to service; in the seventeenth century, the ownership of fifteen peasant households was considered necessary to support a cavalryman.[20] Serfs provided their owners with both cash rent and labor service, ensuring a stable source of income for the large majority of nobles who owned serfs.[21] In addition to having the right to own serfs, the Russian service nobility benefited from an exemption from taxation.[22] Even for the Russian service nobility, however, income received directly from the state remained important, and often crucial, especially for the approximately three-quarters of noblemen who owned fewer than 100 serfs and thus received only modest income from their estates. These nobles, like Qing bannermen, relied on military or bureaucratic service and the salary that accompanied it.[23] Income from military service could provide a much better living to a poor man of *dvorianstvo* status than to one of any other *soslovie*. In this way, the Russian service elite's monopoly on posts in the Russian officer corps can be seen as a form of institutionalized privilege, not just a form of service.

The discourse of service in imperial Russia also echoes that of the Qing. In Russia, as in the Qing, the service nobility was mostly not made up of people who had been enslaved or were descended from slaves. And yet, during the early development of the Russian service elite, some of the same sort of "slave-master" language was used to describe the relationship between noble and tsar as was used for that of bannerman to emperor. During the sixteenth and seventeenth centuries in particular, Russian nobles referred to themselves as "your slave" (Ru. *kholop tvoi*) when addressing the Muscovite ruler. This usage, Juraj Križanić, a Croat visitor during the seventeenth century noted, did not mean that Russian nobles were in economic bondage. Rather, he observed, "to be the slave of the tsar of one's own people, this is honorable and is actually a kind of freedom." As Marshall Poe argues, contrary to the claims of many Western European observers of the time, as well as those of twentieth-century scholars, the idea of slavery here was "ceremonial," not a reflection of some uniquely despotic Russian form of rule.[24] The putative connection to the tsar embedded in the term "slave" elevated nobles above other subjects who lacked the same connection, while also stressing the obligation of "the tsar to care for his men," tied to the requirement of Muscovite law that masters feed their slaves.[25]

Although the pressure of Western European norms that rejected this language as a form of inappropriate servility would eventually lead to its abandonment in the eighteenth century, nobles continued to speak of themselves as "slaves" of the tsar at least as late as the reign of Peter the Great, though they now were using a different Russian term, *rab*, instead of the old *kholop*.[26] So, although it was less central to the service elite institution in its mature form than in the Qing empire, the idea of nobles as slaves of the tsar played a role in the development of the Russian service elite as well, and it was certainly current at the time that their chief economic privilege—the right of serf ownership—was codified.

Expectations of female service were far less important to the Russian service nobility than to the Qing banners. In the early years of the Russian empire, from 1505 until 1689, wives for the tsar and his son were selected via bride shows in a system that bears clear analogies to *xiunü* selection in the Qing.[27] Potential candidates were identified through regional selections held across the country, in which most participating women came from the middle ranks of the service nobility and members of the leading boyar clans were excluded to limit competition among the highest-ranking nobles at court.[28] Participation in the selection process often required substantial travel and expense, so it was viewed by many members of the service class as an unwanted burden; in 1546, for instance, Ivan IV had to warn fathers "not [to] conceal your unwed daughters" when the servitors of Rostov failed to respond to a royal summons to submit their girls for inspection. In addition to concerns over costs, fathers may have worried about removing their daughters from seclusion in the family compound to be subjected to detailed physical inspection, perhaps presenting a challenge to the family's honor.[29]

Yet, as they relate to the position of the service elite, Russian bride shows differed from Qing *xiunü* selection in at least two key respects. First, Russian bride shows were a rare event; where numerous Qing banner girls were chosen for marriage and palace service every three years, Russian bride shows occurred on at most twenty-five occasions over the span of two centuries, and each instance resulted in the choice of only a single girl for a single marriage.[30] Where *xiunü* selection was a routine part of banner life, Russian bride shows were exceptional occurrences, and thus female service in the Russian service elite was perhaps not a normal expectation but instead a rarely imposed burden. Second, while *xiunü* selection was a feature of the mature form of the Qing service elite, in Russia, bride shows were replaced by participation in the European dynastic marriage market during the reign of Peter I, the same tsar who created the rules and bureaucratic apparatus that defined the Russian service elite in its mature form. As such, female service was clearly far more integral to the Qing service elite system than to the Russian one.

When considered comprehensively, the similarities between the Russian and Qing service elites are striking. Despite having imperial co-ethnics at their core, both groups were firmly multicultural, using their inclusiveness to strengthen the court's control over rapidly expanding empires. Both were highly bureaucratized, in part as the result of a ruler's decision to use a preexisting elite to carry out complex administrative functions in institutions modeled to some degree on those of a neighbor and competitor—Ming China for the Qing, Sweden for Russia. And, of course, the privileged position that each group held was tied to its duty to serve the ruling dynasty. Although the next two cases, Edo Japan and the Ottoman Empire, will depart in certain ways from the Russian and Qing examples, in so doing they will enable us to see how the service elite model could work in a wider range of institutional contexts.

The Japanese Samurai

Like the Qing banners, the samurai formed a hereditary group that was nearly impossible to enter for those not born into it. As with all service elites, they originated as warriors, but male samurai also dominated the politics and administration of early modern Japan; indeed, they did so to a much greater extent than did Qing bannermen, who shared power with officials from commoner backgrounds. Unlike members of other service elites, the actual military function of samurai was greatly attenuated during the Edo period (1603–1868), as large-scale warfare became quite rare on the archipelago. Yet samurai remained organized along military lines. The service elite of Japan also differed from its contemporaries in that samurai were not all directly subordinated to a single ruler. Although all domain lords owed allegiance to the shogun, who controlled a very large band of retainers himself, the relationship between the lord and his service elite happened at the level of the domain (Ja. 藩 [han]), not that of the shogunate as a whole. However, despite some differences in the management of samurai across domains, the system was consistent enough that it can be treated as a single model.

Because the Tokugawa state did not incorporate large new populations or territories after the consolidation of its rule over the archipelago, the inclusive functions of service elite status in the Qing and Russian empires were not particularly relevant to Japan. The elites of the few non-Japanese populations that came under Japanese control, most notably the Ainu of Hokkaido and the people of the Ryukyu Islands, were not integrated into the Japan-wide samurai elite.[31] That said, at the founding of his new shogunate, Tokugawa Ieyasu permitted the continuation of nearly all the daimyo houses who opposed him, thus confirming the samurai status of the retainers of those lords. This decision had analogous motives to those of the Qing in permitting soldiers of the Three Feudatories to become bannermen, or to those of the Romanovs in granting noble status to the Crimean Tatar elite. Each case represented an attempt to use privileged status to maintain the loyalty, or at least the quiescence, of an elite who otherwise might exert a destabilizing influence on the broader polity. The fact that this population shared a cultural identity with the ruler in the case of Japan, but not in the case of Russia or the Qing, does not change the structural role played by their incorporation into the service elite.

The early modern Japanese state did not generally create new samurai after the consolidation of the Tokugawa regime. Yet many of the attributes and privileges of samurai status became available, on a temporary basis, to commoners who served in certain government posts, reflecting a similar principle to the Russian rule that men promoted to a sufficiently high rank in state service would receive noble rank. In Edo Japan, a commoner serving in the administration of a magistrate or daimyo was entitled to wear two swords and use a family name in public documents, privileges otherwise reserved to the warrior status group.[32] Although such commoners generally held posts that exclusively employed commoners, like that of magistrate's assistant (Ja. 手代 [tedai]), they could be promoted to warrior-associated posts like that of magistrate's associate (Ja. 手付 [tetsuki]), which constituted a sort of entry into the ranks of shogunal vassals.[33] It is true that such men did not truly enter samurai status because their positions were not heritable, and their very existence caused concern among many government officials.[34] But the idea that samurai should monopolize governance was also quite strong, so magistrate's assistants and even village headmen took on some of the trappings of that status, with the full support of the state, to maintain the link between service and status. And many of the commoners who took on such work conceived of themselves as samurai-like and successfully claimed some of the honor of that status, even occasionally representing themselves as samurai in their own writings.[35]

In Japan, as in the Qing, the standard understanding of the role of the service elite held that their duty, or even more literally, their "main task" (Ja. 本務 [honmu]) was public service (Ja. 公役 [kōeki]).[36] The supposed devotion of the warrior stratum to their service became the ideological justification for their privilege.[37] The Tokugawa samurai had originated as a military class, but the shogunate's attempts to "eliminate the endemic warfare among landed warriors" that characterized earlier periods in Japan's history led to their administrative function as bureaucrats becoming their predominant role in practice.[38] Samurai served as officials both in the *bakufu* government in Edo and in domainal capitals, as well as in regional postings. Indeed, their responsibility for administration exceeded that of Qing banner people, as they had exclusive access to bureaucratic posts, unlike Qing bannermen who were in competition with graduates of the civil service examination system, who largely came from wealthy and landed Han commoner families.[39] Within the shogunal administration, the ruler's own vassals filled the entirety of the 17,000 or so available posts, with all but a handful of the uppermost positions going to men without their own large domains; that is, to "liege vassals" with titles like "bannerman" (Ja. 旗本 [*hatamoto*]) or "houseman" (Ja. 御家人 [*gokenin*]) rather than daimyo.[40]

Yet even as the Pax Tokugawa took away the opportunity for samurai to fight in actual battles, their martial origins remained central to their early modern service roles.[41] The regular *sankin kōtai* (参勤交代) processions of daimyo to Edo functioned as military exercises, involving the organized movement of troops and weaponry over large distances, serving simultaneously as a display of power and as a fulfillment of the service requirements both of daimyo to the shogun and of samurai retainers to their daimyo lords.[42] The obligation to follow one's lord to the capital as part of this system of "alternate attendance," imposed by rotation on the members of a given retainer band, constituted one of the most important duties of samurai.[43] The work that these men did upon arrival in Edo was less martial and often was quite similar to their work back in the domain, including "secretarial and budgetary tasks, personnel management, oversight of shipping," and the like, with the duty most akin to military service being guard work.[44] Related to the guard work was fire prevention, also a key warrior duty, whether in Edo or in castle towns, with firefighting teams organized to prevent disaster in the largely wooden cities.[45]

The bureaucratization of samurai service was far less complete than that of the Qing banners. The most notable difference was the continued role of the daimyo as hereditary rulers of domains. This feudal system was only partly tempered by the development of an impersonal relationship between most domain lords and the shogun and an increase in the authority of the central *bakufu* government over domains, including the only occasionally exercised right to strip daimyo of their power.[46] In addition, low-level vassals of the shogun often occupied hereditary posts with little chance of promotion. The upper ranks of the liege vassals, in contrast, had some room for mobility, though more in the early years of Tokugawa rule than under the mature system.[47] Political power within domains was often similar, with lower-ranking vassals sometimes shut out of high-ranking administrative posts.

But these distinctions among samurai of different ranks did not prevent early modern Japan from developing a substantial role for meritocracy in the selection of officials from among the samurai population. Divisions between lower- and upper-ranking samurai were far less absolute than those between samurai and other status groups. Membership in the service elite, even at a low level, meant that the state, either at the level of the *bakufu* or the domain, could use a warrior in a post where it thought him likely to be of use. In eighteenth-century Yonezawa domain, for instance, a foot soldier named Mori Heiemon 森平右衛門, with a stipend of only six *koku* (the equivalent of thirty bushels of rice per year), rose to the rank of lead secretary (Ja. 小姓頭 [*koshō gashira*]), putting him in control of the domain's inner court.[48] Nyūi Mitsugi 乳井貢 of Hirosaki domain was the son of a copy clerk with a 50-*koku* stipend, but by 1757, he had reached the rank of domain elder (Ja. 家老 [*karō*]) and led a series of major reforms.[49] As discussed in chapter 1, Katsu Kaishū, the son of an unemployed shogunal retainer, rose to serve as the shogunate's chief negotiator during the fall of the *bakufu* in the Meiji Restoration of 1868. Daimyo also could demote misbehaving warriors, removing them from particular duties and reducing their incomes, a further form of centralized control.[50] And, at least in some domains, promotion opportunities for low-ranking samurai were regularized, which helped to incentivize diligence in service.[51] As these examples suggest, even in Edo Japan, where the inheritance of office remained quite important, the service elite system permitted a greater degree of meritocracy than did purely feudal institutions.

In addition to serving their rulers in military and governmental work, the samurai of early modern Japan, like Qing bannermen, were expected to adopt and maintain certain standards of behavior that helped define them as a group. Warriors were required to maintain particular standards of martial appearance and avoid too great an involvement with commerce.[52] They frequently faced lectures from their ruler about the need to maintain frugality and avoid extravagance, themes that were also common in Qing discourse on the "banner way," as discussed in chapter 3.[53] Samurai were expected to control the behavior of their entire household to ensure that it comported with proper standards of propriety, and they were subject to punishment should a scandal come to light.[54] It was this expectation that led, for instance, to the father of the ne'er-do-well samurai Katsu Kokichi imprisoning him in a cage for three years after he ran away from home.[55] As with other service elites, martial masculinity was central to official Tokugawa conceptions of the samurai. Gendered expectations of samurai were tied particularly to ideas about honor that treated the defense of honor as in part a proof of manhood.[56] For instance, ideas about honor specific to the samurai were linked to the right of warriors to murder a wife who committed adultery, as well as her lover.[57]

The economic privileges of the samurai of Edo Japan bore many similarities to those of Qing banner people. The stipends paid to samurai by daimyo constituted the largest portion of government expenditures.[58] In general, samurai retainers in the domains were remunerated according to one of two schemes. Those with landed fiefs (Ja. 地方知行 [*jikata chigyō*]) had direct control over a particular piece of land, receiving tax payments from a particular set of villagers. Those with stipended fiefs (Ja. 蔵米知行 [*kuramai chigyō*]) or salaries (Ja. 俸禄 [*hōroku*]) were paid directly out of the domain treasury in either money or grain. Most domains relied on stipends for their retainers, although landed fiefs were important in some of Japan's largest domains. In practice, though, even many landed fiefholders actually lived in the castle town and played little, if any, role in administration in their nominal fief.[59] Thus, regardless of their official source of income, domainal samurai were usually paid out of the state treasury.

Much the same was true of most of the shogun's own vassals, apart from the daimyo themselves. Of 22,500 vassals of the shogun, 20,000 were supported directly by *bakufu* revenues. Even most of those with their own income from fiefs lived in Edo, with the fiefs themselves managed by a fief intendant (Ja. 代官 [*daikan*]), who collected taxes according to procedures set by the shogun's government. From the perspective of the families that owned them, these fiefs were a source of income little different from the stipends paid to non-fiefholding shogunal vassals.[60] In the end, for nearly all direct retainers of the Tokugawa house, their incomes consisted of the bales of rice, or the cash equivalent thereof, that they received from *bakufu* granaries in Asakusa three times per year.[61] Unlike the Qing system, samurai in both Edo and the domains inherited the right to a particular level of income, which could be supplemented by a salary associated with an actual post. But both systems shared the idea that the service elite would be supported out of the public purse. And like Qing bannermen, most samurai received residences from the state in addition to their cash or grain incomes, meaning that, in theory, the state provided for all their basic needs.[62]

Although Tokugawa Japan lacked a discourse of slavery like those of seventeenth-century Russia or the Qing to describe the relationship between ruler and service elite, there was another potentially analogous discourse of the relationship between daimyo and samurai retainer. Mizubayashi Takeshi points out that the exchange of service and income between daimyo and retainer was not like an economic exchange in a marketplace, but rather like the exchange between master and servant (or slave) in a household. That is, samurai retainers were subordinate to their lords as if they were members of his household.[63] This situation was the result of an early-Tokugawa period move to strip most warrior households of their independent ability to conduct military action and govern territory. Their privilege no longer derived from their exercise of power on their own behalf but came from their hereditary place within the household of their lord.[64] And, on a longer time scale, the warriors who fought for a lord had been understood as members of his household (Ja. 家 [*ie*]) since the Kamakura period (1185–1333), bound by ties "of both actual as well as fictive kinship."[65] So even in Japan, where an explicit discourse of master-slave relations was lacking, the idea that elites were subordinate members of their masters' households defined the scope of both their privilege and service.

In early modern Japan, as in the Qing and Russia, some women of service elite status also faced the duty of service. In general, the clearest burden fell on women of high rank within the samurai status group, in particular the wives of daimyo. As part of the Tokugawa system of alternate attendance, in which daimyo spent every other year in Edo, their wives served as permanent hostages, guaranteeing their husbands' good behavior during years spent in their own domains. During the early seventeenth century, this requirement extended beyond the wives of daimyo to include wives of the highest-ranking retainers.[66] The extremely limited scope of this regulation, which did not apply to wives of men of more ordinary warrior status, means that, as with Russia, female service to the ruler was much less important to the Japanese service elite than to the Qing system. As in the Qing, many women from warrior families served in the women's quarters of the shogun's castle, but in the Tokugawa case, there was no requirement for women of warrior status to submit to selection for service and the female workforce of the Great Interior (Ja. 大奥 [*Ōoku*]) came from a wide variety of status backgrounds, including townspeople and peasants.[67]

The importance of women to the Japanese service elite rested less in their service to their lord and more in the ways in which their marriages helped define the boundaries of the status group, just as they did in the Qing. The 1615 *Laws for the Military Houses* (Ja. 武家諸法度 [*Buke shohatto*]) forbade daimyo and other members of the upper elite from privately contracting marriages, a policy meant to prevent the use of marriage to form political factions. Rules for marriage extended to the entire samurai class and beyond and were implemented by both the shogunate and individual domains. Interstatus marriage was heavily discouraged, in part to prevent strategic marriages across lines of status and wealth. As in the Qing, not only were marriages between commoners and service elites frowned upon, and to some degree legally prohibited, but marriages that cut across divisions within the service elite group also faced impediments.[68] In Japan, these divides were not ethnic, but instead were tied to the different hierarchical gradations of warrior status. Unlike in the Qing, where there is no evidence of official disapproval of interethnic marriage within the banners, the barriers to which appear to have been generated by the choices of banner people themselves, the Tokugawa authorities did attempt to encourage marriages between people of the same social level, counteracting efforts by warrior families to use marriage as a vehicle for improving their status.[69]

In sum, despite early modern Japan's political division into hundreds of domains with substantial autonomy, its samurai did function as a service elite. This is perhaps clearest for the direct retainers of the shogun—his bannermen and housemen whose service enabled the maintenance of shogunal authority across all parts of the archipelago. But even the retainers of daimyo functioned as service elites, as domains replicated the form of the shogun's retainer band in miniature. Most samurai neither inherited particular offices nor exercised genuine authority over hereditary fiefdoms. Their salaries came from their lords' treasuries, and their role in politics came through bureaucratic service in a lord's government. So while the relationship between shogun and daimyo may have been a feudal one, the overwhelming majority of samurai had a relationship to a ruler based in the same kinds of institutional forms that characterized the relationship of bannerman to emperor in the Qing or service noble to tsar in imperial Russia. They were hereditary members of a service elite group. The similarities between the status systems in these three states, as described in chapter 1, suggests that perhaps a social order based on hereditary status was essential for service elites to form. But the case of the Ottoman Empire will test that assumption.

The Ottoman *Askeri*

The final service elite examined here is that of the Ottoman Empire, which consisted of multiple distinct elements that together formed the governing class, the *askeri*. The best known of these, and perhaps the group most often compared to the Qing banners in earlier scholarship, was the janissary infantry corps (Tu. *yeniçeri*) who, along with other less famous imperial military units, consisted of men considered slaves of the sultan (Tu. *kapıkulu*).

These men, at least ideally, were not members of hereditary service elite families, unlike their Qing, Russian, or Japanese counterparts. Rather, they were recruited from among Christian families, mostly in the southeastern European territories of the empire, during regular slave levies, a system known as *devşirme*. This meant that unlike with other service elites, which included the entire families of men who served, women had no place in a core element of the Ottoman service elite system.

The other major portion of the Ottoman service elite consisted of cavalrymen who were granted estates known as *timar*. This group was much more substantially hereditary than the janissaries, although its members were frequently rotated among different estates, and even removed from them entirely during periods of active military service. There was some movement between the janissaries and the *timar*-holders, as the former could receive their own *timar* estates as a reward for service. Top administrators came more frequently from among the *kapıkulu* than from the *timar*-holders, but managing a *timar* was itself a type of administrative service as well, meaning that both sections of the Ottoman service elite were, like other service elites, of great importance to Ottoman administration in addition to serving as the backbone of the empire's military. The lesser role of heredity in defining membership in the Ottoman service elite means that I do not treat it as a status group, unlike the banners, samurai, and service nobility. Thus, the Ottoman case suggests that service elites could develop even outside status-based societies.

The recruitment of slave soldiers as children meant that entry into the Ottoman service elite looked quite different from its early modern Eurasian counterparts. In particular, the Ottoman insistence on enslaving only Christian children produced an elite that was not dominated by Turks, but this approach was not inclusive in the same sense as the willingness of the Russian court to enlist Tatars, Poles, and Germans in its service nobility or the enlistment of Mongols and Han in the Qing banner system. The Ottoman sultan Süleyman I emphasized the importance of caution in carrying out the *devşirme* levies in zones where Christians were mixed with Turks, declaring that anyone who did bring Turks among his "pure blooded slaves" would "be damned by the Prophet 120 thousand times."[70] But this focus on the inclusion of Greeks, Slavs, and the like in his military and bureaucratic elite was probably not principally intended as a way to ensure the loyalty of the empire's non-Turkish population. Two other principles lay at the heart of the Ottoman approach. First, enslaving

Muslims was forbidden under Islamic law. Second, one of the central goals of the Ottoman court was to create an elite with few loyalties outside the palace.[71] Indeed, because *devşirme* recruits were required to convert to Islam, the design of the recruitment process was aimed more at separating elite soldiers from their original communities than at using their links to those communities to maintain control.

That said, some Ottoman bureaucrats saw the diversity of the elite selected via *devşirme* as being important to their function, with the sixteenth-century bureaucrat and intellectual Mustafa Âli arguing that ethnic heterogeneity brought with it new and valuable skills and traits, even if it created the possibility for ethnic conflict.[72] Moreover, their very alienness, Ottoman rulers believed, might prevent Christian *devşirme* recruits from abusing their position and increase their loyalty to the system.[73] And while some Balkan Christians resisted the *devşirme* levies, many others bribed officers to enlist their children, who often remained in contact with their families, creating important ties between the Ottoman dynasty and some of the non-Muslim regions of the empire. So, one consequence of the *devşirme* system was that, between the mid-1400s and the mid-1600s, forty-two out of forty-seven of the empire's grand viziers, the highest-ranking officials in the state, were non-Turkish. Karen Barkey argues that the power held by men of this sort and others of similar background but lower rank, as well as their connections to important non-Turkish family members, contributed "to the control that the Ottoman center garnered from center-periphery relations."[74]

Moreover, non-Turks were included even within the predominantly Turkish portion of the Ottoman ruling class, the *timar*-holding cavalrymen who received revenue from fiefs granted to them as reward for their service.[75] Until about 1520, Christians constituted more than 10 percent of all *timar*-holders in some provinces, and they continued to appear in small numbers into the seventeenth century.[76] This intentional inclusivity helped to encourage loyalty among a diverse group of dynastic followers, analogous to the early period of Qing state-formation, in which Mongols and Han were brought into the banner system alongside Manchus. Neither the early Ottoman nor the early Qing state could have been as successful had it relied only on co-ethnics (or even co-religionists, in the Ottoman case), and the development of their service elites reflected that reality.

Moving beyond the question of ethnic and religious inclusiveness, the Ottoman Empire, like imperial Russia, used grants of service elite membership to certain commoners who served the dynasty as a means of promoting service. The *devşirme* system itself was, of course, a means of granting entry to the service elite to people who otherwise would have been taxpaying subjects. Indeed, in a certain sense, the janissaries and the other *kapıkulu* troops, as well as administrators trained at the Palace School (Tu. *Enderun mektebi*), represent a fuller commitment to the principle of service than the hereditary, status-based systems of Japan, Russia, and the Qing. But opportunities to enter the service elite were used as an incentive even in the *timar* system, which contained a much greater role for heredity. At times, as many as 61 percent of *timar*-holders were what Linda Darling calls "sons of nobodies"—that is, children of men who were not themselves *timar*-holders, nor otherwise members of the ruling *askeri* stratum. She suggests that "these men were probably sons of lesser military men, scribes, or *reaya*," the Ottoman name for the non-*askeri*, taxpaying lower portion of the social order.[77] The numbers of *timar*-holders without elite backgrounds peaked during times of war, perhaps suggesting that, as with Qing grants of banner status to slaves who served in military campaigns with distinction, service in battle was of particular importance to grants of *timar* estates.[78]

The link between entry into the elite and accomplishment in battle reflects the centrality of military service to the Ottoman service elite. Indeed, the term *askeri*, used to designate the governing elite in contrast to the subject population, means "military."[79] Most of the slave recruits of the *devşirme* system served as *kapıkulu*, the household troops of the sultan, who most famously included the janissary infantry but were also comprised of other units, including some cavalry divisions. *Timar* estate holders, the other main branch of the service elite, were mostly cavalrymen.[80] However, as in the Qing, Japan, and Russia, the empire's administrative personnel also came from among the same group of people, particularly from the minority of *devşirme* recruits trained and educated within the palace itself. Various schools in the palace trained boys in a range of tasks and skills, from those necessary to provide personal service to the court, like music, sewing, and embroidery, to preparation for military and administrative work, including instruction in finance.[81] Some of these boys eventually would go on to become bureaucrats, and a few would reach quite high ranks; men from the palace dominated, among other positions, the ranks of provincial governors and governors-general.[82] Trainee janissaries also played some roles that we have already seen associated with samurai, like work as night watchmen and firemen in the cities where they were based.[83] *Timar*-holders, for their part, handled tax collection and administration in the territories assigned to them, which provided the base of their own support in a form of prebendal governance.[84]

The creation of a centralized Ottoman state based on the appointment of bureaucrats from among the service elite, and in particular that portion of the service elite composed of palace slaves selected via *devşirme* levies, dates to the era of Mehmed the Conqueror, in the second half of the fifteenth century.[85] This more centralized system replaced a reliance on powerful warrior families who had allied with the Osmanlı house in the fourteenth century.[86] Although this transition from feudal-style rule based on personal relationships between powerful families with independent authority to more centralized control exercised through service elites paralleled similar shifts in Russia, the Qing, and Japan, it differed in a crucial way. While in the other cases, the older feudal powerholders often continued to exercise power as bureaucrats in the new system, in the Ottoman case, it was a new group of elites who came to dominate the institutions of state power.

The old warrior families continued to be *askeri*, and thus part of the broader service elite, but they were clearly a separate group from the *devşirme* recruits who became politically dominant. The new service elite bureaucrats were selected and promoted meritocratically, with skills, success in lower posts, and the ability to develop useful professional networks determining how far a man might advance in the Ottoman system.[87] Even the *timar*-holding portion of the service elite was bureaucratized through a system of rotation that prevented *timar* holders from maintaining control of the same piece of land over the long term or from passing their *timar* to their sons. Many (perhaps most) sons of *timar* holders would become *timar* holders themselves, but not on the same estate where their father had held sway.[88] Thus, the Ottoman service elite, like its counterparts, was an institution designed to limit hereditary power in favor of centralized control.

As was the case in the Qing, Japan, and Russia, Ottoman service elites, especially the *kapıkulu*, were expected to adopt and maintain certain standards of behavior that helped define them as a group. The court demanded a thoroughgoing transformation from those drafted via the *devşirme* levies. Most selected boys were sent to live with a Turkish family for five years to learn the language and the practice of Islam. Upon their return to the barracks, they were taught to read and write.[89] The idea was to create an Islamicized and Turkified elite out of boys levied from Christian and non-Turkish populations. As in the Qing banners, where Han bannermen were expected to follow cultural practices marked as distinctively Manchu, ideas about the proper culture for the Ottoman elite diverged from their actual backgrounds, even as their ethnic origins remained important. This divergence was indeed far more extreme in the Ottoman case, where Turks were legally excluded from *kapıkulu* regiments entirely, even as the men in those regiments were expected to adopt elements of Turkish culture. Alongside this cultural transformation came certain standards of masculinity. The Ottoman ideal of the service elite was perhaps even more focused on men than any other because *devşirme* recruits, chosen in levies rather than inheriting their positions, were entirely men. The choice of boys reflected an idealized vision of masculinity, with physical appearance being of crucial importance, alongside good health.[90]

Although Ottoman service elites, like their counterparts in Russia, did not rely exclusively on the state treasury for their well-being, their service to the sultan was associated with substantial economic privilege. Janissaries and other men recruited into the elite via the *devşirme* system received salaries. But by the seventeenth century, average members of this portion of the elite earned wages that were actually lower than those of many common laborers, and, moreover, were stagnant over time, even in the face of inflation and currency debasement.[91] And yet, despite the low official income that was offered to janissaries, there are cases of commoner Muslims playing large bribes, perhaps equivalent to one year's worth of earnings for a skilled urban worker, to gain entry into the janissary corps, either for themselves or their sons.[92]

The desirability of janissary membership stemmed from the fact that entry into the corps provided a variety of other economic opportunities, some officially bestowed by the sultanate and some created by janissaries themselves against its orders. The most notable of their official privileges was an exemption from taxation.[93] Moreover, military officers were frequently able to establish substantial political authority over the marketplaces and guilds of Istanbul, both through their domination of the central administration, particularly during the seventeenth century, and through appointment to posts as guild leaders or as market supervisors and tax collectors.[94] These advantages helped janissaries to gain influence within various craft guilds, even as craftsmen sought to bribe their way into the janissary corps to avoid taxation.[95] Janissaries were also frequently able to avoid other kinds of regulations on guild members and to break price ceilings. When they faced prosecution, they were subject to trial by other members of the janissary system, enabling them to often escape punishment.[96] In addition, janissary regiments controlled pious endowments (Tu. *waqf*) that were used as investment vehicles for the benefit of their members.[97] Thus, even as the dynasty repeatedly prohibited janissaries from engaging in commerce or civilian trades, the number of janissaries pursuing these outside occupations exploded in the late sixteenth and early seventeenth centuries.[98] Although official salaries alone may have been enough to provide for the janissaries of the fifteenth and sixteenth centuries, it was the ancillary privileges of service elite membership that became most economically important in the latter half of the Ottoman period.

For *timar*-holders, the economic privileges of service elite membership were more straightforward, as they received revenue directly from the fiefs they held. Thus, superficially, their position was like that of landed fiefholders in Japan. But unlike most fiefholders in Japan, *timar*-holders actually held responsibility for collecting the taxes on their land; their income did not pass through the hands of other officials or the state treasury. In this sense, *timar* privilege was far less institutionalized and far more personal than samurai, banner, or janissary privilege. And yet the same system of rotation that prevented *timar*-holders from maintaining political authority over a single piece of territory over the long term also saw to it that their incomes were not tied to a single territory, either over the course of their lifetimes or across generations. *Timar*-holders possessed the right to the income of a *timar* and could usually pass that right to their sons, but not the right to the income from any particular *timar*. And so, just as their service as tax-collecting administrators was partly bureaucratized, so was their privilege defined institutionally and systematically. Moreover, rotation enabled cavalrymen to receive a better *timar* through service, while during the early seventeenth century, the state became more willing to assign a *timar* to men from other military groups. Thus, the dynasty incentivized military service, helping "create a loyal force in the provinces."[99] The exchange of loyalty for privilege, conducted in bureaucratic-institutional fashion rather than in personal and specific terms, functioned for the *timar*-holding Ottoman cavalry as it did for other service elites.

The link between a discourse of slavery and elite privilege was more apparent in the Ottoman case than in any other. The *devşirme* system developed out of Islamic precedents that dated as far back as the Seljuks and Abbasids, under which non-Muslims were conscripted into slavery in the sultan's household and made to serve as soldiers or administrators.[100] Indeed, the generic term used for men who entered service in this way was *kul*, meaning "slave," the same term applied to personal household slaves purchased on the slave market, who sometimes were called *müştera kul*, meaning "purchased slave," to distinguish them from the sultan's own servitors.[101] And there was a sense, at least among some Ottoman intellectuals, that it was training in the palace that defined who was fit to govern the empire. This was, according to the sixteenth-century Ottoman writer and bureaucrat Mustafa Âli, because household service created a sort of familial bond that inspired loyalty.[102]

Of course, the same principle applied in the opposite direction; the sultan, like the Qing emperor, had a duty to support his "household" and maintain the privileged position of its members, a duty to which janissaries themselves appealed in some of the numerous uprisings that they launched in response to the debasement of coinage or proposals to create new commoner military units to replace them. So when insurrectionary janissaries put Sultan Osman II to death in 1622, they did so because they saw his plan to enlist Anatolian musketmen and Syrian and Egyptian cavalry as a threat to the privileges to which they were entitled.[103] Although the killing of the sultan might appear to run against the idea that service elites were defined by their loyalty to the ruler, it is essential to recognize that in 1622, as in all janissary uprisings, though an individual sultan might be targeted, the rule of the House of Osman was not. The implicit contract between service elite and lord was with the dynastic house in perpetuity, not with a single man. From the janissaries' perspective, a sultan who violated his responsibilities to them could be overthrown, but they still served only one family.

Because the classic Ottoman service elite, consisting of men initially recruited as slaves via *devşirme* levies, was not based on hereditary principles, it is hard to define a group of women with comparable social standing to the daughters of Qing bannermen, Japanese samurai, or men of the Russian service nobility. However, it is possible to identify a female analog to the Ottoman service elite: women of the imperial harem. Indeed, the word "harem" was applied to two spaces of the Ottoman court, as in addition to the women's quarters, there was the "honored harem" (Tu. *harem-i hümayun*), the exclusively male inner courtyard that contained both the sultan's private quarters and the Palace School, in which many of the boy slaves destined for military and administrative careers were trained.

Like men of the Ottoman service elite, all women of the harem, with the exception of the sultan's blood relatives, were slaves, at least by the early sixteenth century. The shift to giving important political offices to slave recruits rather than the hereditary Turkish elite of *timar*-holding cavalrymen occurred at approximately the same time as the shift to reliance on slave concubines for dynastic reproduction. Women of the harem were not only potential concubines for the sultan, but recipients of training and education that prepared them as possible future brides of their male counterparts, Palace School graduates who had been given important administrative posts. Leslie Peirce argues that this system, like that of recruiting and training male slaves, was designed to inculcate loyalty to the ruling house, and former harem slaves, manumitted upon their marriages, frequently acted as agents or supporters of their former mistress upon joining the households of their husbands.[104] As Peirce makes clear, the role of harem women in connecting power holders to the court was much greater for daughters of the sultan than for former harem slaves, a practice more analogous to the marriage of Qing imperial women to Mongol princes than to the service of bannerwomen. Yet the involvement of some female palace slaves in providing political service to the dynasty suggests that female and male service can be conceptually linked in the Ottoman context.

Although the Ottoman *askeri* were only a partly hereditary group, they still fit into a comparative service elite paradigm. The selection of *kapıkulu* as children meant that clear boundaries existed between service elite and commoner; an ordinary subject of the empire could not enter the service elite as an adult through acquiring wealth or cultural capital—membership was marked by boundaries that could be legally surmounted only at the behest of the ruling house. The structure of the Ottoman elite was tied to a process of bureaucratization and centralization that enabled the ruler to work through his elite rather than needing to call upon the support of a class of autonomous fiefholders. Elite privilege, too, derived from an institutional relationship to the ruler rather than the inheritance of a particular position or territory. And the central position that slavery played in defining the Ottoman elite was, as we have seen in our consideration of other service elites, simply a more extreme form of a principle that existed in all service elite systems.

Comparative Patterns in Service Elites

The accounts of the three elite groups given in this chapter, when considered in comparison with the discussion of the Qing banners in chapters 2 through 5, provide sufficient basis for developing a theoretical conception of the service elite as a social form. Service elite membership was used to manage diversity in expanding states like the Qing, Russian, and Ottoman empires. In all three states, conquered populations of ethnicities other than that of the ruling house were routinely included within service elites. The inclusion of new members in these elites was designed to help win loyalty from elites in newly conquered regions and to ensure that elites relied on the ruling dynasty to maintain their advantageous position. In Japan as well, the centrally endorsed institutionalization of samurai status, even in domains that had previously opposed Tokugawa Ieyasu's rise to power, may have marked an attempt to use service elite membership as a way to integrate potentially troublesome populations.

In all four states, paths to membership in the service elite also help underline the extent to which service was essential to elite status. Although entry into service elites was subject to state control—elite status was legally defined, not the product of possessing sufficient economic or cultural capital—when new entrants were permitted, it was usually as a reward for providing service to the state. Service elites across early modern Eurasia developed in part as mechanisms for turning feudal elites into bureaucrats serving as agents of a centralized monarchical state. Like Qing bannermen, members of the service elites in Japan, Russia, and the Ottoman Empire were not just soldiers, but administrators. Indeed, in some ways, each of these states went further than the Qing state, which unlike its counterparts employed large numbers of men from outside the service elite as officials. This is not to say that any of these systems were perfect exemplars of Weberian rational bureaucracy.[105] But they did find in the service elite institution a common answer to the question of how to increase state capacity and central control without destroying the privileged position of preexisting elites, particularly those who had been allies of ruling dynasties in their rise to power.

One consequence of the role played by service elite in all four states was that their populations became highly urbanized. The largest Qing banner garrisons were located in cities, Beijing chief among them, with banner people occupying their own residential zone, often surrounded by a wall.[106] Perhaps half the Ottoman Janissary population lived in Istanbul, making up about 13 percent of the city's population in the seventeenth century, and Cairo also had a large number, perhaps 12,000 to 16,000, or 6 to 8 percent of the city's total.[107] Japanese samurai were concentrated in castle towns, the seats of daimyo rule, as a result of their lords' efforts to bring them out of the fiefs that they had previously controlled.[108] A massive concentration was found in Edo itself, where they made up half the city's population.[109] The Russian nobility was a bit more dispersed, but 30 percent of its population lived in either Moscow or St. Petersburg at around the turn of the nineteenth century.[110] These concentrations of service elites were tied both to their military duties, which required the defense of major cities and of the ruling family itself, and to their administrative work, for which much of the demand existed in the imperial and shogunal capitals.

Analogous to the bureaucratized service that service elites provided to ruling houses was the institutionalized privilege that they received in exchange. That is, just as mature service elite systems abolished most instances of the inheritance of specific duties in favor of turning service elites into civil servants who might be promoted according to merit, the privileges that service elites received were more uniform and centrally controlled than were those of the feudal elites who preceded them. As in a classic feudal relationship, the relationship of service elite to ruler was defined by a set of mutual obligations based on loyalty. But unlike the feudal model, in which the relationship establishing these obligations was personal, with each vassal having a direct and specific relationship to his overlord, service elites had an impersonal, status-based relationship to their ruler.[111] As seen in Qing efforts to provide for banner people, the support that the ruler owed his service elite was owed to them as a group in exchange for their collective loyalty and service. So, although individual members of service elites, like anyone else, could certainly inherit specific sources of wealth, the privilege that was their birthright was not the particular endowment of a single family; rather, it was tied to a broader institutional environment. These privileges were then legitimized via a common framework: the idea that service elites were members of the households of their rulers, a ritual framing that created a simulated personal relationship between lord and servitor.

All service elites were conceived of as fundamentally masculine, and it was the men of these elites who their rulers took the most interest in controlling and putting to use. But although female service was clearly secondary to male service in all service elites, it did exist in some form. Reproduction was as essential a dynastic function as governance or war, and ruling houses often chose to use the same set of people to supply both sets of needs. Even in these cases, however, reproduction required a much smaller group of servitors than did maintaining an army or a bureaucracy, so women were never as likely to serve as men.

Recognizing the service elite as an institutional form that existed in many societies is important not just for those historians or social scientists interested in comparison. It also necessitates a reassessment of the Qing Eight Banner system.[112] The Qing banners have been understood by many historians as a distinctive product of Manchu rule, with their existence intended to ensure the political dominance of an ethnic minority. It is true, of course, that many specific aspects of banner organization are linked to the social structure of pre-1644 Manchuria, just as many features of the Tokugawa samurai are linked to dynamics in pre-1600 Japan and many aspects of the Russian service nobility have roots in pre-Romanov Muscovy. But the existence of an institution like the banner system did not depend on its members being from a minority ethnocultural group that ruled over a majority. After all, the samurai were as Japanese as the population they governed. Nor did the basis of the banners necessarily lie in an ethnic identity that they shared with the imperial family. After all, the janissaries were not Turks. Rather, the banners, like other service elites, were a sociopolitical formation that enabled the centralization of political authority in the hands of a ruling family by supplying it with military force and administrative capacity. Their loyalty to the court depended not only on shared ethnic origins, which most banner people lacked, but also on institutional guarantees of economic privilege that were supported by a claim to membership in the emperor's metaphorical household. It is this bureaucratization of the exchange of privileged status for service that links the elites of the Qing, Japanese, Russian, and Ottoman states and thus is essential to understanding why they persisted for centuries.

CHAPTER 7

Challenging the Service Elite Model

For the first century of Qing rule, the exchange of service for privilege that underlay banner status was understood to be permanent. Banner status was hereditary, and either leaving or entering the banners was possible only under special circumstances, usually requiring the direct intervention of the emperor himself. Although banner people were treated differently from one another on the basis of their ethnic background, which served to define them as members of a status subcategory within the broader banner status group, there was no sense that the permanence of banner status depended on ethnicity. Indeed, in the Qing, as in Tokugawa Japan and imperial Russia, the heritability of service elite status was essential to its purpose. Members of service elites knew that their privilege and that of their children were guaranteed by the ruling dynasty on account of their special relationship with the ruler. But that privilege would be at risk if the dynasty fell, to be replaced by other rulers with no link to the existing elite, very few members of which possessed the degree of influence necessary to make their personal support essential to a new government. As a result, bannermen, like other hereditary service elite groups, were invested in maintaining the power of the Aisin Gioro dynastic line because it enabled them to pass their elite status to their descendants.

Despite the clear importance of indefinite heritability to the logic of banner status, in 1754, the Qing court departed from its commitment to the permanence of membership in the service elite. In April of that year, the Qianlong emperor issued an edict:

> The Eight Banner slaves (Ch. 八旗奴僕 [baqi nupu]) have received the dynasty's grace for more than one hundred years. In that time their population has grown immensely and it is necessary to find a way to handle it. Therefore, as the result of an edict that I issued, Eight Banner Hanjun in the capital who wish to disperse and become commoners have been permitted to become commoners. At present, action in accordance with this practice has not been extended to the Hanjun of the various provincial garrisons. They should also be handled in accord with this [past edict], making them all able to obtain a livelihood. Send Manchus from the capital to fill the posts they leave behind, and capital Manchus will also be somewhat less obstructed [in finding employment]. Let this [edict] be handed over to governor-general Kargišan 喀爾吉善 to work together with Fuzhou general Sinju 新柱 and have them make the Hanjun people of that place either also follow the precedent of the capital Hanjun and be managed by letting them disperse where they like, or, when posts become available in the garrison general's Green Standard regiments, be transferred to fill those. As for the vacancies that are thus created, immediately send Manchus from the capital to fill them. Thus, obstructions for Manchus in the capital will be removed and the local Hanjun will also obtain freedom in [selecting] their way of life; it will truly benefit them both. Once Kargišan and Sinju have devised a thorough plan [for this], let them jointly memorialize.[1]

As a result of this edict, as well as similar ones issued to garrison generals in Guangzhou, Jingkou, Xi'an, and elsewhere over the subsequent twenty-five years, nearly all the Hanjun bannermen assigned to provincial garrisons, along with their families, were expelled from the banners. Other banner populations were targeted at the same time, particularly those descendants of banner slaves who had obtained ordinary banner status via adoption or manumission. Although the language of the 1754 edict emphasized its continuity with past practices, suggesting that expulsion did not represent a major shift in imperial policy toward the banners, this claim is better understood as a reflection of the moral and legal authority that came from apparent adherence to precedent than as an accurate description of the actual significance of the imperial order.² Moreover, despite the emperor's insistence that the decision was made with the best interests of the Hanjun themselves in mind, the reactions of the expelled Hanjun make it clear that they did not agree.

Past scholarship on the expulsion of the Hanjun has mostly emphasized its continuities with preexisting ethnic discrimination within the banners, portraying the expulsion as a culmination of a long-standing policy of using the banners as a vehicle for maintaining the privileged position of Manchus and their ethnic sovereignty over the empire. This chapter argues for a different interpretation, demonstrating that expulsion tried to overturn some of the core assumptions that defined the banner system. Although, as chapter 8 will discuss, the expulsion policy did not ultimately result in the demise of the Qing service elite, or even the end of its ethnic inclusivity, its attack on the security of banner status and the privileges of the dynasty's most loyal Han servants requires explanation.

Records of the first decisions to expel Hanjun and other large groups from the banners indicate that the Qianlong emperor himself initiated the process. This means that expulsion was not a plan developed by bureaucrats attempting to achieve pragmatic goals, like reducing the cost of providing for the entire banner population, within a previously established framework. Rather, it was an extraordinary imperial intervention to redefine the composition and role of the banners in keeping with an ideological direction that was reflected in other aspects of the Qianlong emperor's rule. Qianlong, perhaps more than any other postconquest Qing emperor, was committed to the idea that different ethnic communities should be ruled separately from one another. Moreover, although all Qing emperors certainly understood themselves and their dynasty to be Manchu, the Qianlong emperor was far more committed to the idea that the Qing right to rule was grounded in its sustained connection to Manchu identity and support for Manchu interests than was, for instance, his father and immediate predecessor, the Yongzheng emperor. So, for Qianlong, the preservation of a loyal and multiethnic service elite, though perhaps still of some importance, was subordinated to his desire to protect Manchu ethnic privilege and maintain the dynasty's special connection to its fellow Manchus. Although even Qianlong never went so far as to attempt to expel the entirety of the Hanjun population from the banners, he was willing to treat them as expendable to a degree that had no precedent among his predecessors and would not be reached again by his successors.

Expulsion was thus a product of the contradiction between two distinct imperatives of Qing policy: the dynasty's need to maintain a special connection with its service elite and its desire to preserve such a connection with its fellow Manchus. The Qing was not the only early modern state in which competing ideological priorities challenged the basis of a service elite system. In Russia, at about the same time as the Qing was pursuing Hanjun expulsion, Peter III and Catherine the Great implemented a policy called the "emancipation of the nobility," in part to incorporate Western European ideas about personal liberty into the administration of the elite, even at the risk of undermining the service elite's raison d'être. In some Japanese domains, samurai were encouraged to farm or engage in crafts production to support their daimyo houses' mercantilist economic strategy. No service elite existed in a vacuum; the other ideological proclivities or strategic goals of their ruler did at times threaten their position. It was possible, as in the case of the janissaries of the early nineteenth-century Ottoman Empire, who were bloodily eliminated by the reformist sultan Mahmud II, for these alternative priorities to lead to the abolition of service elite groups. But in many cases, as with the Qing banners, service elites persisted for as long as the ruling house that they served.

This chapter examines the background to the decision to expel many Hanjun, relating a narrative that begins with the 1742 development of a policy to allow Hanjun to leave the banners voluntarily and ends with the first instance of formal Hanjun expulsion: in 1754 at the Fuzhou garrison. A key moment in this narrative was the 1747 removal of the Household Selected Soldiers from the banners. This move swept aside long-standing assumptions that banner status created a permanent and irrevocable right to the privileges that accompanied it, a precedent that had remained in place even after the 1742 policy shift, which had only allowed Han bannermen to choose to give up their status and did not assert the right to force them out. The chapter concludes by presenting an explanation of the ideology that underlay expulsion, recognizing both that the Qianlong emperor's new approach to the banners took inspiration from ideas about the special importance of Manchus and Inner Asian identity that had deep roots in dynastic history, and that it was a genuine and immense break from past precedent. How banner officials and ordinary Han bannermen reacted to this overturning of the service elite framework and how the older model came to be restored will be addressed in chapter 8, which will also take up the analogous challenges faced by other early modern service elites.

The Logic of Livelihood and Precursors to Expulsion

In the fourth month of 1742, the Qianlong emperor issued an edict permitting many Hanjun to leave the banners and live as civilians if they so desired. Although this edict has often been interpreted as the beginning of expulsion, its actual effects were quite different, and it might better be described as foreshadowing expulsion, as it would eventually become part of the emperor's stated justification for the more forceful policy.[3] The edict likely drew on a memorial by the Huguang governor-general Sun Jiagan from earlier in the year, offering suggestions for how to deal with the "problem of livelihood" (Ch. 生計事 [shengji shi]) in the banners.[4] Sun's memorial, though not itself suggesting that any bannerman should be allowed to give up his banner status, advanced a version of the argument that the emperor would use to justify Hanjun being allowed to depart the banners.

First, Sun pointed to the rapid growth in banner population over the preceding decades, which, perhaps to emphasize that the problems faced by bannermen were the result of the successes of dynastic policy rather than its failures, he attributed to the Pax Manjurica supposedly brought about by Qing rule: "In our dynasty's days of peace, the population of the land has flourished, and the [increase of the] Eight Banner population has been especially vigorous." He then suggested that although imperial support was very generous, bannermen would be more secure in the continuance of their livelihoods if they provided for themselves. Sun noted that in his earlier tenure as Zhili governor-general, he had proposed that bannermen in the capital region go to the countryside and make a living through farming, receiving official approval for his idea. Moreover, he remarked, in a recent edict, the emperor himself had given permission for banner people over the age of eighteen to accompany their relatives who were serving in posts outside the capital, which would have the additional benefit of opening up posts and their accompanying stipends for unemployed bannermen in Beijing.[5] Sun argued that when bannermen serving outside the capital left their posts and were required to return to Beijing, they were soon overrun by shiftless friends and relatives asking for loans and by the attempted extortions of minor banner officials, and between those demands and their own idleness, any wealth that they had managed to accumulate soon ran out. Would it not be better, he suggested, to permit retiring bannermen to buy land outside the capital, which they could use as a basis for both agricultural and commercial activity and thus build a foundation for their family's future prosperity?

At this point, Sun finally introduced a distinction between Manchus and Hanjun in order to argue that only the latter were really capable of benefiting from his plan. "In my opinion," he wrote, "Manchus who live for a long time outside the capital may face difficulties. When it comes to Hanjun, though, they are different from Manchus (Ch. 漢軍則與滿洲不同 [*Hanjun ze yu Manzhou bu tong*]). They were originally Han people (Ch. 伊等原係漢人 [*yideng yuan xi Hanren*]), and farming, craftsmanship, commerce, and business are all things they can learn without difficulty."[6] Sun's logic here was to make ethnicity, not status, the basis of livelihood; people of a particular ethnic background were naturally better able to live in ways traditional to people like them than to live in the ways of people of a different ethnicity.[7] Although Hanjun could live like Chinese, Manchus would struggle with such a lifestyle.

This was a new sort of argument for Sun, as his past attempts to find alternative means of livelihood for banner people had not made ethnic distinctions. In fact, the proposal that he had made just two years earlier, for banner people to be given reclaimed banner land if they farmed it themselves, to which he referred in this memorial, had been directed at all banner people, including Manchus as well as Hanjun.[8] Yet even in his new memorial, which distinguished between Manchus and Hanjun on ethnic lines, he did not suggest that Hanjun who found alternative means of supporting themselves should leave the banners. Rather, local officials would be required to maintain special registers of Hanjun living in their jurisdiction, which they would report to both the Board of War and the Board of Revenue, which managed household registration, as part of the regular banner census, enabling bannermen to be called to military service if needed. This system would be, he suggested, "completely consistent with the ancient system of soldiers living as farmers [during times of peace] (Ch. 寓兵於農 [*yu bing yu nong*])."

The Qianlong emperor did not directly endorse Sun's memorial, which never received a rescript, but less than two months later, he issued his own edict, adopting some of Sun's suggestions but offering a somewhat different vision of Hanjun identity. Just as Sun had, the emperor noted that as the empire "recovered and regained strength" in the wake of the dynasty's founding, the Hanjun "population has grown ever-more numerous."[9] Moreover, like Sun, he declared, "I consider the Hanjun people to have originally been Han," a line that is especially striking in Manchu, where the term for "Hanjun" does not already include the ethnonym for Han: *Ujen Coohai urse daci Nikan bihe* ("the Ujen Cooha people were originally Han"). However, the emperor's understanding of the relevance of the Han origins of the Hanjun was somewhat different from Sun's.

First, the emperor distinguished between two types of Hanjun: the "descendants of those officials and people who submitted when the [dynasty's] foundation was erected"—that is, those who had joined the banners prior to the Qing armies entering Shanhai Pass—and the descendants of Hanjun who had entered the banners in any other way.[10] This distinction mattered because those who had been with the dynasty since its early days "had, of old, performed meritorious service (Ma. *fe gung faššan bifi*, Ch. 舊有功勳 [*jiu you gongxun*]), and passed many years [in the dynasty's service]." Those in this category were to be excluded from the edict permitting Hanjun to leave the banners; their record of service to the dynasty meant that their banner status could not be changed.

However, there seems to have been another reason that this distinction mattered: those whose families had served the dynasty prior to 1644 did not necessarily have a place to which they belonged in China proper. This created another discrepancy between Sun's view of how Hanjun differed from Manchus and the view expressed in the edict: rather than emphasizing the natural ability of the Han to live off commerce and agriculture, the emperor pointed out that those Hanjun who had entered the banners after 1644 had somewhere to return to if they left them. It was "*because* some have homes, graves, households, and property in their native place and some have clans, in-laws, and extended families in another province" that they could easily leave the banners.[11] That is, it was their continuing ties to Chinese society, as well as the fact that locations in China could be treated as their native places, that made it fitting for them to leave the banners behind.

The most important difference from Sun's original proposal, however, was that according to the emperor's edict, those Hanjun who chose to take up a new means of livelihood would lose their banner status. This point is made quite clearly; those who moved away from their former banner would be "entered into *baojia* units just like commoners of that place (Ma. *harangga ba i irgen*, Ch. 該處民人 [*gai chu minren*])." The idea that the Hanjun were to be allowed to give up their banner status entirely suggests that the emperor thought of them as fundamentally different from Manchu or Mongol bannermen, who were never permitted to become commoners. However, although this decision to allow Hanjun to leave the banners voluntarily would eventually be cited as the earliest precedent for the decision to forcibly expel

Hanjun bannermen from provincial garrisons, the emperor made it very clear that he was neither attempting to force the Hanjun out nor intending the decision to serve as precedent.[12] The decision, he declared:

> is the result of [an act of] specially bestowed grace; it will not serve as precedent for the future (Ma. *amala kooli oburakū*, Ch. 後不爲例 [*hou bu wei li*]). The thought behind it is my solicitous intention of extraordinarily extending benevolence out of pity for their [the Hanjun's] circumstances. It by no means is meant to force them to leave the banners and become commoners (Ma. *umai cembe bošome gūsaci tucibufi irgen oburengge waka*, Ch. 並非逐伊等使之出旗爲民 [*bingfei zhu yideng shi zhi chuqi weimin*]) nor is it a result of the dynasty having insufficient provisions [to support the Hanjun].

Moreover, even though the edict permitted only Hanjun to leave the banners, it does not seem to have been intended to shift the state's resources from the Hanjun to the Manchus. No salaried posts in the banner armies designated for Hanjun were eliminated or reclassified as Manchu posts, quite unlike what would happen with the Hanjun in many provincial garrisons. In addition, it seems that the policy was genuinely intended to benefit the Hanjun, as the court refused to extend it to a banner group that was perhaps even less favored—the entailed households, who not only were mostly Han in origin but were also descended from slaves rather than ordinary bannermen. One of the justifications proffered for denying entailed householders the right to leave was that they were already forbidden from holding posts in the cavalry or infantry, so an entailed householder leaving the banners would not open up a salaried post for another bannerman.[13] The implication of this claim is that part of the benefit of the Hanjun policy was that it opened up posts to currently unemployed banner people. Since the overall balance of Manchu and Hanjun posts was not changed, one of the ways that Hanjun would have benefited from the policy is that some unemployed Hanjun would find jobs when their employed comrades chose to leave the banners. Thus, although the edict marks the first appearance of the set phrase "remove [them] from the banners and make [them] commoners" (Ma. *gūsaci tucibufi irgen obumbi*, Ch. 出旗爲民 [*chuqi weimin*]), which would become the watchword for the policy of Hanjun expulsion beginning in 1754, the policy that the edict advanced was quite different from that of the later part of the Qianlong period. In fact, the later import of the phrase lends irony to its sole appearance in the edict, in the block quote that ended the previous paragraph, where it was used to describe what the state would *not* do.

Permitting Hanjun to leave the banners voluntarily proved problematic for maintaining clear status divisions between banner people and commoners. One troublesome issue was the possibility that families could be divided by status, which would create problems for a hereditary status system based on the household unit. To some degree, this could be prevented by legal measures, in particular a ban on a son leaving the banners if his father did not and vice versa. Although insufficient oversight by banner officials sometimes permitted violations of this rule, particularly when father and son lived in different jurisdictions on account of the military or administrative service of one or the other, those who were later discovered were returned to the banners.[14]

Conflict between family ties and banner status in cases involving people who left the banners became more complicated in cases of adoption. In 1737, a childless Bordered Yellow Hanjun bannerman named Qi Bin 齊斌 adopted Qi'er 七兒, the son of Yu Zongshun 余宗舜, a Bordered Red Hanjun bannerman who served in the company of Qi's wife's younger brother. At the time, Qi did not make an official report of the adoption, which proved a problem when, in 1743, Yu decided to become a commoner. Three years later, in 1746, while Qi was serving as the left-wing lieutenant general in Hangzhou, he realized that it would soon be time for the now-sixteen-year-old Qi'er, who had taken the name Qi Guangzuo 齊光祚, to be recorded as a man of military age, and thus to become eligible for banner rank. However, Qing law prohibited banner people from adopting the children of commoners, and those who had been adopted anyway would hold only secondary banner status and thus have very little likelihood of receiving a salaried post. Citing his need for an heir, as well as the fact that the Yu family had been banner people at the time of Qi Guangzuo's adoption, Qi Bin begged the Qianlong emperor to permit his adopted son to become his heir and receive regular banner status.[15] The recommendation that the emperor received from the commander of Qi's banner paid particular attention to the fact that Qi Guangzuo was the son by birth of a former Hanjun bannerman, noting that this made the case "slightly different from the adoption of a commoner's son," and thus that, given Qi Bin's age and lack of other children, the adoption should be permitted.[16] Hanjun who left the banners were still not quite the same as ordinary commoners, at least in this respect. But the difficult questions that resulted from the post-1742 weakening of the barrier separating Han bannermen from Han commoners help show why having clear status boundaries had been important to the Qing state in the first place.

The 1742 edict was not the beginning of expulsion. It did not require any Hanjun to leave the banners, nor did it reallocate state resources from Hanjun to Manchus or Mongols.[17] Indeed, the Qianlong emperor explicitly rejected the idea of forcing Hanjun to give up their status. But that is not to say that the edict had little importance. It was, rather, the first clear articulation by a Qing emperor of the idea that being of Han ethnic background should affect the permanence of a bannerman's position in the service elite. The scope of this new idea was limited and still influenced by long-standing ideas about the relationship of service to status. Banner people whose ancestors had served the dynasty since before the Qing conquest of China would not have the option to leave the banners. So even as the edict signaled the rising importance of ethnicity to status, it did not yet claim that Han ethnicity on its own was sufficient to undermine the ties between bannerman and emperor.

Last In, First Out: The Household Selected Soldiers and the First Expulsion

Although the Qianlong emperor's 1742 edict did not start the expulsion process, the 1754 expulsion of the Fuzhou Hanjun, mentioned at the start of this chapter, did have a genuine precedent, albeit one unstated in the edict that initiated it. This was the example of the Household Selected Solders, a group whose elevation from banner slavery to regular banner status in the wake of military service on the frontier, as described in chapter 2, had exemplified the exchange of service for privilege that defined the service elite. In 1747, they became the first victims of the Qianlong emperor's attempts to use ethnicity as a justification for turning banner people into commoners. The judgment of the Yongzheng emperor that the contributions of the Household Selected Soldiers to the dynasty merited a place in the service elite was thus overturned by his son a mere sixteen years later. This rapid reversal in fortune makes clear the scale of the shift in the Qing court's approach to the banners between the 1730s and late 1740s and shows that the logic that led to expulsion was new, not the natural outcome of the ethnic discrimination internal to the banners that had existed for as long as the institution itself.

In 1746, the Suiyuan general Buhi 補熙 wrote a memorial stating that the Household Selected Soldiers, who were all assigned to his garrison, had grown in population to the point that "the salaries and grain stipends that they receive are insufficient to support the people of their households."[18] Moreover, an increasing number of families no longer contained a member who held a salaried post. According to Buhi, there were 1,700 members of households that lacked a man with either a salaried position or sufficient income to support the entire family. In response to Buhi's memorial, Grand Councilor (Ma. *coohai nashūn i amban*, Ch. 軍機大臣 [*junji dachen*]) Necin, likely speaking for the Grand Council (Ma. *coohai nashūn i ba*, Ch. 軍機處 [*junji chu*]) as a whole, suggested that the problem could not be resolved by making simple adjustments. He wrote that already there had been problems with maintaining the livelihood of the soldiers in Suiyuan, which the court had dealt with by granting them their pay entirely in silver instead of a mix of silver and grain, as well as by providing them with gifts of silver to pay off their debts. Since none of this worked, a new approach was required. The solution that Necin proposed is surprising, though, because it did not conform to the system of ethnic division that the Qing seemed to employ in managing its banner population—one in which ethnic Manchus in the Household Selected Soldiers were to be enrolled in the Manchu banners, ethnic Mongols in the Mongol banners, and ethnic Han in the Hanjun banners.

Instead, Necin's memorial argued, the court should consider transferring some members of the Household Selected Soldiers to the Chahar Eight Banners. Although the Chahars were a Mongol group that had initially submitted to Qing rule in 1635, prior to the conquest of China, the Chahar banners were administratively distinct from the Mongol Eight Banners. At the same time, they were not among the forty-nine "banners" of Inner Mongolia, an entirely different form of sociopolitical organization that had been created by fixing the membership and territory of the previously fluid and nomadic political units of the region, which were ruled by *jasaghs* chosen from among their own nobility. Rather, they formed their own separate division of the Qing's Eight Banner system, with their own banner companies organized according to the same system of banner colors applied to the other Eight Banner ethnic divisions.[19] Most households registered in the Chahar banners were expected to support themselves through herding, in a nomadized version of the classic Chinese *tuntian* (屯田) system.[20] Transferring members of the Household Selected Soldiers to the Chahar banners would provide those transferred with a way to support themselves.

But it would also relieve the state of the need to pay their salaries, thereby freeing up funds to help support the livelihoods of the remaining Household Selected Soldiers, "benefitting both" those who were transferred and those who remained in Suiyuan (Ma. *juwe de gemu tusa ombi*).

The details of Necin's proposal for the Household Selected Soldiers make clear that, although he recognized the potential difficulties of attempting to have a group of people with no experience in herding take up a lifestyle that relied on it, he did not see ethnicity as a fundamental obstacle to their incorporation into the Chahar banners. He suggested that every year, each banner should select twenty to thirty families without a salaried soldier, or with one whose income was too small to support the family, to move to the Chahar banner lands, where they would be divided among the various Chahar banner companies.[21] Each household was to receive 30 taels of silver for moving expenses and then, upon arrival in their new homes, six cows, twenty sheep (both rams and ewes), two geldings, four female foals, and one Mongol yurt. This property was to serve as the basis for their support, although there would also still be some stipend-carrying posts for soldiers. Necin did not assume that the new arrivals would know how to manage their new herds productively enough to support the transferred families in perpetuity. He thus proposed that they be entrusted to supervisors (Ma. *uheri da*) who would "properly supervise, guide, and instruct them" so they would, "like Mongols (Ma. *Monggoso i adali*), be made to diligently breed their horses and livestock, and not come to carelessly squander the property granted them by letting their herds die."[22] This final statement suggests that Necin was not unconcerned with ethnic categories and saw the lifestyle that the Household Selected Soldiers would be adopting under his proposal as characteristically Mongol.[23] Moreover, it was a way of life that they as non-Mongols would have to learn, which would require supervision and training. Yet it was also a perfectly appropriate way of life for them. It was one that they were capable of learning to take up, and, for Necin, the fact that the people in question were not themselves Mongols was not an insurmountable obstacle to them entering the Chahar banners and becoming Mongol-like.

The idea that Necin considered it reasonable to send some of the Household Selected Soldiers to take up a way of life that he knew was alien to the skills and livelihood associated with their ethnic background, and for which they had no relevant experience, means that his proposal cannot be explained under a framework that holds ethnicity to be the Qing state's main principle for organizing people. Rather, his proposal is best explained as an attempt to protect the position of the Household Selected Soldiers as members of the Qing service elite. The crisis in Suiyuan, as presented by Buhi, was an inability to adequately support the Household Selected Soldiers. Indeed, prior to coming up with the proposal, Necin and his colleagues asked one follow-up question of Buhi: an inquiry as to the number of households and people who had insufficient resources. The preliminaries to the actual proposal also emphasized the role of the court in meeting the needs of its banner people. Necin both catalogued past imperial aid to the Household Selected Soldiers and worried that, were the problem not dealt with, it would eventually affect all the soldiers of the garrison.

The question of how to support the entire banner population adequately was a long-standing one. As discussed in chapter 4, difficulties with providing sufficient income to Hanjun bannermen in other garrisons had been resolved by granting Green Standard posts to bannermen, who retained their banner status even while serving in a commoner army. This meant that Necin had good reason to assume that the court owed support to its bannermen, and his task was to determine how to provide it without increasing the burden on state finances. The unusual proposal to transfer non-Mongol members of the Household Selected Soldiers into the Chahar banners was, as he explained, a matter of convenience. Suiyuan was located close to the territory of the Chahar Eight Banners, which had a large enough number of statutorily designated posts to be able to absorb additional personnel each year.

One month after he submitted his proposal, Necin received an edict from the Qianlong emperor rejecting his plan. The justification for the emperor's decision was a memorial by the Suiyuan garrison general Buhi suggesting that he did not consider the plan to be feasible, but the emperor's decision to endorse Buhi's judgment over that of the Necin and his fellow members of the Grand Council is likely an indication that his own position on the issue already was in line with Buhi's. According to the edict, Buhi memorialized against Necin's proposal on the following grounds:

> They [the Household Selected Soldiers] cannot live by breeding livestock. After they arrive in that place and have completely consumed the property given to them, they will come to be unable to live normally. His Majesty's profound grace will come to be wasted, and they may not be able to get by.[24]

Buhi's memorial thus reflected a belief that the Household Selected Soldiers were incapable of living as herders. He did not, however, frame this claim in ethnic terms—he may well have simply believed that their lack of experience with herding would lead to problems.

Qianlong's statement of his own views on the matter made a more direct link to ethnicity. According to his edict, the Household Selected Soldiers would "not be able to live by breeding livestock *on the Mongol steppe* (Ma. *Monggo tala de*)."[25] The emperor thus explicitly rejected Necin's claim that the people in question could learn to live "like Mongols," a claim suggesting that ethnicity was an obstacle but not an absolute barrier. For the Qianlong emperor, the steppe was a Mongol space, herding was a Mongol practice, and the Household Selected Soldiers, who were not Mongols, could not be expected to live in such a space or follow such a lifestyle. Necin was not reprimanded for his proposal, as it had not challenged an orthodoxy that was already in place, but his willingness to be flexible about ethnic and cultural divides in service of the status order was no longer in accord with the emperor's preferred approach.

For Qianlong, the dynasty's obligation was not just to protect the privileged status of its loyal bannermen, but to ensure the preservation of proper ethnic distinctions. The emperor's solution to the problem of the Household Selected Soldiers, which he appears to have come up with independently of any ministerial suggestion, confirmed this new position; instead of transferring some of the Household Selected Soldiers to the Chahar banners, he decreed that they "should be managed by making them into Green Standard soldiers." The emperor had an additional practical justification for this decision. A newly established Green Standard camp at Jingyuan 靖遠 had been garrisoned with troops from the "interior" (Ma. *dorgi ba*); surely it would be better to replace the five hundred men there with men from the Household Selected Soldiers, who had extensive experience fighting on the frontier. But the emperor went further. If there were any other such Green Standard camps filled with soldiers from the interior despite lying along the frontier (Ma. *jase*), the remaining Household Selected Soldiers were to be transferred to them. And if those were not enough, they would be sent to similar Green Standard camps in Zhili, the province surrounding the capital.[26]

Unlike past decisions to allow bannermen to hold Green Standard positions and draw Green Standard salaries without sacrificing their status or their right to acquire banner posts in the future, the transfer of the Household Selected Soldiers to the Green Standards quickly came to involve stripping them of banner status and making them into commoners. The emperor's initial edict did not mandate such a change in status. Where it differed from the earlier use of bannermen in Green Standard posts was in its insistence that the entirety of the population should take up such posts. In the past, this had been a supplemental measure to provide employment to idle bannermen; now a group of bannermen would lose the right to hold a regular banner post at all, instead being sent to take positions with lower salary and less prestige. Soon after the emperor's edict, Necin led a group of officials in fleshing out the edict's very rough plan. The 1,900 Household Selected Soldiers not sent to Jingyuan would, along with their families, be divided among multiple Green Standard camps in Zhili and Shanxi. Necin recognized that completely severing these banner people from a garrison raised questions about their status, but he did not opine on how the matter should be handled, instead passing the responsibility to the provincial officials in charge of Zhili and Shanxi: "as for how their household registrations (Ch. 戶口 [*hukou*]) should be inspected, let the respective governor-general and general make a decision and memorialize."[27]

The Suiyuan general Buhi elaborated on the problem of status in a memorial expressing concern about how transferred Household Selected Soldiers could support their families on Green Standard salaries that were lower than those for banner soldiers. He pointed out that "Green Standard soldiers are all commoners of the locality (Ma. *tesu ba i irgen*). Among them are fathers, sons, elder brothers, and younger brothers who farm or engage in trade, and on whom they rely." This was in contrast to the Household Selected Soldiers who "did not originally have property, and, ever since they came to be stationed here, for more than ten years, have relied on the salaries and grain bestowed by the grace of the emperor in order to live." His analysis succinctly laid out the difference between banner and commoner soldiers, and, in requesting that the transferred Household Selected Soldiers be assisted in acquiring property in their new homes, suggested that in the future, they would have to live like commoners, not banner people.[28]

Buhi suggested in addition that there would be problems for elderly, disabled, orphaned, and widowed people in the Household Selected Soldiers: that is, those who could not support themselves and had no immediate family members that could assist them. He noted that "if these people [were] sent [to the Green Standards], there truly would be nothing for them to rely on."[29] This was because, unlike the banners, which constituted a status category including entire populations, not just soldiers, and which were responsible for the support of all people holding banner status, the Green Standard army was a mere military apparatus, responsible for the salaries of its soldiers but nothing else. Buhi seems to have considered it unethical to transfer people who had been promised state support and no longer had the means to support themselves to a system that would not provide for them. Instead, he proposed, the people in question should remain at the Suiyuan garrison and continue to be supported by half-stipends (Ma. *hontoho ciyanliyang*), either for the rest of their lives or, in the case of orphans, until they reached the age of eighteen and could be sent to the Green Standards to serve as soldiers. This proposal was taken up by the Grand Council, and the Qing court allowed that "if there [were] aged, disabled, or widowed [people] who truly had no children and were alone," the Suiyuan garrison would be responsible for taking care of them until their deaths.[30] The general's concern about this group, like his worries about providing property to those being transferred to the Green Standards, suggests that even though there had not yet been any explicit statement of what legal status the Household Selected Soldiers would hold after they moved, it was already clear that in most respects, they would be treated no differently from commoners.

This decision to make the Household Selected Soldiers into commoners was formalized when the Zhili governor-general Nasutu 邢蘇圖 and the acting Shanxi governor Depei 德沛 responded to Necin. The two provincial officials argued:

> The Household Selected Soldiers, in filling vacant posts as Green Standard officers and soldiers, are receiving the special favor of the emperor, whose intention is to broaden their livelihoods. In the future, their sons and grandsons can also enter the army and receive a salary or they can seek alternate employment close at hand; at base they are no different from commoners. They should enter the [commoner] registers (Ch. 入籍 [*ruji*]) in the place where they take up a post, but it should still be clearly indicated that they are banner households. After they have been included together in the commoner registers for five years, another register will be prepared and reported. . . . If there are those who are lazy or do not follow garrison regulations, or those who possess insufficient skills or have gotten old or have suffered an accident, in accordance with the rules for Green Standard soldiers, they will be dismissed from the army, and turned over to local officials to be placed into the *lijia* (里甲) system.

The memorial went on to note that those who committed crimes would be tried by local civil officials (Ch. 地方官 [difang guan]), again as would be the case for regular commoners but not for banner people, who were subject to the jurisdiction of banner officials.[31] Despite the caveat that their banner status would still be noted in the registers for the first five years, these regulations meant that, for all practical purposes, the Household Selected Soldiers would become commoners. Those who left military service for any reason, including age or accident as well as misconduct, would enter the *lijia* system, which divided commoner households into groups of ten and one hundred for tax collection purposes, a function that was irrelevant to banner people, who did not pay taxes.[32] The official endorsement of this memorial, coming in a Board of War memorial, confirmed the essential point of Nasutu and Depei's suggestion by entirely omitting mention of the need to continue to note the banner affiliation of the people in question: "They will enter the commoner registers (Ma. *irgen i dangse*) in the place where they fill their post, and after they have been included together with commoners for five years, another register will be prepared and reported."[33]

Although the initial justification for transferring the Household Selected Soldiers had been the inability of the Suiyuan garrison to provide for them financially, the Qing court soon decided that their posts should not be eliminated, but rather filled by unemployed bannermen of more favored backgrounds. According to the instructions that Buhi received from the Board of War and the Grand Council, though 700 of the 2,400 posts originally allotted to the Household Selected Soldiers would be eliminated, 1,200 of them would be filled by detached household Manchus from the capital, while 500 would be filled by unemployed bannermen from the Suiyuan garrison. In the case of this latter group, there was no specification as to whether Manchus, Mongols, or Hanjun were to be used, suggesting that the Hanjun themselves were not yet seen as undeserving of banner posts.[34] In any case, the fact that most of the Household Selected Soldiers were to be replaced shows that though financial considerations may have played a role, the state was willing to spend the money needed to support a large banner population at Suiyuan, so long as it was benefiting the right people.

This shift in personnel, however, may not have been planned from the beginning, unlike what would happen in Hanjun garrisons over the next few decades. The plan to bring in Manchus from the capital did not appear in any memorial until six months after the decision to transfer the Household Selected Soldiers to the Green Standards. It seems that what would become the basic model of expulsion, removing disfavored banner groups and turning their incomes over to poorly supported members of favored groups, was developed over the course of determining how to deal with the Household Selected Soldiers.

This observation leads to an obvious question: on what basis were the Household Selected Soldiers disfavored? Ethnicity probably played a role. The assumption made in the management of their expulsion—namely, that the Household Selected Soldiers would benefit from receiving farming land but would not have been able to herd—suggests that the court did consider a Han lifestyle appropriate for them, even though it had rejected a Mongol one. This suggests that the group was perceived as Han or mostly Han. Yet ethnicity was not the only factor. Documents from the late Yongzheng era dealing with the Household Selected Soldiers suggest that the group was ethnically mixed to some degree, even though it was likely Han-dominated.[35] Moreover, as noted previously, some of the local Suiyuan bannermen who were eligible to receive the Household Selected Soldiers' vacated posts were themselves Hanjun.

It is likely that any ethnic discrimination involved in the decision was bolstered by the Household Selected Soldiers' status as former slaves. The order to Depei and Nasutu to determine how to deal with the status registration of the transferred soldiers was prefaced by a note that "the aforementioned people were originally Eight Banner household slaves (Ch. 八旗家奴 [baqi jianu]), who by decree became people separately recorded in the registers (Ch. 另記檔案之人 [ling ji dang'an zhi ren])."[36] Clearly, the court believed that this status history was relevant. The phrase "separately recorded in the registers" was used in reference both to banner slaves elevated to detached household status as a reward for their service and to banner slaves or commoners who illicitly gained a place in the banners.[37] The Yongzheng and Qianlong periods featured a campaign to identify those who had illicitly become bannermen. Although the Household Selected Soldiers had clearly gained their banner status legitimately, by emphasizing that they too were "separately recorded in the registers," the court implicitly undermined their right to that status. During the later expulsion period, many of those "separately recorded in the registers" would lose their banner status as well, with no clear indication that either the court or the banner officials in charge of expulsion paid any attention to how they had originally earned that designation.[38]

The rejection of Necin's proposal to move unemployed Household Selected Soldiers to the Chahar banners in favor of the eventual policy of transferring the entire population out of the banners demonstrates how rapidly the court's approach to the banners was shifting. Necin was far from a marginal figure in the Qing court. As a grand councilor, he was one of the highest-ranking officials in the empire, a position that he could not have achieved without close adherence to the basic structures and norms of Qing governance. Even if his willingness to completely bypass ethnic distinctions to protect banner status were not universally shared, his memorial is unlikely to have represented a radical departure from how the banners were usually managed. Moreover, his memorial was framed as a proposal produced after discussion among multiple high-ranking officials, presumably his fellow grand councilors, and thus it likely reflected the views of the council as a whole, or at least views seen as reasonable by multiple high officials.[39]

Although his proposal might appear bizarre, the fact that it was offered before the possibility of expelling the Household Selected Soldiers was even suggested is strong evidence that existing ideas of banner status treated that status as nearly inviolable; expulsion was not yet even an option. The decision to elevate the Household Selected Soldiers out of the ranks of banner slaves and into those of ordinary banner people had been made just fifteen years earlier. As recently as 1739, the descendants of a group of former banner slaves who had died in battle had been elevated in status, with the case of the Household Selected Soldiers cited as precedent. They were promised that "overflowing grace [would] be bestowed eternally (Ma. *enteheme*) unto their children and grandchildren."[40] Necin had been trying to fulfill this eternal promise. The emperor's rejection of his plan suggested that membership in the service elite was no longer guaranteed in perpetuity, even to those who wished to remain in the banners.

The Qing court of the mid-Qianlong era had not ceased to care about maintaining the privileges of its service elite, but the right to continue enjoying those privileges was not absolute, as it had been when the Qianlong emperor took the throne. Rather, that right could be compromised to help the court accomplish other priorities, as it would be on a massive scale during the expulsion of the Hanjun, which began just a few years later.

Hanjun Expulsion Begins in Fuzhou

The imperial edict that began the expulsion process, quoted in the introduction to this chapter, appealed to the precedent of the 1742 edict that had allowed Hanjun to choose to leave the banners. Its actual content, however, was quite different. First, it presented the earlier policy as one option for the Hanjun in Fuzhou, with the only other option being to accept a transfer into the Green Standard army, quite unlike the 1742 edict, which had explicitly stated that no one who wanted to remain in the banners was to be forced to leave. Second, where the previous policy had made no changes to the total number of salaried posts available to Hanjun and Manchus, the 1754 edict specified that posts opened by the departure of Hanjun should be filled by Manchus. That is, the Fuzhou garrison, where all posts had previously been designated for Hanjun, was now to become a fully Manchu garrison. Rather than some Hanjun benefiting from the salaries made available by the departure of their comrades, now Manchus would be the sole beneficiaries.

In their response to the emperor's edict, the Fujian-Zhejiang governor-general Kargišan and the Fuzhou garrison general Sinju explained their understanding of the logic underlying it. They noted that although the garrison at Fuzhou, excluding the naval forces located at Sanjiangkou 三江口, had only about two thousand households that were officially entitled to a salaried post, these households contained a total population of 13,389 people, meaning that between six and seven people had to survive off each soldier's salary. Moreover, the regulations on banner livelihood prevented these people from developing any other source of income. The new edict, they said, was a bountiful extension of the emperor's favor that would allow the Hanjun the freedom to choose their own livelihood and the ability to provide for the long-term future of their families. Even those bannermen who "ordinarily only practice the skills of horsemanship and archery, have no other plan to support themselves, and lack the capital to engage in commerce" would be provided for by being put into the Green Standards. This would, moreover, prevent them from being corrupted by the local customs of Fujian, the influence of which might otherwise lead them to become "brawling thugs and untamed toughs" (Ch. 好勇鬥狠、獷悍不馴之輩 [haoyong douhen, guanghan buxun zhi bei]) or even bandits (Ch. 匪類 [feilei]).[41]

Although the two officials characterized the new policy as being entirely beneficial for the Hanjun, the notion that entry into the Green Standards would help control them suggests that Kargišan and Sinju were aware of the risks of demobilizing so many soldiers at once and the possibility that it would lead to them engaging in unauthorized violence. Moving the

Hanjun into the Green Standards was thus not merely a means to allow former banner people to continue a way of life like the one they had possessed in the banners, but it also was a strategy to prevent them from getting out of control; perhaps Kargišan and Sinju recognized that most Hanjun would not in fact find leaving the banners to be as great an advantage as the emperor had suggested. The two officials thus implicitly recognized the importance of the implied contract between the emperor and his service elite in maintaining the stability of the empire. The loyalty and good behavior of the banner population were tied to their privileged status as banner people; ensuring the continued loyalty and good behavior of Han former banner people after their expulsion from the banners necessitated finding a stable new place for them.

Kargišan and Sinju detailed their plans for carrying out the expulsion of the Fuzhou Hanjun in a memorial to the court that responded to the emperor's edict.[42] Those Hanjun who chose to make their own living as civilians were straightforward to deal with. Just like the Hanjun who had chosen to leave the banners voluntarily in the wake of the 1742 edict, they were to be allowed to move wherever they liked, entered into the commoner registers and local *baojia* units in their new place of residence, and removed from the banner registers. The memorial went to some lengths to specify all the ways in which they would be identical to other commoners: when they took either the military or civil imperial examination, it would be under the same conditions as commoners; they would receive the privileges applicable to commoners of degree status if they already held examination degrees; and they would be permitted to marry commoners, which banner people were banned from doing.[43]

For those Hanjun who chose to enter the Green Standard army, there were quite a few additional complications coming from their continued desire to live off an official salary. First, although the emperor's edict had initially ordered that those who wished to enter the Green Standard ranks would receive posts in the units commanded by the garrison general, in fact there were not enough of those posts available. So Kargišan and Sinju proposed that Hanjun entering the Green Standards should be divided among all nine of the Green Standard companies based in Fuzhou, with posts being made available to them on a rotation system. For every four vacancies occurring in the nine Fuzhou companies, three would be filled by expelled Hanjun, while one would be given to a member of a current Green Standard household.[44] Although no reference was made to the earlier incorporation of the Household Selected Soldiers into Green Standard units in Shanxi and Zhili, a very similar strategy had been used in that earlier case.[45] This continuity in expulsion policy, like the decision in both cases to replace the expelled households with Manchu households from Beijing, provides further justification for treating the expulsion of the Household Selected Soldiers as the first mass banner expulsion.

The two officials also made clear that the entrance of expelled Hanjun into the Green Standard ranks was not merely a variation on the earlier policy of granting Green Standard posts to unemployed Hanjun; their memorial stated explicitly that Hanjun entering the Green Standards as a result of the new policy would "all be changed to commoner registration (Ch. 一體改爲民籍 [*yiti gaiwei minji*])," entered into the registers in the place where their new company was located, and treated as commoners when taking the exams and in all other relevant aspects of their lives. The fact that expelled Hanjun would be enrolled in Green Standard units across the province also differentiated this policy from the earlier use of Hanjun in Green Standard posts, discussed in chapter 4, where keeping Hanjun, as banner people, under the control of the garrison general was considered an important priority.

The Grand Council and the Qianlong emperor quickly embraced the proposals of Kargišan and Sinju. Not only did they grant assent to everything the Fuzhou officials had suggested, but they initiated plans to expand the Fuzhou expulsions to other garrisons, a decision recorded in the *Veritable Records*:

> The Grand Council further memorialized: "As for the Hanjun soldiers of the Fuzhou garrison, in accordance with what the governor-general of that place memorialized, let them disperse to become commoners and be transferred to salaried posts in the Green Standards. Fill the posts they leave behind with Manchus from the capital. All of the Hanjun of the garrisons in Jingkou, Hangzhou, and Guangzhou should also be handled in accordance with this. Let each of the respective governors-general and garrison generals formulate a clear and detailed plan according to the particular situation of each place. When their memorials arrive, we will again arrive at a decision." An edict was received: "There is no need to reconsider this in the future. If it is necessary (to make a determination), carry it out beginning in Jingkou."[46]

Hanjun expulsion was not to be limited to Fuzhou; rather, as the emperor's edict earlier in the year had suggested, it would become general policy for all garrisons in the empire. Yet there is no record of either Jingkou or Hangzhou officials making any move to expel the Hanjun in their garrisons for another nine years, when the emperor issued a new edict ordering removal in both places. Only in Guangzhou did Hanjun expulsion begin quickly, though matters there did not proceed quite as the emperor seemed to expect, as will be explored in the next chapter.

Why Expel the Hanjun?

The expulsion of many Hanjun from the banners marked a challenge to the service elite framework that governed the relationship between the court and the banners for most of the Qing dynasty's history, both before and after expulsion. Although problems with providing for the livelihoods of both Manchu and Hanjun banner people may have contributed to the decision to pursue expulsion, they did not necessitate it.[47] Indeed, in the nineteenth century, as in the first half of the eighteenth century, the Qing court repeatedly developed creative plans for financing the support of the banner population in the face of budgetary limitations.[48] Practical factors help explain the timing of expulsion in certain garrisons, as well as why expulsion happened over the course of decades rather than in one fell swoop, but the decision in the mid-eighteenth century to pursue expulsion rather than other possible solutions was the result of an ideological shift in the Qing court. Ethnicized ideas about the importance of preserving Manchu identity and practices coded as Manchu, as well as discriminatory ethnic preferences for Manchus over Han, whether of banner or commoner status, had always had influence at the court.[49] But only in the period from the 1750s to the 1780s did worries about preserving the privileged position of Manchus become powerful enough to trump the principle that banner people of all ethnic backgrounds were, as loyal slaves of the emperor, entitled to permanent access to the privileges of service elite status.

The reason for the temporary triumph of ethnicity over hereditary loyalty as the justification of banner status lies in the ideas of the Qianlong emperor himself. As discussed in this chapter, the initial memorial by Buhi, the Suiyuan general, about the livelihood problems of the Household

Selected Soldiers gives no indication that he intended such a drastic solution as expulsion. Although he opposed Necin's proposal to send some of the men in question to the Chahar banners, Buhi most likely expected his superiors to propose one of the standard solutions for banner overpopulation, such as allowing Hanjun bannermen to hold posts in the Green Standard army while retaining banner status, or creating new funds designed to support unemployed soldiers. The idea that instead, the Household Selected Soldiers should be removed from the banners en masse first appears only in the emperor's own edict, a statement that constituted a rare imperial rejection of a proposal made by the Grand Council, the emperor's closest and most powerful advisory body.[50]

Most Qing officials, even at the highest levels, apparently did not even see expulsion from the banners as a tool available to them until explicitly told to do so by the emperor, in an unusual intervention into normal bureaucratic procedure. Even as they carried out the emperor's order, both in the case of the Household Selected Soldiers and in that of provincial garrison Hanjun, a policy that also originated with an imperial edict rather than a proposal from an official, Qing administrators devised plans designed to ameliorate the effects of expulsion and take into account what they saw as the dynasty's obligation to the bannermen who had served it. In at least one case, that of Guangzhou, which is a focus of the next chapter, the emperor saw these plans as out of keeping with his intentions, and the garrison general, Sitku, was severely reprimanded for his presumptuousness and for generally impeding the expulsion process.

Why did the Qianlong emperor wish to expel so many Hanjun from the banners, and why did he believe that legal privilege should be based on ethnic origin instead of hereditary status and a family history of service in the expansion of the empire? Zhao Bingzhong and Bai Xinliang argue that "the deep-rooted ethnic-class prejudice of the Qianlong emperor" explains why the banner expulsion policy was designed to protect regular Manchu banner people at the expense of Hanjun and secondary-status banner people (who were descended from slaves). The policy, they suggest, was based on a "principle of first [expelling] those who are distant and afterwards those who are close."[51] Indeed, the Qianlong emperor's record of suspicion of the Han as an ethnic category is well documented—the 1768 soul-stealing panic, for instance, was, Philip Kuhn argues, driven in no small part by imperial fears of Han subversion.[52] Yet complaints and worries about Han subjects were not limited to the Qianlong period, and indeed, imperial diatribes denouncing the Hanjun themselves as lazy and untrustworthy were, if anything, more common under Yongzheng.

More promising, perhaps, is to look beyond anti-Han prejudice on the part of the emperor to his belief in the fundamental distinctness of Manchus and Han, a position that clearly distinguished him from his predecessors. Responding to the treasonous plot of a man named Zeng Jing 曾靜, the Yongzheng emperor had argued that "barbarians" (Ch. 夷 [*yí*]), a category in which he included the Manchus, and Han Chinese were fundamentally alike.[53] Manchu rule was, for the Yongzheng emperor, justified in large part by the Manchus' own moral transformation, which made them fit recipients of the Mandate of Heaven.[54] Indeed, a belief in the transformability of barbarians formed the basis of policies for managing the southwestern frontier that were developed in the Yongzheng period.[55]

The Qianlong emperor, however, rejected the idea that Manchus, and his own Aisin Gioro lineage in particular, had required any transformation to be legitimate rulers, insisting instead on their independent origins in the Northeast and their unique and pure cultural identity.[56] Beyond this, the emperor believed in the need to maintain the distinct ethnic character of the various peoples of Manchuria and Mongolia, as well as to prevent their transformation by the Han. This attitude was apparent everywhere, from attempts to preserve the purity of natural spaces associated with Manchus or Mongols, and in particular to prevent Han intrusion into them, to efforts to maintain the cultural practices of New Manchu groups in the northeast by demanding that they hunt with bow and arrow, not muskets.[57] Manchus and Chinese even had to be distinguished by their names; in 1785, Qianlong excoriated a Manchu official for having a name that sounded too Chinese, and he angrily ordered that he be renamed "Worthless Han" (Ma. *Nikan Fusihun*) as punishment for having blurred ethnic lines.[58] It is likely that these various policies of maintaining ethnic difference were linked, and that they influenced the Qianlong emperor's attitude toward the banners; if names, places, and cultural practices were all ethnically delimited, it might make sense that banner membership should be as well.

The fact that Qianlong's ideas about ethnic distinction gained influence as the expulsion policy was formulated does not mean that older notions of the banners as a multiethnic service elite simply disappeared. Thus, expulsion would not result in all Han banner people losing their banner status. Rather, preexisting status-based hierarchies, like those that preferred Beijing bannermen to those in provincial garrisons or those that denied equal access to salaried posts to bannermen descended from household slaves, also helped determine which Han banner people would be expelled. Moreover, even as Hanjun were expelled from the banners, they would be granted posts in the Green Standard army on relatively favorable terms, perhaps reflecting a lingering sense that the state owed them more than it did other commoners.[59] As the following chapter will demonstrate, the revival of older policies toward the banners in the nineteenth century, including the broadly targeted support of Hanjun livelihood discussed in chapter 4, thus constituted a readjustment of the balance between an ethnicizing approach to the banners and the service elite framework, not a wholesale reinvention of the latter approach.

CHAPTER 8

Expulsion, Resistance, and the Return of the Service Elite

The disjuncture between Qing understandings of the banners prior to the middle of the eighteenth century and those that the Qianlong emperor promoted via his expulsion policy is made clear by the reactions of both Han bannermen subject to expulsion and some of the officials charged with carrying it out. Qianlong's view of the banners, which prioritized ethnicity as the defining marker of status to a greater degree than ever before, stripped away the hereditary privilege of tens of thousands of Hanjun. But in the end, his reforms would fail at remaking the banners into an ethnically exclusive institution or further concentrating political power in the hands of Manchus. Instead, in the century of Qing rule that followed Qianlong's reign, even as Han commoner officials gained more power relative to bannermen, the banners continued to include a substantial number of Hanjun. Indeed, in some ways, institutionalized ethnic discrimination within the banner system would be more muted in the nineteenth century than it had been prior to expulsion.

This chapter picks up the story of Hanjun expulsion at the moment that it expanded beyond Fuzhou with the implementation of the same policy in Guangzhou in 1755. In Guangzhou, the extent to which expulsion challenged preexisting assumptions about how the banners worked became clear, as local banner officials, led by the garrison general, repeatedly misunderstood and resisted imperial instructions to replace the entirety of the garrison's Hanjun with Manchus. In ensuing years, officials at other garrisons adapted to the new policy and began to carry out expulsion more smoothly and proactively. Han bannermen themselves were not passive participants in this process. Hanjun in Fuzhou, likely seeing expulsion as an infringement on the privileges that they believed they were owed, staged a large protest directed at halting their removal from the banners. After the protest failed and its ringleaders were punished, Hanjun resistance became more muted, but even years after the expulsion process ended, there were cases of individual former Hanjun seeking to reestablish their families' links to the banners.

In the end, Hanjun expulsion never extended beyond the provincial garrisons, and it remained incomplete even in that setting due to the resistance of the Guangzhou garrison leadership. After the early 1780s, the imperial push to remove the Han from the banners lost steam, and by the nineteenth century, the position of the remaining Hanjun banner population was once again secure. As the final section of this chapter explores, the service elites of Russia, Japan, and the Ottoman Empire also faced ideological challenges to their continued existence in the late eighteenth and early nineteenth centuries. The Russian service nobility and the Tokugawa samurai would survive for the moment, but the Ottoman janissaries were violently destroyed in the service of fundamental reforms to the empire's military system.

Official Pushback

The expansion of the emperor's expulsion policy outside Fuzhou began with a memorial from the Guangzhou garrison general Sitku in 1755. Sitku's memorial noted the 1742 imperial policy that allowed Hanjun to leave the banners voluntarily. He argued that because Hanjun could abandon the capital and go live with relatives serving as officials in the provinces, they were actually better off than Manchu and Mongol bannermen, who were stuck in Beijing, their populations growing without new positions opening up. The general then offered a misunderstanding of the expulsion policy in Fuzhou, which he believed to consist of the replacement of a mere one thousand of the garrison's Hanjun by Manchus from the capital. This initiative was, as he understood it, designed to even out opportunities for Manchus and Hanjun by turning garrisons at which all the soldiers were Hanjun into mixed Manchu/Hanjun garrisons. When it came to his own garrison, Sitku wrote: "Guangdong is like Fujian, and all its soldiers are Hanjun. I ask if the emperor will extend his grace and likewise send out one thousand Manchus to be garrisoned [here]." These Manchus, he suggested, would replace one thousand of his garrison's Hanjun, who could, as in Fuzhou, either become Green Standard soldiers or ordinary civilians.[1] Sitku, it seems, had incorrectly understood the first wave of transfers at Fuzhou as representing the emperor's entire plan for the garrison. This sort of plan fit well with the general's understanding of proper policy for managing the banner population, in which garrisons should mix Manchus and Hanjun to provide fair opportunities for each.

The emperor responded by stating that his original plan had not looked like the one advanced by Sitku. Not only were all the Hanjun at Fuzhou to be replaced, but the expulsion of the Hanjun at other garrisons was supposed to occur in sequence after the Fuzhou process was complete, not simultaneously with it. Yet the emperor decided that since Sitku was already proposing the start of the expulsion of the Hanjun of Guangzhou, he might as well go ahead with it. So he ordered the general to work with the Liangguang governor-general Yang Yingju to carry out the full expulsion, telling the two men to begin by corresponding with Kargišan and Sinju to get an explanation of the procedures that should be followed.[2]

After communicating with Kargišan, Yang and Sitku set to work drawing up plans for the Guangzhou expulsion. Although in many respects their plan was like that of Fuzhou, and even adopted some of the same language that appeared in Kargišan's memorials, there were major differences. Most important, Guangzhou officials continued to propose the removal of only 1,000 of their garrison's more than 3,000 Hanjun soldiers, in addition to half of the 600-strong naval garrison. This meant that it was necessary to choose which soldiers would be expelled. Sitku and Yang proposed that each of the upper three Manchu banners send either 333 or 334 soldiers to Guangzhou, implying that the expelled Hanjun would also come from the upper three banners.[3] There are two potential reasons for this choice, although neither was explicitly stated in the memorial. The first is a belief that Manchus should hold the slightly more prestigious positions in a garrison divided between Manchus and Hanjun, and thus they should hold posts in the upper three banners, while Hanjun were limited to the lower five.

A more intriguing possibility, though, is based on a distinction between the upper three and the lower five banners that was unique to Guangzhou. The upper three banners in Guangzhou were composed of descendants of former soldiers of Shang Zhixin, one of the Three Feudatories who had rebelled against the Qing in the 1670s, while the lower five banners consisted of descendants of Hanjun soldiers transferred from Beijing. The former group had been one of the specific categories of Hanjun whom the emperor had permitted to leave the banners in his 1742 edict. Moreover, although any legal distinction between them and other Hanjun had been eliminated decades earlier, their descent from rebels may still have made them appear to possess less right to banner status than did descendants of men who had always remained loyal. Perhaps Yang and Sitku were attempting to reconcile the new imperial policy of expelling those people from the banners who had the wrong ethnic background with the older service elite value system, in which a family history of loyal military service was the basis of banner membership.

The Qianlong emperor initially paid little attention to the fact that the general's initial proposal had called for the expulsion of only one thousand Hanjun. But when Yang and Sitku's second memorial reached his desk, he noticed the limited scale of their plan and responded with extreme displeasure. The emperor accused Sitku of "presumptuously" (Ch. 冒昧 [*maomei*]) seeking to change the emperor's original plan in order to delay actually accomplishing the task at hand, and he declared that if Sitku had any actual evidence that Guangzhou couldn't expel all its Hanjun, he needed to provide it forthwith.[4] Sitku's response, though apologetic, was to continue to defend his plan, arguing that he should at least be given more time to plan for the expulsion of the other two thousand Hanjun in his garrison. He pointed out that banner salaries were substantially higher than those for Green Standard soldiers, and he argued that "if we now move [all Hanjun] to Green Standard posts, among those households with many adult men as well as those whose clans live nearby, there will be those for whom [the stipends] will be insufficient to support them."[5] It would be necessary, he suggested, for officials to come up with a way to employ many other adult men in the families of the expelled Hanjun to ensure that they would still earn enough to survive.

The Qianlong emperor remained unimpressed by Sitku's argument, declaring that the general was still "distinctly unclear as to the intention underlying this" policy of Hanjun expulsion. The emperor went on to explain once again that

> the Hanjun population grows incessantly. If they are made to be concentrated in the Eight Banners, and occupy posts in the provincial garrisons, then they will not be able to freely seek their own livelihood like Han people. Therefore, ordering them to leave the banners is truly motivated by [concern for] their livelihoods.[6]

Even Yang and Sitku's plan to provide employment to the family members of expelled Hanjun who entered the Green Standard army was, the emperor argued, fundamentally misguided. By providing them with official employment, Guangzhou garrison officials would be continuing to restrict their livelihoods and preventing them from freely deciding what to do; how, he asked, "is it any different from not even expelling them from the banners at all?" The option to enter the Green Standard forces, he proclaimed, was not meant to be the method of managing *all* Hanjun—it was meant to be limited to those who were only capable of serving as soldiers. For Sitku and his fellow officials to simply compare the salaries of banner soldiers and Green Standard soldiers was to miss the point entirely. These men were to be commoners; it was no longer the state's job to be concerned about how each of them provided for himself and his family.

To drive home the point, the emperor pointed out how absurd it would be if officials tried to do this for all commoners: "Consider the commoners of the directly administered provinces, who are exceedingly numerous. How could officials possibly manage individually the increase and decrease of their daily expenses?" Officials in Guangzhou were "playing the zither with glued pegs" (Ch. 膠柱鼓瑟 [*jiaozhu guse*]), stubbornly sticking to an old way of doing things despite the newly decreed imperial policy. Hanjun were now to be treated just like Han commoners; why couldn't Sitku adapt to the new circumstances? It wouldn't even require any creativity on his part; all he had to do, the emperor said, was simply to copy the regulations that Fuzhou garrison officials had already developed.[7] The emperor's frustration with Sitku was obvious, and just nine days after issuing this edict, he ordered him transferred to serve as garrison commander in distant Barköl, to be replaced as the Guangzhou general by Li Shiyao 李侍堯, the vice president (Ma. *ashan i amban*, Ch. 侍郎 [*shilang*]) of the Board of Revenue.[8]

This back-and-forth between Sitku and the Qianlong emperor demonstrates that the Hanjun expulsion policy represented a major shift in the court's approach to banner status. There are clear parallels to the rejection of Grand Councilor Necin's first proposal for the Household Selected Soldiers prior to the emperor's decision to expel them from the banners, as discussed in chapter 7. Necin had wanted to put the Household Selected Soldiers into the Chahar Mongol banners, which had fewer men than called for in their official quotas, to ensure that they could continue to receive the support appropriate to banner people. Sitku, for his part, had argued that he needed to find sufficient employment to replace the incomes of the Hanjun families who were losing their place in the banners. Both Sitku and Necin had made the mistake of thinking that their priority was to find the best way to provide a livelihood to the banner people in question. Instead, as the emperor explained in both cases, their banner status was no longer relevant; it was now necessary to treat them in accordance with their ethnic background. Although officials in Fuzhou and Guangzhou, like those in Suiyuan who had been responsible for the Household Selected Soldiers, still made some special accommodations for their now former bannermen, from continuing to support the elderly and infirm to helping provide housing, property, and jobs for family members in their new roles, the emperor's view was absolute: former bannermen must now, like ordinary Han, seek their own livelihood, without the structures of the Eight Banners to either support or restrict them.

Sitku's drive to protect the Hanjun under his command and resist the edict to expel all of them was not the product of his own ethnic background. He was himself a Manchu, and were he operating based on ethnic loyalty alone, he might have been expected to support a plan that would benefit Manchus at the expense of Hanjun.[9] Perhaps the general's relatively long term of service in Guangzhou meant that he had developed a personal concern for his men there. But the best explanation for his conduct is probably the one offered by the Qianlong emperor: Sitku simply did not understand the new direction that the banners were taking. The Guangzhou general had tried to deal with the new policy in accordance with the long-standing terms of the relationship between the Qing court and the Qing service elite. As a banner official, he was responsible for protecting the privileged position of the banner people under his authority and ensuring their continued well-being. Although he did not reject the possibility of expulsion entirely—the case of the Household Selected Soldiers had perhaps already shattered the notion that banner status was inviolable—Sitku may have looked to the principles underlying service elite status in determining who should be expelled. If indeed his proposal to expel the Hanjun of the upper three banners was a result of their descent from Shang Zhixin's soldiers, then he was singling them out due to their ancestors' failure to exemplify the loyalty to the throne required of members of the service elite.

Even if this was not Sitku's rationale, he certainly did not see ethnic preference for Manchus as a legitimate justification for expulsion. Rather, he expressly suggested that the purpose of remaking the Guangzhou garrison was to create ethnic equality within the context of the banners by giving Manchus and Hanjun an equal share of the garrison's resources. Moreover, Sitku sought to ensure that even those Hanjun who were expelled from the banners would be provided for by the state, maintaining the special relationship between emperor and servitor that existed within the banner system. The emperor's excoriation of Sitku recognized this fact; the problem that Qianlong identified in the general's proposal was that it did not put expelled Hanjun in the position of ordinary commoners. Sitku's resistance to the emperor's proposed expulsion policy thus marked a clash between the traditional Qing understanding of the banners as a multiethnic service elite, whose hereditary privilege was guaranteed as a reward for their loyalty, and Qianlong's new vision, in which the privileges of banner membership were guaranteed to Manchus, and perhaps to Mongols, but not to Hanjun. His inability to recognize that the emperor had changed the rules of the game was probably exacerbated by the Qing court's refusal to admit that treating Hanjun as unworthy of banner status was an entirely novel approach, as well as its insistence on presenting expulsion as a natural outgrowth of earlier policies. The emperor, of course, did not take a kind view of Sitku's inability to adjust his approach to managing the garrison, so it was necessary for the general to be replaced.

Perhaps surprisingly, the removal of Sitku did not result in the expulsion of all Guangzhou's Hanjun. At the time that Li Shiyao, himself a Hanjun bannerman, arrived in Guangzhou, he carried instructions from the emperor allowing that Guangzhou could become a half-Manchu, half-Hanjun garrison. This would still necessitate the expulsion of 1,500 Hanjun soldiers, 500 more than Sitku had wanted, but it did not mean their total elimination. No clear explanation was ever given for this change in policy, although it may have been related to the difficulty of finding enough unemployed Manchu men from the capital to fill all the posts being vacated in both Guangzhou and Fuzhou.

Indeed, in 1758, the court decided to send large groups of secondary-status bannermen, officially classified as either entailed households or people separately recorded in the registers, to the two garrisons to fill the newly vacant posts.[10] As secondary-status banner people, they were, like the Household Selected Soldiers, former banner slaves or their descendants. Fuheng, a member of the Grand Council, had declared the backgrounds of these people to be inferior to those of Hanjun, and even to those of Green Standard soldiers. Moreover, just months after ordering the expulsion of the Fuzhou Hanjun, the emperor had decreed that those entailed households and people separately recorded in the registers who were assigned to provincial garrisons would eventually lose their banner status as well.[11] Although this expulsion order had not extended to secondary-status households in the capital, the fact that it was necessary to send such people to Guangzhou and Fuzhou to fully replace the expelled Hanjun from those garrisons suggests that the number of Beijing Manchus of regular banner status who could be transferred was insufficient. This may also have been part of the reason that the emperor had not originally planned to start expulsion in Guangzhou while the process was still ongoing in Fuzhou. In any case, half of the Hanjun garrison in Guangzhou was allowed to remain, in what was probably intended initially as only a temporary delay. The reprieve would eventually prove permanent, though, with Hanjun banner people remaining in Guangzhou until the fall of the dynasty. A similar rationale rescued the Hanjun in Fuzhou's naval garrison from expulsion, a state of affairs that would also become permanent. Further expulsions were carried out in the two garrisons in 1762, but they targeted the very secondary-status bannermen who had been transferred to them just four years earlier.[12]

Expulsion Becomes Established Policy

Even as the remaining Hanjun of Fuzhou and Guangzhou were allowed to remain in the banners, a new round of Hanjun expulsion began in garrisons across the rest of the empire. In 1763, the expulsion process began in Hangzhou, Jingkou, Liangzhou 涼州 (present-day Wuwei, Gansu), and Zhuanglang 莊浪 (also in Gansu), and in 1764, it was extended to Suiyuan and Youwei 右衛 (present-day Youyu County, Shanxi). As had happened in Fuzhou and Guangzhou, the Hanjun in each garrison were given the choice of either becoming ordinary civilians or entering the Green Standard army. But the process in each of these garrisons differed from that of Fuzhou and Guangzhou in one crucial way: in no case were the expelled Hanjun replaced by Manchus from the capital. In Jingkou, some of the newly vacant posts would be occupied by unemployed Mongol bannermen from Jiangning 江寧 (present-day Nanjing), even though only 1,100 of the more than 3,000 vacancies created by the departure of the Hanjun would be filled. In the garrisons other than Jingkou, positions for Hanjun were simply eliminated—the Liangzhou and Zhuanglang garrisons were shut down entirely. The extra salaried posts from Hangzhou and Jingkou that became available were given to Chahar and Solon (a New Manchu group from Manchuria) banner people who were sent to Ili, the base of Qing power in newly conquered Xinjiang.[13]

The timing of this second wave of Hanjun expulsions was explicitly linked to the final Qing victory over the Zunghar Khanate after a period of warfare that had lasted for decades along the empire's Inner Asian frontier. The Qing court now needed to establish garrisons in the newly conquered territory of Xinjiang, while certain garrisons that were no longer anywhere near the empire's external borders had lost much of their strategic importance. The case of Zhuanglang and Liangzhou makes this particularly clear. The 3,200 Manchu and Mongol bannermen in the two garrisons were transferred directly to Ili to serve in the new banner garrison established there. The 1,000 Hanjun were dealt with according to the same standards as had been applied in Fuzhou and Guangzhou and so were divided among various Green Standard garrisons in both Gansu and Shaanxi.[14]

As such, it seems clear that the court was using a major redeployment of its western military garrisons as an opportunity to clear out many of the remaining Hanjun in provincial garrisons. The court framed the expulsion as in part a result of the defeat of the Zunghars, which meant that it was "no longer necessary to station excess troops" at garrisons like Zhuanglang, Liangzhou, Suiyuan, and Youwei, and thus that the Hanjun there could be eliminated.[15] Yet, from a logistical perspective, it probably would have been easier to simply transfer Hanjun westward to serve in Ili, keeping them in the banners, rather than sending different groups of soldiers there as it expelled the Hanjun. The court was once again redefining who belonged in the banners along ethnic lines, removing ethnically Han banner people from its metaphorical household to incorporate Manchu-adjacent groups like the Solon, whose history of service to the dynasty was actually shorter than that of most of the Hanjun.

The expulsions in Suiyuan and Youwei also provide further evidence that Qing officials understood the Hanjun expulsion to follow the same principles as those employed in expelling the Household Selected Soldiers. In fact, for the first time, the Household Selected Soldiers became an explicit precedent for Hanjun expulsion. The Suiyuan garrison general Yunju 蘊著 repeatedly cited the precedent of the Household Selected Soldiers, the expulsion of whom some of the officers and staff at his garrison had likely helped to manage, in explaining how and where he would transfer his expelled Hanjun.[16]

The final group of Hanjun to be expelled from the banners were those in Xi'an, who remained in their garrison until 1778. Rejecting a plan created by the Shaan-Gan governor-general Lergiyen 勒爾謹 to simply eliminate a set of Green Standard positions in Shaanxi in order to transfer the men employed in them to Ili, the emperor instead ordered that 1,500 of the more than 2,300 Hanjun soldiers in the Xi'an garrison be expelled from the banners and made to fill the newly opened Green Standard posts. According to this plan, 1,000 of these Hanjun would then be replaced by Manchus from the capital.[17] The movement of Green Standard troops to Ili makes it clear that the court did not consider the frontier to be a military zone suited only to Manchus, challenging explanations of Hanjun expulsion that rely on the changing geography of Qing military needs combined with a sense that Han were unfit for frontier service.[18] Instead, Hanjun were removed from the banners ostensibly to permit the transfer of a group of nonbanner Han soldiers to Xinjiang.

As with the expulsions of fifteen years earlier, the impetus for this final expulsion of Hanjun was military redeployment tied to the completion of the conquest of Xinjiang. But, unlike all previous expulsions of Hanjun, there was no longer any pretext that this was being done for the benefit of Han banner people themselves. Rather than issuing justifications for the decision as something that would reduce restrictions on Hanjun livelihood or deal with their overpopulation and resulting poverty, both the court and officials in Xi'an treated the process of Hanjun expulsion as nothing more than a military matter. Indeed, for the first and only time, Hanjun were not even given the choice of becoming ordinary commoners; they were simply removed from the banners and moved into Green Standard units.[19]

Hanjun expulsion in Xi'an can only be understood as the result of an unspoken assumption on the part of all officials involved that Manchus belonged in the banners and Hanjun did not, an assumption that had not existed in the early years of Hanjun expulsion. The proposal for the removal of the final 800 Hanjun soldiers from Xi'an makes this particularly clear. According to the Xi'an general Umitai 伍米泰, if 800 Hanjun were left in the garrison, "the troop formation in the garrison would not seem very well-ordered," so they should be eliminated, a justification that would have been laughably flimsy were the need to expel Hanjun from provincial garrisons not already an operating principle of banner management. To make the ethnic principle at work even clearer, Umitai then went on to complain that even after the transfer of 1,000 Manchus from the capital, the garrison would have only 2,700 Manchu and Mongol troops, which was not enough for a provincial capital and strategic location, adjacent to all sorts of "barbarians" (Ch. 番夷 [*fanyi*]). As such, even as he proposed the removal of more than 800 Hanjun soldiers, he asked permission to select 300 men from among the garrison's unemployed Manchu and Mongol population to receive official posts, bringing the total size of the garrison force to 3,000.[20] The contrast with the Guangzhou general Sitku's actions just two decades earlier is clear. The Qing bureaucracy finally had internalized the principle that underlay the court's new policy toward the banners: banner status was no longer a privilege guaranteed as a reward for one's own efforts or those of one's ancestors. Having the right ethnic background was necessary to be certain of one's continued place in the service elite.

Experiencing Expulsion: Hanjun Reactions (and Resistance) to the Expulsion Policy

Reactions to expulsion by the Hanjun themselves, like the policy proposals of Necin and Sitku, help make clear that the emperor's new approach to the banners constituted a radical shift. The most notable incident occurred in the first site of forced Hanjun expulsion: Fuzhou. On the morning of November 7, 1756, the Fuzhou garrison general Sinju was met by a large group of Hanjun soldiers, numbering more than four hundred according to his count. One of their number, an ordinary soldier named Liu Yuanzhang, presented Sinju with a petition asking that half of the garrison's Hanjun population be permitted to remain in the banners. Sinju reported that he strictly admonished the petitioners, telling them that their departure from the banners was an expression of the emperor's overflowing grace (Ma. *desereke kesi*), for which they ought to be thankful. These words, Sinju claimed, were sufficient to calm the crowd, which then knelt before him with no reply.

Whether or not one accepts Sinju's assertion that it took nothing more than him speaking a couple sentences of reproach to calm a crowd of hundreds, his pacification of the protesters was surely aided by the arrest of several of their ringleaders, whose identities were revealed by interrogating Liu Yuanzhang. The instigator of the petition was a Plain White Banner soldier named Zheng Lang, who had learned that the Guangzhou garrison was planning to expel only half of its Hanjun. There is no indication as to whether he was aware of the emperor's anger at Sitku, the garrison general who had managed to protect the posts of Guangzhou's remaining Hanjun during the back-and-forth over expulsion in the previous year. In any case, Zheng Lang believed that if many of Guangzhou's Hanjun could keep their jobs and banner status, it should be possible for some of his fellow Fuzhou Hanjun to avoid expulsion as well.

Zheng Lang assembled a group of co-conspirators, among whom were included corporals, the lowest rank of banner officer, in addition to ordinary soldiers. Having drafted the text of the petition and determined when to present it, they gathered a much larger set of Hanjun who were willing to participate and met in the Yulian Temple on November 6. There, they cast lots to determine who should present the petition to Sinju, and Liu Yuanzhang, who had not participated in the initial planning but was one of a large but unspecified number of men who agreed to participate in the protest itself, was chosen.

Sinju's official judicial report on the matter took for granted the idea that it was wholly unacceptable for bannermen to engage in this sort of public protest. Both the testimony of the men involved, the phrasing of which was likely adjusted to accord with judicial standards, and Sinju's summary of the case invoked Manchu phrases like *geren be isabumbi* and *geren be guilembi*, which appear in legal texts with the meaning "assemble a mob," equivalent to the Chinese *jiuzhong* (糾眾).[21] The association of this term in legal texts with violent behavior like armed robbery, the crime to which activities that involved "assembling a mob" were often analogized, meant that Sinju was treating the petitions as a sort of violent uprising, albeit one that was easily suppressed.[22]

Sinju suggested that the involvement of so many banner people in this sort of crime meant that they had been corrupted by Zheng Lang and the other ringleaders, who had "agitated them by rabble-rousing" (Ma. *niyalmai mujilen be hūlimbume hoššome*, Ch. 扇惑人心 [*shanhuo renxin*]). We see here hints at broader worries that some Qing officials may have had about the potential risks of breaking the implicit contract between the ruling house and its banner people by expelling so many Hanjun from the banners. As Sinju put it, "For just a few people to be able to thus deceive and agitate a crowd of soldiers of the four banners is exceedingly disquieting." Why they had been susceptible to misbehavior was clear: as Zheng Lang's confession reported, "the soldiers of the four banners, after hearing that the purpose was to remain in the banners, were led astray for a time." The desire of Hanjun bannermen to remain in the banners, not to mention the possibility that they might engage in disorderly, even perhaps violent, behavior to that end, were clear concerns for Sinju. Even if it had not previously recognized the possibility that expulsion would lead to unrest, Sinju's report brought those concerns before the imperial court as well.

From the protesting bannermen's perspective, the action that they took may not have been anything unusual. Ho-fung Hung has identified the years 1740–1759, an era that included the Fuzhou banner protests, as a period in which nonviolent, state-engaging protest meant to affect government policy became quite common. In these "filial-loyal demonstrations," large rallies in front of a government office, culminating with the presentation of a written petition, were perhaps the most common act of protest.[23] Despite the rhetoric of violence that Sinju applied to the protesters, he reported no actual acts of destruction or use of force. Moreover, as in the typical protest form that Hung describes for this period, the Hanjun protesters appear to have been acting under the belief that a moral appeal to the authorities for the state to protect their interests was a practical way to achieve their goals. Hung's analysis suggests that protesters in this period had a strong belief in the legitimacy of the paternalist authority of the state, which they believed was susceptible to appeals based on loyalty and filiality.[24] For bannermen, the ideological power of this model would have been reinforced by the special relationship that they had to the emperor as his slaves, and thus members of his household. As such, adopting a common protest repertoire designed to engage with and appeal to the banner authorities made a great deal of sense.

However, as we have learned from the language with which the protest was described, Sinju did not see things this way. This is further demonstrated by his handling of Zheng Lang and the other leaders of the action. The Fuzhou garrison general sentenced Zheng and three others to lifelong exile and military labor in Ningguta, and six others deemed to have been accomplices rather than ringleaders to three years of penal servitude and a heavy beating. Liu Yuanzhang, the presenter of the petition, was recognized to have simply been unlucky, but he was still sentenced to eighty blows with the heavy bamboo, which was commuted to a whipping because he remained a bannerman.²⁵ (Even those who were soon to be expelled, it seems, retained the privileges of their status.) For the court, though, Sinju's verdict was not severe enough. An imperially ordered review of the decision by the Grand Council determined that Zheng Lang, as the chief ringleader, should be executed by strangulation forthwith. Perhaps more important, Sinju was given instructions to assemble all the garrison's soldiers inside the marketplace to watch the execution, "in order to serve as a warning."²⁶ The court had adopted Sinju's basic outlook on the protests: they were a threat that needed to be contained. The expelled Hanjun would no longer be bound to the court as members of the service elite, the deal that had previously guaranteed their loyalty. Zheng's execution was an act of intimidation, designed to use fear to ensure the docility of a group of soldiers previously controlled by the privilege that had accompanied their special relationship to the court.

Other banner people subject to expulsion took a less confrontational approach to retaining a connection to the banners, illicitly gaining reentry to the banner registers. This seems to have been a larger problem among expelled households of secondary banner status than among provincial garrison Hanjun, likely because the former retained clear ties to their old companies while the latter had in most cases been replaced wholesale by newcomers, who would have had no incentive to help them. Of the 268 secondary-status banner people expelled from the Plain Yellow Mongol banner in 1757, for instance, seventy of them managed to return to the banners that same year by being adopted by a household that remained in the banners. Given that illegally claiming banner status—and the adoption of a commoner into a banner household was illegal—carried criminal penalties as severe as exile to Xinjiang, the fact that such a high percentage of expelled bannermen would attempt it suggests that many were desperate to regain their status.²⁷ This extreme desire to remain in the banners is suggestive both of the extent of the privilege that came with banner status and the extent to which being a person of the banners was central to the identity of members of the Qing service elite.

One particularly compelling case of illicit reentry to the banners, taking place decades after expulsion, did involve a Hanjun household. In late 1793 in Guangzhou, a Manchu bannerman named He-quan 和全 was approached by the husband of his wife's maternal cousin, a man named Zhao Quan 趙權. Zhao, as he would later tell the local authorities, was "a person expelled from the banners, with no means of support." When his wife gave birth to a son, he concocted a plan to improve his situation by getting He-quan to adopt the boy and raise him in the Manchu banners. When the boy reached maturity and received a salaried post, Zhao and He-quan would split his salary to help support themselves in their old age. He-quan quickly agreed to the plan, likely recognizing that a shortage of Manchu personnel in the Guangzhou garrison meant that it was almost a sure thing that his newly adopted son would be able to receive a salary. The son, whom Zhao Quan had named Zhao Tianlu 趙添祿—his given name literally meant "add an official salary"—was entered into the Manchu banner registers under the false name Quan-heng 全恆 to help pass him off as a Manchu.

As a child, Quan-heng was unaware of his real parentage, and Zhao Quan and He-quan's scheme went smoothly for twenty years, with He-quan sharing 2.5 *dou* (about 25 liters) of rice per month with Zhao out of the small stipend that Quan-heng received from a post as an auxiliary. However, in 1813, Quan-heng obtained a post in the cavalry, and when Zhao went to He-quan to ask for his share of his son's now much-increased salary, He-quan refused to share. Hoping that Quan-heng would help him if he knew his true parentage, Zhao revealed everything to the young man, but things did not go as he hoped. In fear that he would be implicated in what constituted a serious crime, Quan-heng went straight to the yamen of his banner commander to explain the situation, resulting in the loss of his banner status and his cavalry post. He-quan was sentenced under the statute prohibiting "falsely obtaining military provisions for oneself" (Ch. 冒支軍糧入己 [*maozhi junliang ruji*]), which carried a punishment only one degree less than death—one hundred blows with the heavy bamboo and exile to Xinjiang—though as a banner person, his sentence was commuted to sixty days in the cangue and one hundred strokes of the whip. Zhao Quan "fell ill" in custody—likely a euphemism for a failure to recover from judicial torture—and died before his case could be fully adjudicated.[28]

Zhao's attempt to sneak his son into the banner registers reveals the conflict between new ideas about who belonged in the banners and many Hanjun banner people's understandings of their own status. Although he was no longer in the banners, Zhao clearly still sought to live as a banner person; he saw his livelihood as bound up with banner status and continued to think of the banners as a potential source of income. Neither he nor He-quan seems to have believed in a strict division between Manchu and Han; indeed, the two men were relatives by marriage. Yet Zhao understood the official perspective of the expulsion era, which held Manchus to be more deserving of banner status than Hanjun, so he chose to find a Manchu, rather than one of Guangzhou's remaining Hanjun, to adopt his son. Even though Zhao saw himself as a bannerman, he knew that pretending his son was a Manchu was necessary to ensure his access to banner status. For Qing banner officials dealing with the matter, former Hanjun were no different from any other Han person. In adjudicating the case, there is no suggestion that either Zhao's own past status or his familial relationship to He-quan made He-quan's adoption of Quan-heng legal, or even mitigated the punishment of the people involved.

The desire of banner people to retain banner status (and, if possible, state employment) is also attested to by larger-scale data. In response to the 1742 edict that had allowed Hanjun to leave the banners, only a tiny number voluntarily did so. In 1720, the total adult male population of the Hanjun banners had been just over 200,000, and by 1742, it was surely larger.[29] According to demographic estimates produced by Mark Elliott, Cameron Campbell, and James Lee, the overall Hanjun population in 1720 was probably between 760,000 and 1.45 million, meaning that the Hanjun population in 1742 was most likely at least approaching 1 million, if not substantially higher.[30] Three months after the edict, a report from the generals of the Hanjun banners reported a total of only 1,075 people choosing to leave the banners.[31] Thus, the number of Hanjun who had chosen to leave within the banners was barely 0.1 percent of the population. Moreover, of those, 929 came from families that did not hold a paid post of any sort, and only 53 came from the families of actual soldiers—that is, people whose employment depended on their banner status.[32] This means that bannermen employed within the banners almost universally preferred to remain in the banners. And the small total number of voluntary departures suggests that even unemployed banner people generally saw their connection to the banners as too important to give up, whether on account of the prospect of future employment, a strong sense of banner identity, or the other privileges that accompanied membership in the Qing service elite.

A related phenomenon was apparent among Hanjun who faced mandatory expulsion from the banners. As discussed previously, after forced expulsions began in 1754, many Hanjun had the choice of either entering the Green Standard army or becoming commoners. Although Green Standard service was certainly inferior to banner service, in terms of both salary and the other privileges that banner people received, the large majority of expelled Hanjun chose to remain soldiers. As the Suiyuan general Yunju reported to the throne, when told about their choice, his soldiers responded, "For generation after generation, we have relied on the salaries granted by his Majesty to support the people of our households. At this moment when we have learned how to serve in the military ranks, we cannot leave the ranks and seek another way of life." As such, according to Yunju, it would be best to simply put the entire group of Hanjun from his garrison into the Green Standards.[33] Indeed, as seen in table 8.1, although there was some variation from garrison to garrison, 77 percent

TABLE 8.1

Number of expelled Hanjun choosing to enter the Green Standard army versus choosing to become civilians

Expulsion group	Entered Green Standard army	Became civilians	Total	Percent entering Green Standard army
Fuzhou[a]	1,851	195	2,046	90
Guangzhou (first group)[b]	338	162	500	68
Guangzhou (second group)[c]	474	26	500	95
Guangzhou (third group)[d]	458	40	498	92
Jingkou[e]	1,378	1,320	2,698	51
Hangzhou[f]	985	918	1,903	52
Suiyuan and Youwei[g]	3,381	0	3,381	100
Total	**8,865**	**2,661**	**11,526**	**77**
Total excluding Suiyuan and Youwei	**5,484**	**2,661**	**8,145**	**67**

[a] Šetuken, MWLFZZ, FHA 03-0178-1850-026, QL 25.10.21 (November 28, 1760).

[b] Yang Yingju, HWZPZZ, FHA 04-01-01-0216-008, QL 22.2.9 (March 28, 1757).

[c] Tondo 托恩多, MWLFZZ, FHA 03-0177-1750-002, QL 24.2.25 (March 23, 1759).

[d] Li Shiyao, MWLFZZ, FHA 03-0178-1815-002, QL 25.2.28 (April 13, 1760).

[e] Žungboo, MWLFZZ, FHA 03-0180-2057-007, QL 28.10.24 (November 28, 1763).

[f] Fulu 福祿, MWLFZZ, FHA 03-0180-2030-032, QL 28.5.19 (June 29, 1763).

[g] Yunju, MWLFZZ, FHA 03-0182-2108-032, QL 29.9.21 (October 16, 1764), says that all of the men being expelled wished to continue to serve as soldiers. The total number is given in Jangboo 彰寶, HWZPZZ, NPM 403021809, QL 30.11.9 (December 20, 1765).

of the expelled Hanjun who were granted a choice elected to remain soldiers, and even if we exclude the soldiers from Suiyuan and Youwei on the grounds that it is unlikely that none of the more than three thousand men there would have chosen to become civilians if Yunju had not decided to transfer them en masse, 67 percent of the expelled Hanjun chose to enter the Green Standard forces. This choice may reflect the power of the service elite relationship to shape the lives and values of members of the Eight Banners. The livelihoods, and perhaps the identities, of banner people were so tied to state service that most wished to continue in it, even after losing the privileges of banner status.

The Abandonment of Expulsion

From the late 1780s onward, the Qing court abandoned the policy of large-scale expulsions from the banners. There is no evidence of discussion within the court or the banner bureaucracy about ending expulsion, nor of any clear decision to cease expelling Han bannermen. Yet census records make clear that the flow of Hanjun out of the banners slowed markedly around the turn of the nineteenth century before ceasing almost entirely. Between 1720 and 1788, the Hanjun population declined by about 27 percent, or 0.47 percent per year, while the Manchu population *increased* by about 31 percent, or 0.39 percent per year, for a gap of 0.86 percent per year.[34] Between 1788 and 1812, Hanjun population loss slowed, with a decline of less than 4 percent, or 0.15 percent per year, while Manchu population growth remained steady, with a rise of about 11 percent, or 0.42 percent per year, for a gap of 0.58 percent per year. For the remainder of the nineteenth century, from 1812–1887, the gap in population growth between Hanjun and Manchus disappeared almost entirely: the Hanjun population was almost totally flat, declining by just 0.16 percent over the entire seventy-five-year period, while the Manchu population rose by just 2.7 percent, for an average yearly increase of 0.04 percent, a number that thus also represents the gap between Manchu and Hanjun population growth in that period.[35] At the end of this period, in 1887, banner censuses found 143,322 able-bodied adult men (Ma. *ciksin haha*, Ch. 男丁 [*nanding*]) in the Hanjun banners, as compared to 229,011 in the Manchu banners. Not only had expulsion ceased, but the remaining Hanjun population was still quite large; the banners had remained definitively multiethnic.[36]

This population data suggests that from the early nineteenth century on, the right of Hanjun to keep and pass on their banner status was once again no different from that of Manchus. Moreover, during the postexpulsion period, the Qing court and local banner officials made active efforts to provide Han banner people with access to income and a livelihood. In the Guangzhou garrison, in which Hanjun continued to hold half the salaried posts in the immediate wake of expulsion, garrison generals, with the support of the court in Beijing, repeatedly created new supernumerary posts to provide income for otherwise unemployed Hanjun.[37] The garrison even allowed Hanjun to take posts originally designated for Manchus when they were left vacant, with the authorities recognizing that Guangzhou's Hanjun population was much larger than its Manchu population, making an equal division of posts artificial, inconvenient, and damaging to the well-being of the garrison's Hanjun. As a result, by 1884, 6,099 Guangzhou Hanjun received a regular monthly income from the treasury, as compared to only 2,005 Manchus—a far cry from the split of 1,800 Hanjun and 1,800 Manchus envisioned by the emperor and Li Shiyao in the 1750s.[38]

Expulsion thus must be understood as one era in the history of the Eight Banners. It was an era of great importance and one that reshaped the banners demographically. Had the Hanjun population grown at the same rate as the Manchu population between 1720 and 1788, it would have been nearly 80 percent larger at the end of expulsion that it actually was (one-third larger than the Manchu population rather than 25 percent smaller). But although expulsion has often been treated as the culmination of pervasive ethnic discrimination within the banners, marking what Sun Jing describes as the final transformation of the banners from a military organization into a "special interest group," the abandonment of expulsion as a policy suggests that this view is mistaken.[39] Nor do suggestions that the Hanjun no longer served a valuable function to the Qing court explain why so many Hanjun were allowed to remain in the banners in the nineteenth century, when no new function had been developed for them.[40] The court's approach to the banners in the nineteenth century was more like its approach prior to the middle of the eighteenth century than like its approach during the expulsion era. The idea of the banners as service elite was powerful, and although the importance of the banners to both the Qing military and Qing administration dwindled over the dynasty's final century, the special relationship between ruler and banner subject remained. Banner people continued to see service to the court as fundamental to their identities.

This connection between banner service and identity was important to both Manchu and Hanjun bannermen even in the dynasty's final years and after its fall. Donjina, an early-twentieth-century Daur bannerman based in Ili, made the dynastic service of bannermen into a central part of his conception of Manchu racial identity.[41] But although Donjina's ideas could be read as the legacy of an ethnic conception of banner status, the genealogy of the Yang clan of the Guangzhou Plain Yellow Hanjun Banner suggests that many Hanjun thought in similar ways. The genealogy's most recent form, published in 2010, puts extreme emphasis on the family's banner background, with the phrase "Plain Yellow Hanjun Banner garrisoned in Guangdong" (Ch. 駐粵漢軍正黃旗 [zhu Yue Hanjun zhenghuang qi]) appearing as the only words on the cover other than the title, and with the preface defining the clan by its historic banner membership.

But the turn-of-the-twentieth-century Yang clan was equally focused on banner service and banner identity. The family biographies written by the eighth-generation clan member Yang Da 楊達, who died in 1902, go beyond providing basic information about marriages, children, and burial places only when a given individual had a particularly distinguished career of service to the Qing state. These biographies mention when a clan member was "proficient in Manchu and Chinese writing" (Ch. 精通滿漢文字 [jingtong Man Han wenzi]), discuss clan members' service in military campaigns, and commemorate imperial honors bestowed for that service. This genealogy provides the sense that successful banner service and the skills associated with it, like Manchu-language knowledge, were the markers of successful members of the Yang clan, creating a close link between family identity and membership in the service elite.[42]

Ideological Challenges to Eurasian Service Elites

Challenges to service elite frameworks from competing ideological priorities were not unique to the Qing banners. At the same time as the Qing state was expelling Han bannermen from the banners, the imperial Russian state was implementing a policy of "emancipating the nobility." The emancipation of the nobility began as part of a project of meritocratic reform initiated by Peter III, whose 1762 "Manifesto on the Liberty of the Nobility" permitted many nobles currently serving in the army to retire from military service and exempted the children of nobles from future compulsory service.[43]

The Manifesto did not eliminate state expectations of noble service or official expectations for the proper behavior of those with noble status. Rather, it suggested that: "Russian nobles, realizing what great concern we have shown toward them and toward their descendants, will continue to serve Us loyally and zealously and will not withdraw from Our service; on the contrary, . . . they will seek the service eagerly and will continue it as long as possible." Moreover, it required that upon reaching the age of twelve, all noble boys were to be presented to the Heraldry Office with a report on their previous education and plans for continuing it, with the intention of assuring that they would be capable of pursuing useful employment.[44] This requirement continued the expectation, established under Peter the Great, that young noblemen would receive what the court considered a modern, Western-style education, enabling them to contribute to the development of Russia as a European power.[45]

As with banner expulsions, Peter III's Manifesto coincided with the end of a period of military conflict: in Russia's case it was the Seven Years' War; in the Qing case, the wars with the Zunghar Khanate that had driven much of the empire's expansion into Inner Asia. But although a decline in the need for military men made the reform possible, Peter's court was likely motivated by a desire to further professionalize state service through eliminating the compulsory recruitment of nobility into the officer corps.[46] Here again, Peter III followed the ideological line of his grandfather, Peter the Great, who had seen professionalization and bureaucratization as key to Russia's future. The similarity to the Qing expulsion era is clear. Qianlong used the idea that the court had an obligation to support the interests of Manchus and Mongols in order to maintain the dynasty's native Inner Asian character, an idea long established in Qing imperial discourse and associated with the dynasty's founders, as a justification for abrogating hereditary banner privilege. Peter III analogously used the well-established idea that improving Russia required the development of a more meritocratic and professional military and civil service, a principle associated with his most admired dynastic predecessor, to justify the end of a long-standing requirement that the nobility serve in the military.

The Russian court's approach to emancipating the nobility evolved over the subsequent reign of Peter III's wife, Catherine the Great, a participant in the coup that overthrew him. Catherine did not immediately confirm Peter's Manifesto, at least in part because she was skeptical about breaking the link between privilege and service, which she saw as underlying noble status.⁴⁷ As Catherine considered her options, some members of the noble status group expressed support for a confirmation of their right to avoid service, while others opposed the new policy, perhaps out of fear of the potential effects on noble privilege—particularly of separating those who served the state from those of hereditary noble status.⁴⁸ At the same time, the court was contemplating the possibility of other reforms to noble status, including the creation of noble assemblies and providing for nobles to elect low-level provincial officials.

Catherine's final resolution of the questions of noble service and rights of the nobility came in the form of the 1785 Charter to the Nobility. The Charter confirmed the connection of service to noble status, although it placed that connection in the past by stating that noble status was the possession of the descendants of "outstanding men of former times who distinguished themselves by their deeds and who, having thereby made their service worthy of honor, acquired the title of nobility for their posterity."⁴⁹ At the same time, it continued the policy of granting noble status to those officers and civil servants who reached sufficient rank in the military or bureaucracy, rejecting the wishes of some noblemen who sought to close off the nobility to new entrants. The right of those already of noble status to avoid service was confirmed, although the Charter, like Peter III's Manifesto, included exhortations to nobles of their moral obligation to serve the state, and denied certain privileges, particularly the right to vote or be elected to office, to those who did not serve.

Indeed, in the wake of the Manifesto, it appears that many Russian nobles continued to feel great pressure to serve. Even in the middle of the nineteenth century, for a noble to retire from government service was seen as giving up his claim to social usefulness, and was perhaps even shameful for a man of middle age.⁵⁰ This phenomenon is easily recognized in the novels of Leo Tolstoy, in which state service is the default social milieu of the high-ranking nobles that he portrays, with the relationship between status and service frequently of explicit interest to his characters. In *War and Peace*, for instance, Prince Andrei meets with the historical Mikhail Speransky, the reformist who was the dominant political figure of the early nineteenth century, to discuss a proposal to strip the right to court rank from any noble who did not serve. In an attempt to resist Speransky's influence, Andrei advances an alternative theory of nobility, which he attributes to Montesquieu, in which the privileges of nobility under a monarchy are supported to encourage feelings of honor. That service and privilege are linked is assumed by both men to remain an important principle of noble status in Russia; the challenge to it, whether right or wrong, is a foreign one.[51]

Catherine, following in part what she had learned from and admired in her readings on Western European law and the organization of local society, used the Charter to tie nobles to provincial society and the land.[52] Nobles were to be enrolled in provincial associations in the places where they owned estates and were supposed to take an interest in the public affairs of those provinces.[53] This decentralization of the nobility ran against the principles that underlay service elite formations in both Russia itself and the Qing, Ottoman, and Tokugawa polities. Where the Qing under Qianlong had undermined the relationship between service elite and ruler by seeking to redirect privilege from those of banner status to Manchus specifically, Catherine's reforms weakened that relationship by granting nobles a degree of autonomy from court authority and a set of civil liberties that she, like Tolstoy's Prince Andrei, took from the ideas of Montesquieu.[54]

Yet neither Qianlong's elevation of ethnic chauvinism nor Catherine's partial embrace of Enlightenment ideas would mean an end to the basic form of their dynasties' service elite, which operated on similar principles in the mid-1800s as they had in the mid-1700s. In fact, as seen in Tolstoy's *Anna Karenina*, for many nineteenth-century nobles, participation in the assemblies that Catherine had intended to be a source of noble autonomy became a kind of service duty itself. The elections of provincial nobility themselves, as explained to Levin by a landowner, constitute "an obsolete institution that goes on moving only by the force of inertia. Look at the uniforms—even they tell you: this is an assembly of justices of the peace, of permanent members and so on, and not of the nobility."[55] That is, those who showed up to an election that was a product of Catherine's reforms were in fact acting just like the service nobility of old, doing their duty as agents of the state, in uniform, despite seeing little advantage in it to themselves except perhaps to gain a salary by being elected to office.

Meanwhile, because of the relative autonomy of domains in the Tokugawa system, challenges to the role of the samurai as service elite in Japan came not from the shogunal court at Edo but instead occurred within individual domains. One ideological tendency that prompted a rethinking of the nature of samurai status in several domains was what Luke Roberts calls domain-level "mercantilism," under which many eighteenth-century daimyo and their advisors focused on maintaining the "prosperity of the country" (Ja. 国益 [*kokueki*]) by building up profit-making industries that would help secure domain finances.[56] In Yonezawa domain, in the north-central part of Honshu, for instance, the powerful reformist magistrate (Ja. 奉行 [*bugyō*]) Nozoki Yoshimasa 莅戸善政 promoted by-employments, particularly weaving, for the domain's samurai retainers as part of a set of economic reforms in the 1790s. He also pushed rural resettlement for members of samurai families who lacked stipends from official employment, a group analogous to the unemployed bannermen of the Qing.

Unlike the expulsion of Hanjun and secondary-status bannermen in the Qing, Nozoki's policies did not require samurai to give up their status; instead, he suggested that there was honor in farming, sericulture, and weaving, and these tasks were thus appropriate for Yonezawa retainers. By participating in cloth production, men and women of samurai status were providing for the "prosperity of the country," declared a 1792 edict from the domain. Weaving itself became a form of service, with the domain suggesting that poorly made products were a "stain on samurai [honor]." These ideas about the employment of retainers ran against the historically dominant ideological discourse on proper samurai behavior. As Warashina Ryūen 藁科立遠, a conservative critic of domain policy, wrote in 1790, while it was right for farmers, artisans, and merchants to seek profit, the pursuit of profit and the pursuit of duty were incompatible, and it was impossible for the profit-seeking status groups to have "loyal hearts."[57]

In the wake of the Tenmei famine of the 1780s, the far-northern domain of Hirosaki pursued its own samurai resettlement program. In 1784, the retainer Mōnai Giō 毛内宜応 proposed resettling as many as 20,000 people, including retainers and members of their households, to the countryside to replenish a rural population that had collapsed during the famine, thereby enabling a faster return to prior levels of taxation. Mōnai suggested that this policy was in keeping with domain tradition, as the ancestors of the retainers of his day had lived in the countryside rather than in the castle town. A return to the land, he argued, would restore the strength and spirit of the samurai by removing them from the "luxury and pomp" of urban life. Mōnai envisioned an ideal rural samurai who would not only engage in production himself but would govern and administer justice to the commoner population of his area. Overcoming resistance from other administrators, Mōnai convinced the domain leadership to issue multiple edicts allowing voluntary resettlement, incentivized by an allowance and a year of tax relief.

As with the Qing state's 1742 edict permitting voluntary departure from the banners, there were few takers, with Hirosaki's retainers having little interest in giving up a life of urban service for one of rural toil. So, beginning in the 1790s, the domain made resettlement mandatory, dismantling samurai housing to force retainers to leave the castle town. The domain not only moved to restructure the livelihoods of samurai but began to challenge the status order itself by reforming marriage laws to permit samurai-peasant intermarriage, cutting stipends, and sending fief-holding (Ja. 知行取 [*chigyōtori*]) retainers back to the villages that previously they had owned only in name.[58] These reforms did not win the support of Hirosaki retainers, who reportedly launched violent attacks against the residence of one of the officials who had decided to implement them. By 1798, faced with opposition from rural landlords and peasants, as well as its samurai, the domain abandoned mandatory resettlement.[59]

The policies of domains like Yonezawa and Hirosaki have much in common with those implemented by the Qing both immediately prior to and during the expulsion period. Although neither domain resorted to forcibly stripping its samurai of their status, both required that they take up productive labor in place of service and reduced the obligation of the domain treasury to provide for them.[60] It is possible to make sense of these policies solely through financial motivations. However, as Roberts and Mark Ravina have argued, the approach to economic policy that underlay these reforms was the offshoot of a genuine ideological movement. Challenges to the prevailing social and economic role of samurai retainers faced bitter opposition even when they drew on historical precedent as a justification, as did the proposals of Mōnai. The service elite of Edo Japan was potentially just as vulnerable to ideological challenge as was that of the Qing or Russian empires. But in all three places, the importance of the service elite–ruler relationship and the reliance of the state on the service elite were sufficient to ensure that service elites would survive as long as the regimes that employed them.

In the Ottoman Empire, however, the ideological challenge to the service elite became strong enough to destroy its most prominent component: the janissaries, whose demise would predate that of the empire by nearly a century. In 1826, in the so-called Auspicious Incident, new imperial military units created in the late eighteenth and early nineteenth centuries slaughtered between 5,000 and 6,000 janissaries while putting down a janissary uprising in response to a new set of military reforms. The Ottoman court then proceeded to abolish the Janissary Corps entirely, expelling nearly 20,000 janissaries and sending them back to their home provinces.[61]

The modernizing reforms of the sultans Selim III (r. 1789–1807) and Mahmud II (r. 1808–1839), which aimed at enabling more successful military competition with the empire's European rivals, the Habsburg and Russian empires, were the direct cause of this disastrous final janissary uprising. As the Ottoman state presented the matter, the janissaries were agents of disorder and decay, impeding administrative centralization and the Westernization of the army. Most janissaries of this period never actually went to war, and the state thus came to view their continued maintenance as a waste of resources.[62] The conflict between Mahmud II's desire to create a restructured janissary army, a prelude to a broader set of reforms known as the Tanzimat, and the desire of the janissaries to retain their old privileges and forms of organization can be understood as a sort of ideological conflict like those that challenged the service elite formations of the Qing, Russian, and Tokugawa states. Indeed, just as Qianlong, Catherine, and the officials in charge of Hirosaki domain had done, Mahmud attempted to justify his position in an older ideological language, that of Islam. He recruited the clergy to support his reforms, declared that the new army should be seen as Muslim-inspired, not Western-inspired, and even named the new corps *eşkinci*, the same name used for a type of soldier that had served Mehmed the Conqueror.[63]

So why did Mahmud II's challenge to the janissaries result in their destruction while the service elites of other Eurasian empires survived? The fact that the janissaries organized an uprising while resistance in the other cases was less extreme certainly mattered; it was only after that uprising that Mahmud decided to eliminate the janissaries for good. But janissary uprisings had been common for centuries; an uprising alone could not have eliminated the moral claim that janissaries had to their position in the Ottoman version of the service elite framework. As important to consider, perhaps, is how the social position of the janissaries had evolved to distinguish them from service elite groups elsewhere. Beginning in the sixteenth century, the Janissary Corps had transitioned away from complete reliance on *devşirme* levies of Christian boys to fill its ranks, instead enlisting volunteers from among local Muslim populations, to the dismay of much of the Ottoman elite of the time.[64] Although straightforward narratives that treat janissary decline as a result of this shift are probably too simplistic, the change did fundamentally alter the social positioning of the janissaries.

Service elite status was based on a clear separation between members of the service elite and ordinary commoners. In Russia, Japan, and the Qing, this was achieved by making service elite status heritable and limiting movement among status categories and, particularly in the Qing, discouraging or outright banning intermarriage. The Ottomans, in contrast, had relied on selecting elite recruits from a population distinct from the one in which those recruits would live as adults. But both methods ensured that the social position of the service elite relied on its connection to the ruler; service elites were socially and institutionally separate from the rest of the population. This was increasingly not the case for janissaries in the second half of the Ottoman period. Instead, they became ever more embedded in the societies of the cities in which they were based, particularly Istanbul and Edirne, with many of them becoming members of urban guilds over the course of the seventeenth century.[65] Janissaries, then, no longer clearly relied on the House of Osman for their livelihood, and as such they could not be counted on to defend it from challenges from among the empire's subjects. Mahmud therefore had less need to preserve the janissaries than did his near-contemporaries in Japan, Russia, and the Qing, and so they, unlike bannermen, service nobles, and samurai, could be dispensed with when a serious challenge to their position arose.

Service elites were not taken for granted in any of the states where they played an important role. The primacy of the relationship between lord and elite servant or slave was subject to ideological challenge, both from ideas imported from abroad and from longstanding dynastic concerns. However, so long as service elites and their dynastic masters continued to have a relationship of mutual dependence, the total elimination of the service elite was not a legitimate or viable option. The continued service of Hanjun bannermen and their renewed participation in both the discourse and the material rewards of banner privilege in the nineteenth century, as discussed in chapters 3 and 4, show that the multiethnic service elite was a feature of the entire period of Qing rule.

Hanjun expulsion did not mark the replacement of status by ethnicity as the governing principle for membership in the service elite, nor did it reveal that the Hanjun did not fully belong in the banner system. Rather, the failure to complete the process shows that the value of the service elite was sufficient to withstand a serious attack on the system. So the Qing banners, like their counterparts in Russia and Japan, would survive the eighteenth-century challenge to the service elite ideal, shaken but intact.

Conclusion

The End of the Service Elite

Although the Japanese samurai, Russian service nobility, and Qing bannermen all outlasted their eighteenth-century challenges, they would not survive for long following the overthrow of the regimes that they served and the creation of new nation-states. The first to be abolished were the samurai. The fall of the Tokugawa shogunate and its replacement by a government centered on the Meiji emperor, whose predecessors had been powerless figureheads during the period of *bakufu* governance, was the consequence of a political movement that initially had no intention of eliminating samurai status. Indeed, it was led by samurai from the domains of Chōshū and Satsuma concerned about increasing foreign influence on the archipelago in the wake of the American admiral Matthew Perry's 1853 visit to Uraga Bay, which had forced the shogunate to open new ports to Western trade and residence.

Over the ensuing decade-and-a-half, the *bakufu* lost power both to the imperial court and to the domains, even as it attempted to create a "modern" Western-style army and more centralized institutions, particularly in its very last years.[1] However, in many ways, reformers attempted to respect the status system and the hereditary privilege of samurai. The new Tokugawa army, for instance, recruited commoners by temporarily promoting them to warrior status and giving them the possibility of making that elevation permanent through demonstrations of valor, a policy new to the Tokugawa state but reminiscent of how the Qing elevated banner slaves to regular banner status as a reward for service in combat.[2]

The post-1868 Meiji state would not be faced with the same limits and could more aggressively dismantle the social and institutional legacies of the Edo period, justifying its actions both in terms of a need to modernize and compete with Western powers and as a return to Japan's own ancient traditions of imperial rule.[3] The first step was the elimination of the domains and of the independent authority of daimyo, a move supported by the same adherents to the imperial cause who had led the military destruction of the shogunate and its allies during the Boshin War of 1868–1869. Although it had been the power of domains like Satsuma and Chōshū that enabled the imperial victory over forces loyal to the Tokugawa, few daimyo attempted to defend their position, contenting themselves instead with compensation for the income that they gave up and, in many cases, appointments in the new government.[4]

The Meiji state did not immediately attempt to put an end to warrior status or to the role of the samurai. But samurai recognized the risk to their position and moreover were inconsistently loyal to the central state, having been accustomed to serving the lords of their own domains. The warrior-dominated army of the early Meiji thus had substantial problems with discipline, including conflicts between soldiers from different domains, and even a number of small revolts.[5] In 1873, the government decided to impose conscription on commoners and, theoretically at least, eliminated the distinctions between warriors and commoners, who would now be "equally the people of the imperial state."[6] It soon imposed taxes on samurai stipends and banned practices associated with warrior status like ritual suicide, revenge killing, and even, in 1876, sword-wearing, which had been the distinctive sumptuary mark of a member of the warrior status group.[7]

These reforms provoked a final, violent attempt to defend samurai privilege. Rebellions of former samurai broke out in the former domains of Kumamoto, Akizuki, Chōshū, and, finally in 1877, Satsuma, where eight months of fighting were required to end samurai resistance.[8] The Satsuma Rebellion was led by Saigō Takamori 西郷隆盛, who had himself been one of the leading advocates of abolishing the *bakufu* and restoring imperial control, and who had even led the imperial army in the Boshin War. But warriors were not united behind Saigō. Indeed, many volunteered for the imperial army that suppressed the rebellion, in large part due to a need for money after the abolition of samurai stipends in 1876.[9] The loss of the institutions that sustained the position of the service elite under Tokugawa rule had not left samurai uninterested in service, which would continue to provide a livelihood for many ex-warriors. But it changed the terms on which that service was performed. With the defeat of the Satsuma Rebellion, the Meiji state was well on its way toward remaking an idea of service based on status privilege into one of service based on national identity. Its army and its bureaucracy no longer consisted of a service elite bound to a ruler by the exchange of loyalty for privilege, but rather of men who served out of a common sense of membership in the Japanese nation and the common status of citizen that underlay it.

In Russia, too, the service elite helped enable the success of the revolution that would lead to its demise. The nobility had lost some of its most important traditional prerogatives with the 1861 emancipation of the serfs, itself a proposal developed by reformist noble bureaucrats in the court of Alexander II.[10] In the subsequent decades, many hereditary noble families fell into poverty, while others moved into a variety of industries, professions, and trades, leaving behind a life based primarily in service and landholding. And yet the nobility continued to dominate the politics of the empire. Hereditary nobles—that is, not including those who received entry into the nobility via their own service—made up 90 percent of government ministers, 80 percent of deputy ministers, and 97 percent of provincial governors as late as 1914. Even the Duma, an elected legislative body created in the wake of the 1905 Revolution, drew 50 percent of its membership from the hereditary nobility, far out of proportion to their approximately 1 percent share of the population.[11] Over the course of World War I, the clear failures of the government led to such disillusionment within the nobility that many chose to abandon the tsar during the February Revolution of 1917. Local noble assemblies sent messages of support to the Provisional Government, while nobles in the Duma attempted to expand that body's authority. Although nobles certainly did not lead the revolution, they did little to stand in its way.[12]

In the months between the February and October Revolutions, the vast majority of noble privileges were officially abolished, even as the noble status group remained formally intact. Although nobles were probably no more subject to violence or the loss of property than other property holders, incidents of these types, as well as a general loss of the symbols of noble status and an apparent overturning of the social order, inspired fear among many members of the old service elite.[13] Attempts by nobles to organize to defend their interests had little success in the face of their overwhelming numerical disadvantage. But such organization as they did manage proved sufficient to inspire fear of counterrevolution among Russian socialists, particularly in the wake of a failed coup attempt by L. G. Kornilov, the commander-in-chief of the army, in September. Although Kornilov's putsch failed quickly and drew only weak support from the broader noble group, the entirety of the nobility and other members of the elite immediately fell under suspicion. When the Bolsheviks took power, they moved rapidly to formally abolish the nobility and denied them, along with other "nontoiling" groups, the right to vote. Many former nobles would either emigrate or join the White armies in resistance to Communist rule. But others attempted to integrate into the new society and sought, as had many Japanese samurai, to continue careers of service. Approximately 30 percent of officers in the prerevolutionary army would serve in the Red Army, and perhaps 20 percent of state administrative personnel in 1920 were drawn from the ranks of the old service classes. But their hereditary position would no longer provide them with legal privilege; instead, it became something to hide, with multiple state attacks on class enemies in the 1920s and 1930s focused on former members of the nobility.[14]

Although the Qing state fell in 1912, prior to the collapse of the tsarist regime in Russia, the banners would persist longer than any of the other service elites, at least officially. In its final years, the dynasty had given serious consideration to abolishing the banner system. The Guangxu Emperor's Hundred Days of Reform initiated and aborted in 1898, included proposals to reclassify banner people as commoners, abolish the practice of designating bureaucratic posts for bannermen, and set up schools to train bannermen in new trades. The Manchu author Lao She wrote that his family had been terrified by the possibility of losing their stipends at this time.[15] The emperor did not endorse such sweeping initiatives, but he did order the development of programs to resettle banner populations on open land and provide vocational education to bannermen.[16] Even after conservatives regained control of the court, similar proposals returned over the course of the next decade. The empress dowager Cixi moved in 1902 to eliminate prohibitions on banner-commoner intermarriage, and in 1903 she appointed a commoner as banner general in Qiqihar, ending the total monopoly of banner people on posts in the banner system. In 1907, the entirety of Manchuria, previously mostly subject to banner administration, was converted to civilian provincial administration.[17] That same year, the government declared that provincial garrisons would be abolished, with 10 percent of bannermen losing their stipends each year and ordered to take up farming. Angry bannermen challenged the decision, with the Chengdu garrison even rioting. This resistance, combined with the lack of land controlled by garrisons on which banner people could be resettled, led to the reversal of the edict in December 1908.[18]

Thus, in 1911, when the Xinhai Revolution broke out, the banners still limped along, clinging to institutional life. The revolution would destroy their privileged position. Although bannermen in Beijing and Manchuria were mostly spared from violence, bannermen in garrisons elsewhere in China were massacred mercilessly by Han revolutionaries inspired by the virulent anti-Manchu sentiment that had spread in the first decade of the twentieth century. In Wuchang, where the uprising began, 200 bannermen were killed; in Xi'an, 20,000–30,000 were slaughtered, driven to suicide, or forced to flee the city. The Hubei commissioner-in-chief, and future president of the Republic of China, Li Yuanhong 黎元洪 issued a regulation that all persons who hid a Manchu would be killed.[19] Manchu officials serving in civilian posts also faced the wrath of the revolutionaries, and even those who had been supportive of reform were not safe. Duanfang 端方, a former governor-general and an early supporter of ending the banner system, was hacked to death in Zizhou, Sichuan, despite his pleas for his life on the grounds that his ancestors were originally Han.[20] After the establishment of the new Republic of China, bannermen associated with the new Ancestral Temple Party (Ch. 宗社黨 [zongshe dang]), founded by the uncle of the deposed Xuantong emperor, were repeatedly suspected of sedition and insurrection in collaboration with Japan.[21]

But despite these attacks, the banners were not formally eliminated. The Articles of Favorable Treatment, negotiated by the Qing court at its abdication, called for stipends to continue to be distributed to banner people, although they were no longer to face any limits on residence or profession and were to be legally equal to commoners.[22] Continued payments to bannermen were a feature of governance across the country in the first years of the Republic. Even in provincial garrisons, local officials claimed to be continuing payments. For instance, in December 1912, the chief military official in Shaanxi reported that every month, each adult banner person in Xi'an was provided with 2 *dou* of grain, with a half-share for children; and in addition, banner people were supplied with cotton-padded clothes, firewood, salt, and copper cash, with an extra food ration provided in the winter months.²³ Although the distribution of these goods was framed as a sort of humanitarian relief, rather than as the payment of official stipends, the fact that it was directed exclusively at bannermen demonstrates that the banners continued to be a structure for the provision of state welfare even when stipends had ceased.

Early Republican leaders, including Yuan Shikai 袁世凱, the first president of the Republic, attempted to assume a relationship with the banners that bore some resemblance to that between the banners and the Qing dynasty. Yuan portrayed himself as a protector of bannermen. On multiple occasions, he ordered investigations into reports that provinces were illicitly taking control of banner property, stating that property should be dealt with according to the Articles of Favorable Treatment, under which the private property of bannermen was to be protected. Moreover, banner lands belonging to the state were not simply to be taken over, but should rather be used, Yuan declared, to help provide for banner livelihood.²⁴ How effective Yuan's orders were at actually benefiting bannermen is unclear—the fact that complaints about illegal confiscation continued suggests that he may not have achieved much—but the language that Yuan used explicitly set him up as a defender of banner interests. The rescript on one memorial began: "the order of the President protecting Eight Banner property."²⁵

In addition, Yuan did not expend much effort in speeding up the demobilization of the banners, at least in the capital. His policy in one document is explicitly described as "advancing gradually" (Ch. 漸進 [*jianjin*]) in changing the registration of bannermen.²⁶ On one occasion, in response to a proposal to use certain lands in Weichang County, near the old imperial summer retreat in Chengde, to resettle bannermen from that region, Yuan approved the plan even though the same land was originally intended to be used to resettle bannermen from the capital.²⁷ Similarly, in 1913, he refused permission to use government funds to help banner people in Ningxia become farmers, on the grounds of budgetary problems, but he still approved 30,000 yuan in salaries to be issued the group in question.²⁸ Putting an end to the system was not, it seems, a priority.

Under the Republic, bannermen continued to disproportionately provide service to the state in ways consonant with their history as a military force. In Beijing in the 1920s, more than three-quarters of the city's police force consisted of bannermen.²⁹ Certain official military units, most notably the Palace Guard, continued to consist predominantly of banner people; this remained true for the Guard even after it was taken out of the control of the imperial court and moved to Nanjing, serving Feng Guozhang 馮國章 in his role as the military governor of Jiangsu.[30] Outside of the official army, local generals also used bannermen as soldiers. In Hubei in 1913, with the forces of the Guomindang-backed "Second Revolution" pressing General Ding Huai 丁槐, who had only three battalions at his disposal, Ding turned to the bannermen of the Jingzhou garrison. Ding recruited 1,500 of them, and they remained in the army when Shi Xingchuan 石星川 came to take command of Hubei, reportedly because Shi "did not dare to use only Hubei people." This attitude suggests that not only were bannermen considered natural recruits for military purposes, but that they were still considered fundamentally distinct from the local population, to the point that a general might trust them as soldiers even as he worried about enlisting other locals. As of 1917, despite some efforts to eliminate the garrison, many Jingzhou bannermen remained employed as soldiers.[31]

The continued use and support of bannermen by the government of Yuan Shikai may have been the result of his own imperial ambitions and an attempt to make use of the same institutions that had benefited his Qing predecessors. Indeed, some of the early supporters of Yuan's proclamation of himself as emperor in 1915 included prominent bannermen like Wuzesheng 烏澤聲, who had been elected to the National Assembly in 1913, and Guan Zhonghe 關忠和, the commander of the First Brigade of the Palace Guard.[32] Yuan's abandonment of the imperial project and death soon afterward were followed by less attention being paid to the banners from the succession of military men who held power in Beijing over subsequent years. However, especially in the capital, the institution hung on. In 1918, the American sociologist C. G. Dittmer reported that 75 percent of the income of Manchu families in Beijing came from the "pension" that they received from the state.[33] And the Beijing government would continue to recognize the metropolitan banners and appoint officials to govern them until the capture of the city by Guomindang-allied forces under Yan Xishan 閻錫山 in June 1928.[34]

The final demise of the banner system, like that of the samurai and the *dvorianstvo*, was thus the result of the triumph of a new type of government, premised on a radically different form of legitimacy. Russia was to be a workers' state, while Japan and China were nation-states. None had a place for a ruling elite whose authority and privilege derived from their unique relationship to a dynastic house possessed of unchecked power. Although service elites developed as a way to provide specialized, bureaucratic governance to states growing in complexity, they were not simply a step along a smooth path toward the modern state. Rather, they were a technology of administration suitable to their context, that of early modern imperial rule. When the political systems they had served ceased to exist, early modern service elite institutions would not evolve into new forms; rather, they would disappear entirely.

Hereditary status, the social and legal formation that underlay service elite institutions in Japan, Russia, and the Qing empire, similarly no longer exists in its early modern form. But it is not entirely irrelevant to the modern world. One feature of all modern states bears a clear relationship to status: the division of the population into citizens and various legal categories of noncitizen aliens. The link does not exist only at the linguistic level, with the common use of terms like "citizenship status" and "immigration status" to discuss a person's legal relationship to the state in whose territory they reside. Rather, these categories have much in common with early modern status categories. They are substantially hereditary. Although many states, particularly the New World states descended from European settler colonies, grant citizenship to all persons born in their territory, many others, including China, Japan, and Russia, follow the principle of jus sanguinis, under which only the child of a citizen of a nation automatically receives citizenship at birth. Yet, like status, citizenship is recognized as an artificial category tied to the political relationship between an individual and the state, and thus the acquisition of citizenship by a noncitizen is possible, though the difficulty of the process varies.

A variety of complex substatuses are possible as well, as seen with categories like British overseas citizens or Hong Kong permanent residents with Chinese citizenship. People are subject to different laws and criminal punishments depending on their citizenship or immigration status. For instance, states frequently deport noncitizens convicted of crimes. One's rights and duties in relation to the state often depend on citizenship status, including voting rights, access to government employment or to welfare benefits, and the requirement to perform military service. Although citizenship and occupation are not generally linked, rules about who is expected or permitted to serve in the military bear some resemblance to the occupational aspects of status systems, where membership in the highest-ranking status categories was often associated with military service.

These connections are not merely visible in retrospect. In an article on the creation of China's new legal approach to nationality in the early twentieth century, Shao Dan tells the story of a Han bannerman who "misunderstood" nationality as being like banner identity. During the early years of the Republican period, the man referenced a new nationality law in support of his application for household registration near Beijing. The Department of the Interior ordered him to redo his application, describing his reference to the nationality law as "being really a mistake." Shao argues that the case shows "how many people misunderstood nationality—an unprecedented category of identity in early twentieth-century China," by treating it as akin to banner membership, which did indeed help determine where one could live.[35] Although both the Republican government and Shao are surely correct that the man was applying the new nationality law in an irrelevant and mistaken way, I question whether he indeed completely failed to grasp the concept of nationality. Rather, perhaps he analogized nationality to a newly defunct category with which it shared genuine and meaningful similarities. Citizenship replaced status, but in so doing, it took on many of the functions of status in defining a new relationship between people and the state that governed them.

The Importance of Service Elites

Even though the Qing banners, Tokugawa samurai, Russian service nobility, and Ottoman *askeri* no longer exist, understanding the role of service elites across Eurasia is important to making sense of the continent's history between the sixteenth and nineteenth centuries. Service elites were effective tools of governance that enabled the creation and continuation for centuries of powerful empires under the unbroken control of a single dynastic house. The four polities discussed in this book are often seen as relative failures in comparison with the powerful states that emerged in Western Europe during the same period, particularly Great Britain. Yet if one looks not from the perspective of the state or nation as an abstract entity, but from that of the ruling dynasty as a family, one sees a different picture. The Aisin Gioro, Tokugawa, Romanov, and Osmanlı houses maintained absolute power over the states they ruled far later into the modern era than did the Tudor/Stuart/Hanoverian dynasty in Britain or the Bourbons in France. As a method of managing elites and developing a military and bureaucratic administration bound to the interests of a ruling family, the service elite model was quite successful.

The role of service elites in maintaining the authority of hereditary dynasties is tied to the role of the service elite model in enhancing two dimensions of state capacity: coordination capacity and compliance capacity. Coordination capacity, meaning the ability "of state agents to organize collective action," is normally associated with the development of professionalized and rationalized Weberian bureaucracies.[36] The service elite model represents an alternative to the Weberian approach. Service elites developed specialized functions, were subject to meritocratic norms of selection and promotion, and engaged to some extent in rational rule-based governance.[37] Yet, unlike Weberian bureaucrats, they were not autonomous but instead were subject to the arbitrary authority of a hereditary monarch. Moreover, far from representing a departure from "rule by social rank," service elites derived their right to political authority precisely from their distinct social position, one often based in hereditary status.[38] In this way, service elites enabled dynastic houses to take advantage of many of the benefits of bureaucratic rule without sacrificing their own authority.

The ability of ruling families to maintain the loyalty of service elites and their dedication to their military and administrative tasks without granting them independent authority is due in large part to the unique approach to the development of compliance capacity, or the "ability of state leaders to secure compliance for their goals," represented by the service elite model.[39] By strictly limiting, or even entirely preventing, the entry of newcomers into a service elite, dynastic rulers ensured that the position of these elites depended on the continuation of the existing political system. This incentive structure was strongest in the fully hereditary service elites of Japan, Russia, and the Qing, where the continued well-being of one's descendants was linked to the longevity of dynastic control. These practical incentives were then reinforced by ideological ones, particularly the idea that members of service elites made up the household of the ruler whom they served. But because service elite populations were many times larger than actual households, even those of powerful monarchs, they avoided some of the typical problems of patrimonialism, like a near-complete reliance on the ruler's favor as the criterion of selection and promotion.[40]

The immense size of service elite populations relative to the aristocracies of, for instance, Western Europe, meant that a system ensuring their loyalty offered a great deal of protection to the monarchies that they served. Service elite armies were quite unlikely to attempt to overturn the states that sustained them and so, as long as they formed the central element of dynastic defense, military mutiny was unlikely. Even the Ottoman case, where janissaries repeatedly participated in dethroning sultans, does not truly contradict this principle, as successful janissary uprisings consistently resulted in the installation of another member of the Osmanlı house on the throne. In the states that we have examined in this book, it was only as service elites ceased to dominate the personnel of their armies that their rulers fell to internal rebellion. Only in Japan did a dynasty meet its end in a rebellion led by its service elite, but even there, the story is complicated by the bifurcated nature of state power in the archipelago. The samurai who brought down the Tokugawa were not direct retainers of the shogun, but rather, most notably, of domains like Satsuma and Chōshū with histories of fraught relationships with the Tokugawa family. Indeed, many Tokugawa retainers remained loyal and fought in defense of the shogunate during the Boshin War, which marked the *bakufu*'s final defeat. Moreover, in the lead-up to the Meiji Restoration, both the shogunate itself and certain key domains had begun to include commoners to a much greater degree in their military forces, undermining the role of the samurai status group as a bulwark of dynastic power.

In the Russian and Qing empires, the link between military reforms that reduced the importance of service elites and the demise of the dynasty was particularly clear. In Russia, participation in World War I had necessitated mass-mobilization and, particularly as long-serving officers died in battle, led to the partial democratization of the officer corps, which came to include men from a wider variety of social backgrounds.[41] This contributed to a much greater openness toward participation in oppositional movements, and, indeed, in addition to the mutinies of ordinary soldiers, a significant minority of officers joined the opposition to the monarchy during the February Revolution.[42] Meanwhile, the Wuchang Uprising that sparked the 1911 Revolution in China occurred among units in the New Army, an organization dominated by commoner recruits outside banner control. There is a parallel here to the observation that Benjamin Elman has made about the Qing abolition of the civil service exams in 1905, which, he suggests, severed the bonds of mutual interest that tied the dynasty to its wealthy and educated commoner elite, reducing literati support for Aisin Gioro rule in the final years of the Qing.[43] Modernizing reforms designed to make the Qing competitive with the Western powers and Meiji Japan in fact undermined the key institutions that enabled dynastic rule in the first place. Whether or not reformists within the court were right that the empire would be unable to compete economically or militarily with its rivals without abandoning core elements of its internal structure, they underestimated the extent to which that structure was essential to supporting the reign of the imperial clan.

In short, service elites present a compelling alternative explanation to culturally essentialist ideas of "Oriental despotism" or Eastern backwardness for the continuation of absolutist monarchical systems in much of eastern Eurasia into the late nineteenth or twentieth century. Service elites permitted the development of more complex state organizations and the maintenance of elite loyalty to the ruler without the development of democratic institutions or autonomous bureaucracies. Russian, Ottoman, Japanese, and Tokugawa elites embraced service to their lords, couched within a discourse of slavery, not out of a culturally ingrained servility but because the structure of their service elite systems successfully aligned their interests with those of the ruling dynasty.

The Qing Governing Class:
Bannermen, Examination Graduates, and Inner Asian Elites

The service elite framework shifts our understanding of how the banner system functioned and the role that it played in maintaining the authority of the Qing court. However, unlike in Russia, Japan, or the Ottoman Empire, bannermen did not monopolize control of official posts in the Qing empire. Rather, they shared power with a number of other groups, from graduates of the civil service examinations to hereditary Mongol princes to *tusi* native officials of the southwest to Gelug lamas. This coexistence of multiple forms of political power raises two questions. First, were these other political authorities also service elites? Second, if they were not service elites, then how did a service elite system coexist with other types of elites?

The service elite model does not apply well to any of the Qing state's nonbanner elites. The overwhelming majority of civil service examination graduates, who held most local posts in the former territory of the Ming state as well as nearly all the central government posts that were not occupied by bannermen, did come from what many scholars have identified as a single social class, one usually described by the term "gentry" (Ch. 紳士 [*shenshi*]). But the boundaries of this group were defined quite fuzzily, unlike those that set banner people apart from commoners, and almost all male commoners possessed the theoretical right to sit for the examinations. The gentry were hereditarily privileged, but that privilege was passed down largely through the transmission of wealth and cultural resources, which enabled the future production of more examination graduates, rather than via the hereditary right to a particular legal status. Indeed, the importance of the hereditary *yin* (蔭) privilege had already receded greatly by the Ming period, with inheritance of the right to hold office only rarely leading to any sort of position, and never to one with much importance.[44] In this way, neither the gentry in general nor civil examination graduates specifically formed a hereditary status group. Although degree holders were differentiated from other commoners in certain ways, including exemptions from particular types of criminal punishments and the acquisition of tax benefits, those rights could not be passed to their descendants indefinitely.

Nor did the exchange of service for privilege operate for the examination elite in the way that it did for the banners. Even as wealthy merchant families began to enjoy success in the examinations, they often made the pursuit of a degree and a potential official career the work of just one son, while arranging for others to continue to conduct business.[45] This was quite unlike expectations for bannermen, for whom state service was a universal duty, not one to be pursued selectively. And the privileged position of the gentry was less firmly tied to serving the state than was the privilege of bannermen. Landholding elites held local power through their economic and social positions within their communities, not just through the support of the court or their relationship to it. So, although much of this elite did both serve the court (even taking the examinations without success can be seen as a form of state service) and hold a privileged social position, the links between service and privilege were much more attenuated than they were for a service elite like the banners.

Similarly, the non-Han, nonbanner elites of the Qing frontiers did not act as service elites. Mongol *jasagh* princes held positions more like those of feudal lords than those of the bureaucratized military and administrative status group constituted by the people of the banners. They inherited control of specific territories and groups of people rather than being appointed based on merit. Much the same was true of *tusi* headmen. And although both groups officially required the imprimatur of the Qing state to be allowed to legally assume their positions of power, in practice their ability to exercise local authority did not depend on any decision from Beijing, as they, like the gentry of China, possessed a local legitimacy independent of imperial authority.

As for the powerful Buddhist figures of the broader Tibetan world, they did maintain patron-priest relationships with the Qing emperor and, especially from the end of the eighteenth century on, depended on imperial approval to come into their posts.[46] But their legitimacy sprang from their inheritance, via reincarnation, of a particular religious lineage. Thus, for all these groups too, though they frequently worked on behalf of the Qing state and possessed substantial power and privilege, their service and privilege were not closely linked.

To explain the coexistence of these multiple forms of political authority in the Qing, it is first worth recognizing that the Aisin Gioro family was not unique in its endorsement of multiple types of political power. Certainly, the prominence and pervasiveness of nonbanner power, especially that held by examination graduates, went beyond that of nonservice elites in other states of the time. But both the Ottoman and Russian states recognized the authority of religious figures who were not members of the service elite to govern particular aspects of the lives of their communities. In Russia, this went beyond even the Orthodox Church, which of course wielded a great deal of influence in local life and whose priests carried out important state functions like reading laws aloud. The Orenburg Muslim Spiritual Assembly governed Muslim religious life, including such practical matters as marriage, divorce, inheritance, and the licensing of religious practitioners in addition to questions of religious doctrine, on behalf of the Russian state. Its staff were not members of the service elite but Muslim clerics.[47] The Ottoman state organized three non-Muslim *millets* for the Greek Orthodox, Armenian, and Jewish communities, each of which handled many matters of daily life internally, even including issues of state-society relations like tax collection.[48] As in Russia, this meant a form of political authority for people outside the service elite. In Japan, where religion was less important as an identity marker, analogous institutions existed within nonsamurai status groups. Village headmen and outcaste leaders managed many of the affairs of their communities. For instance, Danzaemon, the leader of the *eta* outcastes of the area around Edo, ran his own judicial affairs and controlled his own jail.[49]

The common thread in these comparative examples is that states that relied on a service elite to carry out bureaucratic and judicial functions on behalf of the ruling dynasty still allowed a degree of community self-governance conducted by people who were not part of the service elite. The diversity of forms of political power in the Qing empire can be understood in a similar way. The Qing state recognized that preexisting forms of local authority carried a great deal of legitimacy in the territories that it conquered. So, rather than eliminating those forms, it attempted to coopt them and largely succeeded at doing so. But one of the societies that it conquered, Ming China, was far, far larger than the Qing empire itself had been prior to that conquest. Had the banner system merely coexisted with groups like the *jasaghs*, lamas, *tusi*, and the Muslim *begs* of southern Xinjiang, this system would have been unremarkable compared to that of other contemporary service elite–based states. But because Ming China made up the vast majority of the empire's population, and because the Chinese administrative system became a model for the nascent Qing empire in developing its own bureaucracy, China's traditional system of administration was far more integral to the Qing state than was any other local system.

Yet the political system of the Qing empire as a whole was still based around the service elite. Han commoner administrators dominated only one portion of the bureaucracy—local administration in the former territory of the Ming. They played no role in the local or regional administration of the rest of the empire's territory, at least prior to the late nineteenth century, with all positions of power held either by the traditional local elites of Inner Asia or by bannermen. Despite their vastly lower population, and even ignoring officer posts within the banners themselves, which were held only by bannermen, bannermen were at least on par with Han commoners in terms of controlling the most powerful posts in the central administration. And they dominated the middle and bottom-ranking posts in Beijing, meaning that the actual functioning of the central state depended on the efforts of bannermen.[50] Our classic vision of the Qing bureaucrat may be the county magistrate, and the importance of his role cannot be denied. But to suggest that the Qing state was governed primarily by the gentry-literati is to assume that local administration in China proper was all that mattered. The empire, and the dynasty that ruled it, relied above all on its service elite—the Eight Banners—and the loyal service that they offered in exchange for their privileged status.

Appendix

Reign Names, Dates, and Abbreviations

CD: Chongde 崇德 (1636–1643)
DG: Daoguang 道光 (1821–1850)
GX: Guangxu 光緒 (1875–1908)
JQ: Jiaqing 嘉慶 (1796–1820)
KX: Kangxi 康熙 (1662–1722)
QL: Qianlong 乾隆 (1736–1795)
SZ: Shunzhi 順治 (1644–1661)
TC: Tiancong 天聰 (1627–1635)
TZ: Tongzhi 同治 (1862–1874)
XF: Xianfeng 咸豐 (1851–1861)
XT: Xuantong 宣統 (1909–1911)
YZ: Yongzheng 雍正 (1723–1735)

Source Abbreviations

Documents

DQHD: *Da Qing huidian* 大清會典. See Bibliography.

DQHDSL: *Da Qing huidian shili* 大清會典事例 (*Precedents of the Administrative Code of the Qing Dynasty*). 1899. Accessed via *Legalizing Space in China*. Institut d'Asie Orientale. Lyon, France. https://lsc.chineselegalculture.org/eC/HDSLXB/.

DQLL: *Da Qing lüli* 大清律例 (*Great Qing Code*). 1740. Accessed via *Legalizing Space in China*. Institut d'Asie Orientale. Lyon, France. https://lsc.chineselegalculture.org/eC/DQLL_1740/.

GZSL: *Gaozong Chun huangdi shilu* 高宗純皇帝實錄 (*Veritable Records of the Qianlong Emperor*). See QSL.

HKTB: *Huke tiben* 戶科題本 (Routine memorial of the Board of Revenue, bilingual).

HWCG: *Hanwen chenggao* 漢文呈稿 (Chinese-language draft petition).

HWLFZZ: *Hanwen lufu zouzhe* 漢文錄副奏折 (Chinese-language palace memorial, Grand Council copy).

HWZPZZ: *Hanwen zhupi zouzhe* 漢文硃批奏摺 (Chinese-language vermillion-rescripted palace memorial).

HWZW: *Hanwen ziwen* 漢文咨文 (Chinese-language lateral communication).

HWZZ: *Hanwen zouzhe* 漢文奏折 (Chinese-language memorial).

KXCMWZPZZ: *Kangxi chao manwen zhupi zouzhe quanyi* 康熙朝滿文朱批奏折全译. See Bibliography.

MHHBLFZZ: *Man-Han hebi lufu zouzhe* 滿漢合璧錄副奏摺 (Manchu-Chinese bilingual palace memorial, Grand Council copy).

MHHBZPZZ: *Man-Han hebi zhupi zouzhe* 滿漢合璧硃批奏摺 (Manchu-Chinese bilingual vermillion-rescripted palace memorial).

MWCW: *Manwen chengwen* 滿文呈文 (Manchu-language petition).

MWHKTB: *Manwen huke tiben* 滿文戶科題本 (Manchu-language routine memorial of the Board of Revenue).

MWJXSY: *Manwen jixin shangyu* 滿文寄信上諭 (Manchu-language court letter—a nonpublic edict).

MWLFZZ: *Manwen lufu zouzhe* 滿文錄副奏摺 (Manchu-language palace memorial, Grand Council copy).

MWMFSY: *Manwen mingfa shangyu* 滿文明發上諭 (Manchu-language edicts publicly issued through the Grand Secretariat).

MWZPZZ: *Manwen zhupi zouzhe* 滿文硃批奏摺 (Manchu-language, vermillion-rescripted palace memorial).

QDBQTZ: *Qinding baqi tongzhi* 欽定八旗通志. See Bibliography.

RZSL: *Renzong Rui huangdi shilu* 仁宗睿皇帝實錄 (*Veritable Records of the Jiaqing Emperor*). See QSL.

SYBQ: *Shangyu baqi* 上諭八旗 (*Imperial Edicts to the Eight Banners*). HYL version. Available digitally at https://iiif.lib.harvard.edu/manifests/view/drs:44313381$1i.

SZRSL: *Shengzu Ren huangdi shilu* 聖祖仁皇帝實錄 (*Veritable Records of the Kangxi Emperor*). See QSL.

SZXSL: *Shizong Xian huangdi shilu* 世宗憲皇帝實錄 (*Veritable Records of the Yongzheng Emperor*). See QSL.

SZZPYZ: *Shizong Xian huangdi zhupi yuzhi* 世宗憲皇帝硃批諭旨. See Bibliography.

SZZSL: *Shizu Zhang huangdi shilu* 世祖章皇帝實錄 (*Veritable Records of the Shunzhi Emperor*). See QSL.

TZWSL: *Taizong Wen huangdi shilu* 太宗文皇帝實錄 (*Veritable Records of the Reign of Hong Taiji*). See QSL.

XKTB: *Xingke tiben* 刑科題本 (Routine memorial of the Board of Punishments, bilingual).

XTZJ: *Xuantong zhengji* 宣統政紀 (*A Record of Political Affairs in the Xuantong Period*). This constitutes the *Veritable Records* of the Xuantong period. See QSL.

XZSL: *Xuanzong Cheng huangdi shilu* 宣宗成皇帝實錄 (*Veritable Records of the Daoguang Emperor*). See QSL.

YZBQSY: *Yongzheng baqi shengyu* 雍正八旗聖諭 (*Imperial Edicts to the Eight Banners Issued by the Yongzheng Emperor*). Manchu edition titled *Dergi hese jakūn gūsade wasimbuhangge* (Imperial Edicts Issued to the Eight Banners). HYL version.

YZCMWZPZZ: *Yongzheng chao manwen zhupi zouzhe quanyi* 雍正朝滿文朱批奏折全译. See Bibliography.

ZHMGSDAZL: *Zhonghua minguo shi dang'an ziliao huibian* 中华民国史档案资料汇编. See Bibliography.

Archives and Databases

FHA: First Historical Archives 中国第一历史档案馆, Beijing.

HYL: Harvard-Yenching Library, Rare Books Room, Cambridge, MA.

MQNAF: Ming-Qing Archives Name Authority File 人名權威資料查詢, Institute of History and Philology of Academia Sinica, Taipei. https://newarchive.ihp.sinica.edu.tw/sncaccgi/sncacFtp?@@1204518815.

NGDK: Archives of the Grand Secretariat 內閣大庫檔案, maintained by the Institute of History and Philology of Academia Sinica, Taipei. https://newarchive.ihp.sinica.edu.tw/mcttp/.

NPM: National Palace Museum 國立故宮博物院, Taipei. Accessed on site in Taipei, but archival materials now also available digitally at https://qingarchives.npm.edu.tw/.

QSG: *Qing shi gao* 清史稿 (Draft History of the Qing). Chief Editor Zhao Erxun 趙爾巽. Accessed via Scripta Sinica.

QSL: *Qing shilu* 清實錄 (*Veritable Records of the Qing Dynasty*), cited by reign (see abbreviations in the list of document abbreviations above). Accessed via Scripta Sinica.

Scripta Sinica database 漢籍全文資料庫, maintained by the Institute of History and Philology of Academia Sinica, Taipei. http://hanchi.ihp.sinica.edu.tw/.

SYD: *Shangyu dang* 上諭檔 (Archive of Imperial Edicts). Accessed at FHA.

Notes

Introduction

1. See, perhaps most famously, Zou Rong, *The Revolutionary Army: A Chinese Nationalist Tract of 1903*, trans. John Lust (The Hague: Mouton, 1968).
2. The dominance of this narrative in recent Anglophone historiography is apparent in its appearance in recent textbooks. See, for example, R. Keith Schoppa, *Revolution and Its Past: Identities and Change in Modern Chinese History*, 3rd ed. (New York: Routledge, 2016), 25–29.
3. For the idea that the "New Qing History," a (sometimes controversial) term that has often been applied to the study of the banners, among other topics, since the 1990s (particularly in reference to work in Anglophone academia), takes "a comparative approach to understanding the Qing empire" as one of its central tasks, see Mark Elliott, "Frontier Stories: Periphery as Center in Qing History," *Frontiers of History in China* 9, no. 3 (2014): 347.
4. On the rise of the Jin state and the formation of the banners, see Frederic Wakeman, Jr., *The Great Enterprise: The Manchu Reconstruction of Order in Seventeenth-Century China* (Berkeley: University of California Press, 1985), 49–66; and Mark C. Elliott, *The Manchu Way: The Eight Banners and Ethnic Identity in Late Imperial China* (Stanford, CA: Stanford University Press, 2001), 52–63.
5. On the 1625 revolt, see Wakeman, *The Great Enterprise*, 72–74.
6. The former name appears, for instance, in TZWSL, *juan* 14, TC 7.6.19 (July 24, 1633), and the latter in TZWSL, *juan* 18, TC 8.5.5 (May 31, 1634).
7. Elliott, *The Manchu Way*, 76–77. The invention of the name "Hanjun" appears in TZWSL, *juan* 18, TC 8.5.5 (May 31, 1634).

8. Kenneth M. Swope, *The Military Collapse of China's Ming Dynasty, 1618–44* (London: Routledge, 2014), 91–95, describes the role of Han troops and the cannons that they produced and operated in the siege of Dalinghe. The role of Han-operated cannons in the invasion of Korea is clear in a number of sources, such as TZWSL, *juan* 32, CD 1.12.26 (January 21, 1637). On the importance of artillery and new Dutch-style cannons to the creation of the Hanjun, see Huang Yi-Long 黄一农, "Dutch Cannons and the Eight Banner Hanjun Established by Hong Taiji" 红夷大炮与皇太极创立的八旗汉军, *Lishi yanjiu* 2004, no. 4: 74–105.
9. TZWSL, *juan* 37, CD 2.7.29 (September 17, 1637).
10. TZWSL, *juan* 47, CD 4.6.10 (July 10, 1639). For the connection between the attack on Songshan and this division of the Hanjun banners, see Huang, "Dutch Cannons and the Eight Banner Hanjun," 88.
11. Elliott, *The Manchu Way*, 77, describes the transfer of companies from the Manchu banners. The order to divide the Hanjun into eight banners appears in TZWSL, *juan* 61, CD 7.6.6 (July 2, 1642).
12. Bahana 巴哈納, MWHKTB, FHA 02-02-006-000400-027, SZ 11.10.21 (November 29, 1654). These numbers remained stable through the mid-eighteenth century, as shown in Mark C. Elliott, Cameron D. Campbell, and James Z. Lee, "A Demographic Estimate of the Population of the Qing Eight Banners," *Études chinoises* 35, no. 1 (2016): 24.
13. The population estimate of 500,000 is justified in Elliott, *The Manchu Way*, 118.
14. Elliott, *The Manchu Way*, 192–194.
15. Elliott, *The Manchu Way*, 194–197, 316–318.
16. See, for example, Benjamin A. Elman, *A Cultural History of Civil Examinations in Late Imperial China* (Berkeley: University of California Press, 2000), xviii–xix, 240–247.
17. Lawrence Zhang, "Legacy of Success: Office Purchase and State-Elite Relations in Qing China," *Harvard Journal of Asiatic Studies* 73, no. 2 (December 2013): 259–297.
18. James A. Millward, *Eurasian Crossroads: A History of Xinjiang* (New York: Columbia University Press, 2007), gives a sense of the wide range of forms of administration existing in Xinjiang alone. John Herman, "The Cant of Conquest: Tusi Offices and China's Political Incorporation of the Southwest Frontier," in *Empire at the Margins: Culture, Ethnicity, and Frontier in Early Modern China*, ed. Pamela Kyle Crossley, Helen F. Siu, and Donald S. Sutton (Berkeley: University of California Press, 2006), explains the *tusi* system of the southwest, which developed during the Ming era.
19. Numbers based on an analysis of Narakino Shimesu 楢木野宣, *Research on Important Officials in the Qing Dynasty: With Full Details on the Joint Usage of*

Manchus and Han 清代重要職官の研究：滿漢併用の全貌 (Tokyo: Kazama shobō, 1975). Pages 64–81 discuss governors-general, pages 97–114 deal with governors.

20. The Six Boards, carried over from the Ming, were the Boards of Personnel, Revenue, Rites, War, Punishments, and Works.
21. Edward J. M. Rhoads, *Manchus & Han: Ethnic Relations and Political Power in Late Qing and Early Republican China, 1861–1928* (Seattle: University of Washington Press, 2000), 45.
22. Zou, *The Revolutionary Army*.
23. It would be unfair to single out any author for this practice, which is so easy to adopt that I have certainly resorted to it myself.
24. See, for instance, the case of Donjina in David C. Porter, "Manchu Racial Identity on the Qing Frontier: Donjina and Early Twentieth-Century Ili," *Modern China* 44, no. 1 (January 2018): 3–34.
25. Although, as Pamela Crossley argues, this may not have been true in the early years of the Qing, it had certainly become the case by the early eighteenth century. Pamela Kyle Crossley, *A Translucent Mirror: History and Identity in Qing Imperial Ideology* (Berkeley: University of California Press, 1999), 98.
26. Elliott, *The Manchu Way*, 339.
27. Crossley, *A Translucent Mirror*, 107–109, 120–128.
28. Rhoads, *Manchus & Han*, 42–51.
29. For her criticism of the use of ethnicity to understand Qing history, see Crossley, *A Translucent Mirror*, 3–15; and Pamela Kyle Crossley, "Thinking About Ethnicity in Early Modern China," *Late Imperial China* 11, no. 1 (June 1990): 1–35.
30. Mark Elliott, in response to Crossley, has argued strongly in favor of ethnicity as a defining feature of the Qing social order, particularly in Mark C. Elliott, "Ethnicity in the Qing Eight Banners," in *Empire at the Margins: Culture, Ethnicity, and Frontier in Early Modern China*, ed. Pamela Kyle Crossley, Helen F. Siu, and Donald S. Sutton (Berkeley: University of California Press, 2006), 27–57.
31. For the importance of environment to Qing ideas about ethnic identity, see David A. Bello, *Across Forest, Steppe, and Mountain: Environment, Identity, and Empire in Qing China's Borderlands* (Cambridge: Cambridge University Press, 2016), 2–6.
32. For the "ethnic solidarity" formulation, see, for example, Elliott, *The Manchu Way*, 164. Even though scholars like Elliott and Crossley disagree about whether to treat Manchuness (at least before the very late Qing) as an "ethnic" identity, they, as well as other scholars of what is sometimes called the "New Qing History," have shared the assumption that understanding Qing ideas about Manchu and other analogous types of identity (especially Mongol and

Han) and state projects to define and differentiate those identities is at the core of explaining the banner system.

33. For a sense of these debates, see Mario Cams, "Recent Additions to the New Qing History Debate," *Contemporary Chinese Thought* 47, no. 1 (2016): 1–4, and the set of articles by Li Zhiting, Li Aiyong, Zhang Jian, and Yang Nianqun (translated from the Chinese) that follow it in the same issue (pp. 5–58).
34. Rhoads, *Manchus & Han*.
35. A similar formulation, according to which banner people were both privileged as the "[dynastic] basis" and restrained/controlled as "hereditary slaves," is used to describe the role of bannermen in Lu Zhijun 鹿智鈞, *Dynastic Basis and Hereditary Slaves: The Legal Status of Bannermen in Qing China* 根本與世僕：清朝旗人的法律地位 (Taipei: Xiuwei zixun keji, 2017). Lu, however, does not treat the banner model as a generalizable social formation; instead he is most interested in the relationship of the position of bannermen in law to questions of assimilation and Sinicization in "conquest dynasties" in the mid- and late-imperial periods of Chinese history.
36. See Brenda Meehan-Waters, *Autocracy and Aristocracy: The Russian Service Elite of 1730* (New Brunswick, NJ: Rutgers University Press, 1982), 1–4, which makes clear that her use of the term "service elite" applies only to the *generalitet*, "the 179 officials in the top four military and civil ranks."
37. See Pamela Kyle Crossley, "The Conquest Elite of the Ch'ing Empire," in *The Cambridge History of China*, vol. 9, part 1, ed. Willard J. Peterson (Cambridge: Cambridge University Press, 2002), 310–359; and Crossley, *A Translucent Mirror*, 285–290.
38. Crossley, "The Conquest Elite of the Ch'ing Empire," 346.
39. Crossley, *A Translucent Mirror*, 289.
40. Crossley, *A Translucent Mirror*, 287. She uses this point to make a direct analogy to the Ottoman elite, which I also endorse.
41. Jane Burbank and Frederick Cooper, *Empires in World History: Power and the Politics of Difference* (Princeton, NJ: Princeton University Press, 2010), esp. 3–17; Dominic Lieven, *Empire: The Russian Empire and Its Rivals* (New Haven, CT: Yale University Press, 2000).
42. Peter C. Perdue, "Empire and Nation in Comparative Perspective: Frontier Administration in Eighteenth-Century China," *Journal of Early Modern History* 5, no. 4 (2001): 282–288.
43. Sudipta Sen, "The New Frontiers of Manchu China and the Historiography of Asian Empires: A Review Essay," *Journal of Asian Studies* 61, no. 1 (February 2002): 172–174.
44. Pamela Kyle Crossley, *Hammer and Anvil: Nomad Rulers at the Forge of the Modern World* (Lanham, MD: Rowman & Littlefield, 2019).

1. The Qing Status System

1. This book uses the name "Board of Revenue" because it is the standard translation of this agency's name. But note that the literal meaning of its name refers to households (Ma. *boigon*, Ch. 戶 [*hu*],) and those of its functions relevant to this book are mostly tied to its role in registering households, not in administering state finances or taxation.
2. In pre-modern China, ages were counted by *sui* (歲), with children considered 1 *sui* at birth and increasing in age by 1 *sui* at each Lunar New Year (rather than on their birthday).
3. For this case, see Hešen, HWZZ, NGDK 023382, QL 46.11.4 (December 18, 1781).
4. This is true even if one sets aside the question of whether designations like "Han" or "Manchu" should be treated as ethnic categories during the Qing period (or when in the Qing period such identities became ethnic), an important question in the historiography discussed in the introduction.
5. The exact meaning of "new Manchu" is disputed, though it generally referred to Tungusic peoples who came under Qing rule later than the core "old Manchu"/Jurchen population, perhaps after 1635 or 1644. One "new Manchu" group, the Orochen, was divided into the "mounted Orochen" (Ma. *moringga Oronco*), a population enrolled in the Eight Banners, and the "pedestrian Orochen" (Ma. *yafahan Oronco*), a nonbanner, tribute-paying population, suggesting that even groups considered part of the broader Manchu family could be divided by status. See Loretta E. Kim, *Ethnic Chrysalis: China's Orochen People and the Legacy of Qing Borderland Administration* (Cambridge, MA: Harvard Asia Center, 2019), 101–104, for a discussion of the term "new Manchu"; p. 4 for the status division within the Orochen population.
6. Evelyn S. Rawski, "Economic and Social Foundations of Late Imperial Culture," in *Popular Culture in Late Imperial China*, ed. David Johnson, Andrew J. Nathan, and Evelyn S. Rawski (Berkeley: University of California Press, 1985), 8.
7. See, for example, Susan Mann, *Precious Records: Women in China's Long Eighteenth Century* (Stanford, CA: Stanford University Press, 1997), 14, for a statement of this broadly accepted view.
8. For an argument that Yongzheng's reforms were emancipatory, see Anders Hansson, *Chinese Outcasts: Discrimination and Emancipation in Late Imperial China* (Leiden, Netherlands: Brill, 1996), esp. 165–168; for the idea that they were intended to force orthodox norms of sexual morality on the entire population, see Matthew H. Sommer, *Sex, Law, and Society in Late Imperial China* (Stanford, CA: Stanford University Press, 2000), esp. 260–304.

9. Perhaps the most enthusiastic use of these categories in recent scholarship comes in Richard J. Smith, *The Qing Dynasty and Traditional Chinese Culture* (Lanham, MD: Rowman & Littlefield, 2015), 127–149. But even Smith acknowledges that the lines between these groups, "so clean and clear in theory, became increasingly difficult to draw in practice" (143).
10. See, for example, Susan Naquin and Evelyn S. Rawski, *Chinese Society in the Eighteenth Century* (New Haven, CT: Yale University Press, 1987), 116.
11. This centrality of these ideas, or ones like them, to a set of seminal works published around the turn of the millennium was crystallized in a 2004 review essay. See Joanna Waley-Cohen, "The New Qing History," *Radical History Review* 88 (Winter 2004): 196–199. The specific formulation that I have given here is based on James A. Millward, *Beyond the Pass: Economy, Ethnicity, and Empire in Qing Central Asia* (Stanford, CA: Stanford University Press, 1998), 201 (and is also cited in the Waley-Cohen article). This idea grows out of a longer tradition that recognizes the Qing emperor as playing the distinct roles of Chinese emperor and Mongol khan, as in Pamela Kyle Crossley, "The Rulerships of China," *American Historical Review* 97, no. 5 (December 1992): 1472–1475.
12. See, for example, R. Keith Schoppa, *Revolution and Its Past: Identities and Change in Modern Chinese History*, 3rd ed. (New York: Routledge, 2016), 28–39.
13. See, for example, Edwin O. Reischauer, *Japan: The Story of a Nation* (New York: Knopf, 1970), 89–90. Note that the quadripartite analysis of Japanese society was also common among people in the Edo period, despite its substantial divergence from the actual legal institutions in place at the time.
14. John W. Hall, "Rule by Status in Tokugawa Japan," *Journal of Japanese Studies* 1, no. 1 (Autumn 1974): 44–47.
15. Max Weber, *Economy and Society: An Outline of Interpretive Sociology*, ed. Guenther Roth and Claus Wittich (Berkeley: University of California Press, 1978), 215.
16. One partial exception was the clergy, which could be entered by members of other status groups; for instance, many women, including from the warrior elite, became nuns in part from a desire to acquire greater freedom of movement. See Laura Nenzi, *Excursions in Identity: Travel and the Intersection of Place, Gender, and Status in Edo Japan* (Honolulu: University of Hawai'i Press, 2008), 81–84. But membership in the clergy could also be inherited: see, for example, Amy Stanley, *Stranger in the Shogun's City: A Japanese Woman and Her World* (New York: Scribner, 2020), xx. The family discussed by Stanley had, however, initially acquired its clerical status voluntarily by giving up their role as commoner peasants.
17. Maren A. Ehlers, *Give and Take: Poverty and the Status Order in Early Modern Japan* (Cambridge, MA: Harvard Asia Center, 2018), 109–111, 125–129.

18. André Sorensen, *The Making of Edo Japan: Cities and Planning from Edo to the Twenty-First Century* (London: Routledge, 2002), 18–22. On some of the types of administration to which direct retainers of the shogun were subject, see Teruko Craig's introduction to Katsu Kokichi, *Musui's Story: The Autobiography of a Tokugawa Samurai*, trans. Teruko Craig (Tucson: University of Arizona Press, 1998), xi–xiv.
19. On Danzaemon, see Gerald Groemer, "The Creation of the Edo Outcaste Order," *Journal of Japanese Studies* 27, no. 1 (Summer 2001): 269–273. For an example of an outcaste group outside of Kantō and its system of outcaste management, see Ehlers, *Give and Take*, 86–105.
20. Daniel V. Botsman, *Punishment and Power in the Making of Modern Japan* (Princeton, NJ: Princeton University Press, 2005), 61–71.
21. However, in emulation of Qing reforms to standardize laws on sexual misbehavior, many of the status-based differences in adultery law were eliminated in 1742. See Amy Stanley, "Adultery, Punishment, and Reconciliation in Tokugawa Japan," *Journal of Japanese Studies* 33, no. 2 (Summer 2007): 314–318.
22. Botsman, *Punishment and Power*, 72.
23. Ronald P. Toby, *Engaging the Other: 'Japan' and Its Alter Egos, 1550–1850* (Leiden, Netherlands: Brill, 2019), 208–219; and Noah Y. McCormick, *Japan's Outcaste Abolition: The Struggle for National Inclusion and the Making of the Modern State* (Oxford: Routledge, 2013), 99. Note that outcastes frequently flouted the restrictions on their hairstyles to visually pass as commoners, but this behavior was denounced by Tokugawa authorities.
24. David L. Howell, *Geographies of Identity in Nineteenth-Century Japan* (Berkeley: University of California Press, 2005), 142.
25. Howell, *Geographies of Identity*, 136.
26. See Ehlers, *Give and Take*, 4–13.
27. See, for instance, the case of Ōno, described in Ehlers, *Give and Take*, 42–50.
28. It is worth noting, however, that although the state did not prevent movement among occupational groups, the substantial autonomy and right of self-governance possessed by legally recognized guilds meant that occupational groups did restrict their own memberships, allowing them to keep out newcomers and maintain monopolies on particular trades or services.
29. That said, many commoners also had distinct occupations and livelihoods. This was most true in the late Tokugawa period, which saw the development of a large amount of rural commercial and manufacturing activity. See Edward E. Pratt, *Japan's Proto-Industrial Elite: The Economic Foundations of the Gōnō* (Cambridge, MA: Harvard Asia Center, 1999). Howell, *Geographies of Identity*, 48–49, connects Pratt's account of "rich farmers" (Ja. 豪農 [*gōnō*]) to the distinction of occupation and livelihood.

30. Howell, *Geographies of Identity*, 46–66, focuses on the occupation/livelihood distinction.
31. Groemer, "The Creation of the Edo Outcaste Order." As David Howell notes, the relevant geographies of outcaste economic and social organization were often quite different from those for commoners. For instance, the hereditary outcaste headman Suzuki Jin'emon controlled twenty-five villages divided among nineteen domain lords and shogunal deputies. See Howell, *Geographies of Identity*, 37.
32. Within a household, one's legal position varied substantially in accordance with both gender and age, even though status was shared by all household members. On the intersection of gender and status, see Stanley, "Adultery, Punishment, and Reconciliation," esp. 312–313. On age as a social/legal category that intersected with status, see Gregory M. Pflugfelder, "The Nation-State, the Age/Gender System, and the Reconstitution of Erotic Desire in Nineteenth-Century Japan," *Journal of Asian Studies* 71, no. 4 (November 2012): 964–970.
33. On the legal prohibition, see Marcia Yonemoto, *The Problem of Women in Early Modern Japan* (Oakland: University of California Press, 2016), 96. For an example of adoption as a means of circumventing the prohibition, see the case of the commoner Michi Yoshino and her samurai husband, Motonaga Tamura, in Anne Walthall and M.-P. Gaviano, "Fille de paysan, épouse de samouraï: Les lettres de Michi Yoshino," *Annales: Histoire, Sciences Sociales* 54, no. 1 (1999): 70.
34. Gregory L. Freeze, "The Soslovie (Estate) Paradigm and Russian Social History," *American Historical Review* 91, no. 1 (February 1986): 11–12.
35. Michael Confino, "The 'Soslovie' (Estate) Paradigm: Reflections on Some Open Questions," *Cahiers du Monde russe* 49, no. 4 (October–December 2008): 681–699.
36. Elise K. Wirtschafter, "Social Categories in Russian Imperial History," *Cahiers du Monde russe* 50, no. 1 (January–March 2009): 231–250.
37. See Confino, "The 'Soslovie' (Estate) Paradigm," 693–695.
38. Alison K. Smith, *For the Common Good and Their Own Well-Being: Social Estates in Imperial Russia* (New York: Oxford University Press, 2014), 5–6.
39. For information on a classic estate system, see the description of the Swedish system in Harald Gustafsson, *Political Interaction in the Old Regime: Central Power and Local Society in the Eighteenth-Century Nordic States*, trans. Alan Crozier (Lund, Sweden: Studentlitteratur, 1994), 48–50.
40. Smith, *For the Common Good*, 8–9.
41. Elise Kimerling Wirtschafter, *Social Identity in Imperial Russia* (DeKalb: Northern Illinois University Press, 1997), 42–43.
42. Smith, *For the Common Good*, 17–23.

43. Wirtschafter, *Social Identity in Imperial Russia*, 53.
44. Paul W. Werth, "*Soslovie* and the 'Foreign' Clergies of Imperial Russia: Estate Rights or Service Rights?," *Cahiers du Monde russe* 51, no. 2–3 (2010): 428. But note that although non-Christian clergy shared in many of these privileges of clerical status, they were denied full membership in the status group.
45. John P. LeDonne, *Absolutism and Ruling Class: The Formation of the Russian Political Order, 1700–1825* (Oxford: Oxford University Press, 1991), 6–7; Smith, *For the Common Good*, 23–25.
46. Although late-eighteenth and early-nineteenth century reforms made mobility easier and established clearer legal procedures to govern it, Russians remained tied to a particular *soslovie* status in a particular place and required permission to change either their status or their locality of residence. See Smith, *For the Common Good*, 47–71, for the eighteenth-century situation; and 72–94 for how procedures related to *soslovie* registration were reformed.
47. Wirtschafter, *Social Identity in Imperial Russia*, 118–123.
48. Smith, *For the Common Good*, 106–112.
49. However, in many ways, merchants and townspeople were two divisions within a single, broad status group, as movement between the two categories was relatively straightforward and depended largely on wealth. Smith, *For the Common Good*, 113–117.
50. Howell, *Geographies of Identity*, 48–54.
51. Smith, *For the Common Good*, 30–31.
52. Katsu, *Musui's Story*, 77. Note that the term "bannermen" is used here to translate the Japanese term *hatamoto* 旗本, a different concept, expressed in different characters, from the Qing *qiren* 旗人.
53. Stanley, *Stranger in the Shogun's City*, 241–242.
54. Wirtschafter, *Social Identity in Imperial Russia*, 33–34.
55. Smith, *For the Common Good*, 185–191.
56. On the geography of Japanese outcaste administration, see Howell, *Geographies of Identity*, 37–38. The role of the diocese in dispensing justice, including corporal punishment, for Russian priests is discussed in Gregory L. Freeze, *The Russian Levites: Parish Clergy in the Eighteenth Century* (Cambridge, MA: Harvard University Press, 1977), 65–74.
57. On the culture of honor in Tokugawa Japan, see Eiko Ikegami, *The Taming of the Samurai: Honorific Individualism and the Making of Modern Japan* (Cambridge, MA: Harvard University Press, 1995). As Derek Offord, Vladislav Rjéoutski, and Gesine Argent have pointed out, the extent to which the Russia nobility relied on French to the exclusion of Russian is often exaggerated, and use of the language was not uniform within the noble status group; but they also agree that "francophonie was indeed a means of social differentiation, insofar as it served as a marker of nobility." Derek Offord, Vladislav Rjéoutski, and Gesine Argent,

The French Language in Russia: A Social, Political, Cultural, and Literary History (Amsterdam: Amsterdam University Press, 2018), 42.

58. The ability to maintain an ethnic identity can, of course, also depend on whether an ethnic category is state-recognized in, for example, census categories. But states usually claim to identify ethnic categories as features of the underlying social order rather than self-consciously creating them and so, in practice, officially-recognized ethnic categories usually persist through changes in political regime. This remains true even when the state is quite clearly engaged in a practice of constructing ethnic identity. For a clear example of this phenomenon, see Thomas S. Mullaney, *Coming to Terms with the Nation: Ethnic Classification in Modern China* (Berkeley: University of California Press, 2011), especially the table on page 66 that shows clear continuities in the identification of ethnic groups across the Republican and PRC eras (and dating back to European ethnological research of the late Qing).

    Whether early Soviet-era identity categories like kulak (the upper stratum of the peasantry in Bolshevik discourse) can be described as status categories, in spite of their basis in ideas about class, is outside the scope of this book. But the idea that they were certainly seems plausible.

59. That said, the persistence of outcaste identity was uneven, many outcastes did successfully leave that identity behind, and current identification as a *burakumin* is not necessarily linked to descent from Edo-era outcastes. See Timothy D. Amos, *Embodying Difference: The Making of Burakumin in Modern Japan* (Honolulu: University of Hawai'i Press, 2011), 9–14, 46–53.

60. Yonglin Jiang, *The Great Ming Code: Da Ming lü* (Seattle: University of Washington Press, 2005), 70–71. I have lightly modified Jiang's translation. For the Qing version of the statute and its various substatutes, see *DQLL*, "Lü 76: Households Should Be Established According to the Registers" 律76: 人戶以籍爲定. https://lsc.chineselegalculture.org/eC/DQLL_1740/5.3.1.76.

61. Michael Szonyi, *The Art of Being Governed: Everyday Politics in Late Imperial China* (Princeton, NJ: Princeton University Press, 2017), 40–41.

62. Laibao 來保, XKTB, FHA 02-01-07-0087-007, QL 3.10.25 (December 6, 1738).

63. There was meaningful physical separation between the living spaces of the two groups, as banner garrisons were physically separated from the rest of the city where they were located, and often, as in Xi'an, marked off by walls. But jurisdiction over a crime did not depend on which physical space it happened in, but on who was involved. Banner people who committed a crime in Xianning County but outside the walls of the garrison remained subject to banner authorities. Commoners who entered the garrison to misbehave remained subject to county authorities. In cases that involved both a banner person and a commoner (whether perpetrator or victim), a special joint procedure was

necessary. On the history of the institution responsible for adjudicating cases involving both banner people and commoners, see Ding Yizhuang 定宜庄, "A Brief Examination of Qing Judicial Subprefects" 清代理事同知考略, in *A Collection of Scholarly Essays Celebrating the Eightieth Birthday of Wang Zhonghan* 庆祝王钟翰先生八十寿辰学术论文集, ed. Wei Qingyuan 韦庆远, et al. (Shenyang, China: Liaoning daxue chubanshe, 1993), 263–274.

64. Fucang 福昌, MWLFZZ, FHA 03-0195-3443-003, QL 58.7.29 (September 4, 1793).
65. Leping, *Muwa gisun*, n.d. (unpublished manuscript at HYL), 1a. This text is introduced in Devin Fitzgerald, "Manchu Language Pedagogical Practices: The Connections Between Manuscript and Printed Books," *Saksaha* 17 (2021): 20–23.
66. Others have also applied the idea of the "father and mother official" to the position of company captain. See, for instance, Kicengge 承志, "On the Origin and Classification of Eight Banner Niru" 八旗ニルの根源とニル分類について, *Tōyōshi kenkyū* 65, no. 1 (2006): 202.
67. An important reason for this requirement was to ensure that banner girls met their obligation to participate in the draft of palace women, a topic that will be discussed at length in chapter 5.
68. Mark C. Elliott, *The Manchu Way: The Eight Banners and Ethnic Identity in Late Imperial China* (Stanford, CA: Stanford University Press, 2001), 135.
69. On the *baojia* system, see Tong Lam, *A Passion for Facts: Social Surveys and the Construction of the Chinese Nation State, 1900–1949* (Berkeley: University of California Press, 2011), 60–63.
70. Li Wei 李衛, XKTB, FHA 02-01-07-14059-007, QL 2.8.24 (September 18, 1737).
71. On banner censuses, see Lam, *A Passion for Facts*, 54–57.
72. On banner zones, agricultural territory set aside for banner people in the vicinity of northeastern garrisons, see Christopher Mills Isett, *State, Peasant, and Merchant in Qing Manchuria, 1644–1862* (Stanford, CA: Stanford University Press, 2007), 62–64.
73. Sengboo 僧保, MWZPZZ, FHA 04-02-002-000628-0003, QL 39.12.26 (January 27, 1775).
74. James A. Millward, *Eurasian Crossroads: A History of Xinjiang* (New York: Columbia University Press, 2007), 100–101.
75. On the different treatment in law of banner people and commoners as a form of legal pluralism, see Pär Kristoffer Cassel, *Grounds of Judgment: Extraterritoriality and Imperial Power in Nineteenth-Century China and Japan* (Oxford: Oxford University Press, 2012), 20–22.
76. The cangue was a large wooden board locked around the neck, which a convict would be sentenced to wear for a period usually tallied in months rather

than years. The cangue was quite heavy and large enough that people wearing it could not reach their mouths to feed themselves and so would rely on the assistance of family until their sentence expired. On commutations of criminal sentences for banner people, see Elliott, *The Manchu Way*, 197–200.

77. DQLL, "*Lü* 378: Gambling" 律378: 賭博. https://lsc.chineselegalculture.org/eC/DQLL_1740/5.6.12.378.
78. Coociowan 朝銓, MWLFZZ, FHA 03-0179-1926-031, QL 27.2.19 (March 14, 1762). The official requested the implementation of a three-strike system under which third-time offenders would no longer be allowed to have their sentences commuted. Although the proposal was referred to the Board of Punishments for discussion, it does not appear to have been implemented.
79. Dorothea Heuschert, "Legal Pluralism in the Qing Empire: Manchu Legislation for the Mongols," *International History Review* 20, no. 2 (June 1998): 310–324.
80. Frédéric Constant, "The Legal Administration of Qing Mongolia," *Late Imperial China* 40, no. 1 (June 2019): 158.
81. Heuschert, "Legal Pluralism in the Qing Empire," 317–320.
82. Millward, *Beyond the Pass*, 121–122.
83. That the nonbanner Mongols of Qing Mongolia constituted a status category analogous to that of commoners or banner people is a core idea of Wei-chieh Tsai, "Mongolization of Han Chinese and Manchu Settlers in Qing Mongolia, 1700–1911" (PhD dissertation, Indiana University, 2017).
84. The idea was that their ethnic background made them naturally more adept at such work, and thus that they were more capable of leaving the banners than were Manchus. The implication was thus that work in "agriculture, craftsmanship, business, and commerce" (Ch. 農工商賈 [*nong gong shang gu*]) was part of being a commoner rather than a banner person. See Sun Jiagan 孫嘉淦, HWLFZZ, FHA 03-0523-010, QL 7.2.24 (March 30, 1742).
85. This division was in part a result of the late Ming "Single Whip Reform," which aimed to replace corvée requirements with a single tax paid in silver. Siyen Fei, "'We Must Be Taxed': A Case of Populist Urban Fiscal Reform in Ming Nanjing (1368–1644)," *Late Imperial China* 28, no. 2 (December 2007): 20.
86. Wenfu 文孚, HWLFZZ, FHA 03-2520-017, DG 2.2.7 (February 28, 1822).
87. Elena Suet-Ying Chiu, *Bannermen Tales (Zidishu): Manchu Storytelling and Cultural Hybridity in the Qing Dynasty* (Cambridge, MA: Harvard Asia Center, 2018), 36–38.
88. Shuang Chen, *State-Sponsored Inequality: The Banner System and Social Stratification in Northeast China* (Stanford, CA: Stanford University Press, 2017), 34–39.
89. Chen, *State-Sponsored Inequality*, 92–95.
90. For example, see Bolin 伯麟, HWLFZZ, FHA 03-2843-027, DG 1.10.16 (November 10, 1821).

91. Imperial Household Department 總管內務府, *Zongguan neiwufu*, HWZZ, FHA 05-0016-030, QL 2.10.25 (December 16, 1737).
92. The documentation on this case did not provide an exact year, perhaps because it was so long ago that no one remembered.
93. Yongwei 永瑋, MHHBZPZZ, FHA 04-01-01-0423-001, QL 52.8.24 (October 5, 1787).
94. Yongrong 永瑢, HWZZ, FHA 05-0417-021, QL 53.11.6 (December 3, 1788).
95. The fact that ethnic difference was understood to exist naturally outside its reification in officially created categories is clear from the near-constant scholarly and administrative efforts to study and investigate it, as described in, for instance, Laura Hostetler, *Qing Colonial Enterprise: Ethnography and Cartography in Early Modern China* (Chicago: University of Chicago Press, 2001).
96. SZRSL, *juan* 31, KX 8.11.5 (November 27, 1669).
97. SZRSL, *juan* 118, KX 23.2.13 (March 28, 1684).
98. Xing Hang, *Conflict and Commerce in Maritime East Asia: The Zheng Family and the Shaping of the Modern World, c. 1620–1720* (Cambridge: Cambridge University Press, 2015), 238–240.
99. Cheng-Heng Lu 盧正恆, "Banner and Commoner: A Study of the Banner Zheng Clan and the Quanzhou Zheng Lineage of the Qing Dynasty" 旗與民：清代旗人鄭氏家族與泉州鄭氏宗族初探, *Jifeng Yazhou yanjiu* 2, no. 1 (April 2016): 115–151.
100. SYD, JQ 2.9.24 (November 12, 1797).
101. For a description of Sun Shiyi's life and career, which also mentions his connection to Hešen, see Iona D. Man-Cheong, *The Class of 1761: Examinations, State, and Elite in Eighteenth-Century China* (Stanford, CA: Stanford University Press, 2004), 180–195. The edict stripping Sun Jun of banner status can be found in RZSL, *juan* 163, JQ 11.6.17 (August 1, 1806).
102. Frederic Wakeman Jr., *The Great Enterprise: The Manchu Reconstruction of Order in Seventeenth-Century China* (Berkeley: University of California Press, 1985), 894–896. For a table listing the various banner lords in the preconquest period, see Macabe Keliher, *The Board of Rites and the Making of Qing China* (Oakland: University of California Press, 2019), 208.
103. Liu Xiaomeng 刘小萌, *Qing Dynasty Banner Society* 清代北京旗人社会 (Beijing: Zhongguo shehui kexue chubanshe, 2008), 45–49.
104. There were also eight Chahar banners, although these can perhaps be seen as subordinate to the Mongol banners, with which they shared commanders. See Da-li-zha-bu 达力扎布, "A Brief Examination of the Question of the Early Qing Establishment of the Chahar Banners" 清初察哈尔设旗问题考略, *Nei Menggu daxue xuebao* 31, no. 1 (January 1999): 38–44.
105. Elliott, "Ethnicity in the Qing Eight Banners," 36.

106. On institutionalized discrepancies in the treatment of Manchus and Mongols on the one hand and Hanjun on the other, see Ura Ren'ichi 浦廉一, "Regarding the Hanjun (Ujen Cooha)" 漢軍（烏真超哈）に就いて, in *Essay Collection on Oriental History in Honor of the Sixtieth Birthday of Dr. Kuwabara* 桑原博士還歷記念東洋史論叢 (Kyoto: Kōbundō Shōbō, 1931), 836, 848; and David C. Porter, "Ethnic and Status Identity in Qing China: The Hanjun Eight Banners" (PhD dissertation, Harvard University, 2018), 54–56. The expulsion of the Hanjun will be explored at length in chapters 7 and 8 of this book.
107. Analogous companies existed in the Lower Five Banners as well, but they were never institutionally separated out from the rest of the banner system as were those of the Upper Three Banners through their placement within the Imperial Household Department. See Elliott, *The Manchu Way*, 81–84.
108. Preston M. Torbert, *The Ch'ing Imperial Household Department: A Study of Its Organization and Principal Functions, 1662–1796* (Cambridge, MA: Harvard Asia Center, 1977), 25–26.
109. Jonathan D. Spence, *Ts'ao Yin and the K'ang-hsi Emperor: Bondservant and Master* (New Haven, CT: Yale University Press, 1966). On the origin of the bondservant banners and their replacement of the role of eunuchs, see 1–17; on Cao Yin's role as informant, see 213–254. Cao Yin's lasting claim to fame is as grandfather of Cao Xueqin 曹雪芹, author of the great Qing novel *The Dream of the Red Chamber*, which tells the story of a fictional family closely based on Cao's own.
110. Yulian Wu, *Luxurious Networks: Salt Merchants, Status, and Statecraft in Eighteenth-Century China* (Stanford, CA: Stanford University Press, 2017), 40–43.
111. Isett, *State, Peasant, and Merchant*, 44–50.
112. Chang-lin 長麟, XKTB, FHA 02-01-07-09109-015, JQ 10.8.19 (October 11, 1805).
113. Jangge, MWLFZZ, FHA 03-0172-0793-001, YZ 10.4.22 (May 16, 1732).
114. Elliott, *The Manchu Way*, 191–197.
115. Pamela Kyle Crossley, *Orphan Warriors: Three Manchu Generations and the End of the Qing World* (Princeton, NJ: Princeton University Press, 1990), 6–7, 56–57.
116. Chen, *State-Sponsored Inequality*, 68–69.
117. The other major group consisted of people illegally adopted by bannermen, although in many cases such people were also descended from slave families, who, due to their place in banner households, were an obvious source of potential adoptees for banner families seeking to carry on the family line.
118. In 1720, there were 239,494 fighting-age men (Ch. 男丁 [*nanding*]) listed as "Han household slaves of Manchus and Mongols" in the banner census. By 1887, that number had dropped by nearly 90 percent, to 27,172, even as the total number of nonslave *nanding* grew from 454,989 to 482,176 (about a 6 percent increase). See An Shuangcheng 安双成, "A Simple Analysis of the Number

of Military-Age Men in the Eight Banners during the Shunzhi, Kangxi, and Yongzheng Periods" 顺康雍三朝八旗丁额浅析, *Lishi dang'an* 1983, no. 2 (July 1983): 100–103 for the 1720 numbers and *DQHD* (1899), *juan* 19, 21b–22a for the 1887 numbers.

119. Elliott, *The Manchu Way*, 227–230.
120. Indeed, in the case that produced the precedent, the dispute centered around the son of a freed slave, who hadn't even been born at the time that his father was freed, fifty years before the case came to the attention of the state. The son of the owner who had freed the family was trying to reassert ownership over the family, but the officials dealing with the case suspected that his motives were not legitimate. See Yunxiang 允祥, HWZPZZ, FHA 04-01-30-0083-025, YZ 3.2.24 (April 6, 1725).
121. The term "entailed," applied to the first type of household, follows the usage of Mark Elliott, as does the term "secondary status" itself. See Elliott, *The Manchu Way*, 323.
122. Such adoptions were still illegal, but a person adopted in this fashion who had served with merit and voluntarily reported the situation could be pardoned and remain in a salaried post. See Bodi 博第, MWLFZZ, FHA 03-0174-1496-001, QL 8.6.22 (August 11, 1743).
123. DQHDSL, "*Lü* 84: Households Should Be Established According to the Registers" 律84人戶以籍爲定, 條例 *tiaoli* 19. http://lsc.chineselegalculture.org/eC/HDSLXB/2.3.1.84.0.19.

2. Who Belonged in the Banners? The Makeup of the Qing Service Elite

1. The conclusion of this process is described in Pei Huang, *Autocracy at Work: A Study of the Yung-cheng Period, 1722–1735* (Bloomington: Indiana University Press, 1974), 168–180, although Huang mischaracterizes the banners as clearly in decline and ignores the extent to which the Yongzheng emperor's reforms continued a process that began as early as the reign of Hong Taiji.
2. Frederic Wakeman Jr., *The Great Enterprise: The Manchu Reconstruction of Order in Seventeenth-Century China* (Berkeley: University of California Press, 1985), 63.
3. One presumes that all these men were members of the prominent Li clan of Tieling, mentioned in Kenneth M. Swope, *The Military Collapse of China's Ming Dynasty, 1618–44* (London: Routledge, 2014), 24.
4. The biographies of Li Sizhong and Li Yinzu are found in QSG, *juan* 231.
5. Gadahūn, HKTB, FHA 02-01-02-2129-010, SZ 10.2.20 (March 19, 1653).
6. On the unsuccessful siege of Jinzhou, see Swope, *The Military Collapse of China's Ming Dynasty*, 67–68.

7. The Chinese term for banner companies was the same as that used for their captains, although in the early Qing, the term 牛錄 (*niulu*), a transliteration of the Manchu *niru*, was generally used, rather than the later standard *zuoling*.
8. Ceke, HKTB, FHA 02-01-02-2129-016, SZ 10.5.27 (June 22, 1653).
9. Although agnatic relations were certainly of much greater ritual (and likely practical) importance than cognatic ones in late imperial China, families often maintained close ties to relations through the female line and relied on them for support. See, for example, Susan Mann, *The Talented Women of the Zhang Family* (Berkeley: University of California Press, 2007). This may help explain why Li Ruilong was enrolled in the banners with no more difficulty than Li Guangzu.
10. The number of bondservants and banner slaves, who were also majority Han, increased similarly rapidly, by about 4 percent. The Manchu population decreased negligibly, by about 0.3 percent, while the Mongol population fell 3.1 percent. See Bahana 巴哈納, MWHKTB, FHA 02-02-006-000400-0027, SZ 11.10.21 (November 29, 1654).
11. Gertraude Roth-Li, "State Building Before 1644," in *The Cambridge History of China*, vol. 9, part 1, ed. Willard J. Peterson (Cambridge: Cambridge University Press, 2002), 36.
12. Roth-Li, "State Building Before 1644," 47.
13. At the time of its creation, the Lifan yuan was called the "Mongol Yamen" (Ma. *Monggo yamun*, Ch. 蒙古衙門 [*Menggu yamen*]), reflecting the fact that its primary role was to handle relations with the Qing state's Mongol allies.
14. Da-li-zha-bu 达力扎布, "A Brief Examination of the Question of the Early Qing Establishment of the Chahar Banners" 清初察哈尔设旗问题考略, *Nei Menggu daxue xuebao* 31, no. 1 (January 1999): 38–44.
15. The original three defectors were Wu Sangui, Geng Zhongming, and Shang Kexi. By the outbreak of the rebellion, Shang Kexi had been succeeded by his son Shang Zhixin, and Geng Zhongming by his grandson, Geng Jingzhong.
16. Sinju 新柱, ed., *Fuzhou Garrison Gazetteer* 福州駐防志, compiled 1744 (Fuzhou), reprinted in *Fujian Province National Minority Ancient Book Series: Manchu Volume* 福建省少数民族古籍丛书: 满族卷 (Beijing: Minzu chubanshe, 2004), 27.
17. Yang Yingju 楊應琚, HWZPZZ, NPM 403009753, QL 20.6.21 (July 29, 1755).
18. Cangšan 長善, ed., *Gazetteer for the Eight Banners Garrisoned in Canton* 駐粵八旗志 (Guangzhou, 1884; reprinted Taipei: Wenhai chubanshe, 1997), *juan* 14, 1a.
19. TZWSL, *juan* 62, CD 7.8.27 (September 20, 1642).
20. For an example of the division of Shang Kexi's (the father of Shang Zhixin) army into *niru* and the use of banner titles within it, see SZZSL, *juan* 104, SZ 13.11.8 (December 23, 1656).

21. Li Yanguang 李燕光, "Eight Banner Hanjun in the Qing" 清代的八旗汉军, *Manxue yanjiu* 1992: 94. Li also notes that after the revolt was put down, Wu's troops were assigned to work in post stations in North China and Manchuria rather than being entered into the banners as the troops of Shang and Geng were.
22. For an example of the three former Ming commanders being listed separately from banner commanders, see SZZSL, *juan* 10, SZ 1.10.13 (November 11, 1644), in which an edict is issued to Kong, Geng, Shang, another Ming defector named Shen Zhixiang 沈志祥, and the second son of the Korean king, named Yi Ho 李淏, as well as the "Manchu, Mongol, and Hanjun banner commanders and lieutenant commanders," a group that was clearly different from the defectors. For an example of the troops of the defectors being treated separately, see SZZSL, *juan* 4, SZ 1.4.9 (May 14, 1644), in which the Qing army sets out for Beijing, with its components listed as "two of every three Manchu and Mongol soldiers, as well as the soldiers of the Hanjun, the three princes including the Gongshun Prince [Kong Youde], and the Xushun Duke [Shen Zhixiang]."
23. Li, "Eight Banner Hanjun in the Qing," 94.
24. Sinju, *Fuzhou Garrison Gazetteer*, 19.
25. In support of this latter stance, the Kangxi emperor declared that the troops of Shang Zhixin in fact belonged to his brother Shang Zhixiao 尚之孝, the imperially designated successor to their father, Shang Kexi, and so should not be mistrusted. See SZRSL, *juan* 91, KX 19.8.13 (September 5, 1680).
26. Onuma Takahiro, "250 Years History of the Turkic-Muslim Camp in Beijing," *TIAS Central Eurasian Research Series* no. 2 (2009): 29–30.
27. Onuma, "250 Years History," 31–32.
28. Onuma, "250 Years History," 33–34.
29. For the full story of the Lê entry and exit into the banners, see SYD, QL 54.11.8 (December 24, 1789); SYD, QL 54.11.10 (December 26, 1789); SYD, QL 55.1.9 (February 22, 1790); and RZSL, juan 126, JQ 9.2.13 (March 24, 1804).
30. To this list, we might add the former soldiers of Russian tsars, as reflected in the case of the Russian banner company formed in the late seventeenth century from Cossack soldiers who either voluntarily deserted to the Qing side or were captured in battle during the Qing-Russian frontier wars. See Tatiana A. Pang, "The 'Russian Company' in the Manchu Banner Organization," *Central Asiatic Journal* 43, no. 1 (1999): 132–139.
31. The only such event of comparable scale would be the addition of the former feudatory troops to the banners in 1680.
32. SYBQ, *juan* 9, YZ 9.2.30 (April 6, 1731).
33. Yinzhen 胤禛, MWMFSY, FHA 03-18-009-000001-0001, YZ 9.6.23 (July 26, 1731).

34. See, for instance, Necin 訥親, MWLFZZ, FHA 03-0171-02540-010.1, QL 11.8.30 (October 14, 1746). On their origin, see Necin, MWLFZZ, FHA03-0171-0323-004.1, QL 1.8.26 (September 30, 1736).
35. See Hosoya Yoshio 細谷良夫, "The Transformation of Eight Banner Household Registration Law in the Mid-Qing: With a Focus on *Kaihu*" 清朝中期の八旗戸籍法の変革：開戸を中心にして, *Shūkan tōyōgaku* 15 (May 1966): 51–52. As Hosoya explains later in the article, in the late Yongzheng and Qianlong periods, the term *kaihu* came to be applied mostly to a different group of people: banner slaves who bought their freedom from their masters, as well as nonbanner people adopted illegally by banner people. These latter two groups were members of what Mark Elliott has called "entailed households" in Mark C. Elliott, *The Manchu Way: The Eight Banners and Ethnic Identity in Late Imperial China* (Stanford, CA: Stanford University Press, 2001), 323.
36. Peter C. Perdue, *China Marches West: The Qing Conquest of Central Eurasia* (Cambridge, MA: Harvard University Press, 2005), 241, describes the resumption of Zunghar raids in 1731, as well as the request by Yue Zhongqi 岳鍾琪 for additional troops in Barköl, although he says that that request was refused. But Acengga's intention to head for Barköl is made clear in Acengga, MWLFZZ, FHA 03-0173-1112-020, YZ 9.10.25 (November 24, 1731).
37. Some of the army's difficulties appear in Acengga, MWLFZZ, FHA 03-0173-1112-020, YZ 9.10.25 (November 24, 1731), while descriptions of attempts to locate the army, as well as the attacks on Qing outposts in Aji and Biji in central Outer Mongolia, are found in Nayantai 納延泰, MWLFZZ, FHA 03-0171-1112-017, YZ 9.10.17 (November 16, 1731).
38. Marsai, MWLFZZ, FHA 03-0174-1124-003, YZ 9.10.28 (November 27, 1731).
39. Acengga, MWZPZZ, FHA 04-02-002-000165-0025, YZ 9.11.21 (December 19, 1731).
40. Sirin, MWLFZZ, FHA 03-0171-0385-015, YZ 10.6.21 (August 11, 1732). For more on Fan Yubin's role in supplying the Qing army in Mongolia and Xinjiang, see Kwangmin Kim, "Saintly Brokers: Uyghur Muslims, Trade, and the Making of Qing Central Asia, 1696–1814" (PhD dissertation, University of California at Berkeley, 2008), 372–375.
41. Yongfu 永福, MWZPZZ, FHA 04-02-002-000170-0002, YZ 10.11.18 (January 3, 1733).
42. Acengga, MWLFZZ, FHA 03-0173-1143-008, YZ 10.10.24 (December 11, 1732).
43. By "regular banner people" I refer to two categories: "standard households" (Ma. *jingkini boigon*, Ch. 正戶 [zhenghu]) and "detached households." The original differentiation between the two was that detached households were formed when standard households divided. Only one son could inherit the right to a banner post that had belonged to the original household, but the new detached

household also held the right to a salaried position for one of its adult male members. See Elliott, *The Manchu Way*, 323.

44. Yunlu 允祿, MWLFZZ, FHA 03-0174-1490-006, QL 1.7.17 (August 23, 1736).
45. Elliott, *The Manchu Way*, 192.
46. Yunlu 允祿, MWLFZZ, FHA 03-0174-1490-006, QL 1.7.17 (August 23, 1736).
47. A 1736 memorial reports the division of the Household Selected Soldiers into ethnic units as follows: "once they have achieved merit and returned, make all of them into detached households. If they are Manchu or Mongol, put them in the Manchu or Mongol banners, if they are Han, put them in the Hanjun banners." See Yunlu, MWLFZZ, FHA 03-0174-1490-006, QL 1.7.17 (August 23, 1736). As former slaves, it is likely that the vast majority were Han.
48. Yunlu, MWLFZZ, FHA 03-0174-1490-006, QL 1.7.17 (August 23, 1736).
49. Lake Khoton is referred to as *hotong hūrga*. Another archival document refers to a battle that occurred at *hotong hūrga noor* in YZ 9 (1731); see Coldo 綽勒多, MWLFZZ, FHA 03-0171-0220-002, QL 4.9.6 (October 8, 1739). Since *noor* is the Mongolian word for "lake," and the Qing fought a major battle against the Zunghars at Lake Khoton in 1731, it seems probable that this is the battle in question. There, 80 percent of the 10,000 Qing troops who fought in this battle were wiped out. See Perdue, *China Marches West*, 254. I have been unable to identify "*Usun Juil*."
50. Sanjab, MWLFZZ, FHA 03-0173-1212-017, QL 3.12.9 (January 18, 1739).
51. Agūi, MWZPZZ, FHA 04-02-001-000335-0023, QL 40.8.23 (September 17, 1775).
52. Fuk'anggan, MWZPZZ, FHA 04-02-001-000630-0002, QL 53.1.8 (February 14, 1788).
53. This is probably meant to refer to Qing-era Fengtian or Ming-era Liaodong more generally, not just to the city of Mukden (Ch. 盛京 [Shengjing], now known as Shenyang), which was the Manchu capital prior to Beijing and served as a secondary capital in the Qing period.
54. Arigūn 阿里袞, MHHBLFZZ, FHA 03-0170-0049-004, YZ 10.9.7 (October 25, 1732).
55. The decision to this effect is quoted in Fusen 傅森, MWZPZZ, NPM 412000553, YZ 13.8.27 (October 12, 1735).
56. Yunlu, MWLFZZ, FHA 03-0175-1541-015, YZ 13.9.14 (October 29, 1735).

3. Duty, Service, and Status Performance

1. Mark C. Elliott, *The Manchu Way: The Eight Banners and Ethnic Identity in Late Imperial China* (Stanford, CA: Stanford University Press, 2001), 200. Of course, this did not mean that bannermen never took on other forms of work, beneath

the radar of the state. Officially, these men were considered "idle," even if they worked quite hard in their other pursuits. See Bingyu Zheng, "The Way of the Idle Men: Leisure and Daily Life of Bannermen in Qing Beijing, 1750–1900" (PhD dissertation, Princeton University, 2018), 15–17.

2. Some posts were available only to Manchus, to bannermen of the Imperial Household Department or, for low-level posts within the banner hierarchy, to bannermen from the same garrison or the same banner. But only a relatively small subset of posts, most notably the captaincies of certain banner companies, were hereditary.
3. Pei Huang, *Autocracy at Work: A Study of the Yung-cheng Period, 1722–1735* (Bloomington: Indiana University Press, 1974), 162–184.
4. This process in general was more complicated than a one-way flow of influence from China to the Manchus. See Macabe Keliher, *The Board of Rites and the Making of Qing China* (Oakland: University of California Press, 2019).
5. See, for example, Elliott, *The Manchu Way*, 175–191.
6. For the 1654 population figures, see Bahana 巴哈納, MWHKTB, FHA 02-02-006-000400-0027, SZ 11.10.21 (November 29, 1654).
7. Nicola Di Cosmo, "Introduction," in Dzengšeo, *The Diary of a Manchu Soldier in Seventeenth-Century China*, trans. Nicola Di Cosmo (London: Routledge, 2006), 23–24.
8. On the role of artillery in the formation of the Hanjun banners, see Huang Yi-Long 黃一農, "Dutch Cannons and the Eight Banner Hanjun Established by Hong Taiji" 红夷大炮与皇太极创立的八旗汉军, *Lishi yanjiu* 2004, no 4: 74–105. For an example of such a drill in the nineteenth century, see Cao Zhenyong 曹振镛, MWLFZZ, FHA 03-0202-4063-008, DG 8.9.7 (October 15, 1828).
9. Cangšan 長善, ed., *Gazetteer for the Eight Banners Garrisoned in Canton* 駐粵八旗志 (Guangzhou, 1884; reprinted Taipei: Wenhai chubanshe, 1997), *juan* 1, 2a–5a.
10. For a statement of the negative view, see a summary in a recent encyclopedia of Chinese military history declaring that the banners "were no longer a regular army" as early as the Qianlong reign, and the banner system was replaced by the new Chinese-commanded armies of the mid-nineteenth century on account of their ineffectiveness in the First Opium War and the Taiping Rebellion; Patrick Fuliang Shan, "Banner System (1601–1912)," in *China at War: An Encyclopedia*, ed. Xiaobing Li (Santa Barbara, CA: ABC-CLIO, 2012), 18–20.
11. Mark C. Elliott, "Bannerman and Townsman: Ethnic Tension in Nineteenth-Century Jiangnan," *Late Imperial China* 11, no. 1 (June 1990): 38 (note 3).
12. Pamela Kyle Crossley, *Orphan Warriors: Three Manchu Generations and the End of the Qing World* (Princeton, NJ: Princeton University Press, 1990), 100–118.
13. Crossley, *Orphan Warriors*, 128–137.

14. Eric Schluessel, *Land of Strangers: The Civilizing Project in Qing Central Asia* (New York: Columbia University Press, 2020), 235; David C. Porter, "Manchu Racial Identity on the Qing Frontier: Donjina and Early Twentieth-Century Ili," *Late Imperial China* 44, no. 1 (January 2018): 4.
15. Porter, "Manchu Racial Identity on the Qing Frontier," 26.
16. Cangšan, *Gazetteer for the Eight Banners Garrisoned in Canton*, juan 13, 1a–6b.
17. Cangšan, HWZPZZ, FHA 04-01-01-0942-074, GX 6.6.22 (July 28, 1880).
18. Gige 繼格, MWLFZZ, FHA 03-0209-4554-068, GX 11.2.17 (April 2, 1885).
19. Shou-yin, HWZPZZ, FHA 04-01-19-0072-001, GX 27.12.13 (January 22, 1902).
20. The following discussion draws substantially on David Porter, "Bannermen as Translators: Manchu Language Education in the Hanjun Banners," *Late Imperial China* 40, no. 2 (December 2019): 1–43.
21. On the one obvious exception, the training of Hanlin bachelors in Manchu, see Mårten Söderblom Saarela, "Manchu and the Study of Language in China (1607–1911)" (PhD dissertation, Princeton University, 2015), 167–168.
22. Mårten Söderblom Saarela, "Linguistic Compartmentalization and the Palace Memorial System in the Eighteenth Century," *Late Imperial China* 41, no. 2 (December 2020): 135.
23. The proposal to create the Beijing schools is found in SZXSL, juan 86, YZ 7.9.19 (November 9, 1729). Sinju 新柱, ed., *Fuzhou Garrison Gazetteer* 福州駐防志, compiled 1744 (Fuzhou), reprinted in *Fujian Province National Minority Ancient Book Series: Manchu Volume* 福建省少數民族古籍叢書: 滿族卷 (Beijing: Minzu chubanshe, 2004), 58, describes the first such school in a provincial garrison.
24. Dekiboo 德沁寶, MWLFZZ, FHA 03-0178-1822-021, QL 25.5.7 (June 19, 1760), successfully proposed the opening of such a school in Jingzhou.
25. Wang Jintai 王進泰, HWLFZZ, FHA 03-1188-008, QL 3.5.29 (July 15, 1738).
26. Sinju, *Fuzhou Garrison Gazetteer*, 109–110.
27. Ma Zimu 马子木, "On the Formation and Development of the Qing Translation Examinations (1723–1850)" 论清朝翻译科举的形成与发展 (1723–1850), *Qingshi yanjiu* 2014, no. 3 (August 2014): 31–38, describes the content of these exams.
28. Defu 德福, MHHBLFZZ, FHA 03-0173-1054-008, QL 4.9.16 (October 18, 1739).
29. The remaining individual had no identified affiliation. These figures are derived from a search for 理藩院筆帖式 *Lifan yuan bitieshi* in MQNAF.
30. For a summary of the scholarship on this issue, see Porter, "Bannermen as Translators," 26–27.
31. Wesingge 倭昇額, MWCW, FHA 05-08-018-000002-0001, JQ 1.2.20 (March 28, 1796).

32. See, for instance, the career of a bannerman named Chang-fu 常福, who, after completing his studies at the Muslim school, worked as a Lifan yuan *bithesi* before being transferred to an Imperial Household Department agency that managed livestock herds in Inner Asia. Na-xiang 那祥, HWCG, FHA 05-08-018-000002-0007, JQ 7.7.29 (August 26, 1802).
33. Whether the relevant group here is the Torghuts, who famously returned to the Qing in 1771, is uncertain, although a 1792 reference to the passage of thirty years suggests not, as does the use solely of the Manchu term "Ūlet" rather than "Turgūt" to describe the people in question.
34. Booning, MWLFZZ, FHA 03-0194-3377-028, QL 57.2.17 (March 9, 1792).
35. Booning, MWZPZZ, FHA 04-02-001-000212-0074, QL 60.3.18 (May 6, 1795).
36. Yishan, MWZPZZ, FHA 04-02-002-001349-0043, XF 4.8.3 (September 24, 1854).
37. The third Tongwen Guan, in Shanghai, enrolled commoners, probably in part due to its location in a city that lacked a banner garrison but was nevertheless one of the most important sites of contact with western Europeans.
38. English, Russian, and Japanese instruction is referenced in Shou-yin, HWZPZZ, FHA 04-01-38-0189-008, GX 27.12.16 (January 25, 1902). French instruction is referenced in Shou-yin, HWZPZZ, FHA 04-01-38-0190-009, GX 28.10.23 (November 22, 1902).
39. The structural similarities are detailed in Porter, "Bannermen as Translators," 30–33.
40. Cangšan, ed., *Gazetteer for the Eight Banners Garrisoned in Canton*, juan 3, 17b.
41. Qing recognition of the importance of translators as individuals, in the context of negotiations with European powers, is explored in Henrietta Harrison, "A Faithful Interpreter? Li Zibiao and the 1793 Macartney Embassy to China," *International History Review* 41, no. 5 (2019): 1076–1091.
42. On the strategic importance of garrison locations, see Elliott, *The Manchu Way*, 93–98.
43. Kaijun Chen, "The Rise of Technocratic Culture in High-Qing China: A Case Study of Bondservant (Booi) Tang Ying (1682–1756)" (PhD dissertation, Columbia University, 2014), 1–35.
44. Jonathan D. Spence, *Ts'ao Yin and the K'ang-hsi Emperor: Bondservant and Master* (New Haven, CT: Yale University Press, 1966), 82–89.
45. Yulian Wu, *Luxurious Networks: Salt Merchants, Status, and Statecraft in Eighteenth-Century China* (Stanford, CA: Stanford University Press, 2017), 70–75.
46. Jonathan Schlesinger, *A World Trimmed with Fur: Wild Things, Pristine Places, and the Natural Fringes of Qing Rule* (Stanford, CA: Stanford University Press, 2017), 68–88.

47. Catherine Jami, *The Emperor's New Mathematics: Western Learning and Imperial Authority during the Kangxi Reign (1662–1722)* (Oxford: Oxford University Press, 2012), 376, 382–383.
48. Mario Cams, *Companions in Geography: East-West Collaboration in the Mapping of Qing China (c. 1685–1735)* (Leiden, Netherlands: Brill, 2017), 111–124, 136–150.
49. Cams, *Companions in Geography*, 7.
50. Elliott, *The Manchu Way*, 135.
51. Chia Ning, "Lifanyuan and Libu in Early Qing Empire Building," in *Managing Frontiers in Qing China: The Lifanyuan and Libu Revisited*, ed. Dittmar Schorkowitz and Ning Chia (Leiden, Netherlands: Brill, 2017), 50–52.
52. Perhaps the most extensive and notable change was in Xinjiang, where the recovery of the region in the 1870s after a major Muslim rebellion led to the concentration of authority in the hands of the Han commoner military men who led the reconquest and, in 1884, to the region becoming a province. Similar processes were also getting started in Manchuria, Mongolia, and Tibet by the fall of the dynasty in 1911. See James A. Millward, *Eurasian Crossroads: A History of Xinjiang* (New York: Columbia University Press, 2007), 139; and Joseph W. Esherick, "How the Qing Became China," in *Empire to Nation: Historical Perspectives on the Making of the Modern World*, ed. Joseph W. Esherick, Hasan Kayalı, and Eric Van Young (Lanham, MD: Rowman & Littlefield, 2006), 239–243.
53. And even once commoners did begin developing an interest in Inner Asia, they remained excluded from actual influence there for several decades. See Matthew W. Mosca, "The Literati Rewriting of China in the Qianlong-Jiaqing Transition," *Late Imperial China* 32, no. 2 (December 2011): 89–132.
54. See Pamela Kyle Crossley, "The Conquest Elite of the Ch'ing Empire," in *The Cambridge History of China*, vol. 9, part 1, ed. Willard J. Peterson (Cambridge: Cambridge University Press, 2002), 329–333.
55. Benjamin A. Elman, *A Cultural History of Civil Examinations in Late Imperial China* (Berkeley: University of California Press, 2000), 240–247.
56. Gertraude Roth-Li, "State Building Before 1644," in *The Cambridge History of China*, vol. 9, part 1, ed. Willard J. Peterson (Cambridge: Cambridge University Press, 2002), 37.
57. Keliher, *The Board of Rites*, 130–133.
58. This classification was in force in the Yongzheng period, though it was clearly inherited from a classificatory system created under Kangxi. See Kicengge 承志, "On the Origin and Classification of Eight Banner Niru" 八旗ニルの根源とニル分類について, *Tōyōshi kenkyū* 65, no. 1 (2006): 180–178, 172.
59. See Feng Erkang 冯尔康, *Biography of the Yongzheng Emperor* 雍正传 (Beijing: Renmnin chubanshe, 2014), 256–260.

60. Huang, *Autocracy at Work*, 172, 181.
61. Huang, *Autocracy at Work*, 169.
62. See Yunghing 永興, HWLFZZ, FHA 03-0373-023, QL 4.6.7 (July 12, 1739), which emphasizes the importance of having a large enough candidate pool under consideration for promotions to ensure that there were multiple names that could be presented to the emperor.
63. Hongzhou 弘晝, MWZPZZ, FHA 04-02-002-000441-0025, QL 24.6.4 (July 18, 1759).
64. Elliott, *The Manchu Way*, 8–11.
65. Elliott certainly recognizes that the requirements of the Manchu way applied to all bannermen, but he suggests that this is linked to a process in which "the different people of the banners gradually became, for practical purposes, Manchus." Elliott, *The Manchu Way*, 14. My point is that a clear sense of Manchu-Han difference within the banners coexisted (mostly unproblematically, other than during the expulsion era) with an understanding that all bannermen needed to abide by the Manchu way.
66. Yi Zhaoxiong 宜兆熊, HWZPZZ, FHA 04-01-30-0156-033, YZ 5 (1727). The author of this memorial, Shi's recommender, was himself Hanjun.
67. Sitku, HWZPZZ, FHA 04-01-18-0005-029, QL 10.10.1 (October 25, 1745).
68. Sitku, HWZPZZ, FHA 04-01-01-0133-039, QL 11.5.28 (July 16, 1746).
69. Sinju, *Fuzhou Garrison Gazetteer*, 58.
70. Arigūn, MHHBLFZZ, FHA 03-0170-0049-004, YZ 10.9.7 (October 25, 1732).
71. For an example of both banner and Green Standard soldiers being evaluated on the same set of military skills, see Demin 德敏, MWLFZZ, FHA 03-0177-1689-011, QL 23.3.26 (May 3, 1758). Only the bannermen were evaluated for their Manchu-language abilities.
72. For an example of the use of *jiyi* as the equivalent Chinese-language term, see, for instance, Cangšan, HWZPZZ, FHA 04-01-01-0910-047, TZ 9.6.19 (July 17, 1870).
73. Hongli 弘曆, MWMFSY, FHA 03-18-009-000024-0001, QL 23.2.18 (March 26, 1758).
74. Nicolas Schillinger, *The Body and Military Masculinity in Late Qing and Early Republican China: The Art of Governing Soldiers* (Lanham, MD: Lexington Books, 2016), 24.
75. See, for example, Angela Zito, *Of Body and Brush: Grand Sacrifice as Text/Performance in Eighteenth-Century China* (Chicago: University of Chicago Press, 1997), 23.
76. For an example of Hanjun discussed in terms of "manly virtue," see Arigūn, MHHBLFZZ, FHA 03-0171-0167-004, YZ 11.5.10 (June 21, 1733).
77. For more on Manchu-language education for Hanjun, see Porter, "Bannermen as Translators," 11–23.

78. Zhu Lantai 朱蘭泰, HWZPZZ, NPM 402020296, YZ 11.5.10 (June 21, 1733).
79. Sinju, *Fuzhou Garrison Gazetteer*, 21.
80. Baši, MWZPZZ, NPM 412000039, YZ 13.11.14 (December 27, 1735).
81. Jekune, MWLFZZ, FHA 03-0171-0300-004.1, QL 3.6.12 (July 28, 1738).
82. See, for example, Šuhede 舒和德, HWZPZZ, FHA 04-01-38-0058-027, QL 1.3.27 (May 7, 1736); Arsai, HWZPZZ, FHA 04-01-38-0180-036, QL 2.8.2 (August 27, 1737); Arsai, HWZPZZ, FHA 04-01-12-0013-015, QL 4.1.15 (February 22, 1739); Sinju, HWZPZZ, FHA 04-01-12-0077-038, QL 15.10.11 (November 9, 1750).
83. Arigūn, MWLFZZ, FHA 03-0171-0167-004, YZ 11.5.10 (June 21, 1733). On the use of Hanjun in Green Standard units, including more discussion of the Hangzhou proposal, see chapter 4.
84. Linning, MWZPZZ, FHA 04-02-001-000337-0050, JQ 2.9.19 (November 7, 1797).
85. Yongyan, MWMFSY, FHA 03-18-009-000056-0005, JQ 2.9.27 (November 15, 1797).
86. Deboo, MWZPZZ, FHA 04-02-002-000475-0052, QL 27.6.21 (August 10, 1762).
87. Wang Yi, HWZPZZ, FHA 04-01-01-0025-021, QL 3.2.4 (March 23, 1738).
88. Elliott, *The Manchu Way*, 9.
89. See, for instance, Cirsa 奇爾薩, MWZPZZ, YZ 1.8.10 (September 9, 1723), YZCMWZPZZ 514, p. 276; Bootai 保泰, MWZPZZ, YZ 1.9.23 (October 21, 1723), YZCMWZPZZ 690, p. 373; and YZBQSY, *juan* 1, p. 22, YZ 1.7.28 (August 28, 1723).
90. Gendushe 根都思赫, MWZPZZ, FHA 04-02-002-000180-0061, YZ 12.11.5 (November 29, 1734).
91. Sarhadai, HWZPZZ, FHA 04-01-16-0035-055, QL 16.5R.19 (July 11, 1751).
92. GZSL, *juan* 164, QL 7.4.13 (May 17, 1742). This edict is discussed in chapter 7.
93. For the nineteenth-century use of a term like "banner way," see De'ingga 德英阿, MWZPZZ, FHA 04-02-002-001144-0019, DG 2.9.26 (November 9, 1822). For a late-nineteenth-century example of bannermen, including Hanjun, being judged on their skills in core elements of the banner/Manchu way (namely, standing and mounted archery), see Gige, MWLFZZ, FHA 03-0209-4554-068, GX 11.2.17 (April 2, 1885).
94. The association between Manchuness and the requirements of the Manchu way was, of course, a construct of Qing ideology, as was the very idea that a coherent group called "Manchus" existed at all.
95. Quoted in Mark C. Elliott, "Whose Empire Shall It Be? Manchu Figurations of Historical Process in the Seventeenth Century," in *Time, Temporality, and Imperial Transition: East Asia from Ming to Qing*, ed. Lynn A. Struve (Honolulu: University of Hawai'i Press, 2005), 47.

96. Arguments of this sort are now quite common, but a pioneering work making the case is Crossley, *Orphan Warriors* (see esp. 221–228).
97. For official policy and discourse demonstrating the clear ethnic distinction made between Manchus and Han within the banner system, see David C. Porter, "Ethnic and Status Identity in Qing China: The Hanjun Eight Banners" (PhD dissertation, Harvard University, 2018), 53–58.

4. Privilege and State Support

1. Why the emperor even suggested that Gao Bin leave the banners is unclear, given that both sides were well aware of the privilege associated with being a bannerman. Perhaps he believed it inappropriate that the father of one of his consorts was a slave (in the more literal sense in which that term applied better to bondservants than to other banner people), or perhaps it was intended that Gao refuse this act of emancipation as a demonstration of loyalty.
2. Jonathan D. Spence, *Ts'ao Yin and the K'ang-hsi Emperor: Bondservant and Master* (New Haven, CT: Yale University Press, 1966), 9; Evelyn S. Rawski, *The Last Emperors: A Social History of Qing Imperial Institutions* (Berkeley: University of California Press, 1998), 167.
3. Gao Bin, HWZPZZ, FHA 04-01-30-0040-006, YZ 13.10.8 (November 21, 1735). Elevating imperial in-laws to the Manchu banners, even if they had previously had a lesser banner affiliation, was quite common. See Mark C. Elliott, *The Manchu Way: The Eight Banners and Ethnic Identity in Late Imperial China* (Stanford, CA: Stanford University Press, 2001), 87.
4. Gao Bin, HWZPZZ, FHA 04-01-30-0040-006, YZ 13.10.8 (November 21, 1735).
5. Edward J. M. Rhoads, *Manchus & Han: Ethnic Relations and Political Power in Late Qing and Early Republican China, 1861–1928* (Seattle: University of Washington Press, 2000), 45.
6. Even for most of the nineteenth century, between 20 percent and 70 percent of these top provincial posts were held by bannermen. The only period during which Han commoners consistently held more than 80 percent of such posts was 1871–1894, and in only one year (1881) were bannermen not overrepresented when compared to the proportion they made up of the empire's total population. Narakino Shimesu 楢木野宣, *Research on Important Officials in the Qing Dynasty: With Full Details on the Joint Usage of Manchus and Han* 清代重要職官の研究：滿漢併用の全貌 (Tokyo: Kazama shobō, 1975), pages 64–81 deal with governors-general, while pages 97–114 deal with governors. Even at the bottom ranks of provincial administration, in the post of county magistrate, bannermen were moderately overrepresented. Rhoads, *Manchus & Han*, 47.

7. Elliott, *The Manchu Way*, 206–207.
8. Elliott, *The Manchu Way*, 197–200; Rhoads, *Manchus & Han*, 42–43. However, note that, as Lu Zhijun has pointed out, the court emphasized the need in certain cases to punish banner people more harshly in the hopes of dissuading them from behaving dissolutely and departing from the standards of status performance that were expected of them. See Lu Zhijun 鹿智鈞, *Dynastic Basis and Hereditary Slaves: The Legal Status of Bannermen in Qing China* 根本與世僕：清朝旗人的法律地位 (Taipei: Xiuwei zixun keji, 2017), 103.
9. Elliott, *The Manchu Way*, 191–197; Rhoads, *Manchus & Han*, 48–51; Pamela Kyle Crossley, *Orphan Warriors: Three Manchu Generations and the End of the Qing World* (Princeton, NJ: Princeton University Press, 1990), 51–54.
10. Rhoads, *Manchus & Han*, 122; Lao She, *Beneath the Red Banner*, trans. Don J. Cohn (Beijing: Panda Books, 1982), 58.
11. On the costs of the banner system, see Elliott, *The Manchu Way*, 306–313.
12. The expulsion era is the focus of chapters 7 and 8 of this book.
13. Luo Ergang 罗尔纲, *An Account of the Green Standards* 绿营兵志 (Beijing: Shangwu yinshu guan, 2011), 16–27.
14. Mamboo, MWZPZZ, KX 57.3.24 (April 24, 1718), KXCMWZPZZ 3167, p. 1281.
15. Sinju 新柱, ed., *Fuzhou Garrison Gazetteer* 福州駐防志 (compiled Fuzhou: 1744), reprinted in *Fujian Province National Minority Ancient Book Series: Manchu Volume* 福建省少数民族古籍丛书：满族卷 (Beijing: Minzu chubanshe, 2004), 28.
16. The edict is quoted in Arigūn, MWLFZZ, FHA 03-0171-0167-004, YZ 11.5.10 (June 21, 1733).
17. The passage described here uses Ma. *gūsai amban*.
18. SZXSL, *juan* 88, YZ 7.11.7 (December 26, 1729).
19. Arigūn, MWLFZZ, FHA 03-0171-0167-004, YZ 11.5.10 (June 21, 1733).
20. The administrative scope of the Qing's various governors-general changed frequently during the first half of the Qing era. From 1645 until 1738, Zhejiang and Fujian were variously combined under a single governor-general—sometimes based in Zhejiang, sometimes in Fujian (as was the case when Chen Yuanzhang wrote his memorial)—or each given its own (as was the case when Arigūn wrote his memorial). From 1738 on, they would be combined under a single governor-general based in Fuzhou. See Zhu Taiwen 祝太文, "An Investigation and Discussion of the Establishment of Governor and Governor-General Posts in Qing Zhejiang" 清代浙江督抚设置考述, *Wenzhou daxue xuebao (shehui kexue ban)* 30, no. 5 (September 2017): 85–86.
21. Cheng Yuanzhang, HWZPZZ, NPM 402015949, YZ 13.3.? (April 1735).
22. SZXSL, *juan* 154, YZ 13.4.3 (April 25, 1735).
23. Sinju, *Fuzhou Garrison Gazetteer*, 21–22.

24. Bo Zhifan 栢之蕃, HWZPZZ, NPM 402008802, YZ 11.3.11 (April 24, 1733).
25. This proposal is found in Arsai, HWZPZZ, FHA 04-01-16-0002-038, QL 1.5.2 (June 10, 1736). Sinju, *Fuzhou Garrison Gazetteer*, 32–33, confirms that it was implemented.
26. Luo Ergang, *An Account of the Green Standards*, 8, describes the role of the Malan and Taining garrisons in protecting imperial tombs.
27. Qu Chunhai 屈春海, "Public Order and Defense Organizations in the Qing Capital: An Outline of the Office of the Gendarmerie" 清代京师治安防务机构：步军统领衙门述略, *Gong'an daxue xuebao* 1989, no. 2: 68–70. The original memorial proposing the policy, from Supervisor of Instruction (Ch. 詹事府 [*zhanshi fu*]) Li Fu 李紱, directly argued that the special roles of the Green Standard companies in question (both the ones at Malan and Taining and the police battalions) made them particularly appropriate places to use bannermen. See Zhang Tingyu 張廷玉, MHHBZPZZ, FHA 04-01-01-0120-005, QL 10.5.11 (June 10, 1745).
28. GZSL, *juan* 237, QL 10.3.20 (April 21, 1745).
29. Bulantai, HWZPZZ, FHA 04-01-16-0022-034, QL 10.4.20 (May 21, 1745).
30. Zhang Tingyu, MHHBZPZZ, FHA 04-01-01-0120-005, QL 10.5.11 (June 10, 1745).
31. For the distinction between occupation and livelihood, see the discussion in chapter 1, drawing on the work of David Howell, a historian of Tokugawa Japan.
32. The initial proposal is found in Bulantai, HWLFZZ, FHA 03-0049-021, QL 3.4.17 (June 4, 1738). Imperial approval for his proposal appears in Ortai, MHHBZPZZ, FHA 04-01-16-0006-033, QL 3.5.7 (June 23, 1738).
33. Descendants of the soldiers at Taining, near the Qing's western tomb complex (Ch. 西陵 [*xi ling*]), remember (or at least represent) themselves as Manchus to the present day, although the tomb units were part of the Green Standards until the very end of the dynasty. For Taining as a present-day site of "Manchu" cultural identity, see Jeremiah Jenne, "Making History," *The World of Chinese*, September–October 2017, http://www.theworldofchinese.com/2017/11/making-history/. The continuation of the Malan and Taining garrisons as Green Standard units through the fall of the Qing is confirmed by XTZJ, *juan* 70, XT 3.12.22 (February 9, 1912).
34. See, for instance, Yingcong Dai, *The White Lotus War: Rebellion & Suppression in Late Imperial China* (Seattle: University of Washington Press, 2019), 369–430, for an account of the massive 120-million-tael cost of the White Lotus War of the turn of the nineteenth century. On the generally poor condition of state finances in the middle of the nineteenth century, see Stephen R. Platt, *Autumn in the Heavenly Kingdom: China, the West, and the Epic Story of the Taiping War* (New York: Vintage, 2012), 150.

35. On the Hanjun expulsion, see chapters 7 and 8.
36. Yang Yingju, HWZPZZ, NPM 403012560, QL 21.8.14 (September 8, 1756).
37. This was a reduction from the 800 such posts held by Guangzhou Hanjun prior to expulsion. See Yang Yingju, HWZPZZ, NPM 403011889, QL 21.5.11 (June 8, 1756).
38. Fuhui 福會, HWZPZZ, FHA 04-01-01-0526-042, JQ 16.7.21 (September 8, 1811).
39. In the years around 1760, there was the additional problem that many of the Manchu banner affiliates sent to Guangzhou during the expulsion process of the late 1750s were people designated as entailed households or people "separately recorded in the registers," whom the court soon decided should also be targets for expulsion from the banners. Their removal from the banner registers, and thus from whatever posts they may have held, created a large number of vacancies very quickly.
40. Dzenghai, MWLFZZ, FHA 03-0183-2282-027, QL 33.8.25 (October 5, 1768).
41. Fusengge, MWLFZZ, FHA 03-0179-1885-017, QL 26.?.? (1761), applied this policy to officer posts, while Mingfu, MWLFZZ, FHA 03-0179-1965-010, QL 27.9.? (October–November 1762), applied it to ordinary soldiers.
42. Dzenghai, MWLFZZ, FHA 03-0183-2282-027, QL 33.8.25 (October 5, 1768). The proposal received imperial endorsement in GZSL, *juan* 819, QL 33.9.29 (November 8, 1768).
43. Teksin, MWLFZZ, FHA 03-0184-2386-009, QL 35.8.21 (October 9, 1770).
44. Fuioi 傅玉, MWLFZZ, FHA 03-0189-2894-028, QL 46.8.4 (September 21, 1781). Note that this Hanjun infantry had in fact replaced a larger contingent of 600 Hanjun employed in the Green Standard army, and their positions were financed by the elimination of 200 Hanjun-designated banner cavalry posts. See Dzenghai, MWLFZZ, FHA 03-0183-2303-010, QL 33.12.12 (January 19, 1769).
45. Tsuntai, MWLFZZ, FHA 03-0192-3213-017, QL 53.10.3 (October 31, 1788); Tsuntai, MWLFZZ, FHA 03-0192-3213-010, QL 53.10.22 (November 19, 1788).
46. Fucang, MWLFZZ, FHA 03-0195-3460-019, QL 59.2.? (March 1794).
47. On the *Puji tang*, which began as private institutions but came under increasing state control beginning in the Qianlong period and derived a substantial portion of their income from property donated by the Qing state, see Fuma Susumu 夫馬進, *Research on the History of Charitable and Benevolent Organizations in China* 中国善会善堂史研究 (Kyoto, Japan: Dōhōsha shuppan, 1997).
48. Ji-qing 吉慶, HWLFZZ, FHA 03-1833-033, JQ 2.9.1 (October 20, 1797). Imperial approval for the request can be found in SYD, JQ 2.10.12 (November 29, 1797).
49. Qing-pu, HWZPZZ, FHA 04-01-01-0514-057, JQ 14.12.12 (January 16, 1810).

50. RZSL, *juan* 218, JQ 14.9.15 (October 23, 1809).
51. Qing-pu, HWZPZZ, FHA 04-01-01-0514-057, JQ 14.12.12 (January 16, 1810).
52. SYD, JQ 15.1.21 (February 24, 1810).
53. Elliott, *The Manchu Way*, 318–322.
54. Kingboo 慶保, HWZPZZ, FHA 04-01-01-0706-014, DG 9.9.2 (September 29, 1829). A favorable imperial review of Kingboo's proposal can be found in SYD, DG 9.10.16 (November 12, 1829), although it was referred for further discussion. Confirmation of its final approval can be found in Bahangga 巴杭阿, MWLFZZ, FHA 03-0202-4084-032, DG 9.12.15 (January 9, 1830).
55. Kingboo, HWZPZZ, FHA 04-01-01-0715-034, DG 10.10.26 (December 10, 1830).
56. Cangšan 長善, ed., *Gazetteer for the Eight Banners Garrisoned in Canton* 駐粵八旗志 (Guangzhou, 1884; reprinted Taipei: Wenhai chubanshe, 1997), *juan* 6, 15b.
57. Sulfangga 蘇勒芳阿, HWZPZZ, FHA 04-01-01-0775-025, DG 16.3.17 (May 2, 1836).
58. Muten 穆特恩, HWZPZZ, FHA 04-01-01-0857-033, XF 5.10.27 (December 6, 1855).
59. These schemes are described in Mengju 孟住, HWZPZZ, FHA 04-01-35-0787-044, DG 2.3.21 (April 12, 1822); Cangšan, *Gazetteer for the Eight Banners Garrisoned in Canton*, *juan* 6, 16b, quoting a memorial from Rui-lin 瑞麟 from TZ 8.4 (May–June 1869); Shou-yin, HWZPZZ, FHA 04-01-18-0054-058, GX 26.4.8 (May 6, 1900); and Cangšan, HWZPZZ, FHA 04-01-03-0168-023, GX 2.7.3 (August 21, 1876).
60. SYD, JQ 10.11.10 (December 30, 1805).
61. XZSL, *juan* 110, DG 6.11.22 (December 20, 1826).
62. Sulfangga, HWZPZZ, FHA 04-01-01-0774-004, DG 16.8.17 (September 27, 1836).
63. The emperor ordered that the proposal be "sent down to the Board to discuss and implement"; XZSL, *juan* 289, DG 16.9.22 (October 31, 1836).
64. For a reflection on slavery in Qing Mongolia that engages with the question of comparability, see Samuel H. Bass, "Notes on Encountering Slavery Skepticism in Mongolia," *Critical Asian Studies Commentary* 2019, no. 11 (May 9, 2019), https://criticalasianstudies.org/commentary/2019/5/9/201911-samuel-h-bass-notes-on-encountering-slavery-skepticism-in-mongolia. For recent work on slavery in late imperial China, see Claude Chevaleyre, "Slavery in Late Ming China," in *The Palgrave Handbook of Global Slavery throughout History*, ed. Damian A. Pargas and Juliane Schiel (Cham, Switzerland: Palgrave Macmillan, 2023), 297–317.
65. See Elliott, *The Manchu Way*, 227–230; and Rawski, *The Last Emperors*, 167, 172.
66. This is supported by references in the Qing code, as in a substatute from 1788 that held that although slaves who had been purchased with a "white contract"

(Ch. 白契 [baiqi]) (i.e., not using officially issued forms as a way to avoid government fees) after the ascension of the Qianlong emperor in 1736 would be allowed to redeem themselves to become commoners, those purchased with a white contract prior to 1736 would "still, in accordance with precedent, remain in the household of their master" (Ch. 仍照例在本主戶下 [reng zhaoli zai benzhu huxia]). DQHDSL, "Lü 84: Households Should Be Established According to the Registers" 律84人戶以籍爲定, 條例 tiaoli 11, https://lsc.chineselegalculture.org/eC/HDSLXB/2.3.1.84.0.11.

67. For instance, criminal convicts who had been given as slaves to a person who had performed meritorious service were to be transferred to Xinjiang to become military slaves if their masters could not provide for them (Ch. 養贍 [yangshan]). That is, there was a clear sense in Qing law that part of owning a slave included meeting their basic material needs. DQHDSL, "Lü 51: Criminals Sentenced to Exile Being Moved to Another Place 3" 律51徒留遷徙地方三, 條例 tiaoli 5, https://lsc.chineselegalculture.org/eC/HDSLXB/2.1.20.51.0.5.

   Moreover, one key justification of slavery in late imperial China, reflected in contracts of self-sale from the late Ming dynasty, was that people who sold themselves into slavery "were always given assurance that their basic needs would be taken care of." See Chevaleyre, "Slavery in Late Ming China," 305.

68. Pamela Kyle Crossley, *A Translucent Mirror: History and Identity in Qing Imperial Ideology* (Berkeley: University of California Press, 1999), 140–141.

69. Crossley, *A Translucent Mirror*, 125–128.

70. Zaixun, HWZZ, FHA 04-01-02-0013-007, XT 2.1.28 (March 9, 1910). Though scholars of early China might well note that the Chinese term *chen* also originated as a term referring to servile status, it had lost this sense by the Qing, as clearly reflected by its Manchu equivalent, *amban*, etymologically linked to the Manchu word for "big" or "great": *amba*.

71. See, for instance, Cangšan, HWZPZZ, FHA 04-01-38-0186-36, GX 9.6.15 (July 18, 1883), a joint memorial in which the Hanjun official Shang Changmao 尙昌懋 is introduced as *nucai*.

72. Rhoads, *Manchus & Han*, 141–142. That said, many fewer memorials were written in Manchu than Chinese by this point, making the exception of little practical importance in most cases.

73. Hongli, MWJXSY, FHA 03-18-009-000024-0001, QL 23.2.16 (March 24, 1758).

74. Han bannermen were included in this practice, which depended on status and not ethnicity. See, for example, Wang Yan 王炎, MWZPZZ, FHA 04-02-002-000428-0057, QL 23.4.7 (May 13, 1758).

75. Even very high-ranking Manchu bannermen often referred to themselves as *amban/chen* ("minister") when carrying out official duties in posts like those of governors or governors-general. For instance, a search of the Manchu-language

palace memorials of the famous mid-eighteenth century Manchu official Ortai 鄂爾泰 shows the exclusive use of *amban* to refer to himself, probably because the most important posts that he held were in the nonbanner bureaucracy.

76. As seen in the following discussion, these are often forms of the verbs *hūwašabumbi* and *ujimbi* in Manchu. Similar Chinese documents used compounds featuring the character 養 (*yang*).

77. See, for instance, Ertu 額爾圖, MWLFZZ, FHA 03-0172-0798-001, QL 11.4.21 (June 9, 1746).

78. Although Christopher Atwood points out that the language of "grace" was used in a wide range of contexts, the extension of the idea of nourishment through imperial grace to ordinary Han commoners (those not holding official posts) does not show up in his research (though the same language does seem to appear for nonbanner Mongols). Atwood treats the language of grace and its repayment as inherently linked to Confucian ideas of a parent-child relationship, refuting the notion that Inner Asians and Han had different types of relationships to the emperor (master-slave and parent-child, respectively). But the examples that I identify here show that nourishing imperial grace was understood as being linked to the position of banner people as slaves; it did not exclusively apply to parent-child relationships (real or metaphorical), whatever its origins may have been. See Christopher Pratt Atwood, "'Worshipping Grace': The Language of Loyalty in Qing Mongolia," *Late Imperial China* 21, no. 2 (December 2000): 86–139.

79. Šetuken 舍圖肯, MWLFZZ, FHA 03-0182-2191-011, QL 31.6.6 (July 12, 1766).

80. Fugiyūn 富俊, MWZPZZ, FHA 04-02-002-000921-0060, JQ 7.2.12 (March 15, 1802).

81. I add "imperial" in brackets to reflect that the word *kesi* (grace) is elevated in the text. Bahangga, MWLFZZ, FHA 03-0202-4084-032.1, DG 9.12.15 (January 9, 1830).

82. Hongli, MFSY, FHA 03-18-009-000005-003, QL 7.9.17 (October 15, 1742).

83. Ironically, the answer that Qianlong would reach about how to maintain adequate support for banner people involved denying continued privilege to some of the banner population on the basis of ethnicity, as is explored in chapter 7.

84. Thomas T. Allsen, *The Royal Hunt in Eurasian History* (Philadelphia: University of Pennsylvania Press, 2006), 200.

85. Hou Ching-Lang 侯錦郎 and Michèle Pirazzoli, "Les chasses d'automne de l'empereur Qianlong à Mulan," *T'oung Pao* 65, no. 1–3 (1979): 39.

86. Mark C. Elliott and Ning Chia, "The Qing Hunt at Mulan," in *New Qing Imperial History: The Making of Inner Asian Empire at Qing Chengde*, ed. James A. Millward, Ruth W. Dunnell, Mark C. Elliott, and Phillippe Forêt (London: RoutledgeCurzon, 2004), 73–74.

87. Elliott, *The Manchu Way*, 335.

88. The fact that Hanjun were often exempted from hunting when Manchus and Mongols were not is made clear in a Yongzheng-era memorial that suggests that cannon drills took the place of hunting for the Hanjun. See Barhūda 巴爾呼達, MWZPZZ, FHA 04-02-002-000201-0013, YZ ?.?.?.
89. Fusen, MWZPZZ, FHA 04-02-002-000226-0021, QL 2.12.1 (January 20, 1738).
90. On Tang Xie, see Hongzhou, MWZPZZ, FHA 04-02-002-000281-0041, QL 9.8.28 (October 3, 1744); on Wang Huailiang, see Kitungga 奇通阿, MWZPZZ, FHA 04-02-002-000342-0012, QL 15.12.4 (January 1, 1751). Many similar records exist as well.
91. Yunghing, MWZPZZ, FHA 04-02-002-000356-0009, QL 6.9.24 (November 2, 1741).
92. It seems probable, given Fusen's memorial, that the Hanjun in provincial garrisons were excluded (at least most of the time) from the hunt, unlike their Manchu/Mongol counterparts. So this may be a case where the distinction between capital and provincial garrison bannermen, as well as ethnic distinctions, was important.
93. Michael G. Chang, *A Court on Horseback: Imperial Touring & the Construction of Qing Rule, 1680–1785* (Cambridge, MA: Harvard Asia Center, 2007), 11–27.
94. Max Weber, *Economy and Society: An Outline of Interpretive Sociology*, ed. Guenther Roth and Claus Wittich (Berkeley: University of California Press, 1978), 1027–1031.

5. A Female Service Elite: Status, Ethnicity, and Qing Bannerwomen

1. Shuo Wang, "Qing Imperial Women: Empresses, Concubines, and Aisin Gioro Daughters," in *Servants of the Dynasty: Palace Women in World History*, ed. Anne Walthall (Berkeley: University of California Press, 2008), 137–158.
2. Wang, "Qing Imperial Women," 153.
3. Yue Du, "Legal Justice in Eighteenth-Century Mongolia: Gender, Ethnicity, and Politics in the Manchu-Mongol Marriage Alliance," *Late Imperial China* 37, no. 2 (December 2016): 13–17.
4. There was no special term in Manchu. Manchu-language documents usually refer to "the selection of girls" (*sargan juse be sonjoro*), though some also mention "the examination of girls" (*sargan juse be tuwara*) or "exhibiting girls" (*sargan juse tuwabure*). In no case does any term more specialized than "girls" (*sargan juse*) appear. "Girls" in these phrases might also be understood to mean either "daughters," defining them by their relationship to their fathers in the banners, or "maidens," defining them by their position as qualified potential marriage partners for men in the imperial lineage.

5. Evelyn S. Rawski, "Ch'ing Imperial Marriage and the Problems of Rulership," in *Marriage and Inequality in Chinese Society*, ed. Rubie S. Watson and Patricia Buckley Ebrey (Berkeley: University of California Press, 1991), 183–184. 20 taels of silver was equivalent to five months' worth of the standard salary in silver of a banner soldier in Beijing, or more than six months' salary for a banner soldier in a provincial garrison. See Mark C. Elliott, *The Manchu Way: The Eight Banners and Ethnic Identity in Late Imperial China* (Stanford, CA: Stanford University Press, 2001), 92. Palace women were also fully provided for during their time in palace employment.
6. Despite beginning in the lowest ranks of the imperial harem, such women could be promoted. Empress Xiaoyichun 孝儀純, the Qianlong emperor's third empress and mother of the Jiaqing emperor, was the daughter of a bondservant and probably entered the palace as a maid. The same was true of the Jiaqing emperor's first empress, Empress Xiaoshurui 孝淑睿. See Rawski, "Ch'ing Imperial Marriage," 184–185.
7. On the quantity of Qing marriages to various types of women, Rawski, "Ch'ing Imperial Marriage," p. 187 gives the percentage of marriages to *xiunü*, p. 184 gives the percentage of marriages to palace maids, and pp. 177–179 discuss marriages between the Aisin Gioro lineage and Mongol aristocrats.
8. Shuo Wang, "The Selection of Women for the Qing Imperial Harem," *Chinese Historical Review* 11, no. 2 (Fall 2004): 218. On the requirement of permission from the company captain prior to marriage, see Elliott, *The Manchu Way*, 254.
9. Evelyn S. Rawski, *The Last Emperors: A Social History of Qing Imperial Institutions* (Berkeley: University of California Press, 1998), 133–134. Hence the great excitement when Jia Baoyu's elder sister Yuanchun, an imperial consort, visits her family in the famous eighteenth century novel, *The Dream of the Red Chamber*. Cao Xueqin, *The Story of the Stone*, vol. 1, "The Golden Days," trans. David Hawkes (London: Penguin, 1973), 354.
10. Wang, "Qing Imperial Women," 146.
11. Because the adoption story appeared to have been invented, there is no discussion in the archives of how the marriage would have been dealt with if Yu's daughter really had been adopted from a Hanjun household by a commoner family.
12. Hongshang 弘晌, MWZPZZ, FHA 04-02-002-000689-0041, QL 45.8.24 (September 22, 1780).
13. Wang, "The Selection of Women for the Qing Imperial Harem," 220.
14. Yongyan 顒琰, MWMFSY, FHA 03-18-009-000063-002, JQ 11.5.9 (June 25, 1806).
15. Elliott, *The Manchu Way*, 192.
16. Wenking 文慶, MWZPZZ, FHA 04-02-002-001351-0015, XF 4.10.18 (December 12, 1854). Although I have not found documents with similar detail

for other years, this memorial implies that excluding the daughters of ordinary soldiers was the usual decision.

17. *DQHD* (1818), *juan* 12, 22a–b. Note that Hanjun constituted 34 percent of the population of regular Manchu, Mongol, and Hanjun bannermen when other smaller banner categories, as well as household servants/slaves of banner people, were excluded.

18. Zhou Fu 周馥, HWZPZZ, FHA 04-01-14-0099-055, GX 30.7.19 (August 29, 1904). The edict did not specify what was problematic about the Ming system. Given the context, it seems likely that the implied criticism was that under the Ming system, all ordinary women were potentially subject to selection, posing a burden on the entire population. In practice, however, most Ming consorts from the early fifteenth century on were chosen from low-ranking to mid-ranking families of hereditary military status. As such, this system bore some resemblance to that of the Qing, although the principle underlying it was different. Imperial consorts, per the *Ancestral Instructions* of the Hongwu emperor, the founder of the Ming dynasty, were to come from ordinary, unconnected families to prevent imperial in-laws from becoming too powerful. That is, where the Qing system emphasized the special connection between banner people and the emperor as the reason for selecting palace women from among the banner population, the Ming system viewed military families as good sources for imperial brides precisely because they lacked preexisting connections to the court. On the Ming system, see Ellen Soullière, "The Imperial Marriages of the Ming Dynasty," *Papers on Far Eastern History* 37 (March 1988), esp. 23–25.

19. For the typical Manchu female hairstyle, see Elliott, *The Manchu Way*, 249–251, which includes images.

20. Hongli, MWMFSY, FHA 03-18-009-000027-0001, QL 24.4.12 (May 8, 1759).

21. Yongyan, MWMFSY, FHA 03-18-009-000061-0001, JQ 9.2.4 (March 15, 1804). Although this memorial does not specify which banner ethnic categories were wearing wide sleeves, a later edict associates foot-binding with Hanjun women and wide sleeves with Manchu and Mongol women. See Yongyan, MWMFSY, FHA 03-18-009-000063-0002, JQ 11.5.15 (July 1, 1806).

22. See John E. Vollmer, *Ruling from the Dragon Throne: Costume of the Qing Dynasty (1644–1911)* (Berkeley, CA: Ten Speed, 2002), 27–31, 45, 59–63. Images on pages 31 and 62 make clear the difference in the sleeve styles of Han and Manchu women.

23. Yongyan, MWMFSY, FHA 03-18-009-000063-0002, JQ 11.5.15 (July 1, 1806).

24. There was, however, as seen in the discussions of "Han customs," a worry about a sort of "status acculturation"—that Han (and other) bannerwomen would become too much like Han commoners. Yongyan, MWMFSY, FHA 03-18-009-000063-0002, JQ 11.5.15 (July 1, 1806).

25. Yongyan, MWMFSY, FHA 03-18-009-000063-0002, JQ 11.5.15 (July 1, 1806).
26. Yongyan, MWMFSY, FHA 03-18-009-000061-0001, JQ 9.2.4 (March 15, 1804).
27. Why the Hanjun banner people in question were living in villages is not specified. It is likely that they were from Manchuria or the outskirts of Beijing, where many people of banner status were assigned to agricultural work on imperially owned estates. The implication of the edict seems to be that no bannerwomen from garrison communities were discovered to have bound feet, but as there is no discussion of any of the individual women, it is difficult to be sure.
28. Hongli, MWMFSY, FHA 03-18-009-000007-0002, QL 12.2.1 (March 11, 1747).
29. See Weijing Lu, *True to Her Word: The Faithful Maiden Cult in Late Imperial China* (Stanford, CA: Stanford University Press, 2008), on girls in Qing China who insisted on remaining faithful to deceased fiancés, or even committing suicide in the wake of their deaths, in direct opposition to the wishes of their parents, who hoped to find them new husbands.
30. Elliott, *The Manchu Way*, 254.
31. See, for instance, Edward J. M. Rhoads, *Manchus & Han: Ethnic Relations and Political Power in Late Qing and Early Republican China, 1861–1928* (Seattle: University of Washington Press, 2000), 76. Rhoads notes that the elimination of the prohibition did not produce a wave of intermarriage; it remained relatively rare.
32. Zhou Fu, HWZPZZ, FHA 04-01-14-0099-055, GX 30.7.19 (August 29, 1904).
33. Cited in Ding Yizhuang 定宜庄, *Research on the Lives of Women and Marriage System of the Manchu People* 满族的妇女生活与婚姻制度研究 (Beijing: Peking University Press, 1999), 342.
34. Here, I quote from Yang Yingju, HWZPZZ, NPM 403009753, QL 20.6.21 (July 29, 1755), dealing with the Guangzhou expulsion. But very similar phrases also appear in documents about expulsion in Fuzhou, Liangzhuang, and Hangzhou.
35. DQHDSL, "*Lü* 84: Households Should Be Established According to the Registers" 律 84 人戶以籍爲定, 條例 *tiaoli* 19, http://lsc.chineselegalculture.org/eC/HDSLXB/2.3.1.84.0.19.
36. See the discussion of adoption in chapter 1.
37. See Ding, *Research on the Lives of Women*, 335–342.
38. SYD 52.1.7 (February 24, 1787).
39. GZSL, *juan* 1272, QL 52.1.8 (February 25, 1787).
40. In other contexts, Sino-Muslims (usually referred to today as "Hui"), the community to which Jiang's wife likely belonged, were treated like other commoners for marriage purposes; for instance, they were "subject to antimiscegenation regulations in their relations with non-Chinese-speaking Muslims." See Jonathan Lipman, "'A Fierce and Brutal People': On Islam and Muslims

in Qing Law," in *Empire at the Margins: Culture, Ethnicity, and Frontier in Early Modern China*, ed. Pamela Kyle Crossley, Helen F. Siu, and Donald S. Sutton (Berkeley: University of California Press, 2006), 87.

41. An adopted-in son-in-law lived with his wife's family and became part of her lineage, thus leaving his own patriline. Children would take the wife's surname, although in some cases, one son might be returned to the father's lineage. See, for example, Jack Goody, *The Oriental, the Ancient, and the Primitive: Systems of Marriage and the Family in the Pre-industrial Societies of Eurasia* (Cambridge: Cambridge University Press, 1990), 45–48.
42. Zhong Bao 鐘保, HWZPZZ, NPM 402014976, YZ 13.5.25 (July 15, 1735).
43. In 1732, three years before the Tong case came to light, a ban on Han-Miao marriages in Hunan had just been lifted. See Donald S. Sutton, "Ethnicity and the Miao Frontier in the Eighteenth Century," in *Empire at the Margins: Culture, Ethnicity, and Frontier in Early Modern China*, ed. Pamela Kyle Crossley, Helen F. Siu, and Donald S. Sutton (Berkeley: University of California Press, 2006), 200.
44. Mai-zhu 邁柱, YZ 13.4.24 (May 16, 1735), *SZZPYZ*, juan 213.6.
45. By analogy, perhaps the marriage of bannerwomen to commoner men was prohibited for the same reason: that it meant giving up their status.
46. The dismissal from office is found in SZXSL, *juan* 158, YZ 13.7.5 (August 22, 1735). Although no specific reason is specified in the *Shilu*, Zhun-tai's memorial suggests that this purchase of a banner woman was the cause.
47. Zhun-tai, HWZPZZ, NPM 402001323, YZ 13.8.4 (September 19, 1735).
48. Ding, *Research on the Lives of Women*, 334.
49. On the tendency of Chinese marriage toward female hypergamy, see Patricia Buckley Ebrey, "Introduction," in *Marriage and Inequality in Chinese Society*, ed. Rubie S. Watson and Patricia Buckley Ebrey (Berkeley: University of California Press, 1991), 5.
50. These sections can be found in *QDBQTZ*, juan 241–269. Note that Ch. 列女 is more commonly seen as 烈女 (both are read as *lienü*), but in the published *QDBQTZ*, the former character pair is given.
51. Weijing Lu notes that these records include some women honored for committing suicide upon the deaths of their husbands. See Lu, *True to Her Word*, 285, n32.
52. Mark C. Elliott, "Manchu Widows and Ethnicity in Qing China," *Comparative Studies in Society and History* 41, no. 1 (January 1999): 42 (table 2.2).
53. This is a common usage in scholarship on gender in Qing China; see, for example, Fangqin Du and Susan Mann, "Competing Claims on Womanly Virtue in Late Imperial China," in *Women and Confucian Cultures in Premodern China, Korea, and Japan*, ed. Dorothy Ko, JaHyun Kim Haboush, and Joan R. Piggott (Berkeley: University of California Press, 2003), 219.

54. For the purposes of creating my data set, I treated all one-character, ordinary Chinese surnames as Han, since Manchu clan names derived from Chinese surnames appear to have been consistently identified by the addition of the character 佳 (*jia*), derived from the Manchu *giya*, itself a Manjurization of the Chinese character 家 (*jia*), meaning "family." That is, where a Han woman would be listed as 李氏 (*Li shi*), or "woman of the Li family," a Manchu woman from a clan whose name was based on the same Chinese surname would be listed as 李佳氏 (*Li-jia shi*) (Ma. *Ligiya hala*), or "woman of the Ligiya clan." If a one-character family name from the data set is not defined as a surname in standard Chinese dictionaries, I recorded the ethnicity of the woman who bore it as indeterminate. When distinguishing between native Manchu and Mongol clan names, I relied both on listings of surnames from the *Comprehensive Genealogy of Eight Banner Manchu Clans* (Ch. 八旗滿洲氏族通譜 [*Baqi Manzhou shizu tongpu*]), which also includes many banner Mongol clans, and on phonological characteristics of the name. For instance, names ending in *te* (usually Ch. 特 or 忒) are extremely likely to be Mongol. It was occasionally impossible to determine whether a given clan name was Manchu (or from one of the related New Manchu groups like the Sibe, Solon, and Evenki, which I treated as Manchu for this purpose) or Mongol. In these cases, I recorded the ethnicity of the woman as indeterminate.
55. Ding Yizhuang, *Research on the Lives of Women*, 337–340, 353.
56. Manchu men were the group most likely to marry Manchu women, Mongol men the group most likely to marry Mongol women, and Hanjun men the group most likely to marry Han women. The numbers of Mongol women are also most likely underestimated in both Manchu and Mongol marriages—the percentage of unidentifiable clan names was highest for women married to Mongol men, suggesting that most such clan names were Mongol. The true percentage of Manchu men married to Mongol women may have been as high as 4.5 percent.
57. See Elliott, *The Manchu Way*, 78, which explains this hierarchy as a standard formula by which the banners were discussed in the Qing. Elliott himself is clear that the Hanjun were substantially inferior to both Manchus and Mongols, who were more equal to one another.
58. Note that the spikes in 1732 for Manchu men marrying Hanjun women are misleading—the overwhelming majority of records for this year in the Manchu section are for wives of Imperial Household Department bondservants.
59. A lag of this sort is to be expected, as a woman would not receive a chastity award until at least fifteen years after her husband's death, so any marriage in principle would have occurred at least fifteen years prior to the date of the award.
60. Elliott, "Manchu Widows and Ethnicity," 41. Elliott found an overall total of 59 percent of *jingbiao* going to the Manchu banners, or 63 percent when

bondservant bannermen from the Imperial Household Department are included (I treated bondservants as Manchus in forming my data set because the text included them in its Manchu section). This is roughly in line with my results from a 20 percent sample.

61. Surnames like Bo-er-ji-te 白爾吉特 ("Borjigit" in Mongolian) are clearly identifiable as belonging to Mongols, but, as might be expected in a garrison with no Mongol banner troops, only a tiny number of such surnames appear among the listed women.
62. Cangšan 長善, ed., *Gazetteer for the Eight Banners Garrisoned in Canton* 駐粵八旗志 (Guangzhou, 1884; reprinted Taipei: Wenhai chubanshe, 1997), *juan* 13, 10a–51b.
63. Since women often had to maintain their chastity for two decades or more after their widowhood to receive official honors, the women who received chastity awards in the 1870s and 1880s had likely married around the middle of the century.
64. The extreme asymmetry that I have found in the gender of partners in interethnic marriages within the banners is in striking contrast to the findings of researchers who have worked on ethnic intermarriage in a late-Qing (1866–1913) banner population in Shuangcheng, a banner agricultural settlement in Manchuria established in the early nineteenth century. In Shuangcheng, a surname-based analysis of marriage patterns found that Han bannermen married non-Han bannerwomen much more frequently than non-Han bannermen married Han bannerwomen. See Bijia Chen, Cameron Campbell, and Hao Dong, "Interethnic Marriage in Northeast China, 1866–1913," *Demographic Research* 38, no. 34 (March 2018): esp. 950, table 5. Since the chaste widow records cover a wider geographical and temporal range and provide clearer evidence of ethnic background than the Shuangcheng records (which list only single character surnames with an ambiguous relationship to ethnic origin), I believe that they are more likely to reflect the general state of intermarriage in the Qing.

6. A Comparative History of Service Elites

1. Andreas Kappeler, *The Russian Empire: A Multiethnic History*, trans. Alfred Clayton (Harlow, UK: Pearson Education Limited, 2001), 124.
2. Kappeler, *The Russian Empire*, 42.
3. Kappeler, *The Russian Empire*, 152.
4. Kappeler, *The Russian Empire*, 73–75.
5. Kelly O'Neill, "Rethinking Elite Integration: The Crimean Murzas and the Evolution of Russian Nobility," *Cahiers du Monde russe* 51, no. 2 (2010): 401–403.

6. Kappeler, *The Russian Empire*, 77–83.
7. Lindsey Hughes, *Russia in the Age of Peter the Great* (New Haven, CT: Yale University Press, 1998), 180–185.
8. This is the group that Richard Hellie calls the "middle service class." Their military usefulness declined greatly during the seventeenth-century gunpowder revolution, before they were repurposed by Peter the Great into a new service class. Richard Hellie, *Enserfment and Military Change in Muscovy* (Chicago: University of Chicago Press, 1971), 258.
9. Although the Qing state made extensive use of commoner soldiers as well, it maintained institutional separation between commoner armies and service elite armies, unlike Russia, where commoner soldiers were commanded by noble officers. On the recruitment of both nobles and non-nobles into the Russian army in the Petrine period, see Hughes, *Russia in the Age of Peter the Great*, 65–71.
10. Hughes, *Russia in the Age of Peter the Great*, 180–185.
11. Hughes, *Russia in the Age of Peter the Great*, 107.
12. Elise Kimerling Wirtschafter, *Social Identity in Imperial Russia* (DeKalb: Northern Illinois University Press, 1997), 33.
13. John P. LeDonne, *Absolutism and Ruling Class: The Formation of the Russian Political Order, 1700–1825* (Oxford: Oxford University Press, 1991), 4–5.
14. Wirtschafter, *Social Identity in Imperial Russia*, 27.
15. Alison K. Smith, *For the Common Good and Their Own Well-Being: Social Estates in Imperial Russia* (New York: Oxford University Press, 2014), 9.
16. W. Bruce Lincoln, *In the Vanguard of Reform: Russia's Enlightened Bureaucrats, 1825–1861* (DeKalb: Northern Illinois University Press, 1982), 2–4, 12, 41–48.
17. Hughes, *Russia in the Age of Peter the Great*, 174–175.
18. Nancy Shields Kollman, "'What's Love Got to Do with It?': Changing Models of Masculinity in Muscovite and Petrine Russia," in *Russian Masculinities in History and Culture*, ed. Barbara Evans Clements, Rebecca Friedman, and Dan Healey (New York: Palgrave, 2002), 17.
19. Valerie A. Kivelson, *Autocracy in the Provinces: The Muscovite Gentry and Political Culture in the Seventeenth Century* (Stanford, CA: Stanford University Press, 1996), 220–221.
20. Kivelson, *Autocracy in the Provinces*, 50.
21. Robert O. Crummey, *Aristocrats and Servitors: The Boyar Elite in Russia, 1613–1689* (Princeton, NJ: Princeton University Press, 1983), 128–129.
22. LeDonne, *Absolutism and Ruling Class*, 260.
23. Wirtschafter, *Social Identity in Imperial Russia*, 33. As of 1858, 78 percent of noble landowners owned fewer than 100 serfs, and 44 percent owned fewer than 21 serfs. As of 1834, 17,000 nobles owned no land at all (out of a total of

106,000 who owned fewer than 100 serfs), and thus were entirely dependent on other sources of income, particularly official employment.
24. Marshall Poe, "What Did Russians Mean When They Called Themselves 'Slaves of the Tsar'?," *Slavic Review* 57, no. 3 (Autumn 1998): 601. Some Western observers apparently thought similar things about Qing usage—a 1909 report in the Jesuit journal *America* declared that "the Manchus are awakening to a sense of dignity. Manchu officials are no longer to call themselves 'slaves' in addressing the Throne. They will in future follow the practice of Chinese officials and use the more dignified expression of 'your ministers.'" M. Kennelly, "China's Social and Economic Progress," *America: A Catholic Review of the Week* 1, no. 12 (July 3, 1909): 323.
25. Poe, "What Did Russians Mean," 601–607.
26. Hughes, *Russia in the Age of Peter the Great*, 178. Catherine the Great, however, insisted on the use of "loyal subject"; see Elise Kimerling Wirtschafter, "Power and the 18th-Century Nobility," *Kritika: Explorations in Russian and Eurasian History* 15, no. 3 (Summer 2014): 660.
27. Russell E. Martin, *A Bride for the Tsar: Bride Shows and Marriage Politics in Early Modern Russia* (DeKalb: Northern Illinois University Press, 2012). Martin directly compares the Russian bride shows to the Qing *xiunü* selection process, although he notes that they did not share a common origin (see pp. 28–29).
28. Martin, *A Bride for the Tsar*, 47.
29. Martin, *A Bride for the Tsar*, 66–69.
30. Martin, *A Bride for the Tsar*, 55–56, gives a complete listing of the instances when bride shows occurred.
31. The Ryukyuan elite, known as the *yukatchu* (良人), bore certain resemblances to samurai in their role in the civil service, receipt of government stipends, and clear separation from the broader population. But they had no military role and clearly were distinct from the samurai of Japan proper, whether or not they may have constituted a service elite in their own right. On the *yukatchu*, see Gregory Smits, *Visions of Ryukyu: Identity and Ideology in Early-Modern Thought and Politics* (Honolulu: University of Hawai'i Press, 1999), 40, 167, and 176 n.95.
32. Daniel Robert Stewart, "Temporary Samurai: Status and Service in Early Modern Japan" (PhD dissertation, University of California, Berkeley, 2003), 23.
33. Stewart, "Temporary Samurai," 31.
34. Stewart, "Temporary Samurai," 44.
35. Stewart, "Temporary Samurai," 153–154.
36. Morishita Tōru 森下徹, *The Status of Warriors: The Daimyō Retainer Band of Castle Town Hagi* 武士という身分：城下町萩の大名家臣団 (Tokyo: Yoshikawa kōbunkan, 2012), 31–33.
37. Conrad Totman, *Early Modern Japan* (Berkeley: University of California Press, 1993), 172.

38. Douglas R. Howland, "Samurai Status, Class, and Bureaucracy: A Historiographical Essay," *Journal of Asian Studies* 60, no. 2 (May 2001): 368.
39. Howland, "Samurai Status, Class, and Bureaucracy," 367–370.
40. Conrad Totman, *Politics in the Tokugawa Bakufu, 1600–1843* (Berkeley: University of California Press, 1967), 131.
41. On the long period of peace under Tokugawa rule that challenged the role of the samurai as a military elite, see Mark Ravina, *To Stand with the Nations of the World: Japan's Meiji Restoration in World History* (Oxford: Oxford University Press, 2017), 46; and Eiko Ikegami, *The Taming of the Samurai: Honorific Individualism and the Making of Modern Japan* (Cambridge, MA: Harvard University Press, 1995), 157.
42. Constantine Nomikos Vaporis, *Tour of Duty: Samurai, Military Service in Edo, and the Culture of Early Modern Japan* (Honolulu: University of Hawai'i Press, 2008), 70–73.
43. Vaporis, *Tour of Duty*, 103–105.
44. Vaporis, *Tour of Duty*, 123.
45. Morishita, *The Status of Warriors*, 42–45.
46. John Whitney Hall, "Feudalism in Japan—a Reassessment," *Comparative Studies in Society and History* 5, no. 1 (October 1962): 45–47; Philip C. Brown, *Central Authority and Local Autonomy in the Formation of Early Modern Japan: The Case of Kaga Domain* (Stanford, CA: Stanford University Press, 1993), 24.
47. Totman, *Politics in the Tokugawa Bakufu*, 145–148.
48. Mark Ravina, *Land and Lordship in Early Modern Japan* (Stanford, CA: Stanford University Press, 1999), 84.
49. Rosemary Gray Trott, "The Politics of Famine in a Far-off Place: Nyūi Mitsugi and the Hōreki Crisis in Tsugaru" (PhD dissertation, Australian National University, 2001), 59.
50. For example, see an 1824 case from Tosa domain in which a high-ranking retainer lost his post for failure to maintain proper control of his household, described in Luke Roberts, "Governing the Samurai Family in the Late Edo Period," in *What Is a Family? Answers from Early Modern Japan*, ed. Mary Elizabeth Berry and Marcia Yonemoto (Oakland: University of California Press, 2019), 149.
51. Morishita, *The Status of Warriors*, 126–127.
52. Amy Stanley, *Stranger in the Shogun's City: A Japanese Woman and Her World* (New York: Scribner, 2020), 112–133.
53. See, for example, Luke S. Roberts, *Performing the Great Peace: Political Spaces and Open Secrets in Tokugawa Japan* (Honolulu: University of Hawai'i Press, 2012), 37.
54. Roberts, "Governing the Samurai Family," 162–165.
55. Katsu Kokichi, *Musui's Story: The Autobiography of a Tokugawa Samurai*, trans. Teruko Craig (Tucson: University of Arizona Press, 1998), 68–69. This is the same Katsu Kokichi mentioned previously.

56. Ikegami, *The Taming of the Samurai*, 244.
57. Indeed, this rule was related to the ability of domains to punish samurai for failing to control a wife's adultery—because loss of control of the household threatened a samurai man's position, the offense was considered more grievous than in commoner households. Although the right to revenge killing was extended to commoners in the mid-eighteenth century, they remained less likely to take advantage of it. See Amy Stanley, "Adultery, Punishment, and Reconciliation in Tokugawa Japan," *Journal of Japanese Studies* 33, no. 2 (Summer 2007): 315–319, 324–325.
58. Ravina, *Land and Lordship*, 6.
59. Ravina, *Land and Lordship*, 62–67. Note that in the early years of the Qing, banner people were given large tracts of land, the revenue of which was to be used to support them. Over time, most of this land fell out of banner hands, but the initial imposition of the system offers a possible analog to the landed fief system in the Tokugawa because in both cases, service elites were meant to be supported by particular tracts of land with which they had very little contact. See Mark C. Elliott, *The Manchu Way: The Eight Banners and Ethnic Identity in Late Imperial China* (Stanford, CA: Stanford University Press, 2001), 193–194.
60. Totman, *Politics in the Tokugawa Bakufu*, 133–139.
61. Teruko Craig, "Introduction," in *Musui's Story: The Autobiography of a Tokugawa Samurai*, trans. Teruko Craig (Tucson: University of Arizona Press, 1998), xv.
62. Craig, "Introduction," xv–xvi.
63. Mizubayashi Takeshi 水林彪, *The Restructuring of the Feudal System and the Formation of Japanese Society* 封建制の再編と日本的社会の確立 (Tokyo: Yamakawa shuppansha, 1987), 274–275.
64. Ravina, *Land and Lordship*, 37–40; Ravina draws on the work of both Mizubayashi Takeshi and Kasaya Kazuhiko in formulating this argument.
65. Constantine Nomikos Vaporis, *Samurai: An Encyclopedia of Japan's Cultured Warriors* (Santa Barbara, CA: ABC-CLIO, 2019), 233.
66. Vaporis, *Tour of Duty*, 12–13.
67. Hata Hisako, "Servants of the Inner Quarters: The Women of the Shogun's Great Interior," trans. Anne Walthall, in *Servants of the Dynasty: Palace Women in World History*, ed. Anne Walthall (Berkeley: University of California Press, 2008), 180–181. The "Great Interior" is the name usually used to refer to the women's quarters of Edo Castle, the shogunal residence.
68. Also, as in the Qing, legal impediments to interstatus marriage sometimes depended on the gender of the parties involved. For instance, in Kaga domain, the daughter of a samurai family could marry the son of a priest, but not the other way around.
69. Marcia Yonemoto, *The Problem of Women in Early Modern Japan* (Oakland: University of California Press, 2016), 95–96.

70. Evgeni Radushev, "'Peasant' Janissaries?," *Journal of Social History* 42, no. 2 (Winter 2008): 450.
71. Norman Itzkowitz, *Ottoman Empire and Islamic Tradition* (Chicago: University of Chicago Press, 1972), 60. Also see I. Metin Kunt, *The Sultan's Servants: The Transformation of Ottoman Provincial Government, 1550–1650* (New York: Columbia University Press, 1983), 32–33. There, Kunt makes the point that because the populations from whom *devşirme* were taken were inhabitants of a Muslim state, they should have been safe from enslavement as well according to Islamic law. But despite the Ottomans ignoring this prohibition, it still seems clear that the Ottoman court treated being a non-Muslim as a sufficient and necessary condition to be eligible for the *devşirme* levies.
72. Cornell H. Fleischer, *Bureaucrat and Intellectual in the Ottoman Empire: The Historian Mustafa Ali (1541–1600)* (Princeton, NJ: Princeton University Press, 1986), 255–258.
73. Halil İnalcık, *The Ottoman Empire: The Classical Age 1300–1600* (New York: Weidenfeld and Nicolson, 1973), 78.
74. Karen Barkey, *Empire of Difference: The Ottomans in Comparative Perspective* (New York: Cambridge University Press, 2008), 124–125. For the quote, see 124 n.41.
75. For a clear explanation of *timar*, see Linda T. Darling, "The Sultan's Advisors and Their Opinions on the Identity of the Ottoman Elite, 1580–1653," in *Living in the Ottoman Realm: Empire and Identity, 13th to 20th Centuries*, ed. Christine Isom-Verhaaren and Kent F. Schull (Bloomington: Indiana University Press, 2016), 172. These fiefs were not held in perpetuity; they could be taken away or increased in size, while their holders could also be transferred to new *timar*. See, for instance, Muhsin Soyudoğan, "The Fall of Icarus: The Paradox of the Ottoman Centralization and the Abstraction of Timars," *Turkish Historical Review* 8 (2017): 200; and Victor Ostapchuk, "The Trouble with Timars: An Excursion into a Seventeenth-Century Documentary Landscape," in *Ottoman War and Peace: Studies in Honor of Virginia H. Aksan*, ed. Frank Castiglione, Ethan L. Menchinger, and Veysel Şimşek (Leiden, Netherlands: Brill, 2019), 45–48.
76. Linda T. Darling, "Nasihatnameler, İcmal Defterleri, and the Timar-Holding Ottoman Elite in the Late Sixteenth Century," *Journal of Ottoman Studies* 43 (2014): 203.
77. Linda T. Darling, "Historicizing the Ottoman *Timar* System: Identities of *Timar*-Holders, Fourteenth to Seventeenth Centuries," *Turkish Historical Review* 8 (2017): 153; for the 61 percent figure, which comes from the 1566–1574 reign of Selm II, see page 163.
78. Darling, "Historicizing the Ottoman *Timar* System," 169.
79. Halil İnalcık, "The Nature of Traditional Society: Turkey," in *Political Modernization in Japan and Turkey*, ed. Robert Ward and Dankwart Rostow (Princeton, NJ: Princeton University Press, 1964), 44.

80. Darling, "The Sultan's Advisors," 172.
81. Gulay Yilmaz, "Becoming a *Devşirme*: The Training of Conscripted Children in the Ottoman Empire," in *Children in Slavery Through the Ages*, ed. Gwyn Campbell, Suzanne Miers, and Joseph C. Miller (Athens: University of Ohio Press, 2009), 123.
82. Karen Barkey, *Bandits and Bureaucrats: The Ottoman Route to State Centralization* (Ithaca, NY: Cornell University Press, 1994), 77–80.
83. Yilmaz, "Becoming a *Devşirme*," 124.
84. Barkey, *Bandits and Bureaucrats*, 36.
85. Barkey, *Bandits and Bureaucrats*, 29.
86. These powerful warrior families are the ones called "marcher-lords" in Caroline Finkel, *Osman's Dream: The History of the Ottoman Empire* (New York: Basic Books, 2005), 75.
87. Barkey, *Bandits and Bureaucrats*, 32–34. Although Barkey argues that the importance of networking and patronage was a departure from meritocracy, the value of connections is apparent in all meritocratic systems, whether early modern or contemporary. In any case, promotion through patronage connections is clearly different from simple inheritance of power, as in a hereditary system.
88. Barkey, *Bandits and Bureaucrats*, 65.
89. Yilmaz, "Becoming a *Devşirme*," 124.
90. Gülay Yilmaz, "The Devshirme System and the Levied Children of Bursa in 1603–4 A.D.," *Belleten* 79, no. 286 (December 2015): 919–924.
91. Gülay Yılmaz, "The Economic and Social Roles of Janissaries in a 17th-Century Ottoman City: The Case of Istanbul" (PhD dissertation, McGill University, 2011), 187–188.
92. Baki Tezcan, *The Second Ottoman Empire: Political and Social Transformation in the Early Modern World* (Cambridge: Cambridge University Press, 2010), 205.
93. Andrew Wheatcroft, *The Ottomans* (London: Viking, 1993), 90.
94. Eunjeong Yi, *Guild Dynamics in Seventeenth-Century Istanbul: Fluidity and Leverage* (Leiden, Netherlands: Brill, 2004), 140.
95. Yilmaz, "The Economic and Social Roles of Janissaries," 192–193.
96. Tezcan, *The Second Ottoman Empire*, 207–208.
97. Yilmaz, "Becoming a *Devşirme*," 125–126.
98. Yi, *Guild Dynamics in Seventeenth-Century Istanbul*, 136–137; Tezcan, *The Second Ottoman Empire*, 199–202.
99. Barkey, *Bandits and Bureaucrats*, 60–76.
100. See Kunt, *The Sultan's Servants*, 32–33; and Itzkowitz, *Ottoman Empire and Islamic Tradition*, 49.
101. Fleischer, *Bureaucrat and Intellectual*, 15.
102. Fleischer, *Bureaucrat and Intellectual*, 208–209.
103. Finkel, *Osman's Dream*, 201.

104. Leslie P. Peirce, "Beyond Harem Walls: Ottoman Royal Women and the Exercise of Power," in *Servants of the Dynasty: Palace Women in World History*, ed. Anne Walthall (Berkeley: University of California Press, 2008), 88–91.
105. See Max Weber, *Essays in Sociology*, ed. and trans. H. H. Gerth and C. Wright Mills (New York: Routledge, 1948), 196–244.
106. Elliott, *The Manchu Way*, 89–132.
107. Yılmaz, "The Economic and Social Roles of Janissaries," 110–111.
108. For instance, see James L. McClain, *Kanazawa: A Seventeenth-Century Japanese Castle Town* (New Haven, CT: Yale University Press, 1982), 28, for a description of the process of turning samurai into an urban population in seventeenth century Kaga domain.
109. Stanley, *Stranger in the Shogun's City*, 112.
110. LeDonne, *Absolutism and Ruling Class*, 22.
111. On the centrality of "purely personal loyalty" to feudalism, see Max Weber, *Economy and Society: An Outline of Interpretive Sociology*, ed. Guenther Roth and Claus Wittich (Berkeley: University of California Press, 1978), 256.
112. And this need for reassessment perhaps applies to the other service elites under discussion in this chapter, although specialists in the relevant fields are better qualified to undertake that work.

7. Challenging the Service Elite Model

1. GZSL, *juan* 459, QL 19.3.27 (April 19, 1754). According to the memorial that the two officials sent in response, the original edict was in Manchu and was personally received by Kargišan at an audience with the emperor, but the only available surviving versions are in Chinese. See Kargišan, HWZPZZ, NPM 403006688, QL 19.6.6 (July 25, 1754).
2. Claims of adherence to dynastic precedents were important to Qing emperors even when they in fact sought to reverse those precedents, in part because of the moral necessity of demonstrating obedience to their ancestors. For instance, although the Qianlong emperor let many of his father's fiscal reforms lapse, or even undermined them directly, he did not explicitly overturn them. See Madeleine Zelin, *The Magistrate's Tael: Rationalizing Fiscal Reform in Eighteenth-Century Ch'ing China* (Berkeley: University of California Press, 1984), xv.
3. The idea that 1742 marked the beginning of expulsion occurs in a range of works from multiple different scholarly traditions, including Ura Ren'ichi 浦廉一, "Regarding the Hanjun (Ujen Cooha)" 漢軍（烏真超哈）に就いて, in *Essay Collection on Oriental History in Honor of the Sixtieth Birthday of Dr. Kuwabara* 桑原博士還歴記念東洋史論叢 (Kyoto, Japan: Kōbundō Shōbō, 1931), 842; Liu Xiaomeng 刘小萌, *Eight Banner People of the Qing Dynasty*

清代八旗子弟 (Liaoyang, China: Liaoning minzu chubanshe, 2008), 69–70; and Mark C. Elliott, *The Manchu Way: The Eight Banners and Ethnic Identity in Late Imperial China* (Stanford, CA: Stanford University Press, 2001), 339–340. Elliott recognizes the 1742 policy as distinct from what came later (though he does describe the earlier decision as the "first step" of expulsion), but that distinction is lost entirely in much of the scholarship that relies on his work. See, for example, James Leibold, *Reconfiguring Chinese Nationalism: How the Qing Frontier and Its Indigenes Became Chinese* (New York: Palgrave Macmillan, 2007), 28, which mistakenly claims that in 1742, the Qianlong emperor expelled "all members of the Eight Chinese Banners."

4. Sun Jiagan, HWLFZZ, FHA 03-0523-010, QL 7.2.24 (March 30, 1742). Qianlong did not explicitly mention the memorial, but similarities in some of the ideas that appear in both it and the edict suggest a connection between the two.
5. This edict can be found in GZSL, *juan* 158, QL 7.1.4 (February 8, 1742).
6. This passage is also cited in Elliott, *The Manchu Way*, 338, with slight differences in phrasing. Elliott argues that this passage shows that the Hanjun were viewed as "simply Chinese with peculiar backgrounds" and "no longer were they 'men of the banners.'" I think this somewhat overstates the claim of the memorial, which, as explained later in this discussion and as Elliott himself notes, did not even suggest that Hanjun who took up this offer should lose their banner registry.
7. Sun's suggestion here, probably unlike the emperor's own views, may have reflected a belief that the supposed natural ability of Han to engage in commerce and agriculture was a sign of their superiority over Manchus and Mongols. In 1741, as Zhili governor-general, Sun suggested that Han be allowed to exploit salt lakes in Inner Mongolia on account of the failure of Mongols, to whom he referred in one memorial (for which he was reprimanded) as "barbarians" (Ch. 夷人 [*yiren*]), to do so. See David A. Bello, *Across Forest, Steppe, and Mountain: Environment, Identity, and Empire in Qing China's Borderlands* (Cambridge: Cambridge University Press, 2016), 154–155.
8. In the earlier memorial, he had written: "instruct the Eight Banners: if there are those who wish to go to the countryside and live by cultivating the land, there is no need for them to pay, give them 100 *mu* of superior land, 150 *mu* of medium quality land, or 200 *mu* of lesser quality land, and have them take their wives and children, live in the countryside, and farm." This memorial is found in He Changling 賀長齡, ed., *A Collection of Essays on Statecraft from Our Dynasty* 皇朝經世文編 (1826, reprinted Shanghai: Guangbaisong zhai, 1887), *juan* 35, 10b–11b. It is undated in this collection but quotes an edict from late 1739—see GZSL, *juan* 104, QL 4.11.2 (December 2, 1739). Sun's tenure as Zhili governor-general ended in 1741, so the memorial must date from 1740 or 1741, and given the date of the quoted edict, it is likely from 1740.

9. Much of this edict, including this passage, is also translated in Elliott, *The Manchu Way*, 339–340. My translation differs from his in some particulars, in part because I have also used the Manchu version of the edict, which had been unavailable to Elliott. The Chinese-language text of the entire edict can be found in GZSL, *juan* 164, QL 7.4.13 (May 17, 1742). The Manchu and Chinese texts of the edict are both quoted in their entirety (with the exception of a damaged section at the beginning of the Manchu version) in Hongzhi 弘旺, MHHBZPZZ, FHA 04-01-01-0073-049, QL 7.7.25 (August 25, 1742).

10. The emperor detailed the other ways that Hanjun may have entered the banners as follows: "those who submitted and entered the banners after the establishment of the capital at Beijing, also those who on account of a crime entered the banners and those entered into the banners as people under the Three Feudatories, those raised out of the bondservant companies of the Imperial Household Department or [the bondservant companies] of the nobility and put into the banners, along with those recruited to serve as artillerymen, those adopted as descendants from outside the patriline, and those who followed their mother on account of her marriage [to a banner person]."

11. Emphasis added. The importance of this is much clearer in the Manchu version of the edict, which uses the Manchu word *dahame*, meaning "because," following its claim that Hanjun who had joined up late all had homes to return to, clarifying that this was a reason for the decision that they would have the right to leave. Notably, this established a parallel with the earlier description of Hanjun who joined up before the conquest, who *because* they had spent so many years in service were to be exempted (Ma. *aniya goidahangge be dahame*), perhaps suggesting that the very length of their service had led to them no longer having the sorts of connections to a native place in China that those who entered the banners later still had.

12. The edict that began the process of expelling the Fuzhou Hanjun cited the "precedent of the capital Hanjun" (Ch. 京城漢軍之例 [*Jingcheng Hanjun zhi li*]), who, as the edict said, had been permitted to leave the banners. See GZSL, *juan* 459, QL 19.3.27 (April 19, 1754). According to this edict, this right had never been extended to Hanjun in the provincial garrisons, and indeed the scholarly literature on the Hanjun expulsion also says that it applied only to capital Hanjun (cf. Elliott, *The Manchu Way*, 340). However, at least at the time of the 1742 edict, the emperor seems to have intended Hanjun anywhere in the empire to be able to take advantage of its provisions, decreeing: "For those who wish to change to commoner status and wish to move to the provinces to live, without regard to whether they are in the capital or in the provinces, or to whether they are official soldiers or unemployed, . . . it will be arranged thusly."

13. Guanglu 廣祿, MHHBZPZZ, FHA 04-01-16-0016-054, QL 7.9.2 (September 30, 1742).

14. Yunbi 允祕, MWLFZZ, FHA 03-0181-2109-006, QL 29.10.4 (October 28, 1764).
15. Qi Bin, HWZPZZ, FHA 04-01-01-0131-048, QL 11.11.29 (January 9, 1747).
16. Qi Bin, HWZPZZ, FHA 04-01-01-0142-004, QL 12.1.25 (March 5, 1747).
17. The importance of the first of these points, though not the second, has also been emphasized by Zhang Yuxing 张玉兴, "A Brief Comment on Bondservants with Han Surnames and the Hanjun: A Historical Testimony on the Rise and Decline of the Eight Banner System" 包衣汉姓与汉军简论：八旗制度兴衰的一个历史见证, *Liaoning daxue xuebao (zhexue shehui kexue ban)* 31, no. 4 (July 2003): 43.
18. Quoted in Necin, MWLFZZ, FHA 03-0171-0254-010.1, QL 11.8.30 (October 14, 1746).
19. Although Elliott states that the Chahar were an "auxiliary" force, not structurally linked to the Eight Banners (*The Manchu Way*, 74), until 1762, Mongol Eight Banner generals in fact served simultaneously as Chahar banner commanders, and like the other Eight Banner divisions, the Chahar banners were divided into their own companies. See Da-li-zha-bu 达力扎布, "A Brief Examination of the Question of the Early Qing Establishment of the Chahar Banners" 清初察哈尔设旗问题考略, *Nei Menggu daxue xuebao* 31, no. 1 (January 1999): 38–44.
20. In addition to raising livestock, partly to supply state needs, Chahar bannermen could be (and often were) called to serve in banner armies. See SZXSL, *juan* 120, YZ 10.6.8 (July 29, 1732), which mentions that nearly all adult Chahar men were either serving on the frontier or preparing to do so. Bello, *Across Forest, Steppe, and Mountain*, 122–123, also mentions the role of the Chahars in the Qing state's official herding operations.
21. This is an important point because it means that the transferred Household Selected Soldiers would cease to be a coherent group because they would not have their own companies (Ma. *niru*). Moreover, it challenges our standard understanding of the ethnic basis of the Qing banner system as explained by Mark C. Elliott, "Ethnicity in the Qing Eight Banners," in *Empire at the Margins: Culture, Ethnicity, and Frontier in Early Modern China*, ed. Pamela Kyle Crossley, Helen F. Siu, and Donald S. Sutton (Berkeley: University of California Press, 2006), 46, according to which even when a particular ethnic banner category had soldiers of a different ethnic background, individual companies would consist entirely of soldiers of one ethnicity. Necin did not seem to see this principle as an obstacle to his plan. In addition, his memorial proposed that qualified Household Selected Soldiers could be used as lieutenants (Ma. *funde bošoku*) in their new Chahar companies, suggesting that they would cease to be distinguished from the original members of these companies.
22. Necin, MWLFZZ, FHA 03-0171-0254-010.1, QL 11.8.30 (October 14, 1746).

23. As David Bello has shown, the idea that pastoralism was the proper lifestyle for Mongols was a fundamental part of how the Qing state managed both physical spaces and people. See Bello, *Across Forest, Steppe, and Mountain*, ch. 3.
24. Quoted in Fuheng 傅恒, MWLFZZ, FHA 03-0171-0254-010.2, QL 11.9.26 (November 9, 1746).
25. Emphasis added. Quoted in Fuheng 傅恒, MWLFZZ, FHA 03-0171-0254-010.2, QL 11.9.26 (November 9, 1746).
26. Fuheng 傅恒, MWLFZZ, FHA 03-0171-0254-010.2, QL 11.9.26 (November 9, 1746).
27. GZSL, *juan* 280, QL 11.12.4 (January 14, 1747).
28. Buhi, MWLFZZ, FHA 03-0172-0616-002, QL 12.1.20 (February 28, 1747).
29. Buhi, MWLFZZ, FHA 03-0171-0179-001, QL 12.1.20 (February 28, 1747).
30. Necin, MWLFZZ, FHA 03-0171-0258-009, QL 12.1.28 (March 8, 1747). Later documents show that some people without other means of support were in fact retained at Suiyuan in the banners. In 1753, there were still thirty children being supported by the Suiyuan garrison until they reached the age of eighteen and could be transferred to Green Standard garrisons to support themselves as soldiers. Fucang, MWLFZZ, FHA 03-0172-0545-005, QL 18.4.15 (May 17, 1753).
31. Nasutu, HWZPZZ, FHA 04-01-01-0146-008, QL 12.7.6 (August 11, 1747).
32. Although *lijia* is usually associated with the Ming, it formally existed in the Qing well into the eighteenth century. See Zheng Zhenman, *Family Lineage Organization and Social Change in Ming and Qing Fujian*, trans. Michael Szonyi (Honolulu: University of Hawai'i Press, 2001), for the continued relevance of the system into the Qing era.
33. Peng Weixin 彭維新, MHHBZPZZ, FHA 04-01-01-0146-011, QL 12.8.19 (September 23, 1747).
34. All three groups were found in the Suiyuan garrison. In fact, the very same document describes a decision to split the soldiers in a banner unit transferred from Chengde into Manchu, Mongol, and Hanjun companies on the basis of their ethnic status (five hundred "Old Chinese" [Ma. *fe Nikan*] were to be divided among the eight Hanjun companies at Suiyuan), where they had previously been "mixed among the forty companies, without any regard to whether they were Manchu, Mongol or Hanjun." Buhi, MWLFZZ, FHA 03-0171-0179-004, QL 12.03.23 (May 2, 1747).
35. See the previous discussion of the Household Selected Soldiers' entrance into the banners in chapter 2, note 47, which mentions the division of the group into Manchu, Mongol, and Hanjun banners depending on each soldier's ethnic background.
36. Nasutu, HWZPZZ, FHA 04-01-01-0146-008, QL 12.7.6 (August 11, 1747).

37. See Qu Cheng 屈成, "The Auditing of the 'Separate Registers' during the Yongzheng and Qianlong Reigns" 清雍乾时期的"另记档案"清查, *Qing shi yanjiu* 2018, no. 3 (August 2018): 17–18, 21.
38. Qu Cheng argues that the two types of banner households that were "separately recorded in the registers" had fully distinct statuses. This was probably true in the Yongzheng and early Qianlong periods, and the distinction reappeared occasionally in later periods as well. But neither the example of the Household Selected Soldiers themselves nor Qu's own description of the later campaign to expel such households from the banners shows any evidence that the court still made this distinction during the expulsion era. See Qu, "The Auditing of the 'Separate Registers,'" 24–29, for Qu's account of the expulsion.
39. The opening to the memorial is signed "Necin, et al" (Ma. *Necin se*), and the edict responding to it begins, "You all discussed and memorialized" (Ma. *suweni gisurefi wesimbuhe*—that is, it uses the second person plural form *suweni*).
40. Sanjab, MWZZ, FHA 03-0173-1212-017, QL 3.12.9 (January 18, 1739).
41. This was the opposite problem from the one that banner officials usually brought up when discussing the effects of local commoner customs on banner people, whom they usually worried would lose their marital spirit. Kargišan, HWZPZZ, NPM 403006689, QL 19.6.6 (July 25, 1754).
42. Kargišan, HWZPZZ, NPM 403006688, QL 19.6.6 (July 25, 1754).
43. Presumably, they would also no longer be able to marry banner people themselves, although this fact is not mentioned. Although, as discussed in chapter 5, there is no clear evidence for a total prohibition of intermarriage (particularly between bannermen and commoner women), the memorial quite clearly states that "when it comes to the prior regulation that Hanjun men and women must not marry commoners, now those who have already dispersed [from the garrison] and become commoners are permitted to contract marriage with commoner households as a single group."
44. Normally, younger male relatives of Green Standard soldiers had the right to fill supernumerary posts (Ch. 餘丁 [*yuding*]), from which regular soldiers would be selected. If a vacancy appeared in the ranks of regular soldiers, men would first be taken from among the supernumeraries to fill it. Only if the number of available supernumeraries was insufficient would military officials recruit from among the general commoner population. As such, there was a strong hereditary component to Green Standard service, though unlike with bannermen, there was no requirement that sons of Green Standard soldiers take up military service. Guo Taifeng 郭太风, "An Initial Survey of the Salary System of the Eight Banners and Green Standards" 八旗绿营俸饷制度初探, *Fudan xuebao (shehui kexue ban)* 1982, no. 4: 106–107.

45. The only change was offering the expelled bannermen three-fourths of the available vacancies rather than the seven-tenths that had been offered to the Household Selected Soldiers who were expelled. See Nasutu, HWZPZZ, FHA 04-01-01-0146-008, QL 12.07.06 (August 11, 1747).
46. GZSL, *juan* 469, QL 19.7.17 (September 3, 1754).
47. This explanation of expulsion is preferred by Mark Elliott. See Elliott, *The Manchu Way*, 306–313. A related argument, made most explicitly by Zhao Bingzhong 赵秉忠 and Bai Xinliang 白新良, "An Investigation Regarding Qianlong-era Eight Banner Policy" 关于乾隆时期八旗政策的考察 *Shixue yuekan* 1991, no. 2: 40, suggests that the court was not necessarily trying to save money; rather, it wanted to better provide for Manchus in the banners without having to increase spending.
48. Some of these plans were discussed in chapter 4.
49. Ethnic discrimination within the banners was discussed in chapter 1; for worries in the preconquest period about the loss of Jurchen ways, see, for example, Mark C. Elliott, "Whose Empire Shall It Be? Manchu Figurations of Historical Process in the Seventeenth Century," in *Time, Temporality, and Imperial Transition: East Asia from Ming to Qing*, ed. Lynn A. Struve (Honolulu: University of Hawai'i Press, 2005), 47.
50. According to Beatrice Bartlett, under Qianlong and later emperors, recommendations produced after discussion by high-ranking officials, as Necin's had been, received imperial approval between 98 and 99 percent of the time. Beatrice S. Bartlett, *Monarchs and Ministers: The Grand Council in Mid-Qing China* (Berkeley: University of California Press, 1991), 276.
51. Zhao and Bai, "An Investigation Regarding Qianlong-era Eight Banner Policy," 40.
52. Philip A. Kuhn, *Soulstealers: The Chinese Sorcery Scare of 1768* (Cambridge, MA: Harvard University Press, 1990).
53. Jonathan D. Spence, *Treason by the Book* (New York: Viking Penguin, 2001), 171.
54. Pamela Kyle Crossley, *A Translucent Mirror: History and Identity in Qing Imperial Ideology* (Berkeley: University of California Press, 1999), 256.
55. C. Patterson Giersch, *Asian Borderlands: The Transformation of Qing China's Yunnan Frontier* (Cambridge, MA: Harvard University Press, 2006), 66–67, 90.
56. Crossley, *A Translucent Mirror*, 260–262.
57. On the connection between the natural spaces of Manchuria and the identity of the Manchus, see Jonathan Schlesinger, *A World Trimmed with Fur: Wild Things, Pristine Places, and the Natural Fringes of Qing Rule* (Stanford, CA: Stanford University Press, 2017), 57. Bello, *Across Forest, Steppe, and Mountain*, 36–38, 45–48, suggests a much stronger sense of the importance of protecting divisions between Han and Inner Asian physical spaces on the part of Qianlong, as compared to Kangxi, who saw value in the expansion of Han cultivation practices

into the frontier zone, and especially when compared with Yongzheng, who encompassed Manchuria within the geomantic space of China. An edict ordering the Solon, a New Manchu group, to follow supposedly traditional practices of archery and eschew the use of muskets can be found in GZSL, *juan* 374, QL 15.10.8 (November 6, 1750).
58. The Manchu literally means "less than a Han." Nikan Fusihun 尼堪富什渾, MWLFZZ, FHA 03-0191-0357-009, QL 50.10.12 (November 13, 1785).
59. As discussed previously, this was part of the expulsion process of the Household Selected Soldiers, as well as the Hanjun in Fuzhou. It was also important in Xi'an, for instance, where some expelled Hanjun were allowed to continue living in garrison housing for free. See Yu Minzhong 于敏中, HWLFZZ, NPM 024451, QL 44.7.26 (September 6, 1779).

8. Expulsion, Resistance, and the Return of the Service Elite

1. Sitku, MWLFZZ, FHA 03-0171-0341-002, QL 20.3.7 (April 17, 1755).
2. GZSL, *juan* 486, QL 20.4.8 (May 18, 1755).
3. Yang Yingju, HWZPZZ, NPM 403009753, QL 20.6.21 (July 29, 1755).
4. GZSL, *juan* 493, QL 20.7.27 (September 3, 1755).
5. Sitku, HWZPZZ, NPM 403010464, QL 20.9.28 (November 2, 1755).
6. GZSL, *juan* 500, QL 20.11.4 (December 6, 1755).
7. GZSL, *juan* 500, QL 20.11.4 (December 6, 1755).
8. GZSL, *juan* 500, QL 20.11.13 (December 15, 1755). No reason is given for the transfer, but Barköl, on the edge of the far-off, newly conquered territories that would later be named Xinjiang, was almost certainly a less favorable assignment than Guangzhou, and it seems unlikely to be coincidental that Sitku was transferred after ten years of service in Guangzhou only days after receiving a harsh rebuke for his plan for Hanjun expulsion. The Guangzhou garrison gazetteer also claims that Li Shiyao was specially appointed for the purposes of managing the expulsion. See Cangšan 長善, ed., *Gazetteer for the Eight Banners Garrisoned in Canton* 駐粤八旗志 (Guangzhou, 1884; reprinted Taipei: Wenhai chubanshe, 1997), *juan* 14, 8a.
9. A brief description of Sitku's service as garrison general can be found in Cangšan, *Gazetteer for the Eight Banners Garrisoned in Canton*, *juan* 14, 7b–8a.
10. GZSL, *juan* 557, QL 23.2.24 (April 1, 1758). That this edict was carried out is confirmed in Fusengge, MWLFZZ, FHA 03-0180-1976-015, QL 27.10.? (November–December 1762), which proposed using some of the secondary-status bannermen sent to Fuzhou to fill posts in the naval garrison that were to be vacated by Hanjun.

11. SYD, QL 21.5.9 (June 6, 1756). Only those who did not already hold salaried posts were to be expelled immediately; those currently employed were to be allowed to serve until their retirement. However, unlike the Hanjun, those members of secondary-status groups who were expelled were not to be given employment in the Green Standards. For more on the expulsion of the secondary-status banner groups, see David C. Porter, "Ethnic and Status Identity in Qing China: The Hanjun Eight Banners" (PhD dissertation, Harvard University, 2018), 157–161.
12. See Fusengge, MWLFZZ, FHA 03-0180-2005-001, QL 28.1.9 (February 21, 1763), for the expulsion of this group from Fuzhou; and Mingfu, MWLFZZ, FHA 03-0180-2027-040, QL 28.4.22 (June 3, 1763), for the same policy in Guangzhou.
13. The edict relating to Zhuanglang, Liangzhou, Hangzhou, and Jingkou can be found in GZSL, *juan* 677, QL 27.12.26 (February 8, 1763). The number of Mongols sent from Jiangning to Jingkou is in GZSL, *juan* 780, QL 32.3.14 (April 12, 1767). The edict ordering Hanjun expulsion at Suiyuan, which provided no guidance as to what to do with the posts thereby made available, is in GZSL, *juan* 715, QL 29.7.22 (August 19, 1764).
14. See Balu 巴祿, HWZPZZ, NPM 403014224, QL 28.2.13 (March 27, 1763); and Balu, MWLFZZ, FHA 03-0180-2020-009, QL 28.4.4 (May 16, 1763).
15. Hokijung 和其衷, MWLFZZ, FHA 03-0181-2099-031, QL 29.8.1 (August 27, 1764).
16. See Yunju, MWLFZZ, FHA 03-0181-2108-031 and FHA 03-0181-2108-032, QL 29.9.21 (October 16, 1764).
17. GZSL, *juan* 1065, QL 43.8.19 (October 9, 1778). The specifics of which Green Standard soldiers were to be transferred also differentiated the emperor's plan from Lergiyen's.
18. For an example of this sort of argument, see Sun Jing 孙静, "A Discussion of the Change in Status of the Eight Banner Hanjun during the Qianlong Period" 乾隆朝八旗汉军身份变化述论, *Heilongjiang minzu congkan* 2005, no. 2: 61.
19. A detailed description of the procedures can be found in Yu Minzhong, HWLFZZ, NPM 024451, QL 44.7.26 (September 6, 1779).
20. Umitai, HWZPZZ, NPM 403036532, QL 43.10.26 (December 14, 1778).
21. The equivalent between the Manchu *geren be guilembi* and the Chinese *jiuzhong* can be verified through an examination of the Manchu and Chinese versions of the 1740 大清律例 *Da Qing lüli*. In statute 276, 發塚 *fazhong* ("opening a tomb"), the first substatute (Ma. *kooli hacin*, Ch. 條例 [*tiaoli*]) uses the phrase *geren be guilefi* in the Manchu version and *jiuzhong* in the Chinese. For the Manchu version, see Hongzhou 弘晝, ed., *Statutes and Regulations of the Great Qing Dynasty, Compiled at Imperial Order* (*Hesei toktobuha Daicing gurun i fafun i bithe kooli*) (Beijing, 1741). The Staatsbibliothek zu

Berlin version is available digitally at https://digital.staatsbibliothek-berlin.de/werkansicht/?PPN=PPN3346157741, and the substatute in question can be found at location 2173. For the Chinese version, see DQLL, "*Lü* 276: Opening Graves" 律276: 發塚, http://lsc.chineselegalculture.org/eC/DQLL_1740/5.6.3.276.

22. For relevant analogies, see the following substatutes in DQLL: *Lü* 73, *tiaoli* 4 http://lsc.chineselegalculture.org/eC/DQLL_1740/5.6.3.273.4; *Lü* 276, *tiaoli* 1 http://lsc.chineselegalculture.org/eC/DQLL_1740/5.6.3.276.1; and *Lü* 382, *tiaoli* 2 http://lsc.chineselegalculture.org/eC/DQLL_1740/5.6.12.383.2.
23. Ho-fung Hung, *Protest with Chinese Characteristics: Demonstrations, Riots, and Petitions in the Mid-Qing Dynasty* (New York: Columbia University Press, 2011), 68–71.
24. Hung, *Protest with Chinese Characteristics*, 86.
25. The preceding discussion of the protest case is based on Sinju, MWZPZZ, FHA 04-02-002-00412-0059, QL 21.R9.20 (November 12, 1756).
26. Sinju, MWZPZZ, 04-02-002-000414-0036, QL 21.11.15 (January 4, 1757).
27. Fuheng, MWLFZZ, FHA 03-0179-1948-002, QL 27.6.9 (July 29, 1762).
28. Ben-zhi 本智, HWZPZZ, FHA 04-01-01-0544-025, JQ 18.8.24 (September 18, 1813).
29. An Shuangcheng 安双成, "A Simple Analysis of the Number of Military-Age Men in the Eight Banners during the Shunzhi, Kangxi, and Yongzheng Periods (顺康雍三朝八旗丁额浅析)," *Lishi dang'an* 1983, no. 2 (July 1983): 100–103.
30. Mark C. Elliott, Cameron D. Campbell, and James Z. Lee, "A Demographic Estimate of the Population of the Qing Eight Banners," *Études chinoises* 35, no. 1 (2016): 37.
31. This number increased to only 1,396 a full year after the date of the original edict. The report containing this larger number, which is frequently cited in scholarship on the Hanjun expulsion (see, e.g., Ding Yizhuang 定宜庄, "A Brief Discussion of the Garrison Hanjun Leaving the Banners in the Qianlong Period" 乾隆朝驻防汉军出旗浅议, *Qingshi yanjiu tongxun* 1990, no. 3: 14), does not include a breakdown of the total that distinguishes unemployed bannermen from ordinary soldiers, so it obscures the fact that even this fairly small number included almost no one who had employment options within the banners. See GZSL, *juan* 189, QL 8.4.25 (May 18, 1743).
32. The others held posts in civil administration. Hongzhi, MHHBZPZZ, FHA 04-01-01-0073-049, QL 7.7.25 (August 25, 1742).
33. Yunju, MWLFZZ, FHA 03-0182-2108-032, QL 29.9.21 (October 16, 1764).
34. Annualized rates were calculated by subtracting the natural log of the initial population from the natural log of the final population, dividing by the number of years in the period covered, and multiplying by 100 (to produce a percentage). Note that the original population figures are all for able-bodied adult

men, and this analysis assumes that the ratio of total population to able-bodied adult men is constant.

35. The change from 1720–1788 includes a long period prior to expulsion; unfortunately, comparable population figures are not available for any date after 1720 but before the start of expulsion. As such, the difference between annual rates of change in Manchu and Hanjun populations in the expulsion period is almost certainly much greater than it is for the 1720–1788 period as a whole. The decline in Hanjun expulsion between 1788 and 1812 is thus probably greater than a simple comparison in average rate of population change between that period and the previous period would suggest. More detail on changes in population are provided in Porter, "Ethnic and Status Identity," 187–190. The 1720 population numbers come from An, "A Simple Analysis of the Number of Military-Age Men in the Eight Banners"; the 1788 population numbers come from Board of Revenue, HWZW, FHA 03-0193-3244-007, QL 54.6 (July–August 1789); the 1812 population numbers come from *DQHD* (1818), *juan* 12, 22a–b; and the 1887 population numbers come from *DQHD* (1899), *juan* 19, 21b–22a.
36. There were also nearly 57,000 Mongols and more than 15,000 Chahars, in addition to other smaller groups.
37. This topic was discussed in detail in chapter 4.
38. These numbers include both the 1,500/1,500 split in the main garrison, as described previously, and a 300/300 division of the banner naval garrison attached to Guangzhou. The number of Hanjun receiving monthly income in 1884 comes from Cangšan, *Gazetteer for the Eight Banners Garrisoned in Canton*, *juan* 1, 2a–5a. See also table 4.1, where I provide a complete breakdown of the salaried posts in the late nineteenth century Guangzhou garrison.
39. See Sun, "The Change in Status of the Eight Banner Hanjun," 65.
40. For scholars suggesting that the cause of Hanjun expulsion was the loss of a previously existing special function for them, whether a particular set of military skills that was either eventually acquired by Manchus or ceased to be of use to the court, or an ability to serve as intermediaries between Manchus and Han commoners that was obviated by various forms of Manchu Sinicization, see Ding, "Garrison Hanjun Leaving the Banners," and Sun, "The Change in Status of the Eight Banner Hanjun." A related argument—namely, that Hanjun banner people were intended to serve as part of a universalist elite that was never successfully created, with the court instead relying on two groups of specialists (Manchu/Mongol bannermen and Han commoners); and that the abandonment of this universalist idea helps explain expulsion—appears in Pamela Kyle Crossley, *A Translucent Mirror: History and Identity in Qing Imperial Ideology* (Berkeley: University of California Press, 1999), 286–290.

41. See David C. Porter, "Manchu Racial Identity on the Qing Frontier: Donjina and Early Twentieth-Century Ili," *Late Imperial China* 44, no. 1 (January 2018): 3–34.
42. Yang Zongjiong 楊宗炯, *Yang Charitable Hall Genealogy* 楊樂善堂族譜 (privately published, 2010), 17–30. Similar sorts of details appear on occasion in the handwritten facsimiles of an earlier version of the genealogy (see pp. 135–157). I owe thanks to Elena Chiu, whose husband, Kenneth Yeung, is a member of the Yang clan, for providing me with a copy of this genealogy.
43. However, nobles who did not hold officer rank were not permitted to retire unless they had already served twelve years, and permission to retire could be denied to other nobles if the military needs of the empire required their continued service.
44. Robert E. Jones, *Emancipation of Russian Nobility, 1762–1785* (Princeton, NJ: Princeton University Press, 1973), 28–34.
45. See Lindsey Hughes, *Russia in the Age of Peter the Great* (New Haven, CT: Yale University Press, 1998), 298–299, on Peter's desire to use education to create a kind of "new man" and close the gap with the West, and pages 174–175, on how education mandates were applied to the nobility in particular.
46. Jones, *Emancipation of Russian Nobility*, 34–37.
47. Isabel de Madariaga, *Russia in the Age of Catherine the Great* (New Haven, CT: Yale University Press, 1981), 83.
48. Jones, *Emancipation of Russian Nobility*, 167.
49. Jones, *Emancipation of Russian Nobility*, 275–276.
50. Thomas Newlin, *The Voice in the Garden: Andrei Bolotov and the Anxieties of Russian Pastoral, 1738–1833* (Evanston, IL: Northwestern University Press, 2001), 67–68.
51. See Leo Tolstoy, *War and Peace*, trans. Richard Pevear and Larissa Volokhonsky (New York: Knopf, 2007), 429–430.
52. On Catherine's interest in the institutions of Western Europe, see de Madariaga, *Russia in the Age of Catherine the Great*, 306–307; she had a particular interest in Blackstone's *Commentaries on the Laws of England*, on which see Jones, *Emancipation of Russian Nobility*, 218–220.
53. Jones, *Emancipation of Russian Nobility*, 283–285.
54. Jones, *Emancipation of Russian Nobility*, 288–289.
55. Leo Tolstoy, *Anna Karenina*, trans. Richard Pevear and Larissa Volkhonsky (New York: Viking, 2000), 656.
56. By "country," these men referred to the domain, not to Japan as a whole. See Luke S. Roberts, *Mercantilism in a Japanese Domain: The Merchant Origins of Economic Nationalism in 18th-Century Tosa* (Cambridge: Cambridge University Press, 1998).
57. This material, including quotations, is taken from Mark Ravina, *Land and Lordship in Early Modern Japan* (Stanford, CA: Stanford University Press, 1999),

103–110. Ravina gives Warashina's name as Ritsutada, but other scholars (e.g., Kozo Yamamura, "The Increasing Poverty of the Samurai in Tokugawa Japan, 1600–1868," *Journal of Economic History* 31, no. 2 [June 1971]: 401) give Ryūen, which seems a better fit for the characters.

58. That is, they had lived in the castle town off of incomes that were paid out of the domain treasury and had exercised no authority in the villages that they supposedly owned, even though the amount of their income was tied to the official production of those villages.
59. Ravina, *Land and Lordship*, 130–141.
60. After the abandonment of mandatory resettlement, however, a few Hirosaki samurai decided to voluntarily send their younger sons to the countryside as a means of providing for them, and these sons were required to register as farmers rather than samurai.
61. On death totals, see Mehmet Mert Sunar, "Cauldron of Dissent: A Study of the Janissary Corps, 1807–1826" (PhD dissertation, SUNY Binghamton, 2006), 209. On expulsions, see Mehmet Mert Sunar, " 'When Grocers, Porters, and Other Riff-raff Become Soldiers': Janissary Artisans and Laborers in the Nineteenth Century Istanbul and Edirne," *Kocaeli Üniversitesi Sosyal Bilimler Enstitüsü Dergisi* 17 (2009): 190.
62. Karen Barkey, *Empire of Difference: The Ottomans in Comparative Perspective* (New York: Cambridge University Press, 2008), 267–269.
63. Caroline Finkel, *Osman's Dream: The History of the Ottoman Empire* (New York: Basic Books, 2005), 433–434.
64. Sunar, "Cauldron of Dissent," 34–37.
65. On the close connections between janissaries and the urban commercial and craftsman classes, see Sunar, "Cauldron of Dissent." For the origins of this phenomenon in the height of the Ottoman period, see Cemal Kafadar, "On the Purity and Corruption of the Janissaries," *Turkish Studies Association Bulletin* 15, no. 2 (September 1991): 273–280.

Conclusion

1. On the rise of daimyo and imperial power, see Mark Ravina, *To Stand with the Nations of the World: Japan's Meiji Restoration in World History* (Oxford: Oxford University Press, 2017), 96–97; see 106–108 for the shogunate's attempts to centralize administration.
2. Colin Jaundrill, *Samurai to Soldier: Remaking Military Service in Nineteenth-Century Japan* (Ithaca, NY: Cornell University Press, 2016), 49–52.
3. Ravina, *To Stand with the Nations of the World*, 84.
4. Ravina, *To Stand with the Nations of the World*, 134–135.

5. Jaundrill, *Samurai to Soldier*, 96–101.
6. Jaundrill, *Samurai to Soldier*, 109.
7. Constantine Nomikos Vaporis, *Samurai: An Encyclopedia of Japan's Cultured Warriors* (Santa Barbara, CA: ABC-CLIO, 2019), 349–350.
8. Vaporis, *Samurai: An Encyclopedia*, 350–351.
9. Jaundrill, *Samurai to Soldier*, 146.
10. W. Bruce Lincoln, *In the Vanguard of Reform: Russia's Enlightened Bureaucrats, 1825–1861* (DeKalb: Northern Illinois University Press, 1982), 168–211.
11. Matthew Rendle, *Defenders of the Motherland: The Tsarist Elite in Revolutionary Russia* (Oxford: Oxford University Press, 2010), 4–6.
12. Matthew Rendle, "Counter-Revolution and the Tsarist Elite," in *A Companion to the Russian Revolution*, ed. Daniel Orlovsky (Hoboken, NJ: Wiley, 2020), 188–189.
13. Rendle, *Defenders of the Motherland*, 67–73.
14. Rendle, "Counter-Revolution and the Tsarist Elite," 189–193.
15. Lao She, *Beneath the Red Banner*, trans. Don J. Cohn (Beijing: Panda Books, 1982), 58.
16. Edward J. M. Rhoads, *Manchus & Han: Ethnic Relations and Political Power in Late Qing and Early Republican China, 1861–1928* (Seattle: University of Washington Press, 2000), 65–66. The reforms were aborted due to a conservative coup that stripped the emperor of his powers and returned authority to Empress Dowager Cixi.
17. Rhoads, *Manchus & Han*, 76–77.
18. Dai Yinghua 戴迎华, *Research on the Living Conditions of Banner People in the Late Qing and Early Republic* 清末民初旗民生存状态研究 (Beijing: Renmin chubanshe, 2010), 80–81; also see Rhoads, *Manchus & Han*, 122.
19. Shao Dan, *Remote Homeland, Recovered Borderland: Manchus, Manchoukuo, and Manchuria, 1907–1985* (Honolulu: University of Hawai'i Press), 71–75.
20. Rhoads, *Manchus & Han*, 202–203.
21. See, for instance, documentary reports in *ZHMGSDAZL*, vol. 1, 632–635.
22. The Articles of Favorable Treatment are quoted in full in Dai, *Research on the Living Conditions of Banner People*, 123.
23. Lei Jin 雷瑨, ed., *Banner Affairs* 旗務, vol. 38 of *A Classified Compilation of the Government Gazette* 政府公報分類彙編 (Shanghai: Saoye shanfang, 1915), 13–14.
24. For a June 1912 edict dealing with this problem nationwide, see Lei, *Banner Affairs*, 1. For another example in Jiangsu in 1914, see *Banner Affairs*, 24–26.
25. Lei, *Banner Affairs*, 6.
26. Lei, *Banner Affairs*, 7.
27. Lei, *Banner Affairs*, 11–13.
28. Lei, *Banner Affairs*, 13–14.
29. David Strand, *Rickshaw Beijing: City People and Politics in the 1920s* (Berkeley: University of California Press, 1989), 73.
30. Rhoads, *Manchus & Han*, 238.

31. "Jingzhou Bannermen in the Aftermath of the Failure of the Restoration" 復辟失敗後之荊州旗人, *Shenbao* 申報, July 22, 1917.
32. Rhoads, *Manchus & Han*, 238.
33. C. G. Dittmer, "An Estimate of the Standard of Living in China," *Quarterly Journal of Economics* 33, no. 1 (1918): 113.
34. Tong Jiajiang 佟佳江, "A New Opinion on When the Qing Eight Banner System Perished" 清代八旗制度消亡时间新议, *Minzu yanjiu* no. 5 (1994): 101–108.
35. Shao Dan, "Chinese by Definition: Nationality Law, Jus Sanguinis, and State Succession, 1909–1980," *Twentieth-Century China* 35, no. 1 (November 2009): 13.
36. Elissa Berwick and Fotini Christia, "State Capacity Redux: Integrating Classical and Experimental Contributions to an Enduring Debate," *Annual Review of Political Science* 21 (2018): 78.
37. In the banners, this was perhaps most apparent in their internal management, with the carrying out of regular and standardized censuses, maintenance of population registers, payment of salaries, and provision of welfare benefits.
38. On the characteristics of Weberian bureaucracy, see Max Weber, *Economy and Society: A New Translation*, ed. and trans. Keith Tribe (Cambridge, MA: Harvard University Press, 2019), 347–354.
39. Berwick and Christia, "State Capacity Redux," 79.
40. Weber, *Economy and Society: A New Translation*, 359.
41. I. N. Grebenkin, "From War to Revolution: Political Aspects of the Mood of Russian Officers between 1914 and 1917," trans. Kenneth Cargill, *Russian Studies in History* 56, no. 3 (January 2018): 146–147.
42. Grebenkin, "From War to Revolution," 156–157; Rendle, *Defenders of the Motherland*, 38–45.
43. Benjamin A. Elman, *A Cultural History of Civil Examinations in Late Imperial China* (Berkeley: University of California Press, 2000), 620–625.
44. Elman, *A Cultural History of Civil Examinations*, 248–249, 252.
45. Yulian Wu, *Luxurious Networks: Salt Merchants, Status, and Statecraft in Eighteenth-Century China* (Stanford, CA: Stanford University Press, 2017), 14.
46. Max Oidtmann, *Forging the Golden Urn: The Qing Empire and the Politics of Reincarnation in Tibet* (New York: Columbia University Press, 2018).
47. Charles Steinwedel, "How Bashkiria Became Part of European Russian, 1762–1881," in *Russian Empire: Spaces, People, Power, 1700–1930*, ed. Jane Burbank, Mark von Hagen, and Anatolyi Remnev (Bloomington: Indiana University Press, 2007), 99–102.
48. Karen Barkey, *Empire of Difference: The Ottomans in Comparative Perspective* (New York: Cambridge University Press, 2008), 130–142.
49. Gerald Groemer, "The Creation of the Edo Outcaste Order," *Journal of Japanese Studies* 27, no. 1 (Summer 2001): 269–273.
50. Rhoads, *Manchus & Han*, 45–47.

Bibliography

Allsen, Thomas T. *The Royal Hunt in Eurasian History*. Philadelphia: University of Pennsylvania Press, 2006.

Amos, Timothy D. *Embodying Difference: The Making of Burakumin in Modern Japan*. Honolulu: University of Hawai'i Press, 2011.

An Shuangcheng 安双成. "A Simple Analysis of the Number of Military-Age Men in the Eight Banners during the Shunzhi, Kangxi, and Yongzheng Periods" 顺康雍三朝八旗丁额浅析. *Lishi dang'an* 1983, no. 2 (July 1983): 100–103.

Atwood, Christopher Pratt. "'Worshipping Grace': The Language of Loyalty in Qing Mongolia." *Late Imperial China* 21, no. 2 (December 2000): 86–139.

Barkey, Karen. *Bandits and Bureaucrats: The Ottoman Road to State Centralization*. Ithaca, NY: Cornell University Press, 1994.

———. *Empire of Difference: The Ottomans in Comparative Perspective*. Cambridge: Cambridge University Press, 2008.

Bartlett, Beatrice S. *Monarchs and Ministers: The Grand Council in Mid-Ch'ing China*. Berkeley: University of California Press, 1991.

Bass, Samuel H. "Notes on Encountering Slavery Skepticism in Mongolia." *Critical Asian Studies Commentary* 2019, no. 11 (May 9, 2019). https://criticalasianstudies.org/commentary/2019/5/9/201911-samuel-h-bass-notes-on-encountering-slavery-skepticism-in-mongolia.

Bello, David A. *Across Forest, Steppe, and Mountain: Environment, Identity, and Empire in Qing China's Borderlands*. Cambridge: Cambridge University Press, 2016.

Berwick, Elissa, and Fotini Christia. "State Capacity Redux: Integrating Classical and Experimental Contributions to an Enduring Debate." *Annual Review of Political Science* 21 (2018): 71–91.

Botsman, Daniel V. *Punishment and Power in the Making of Modern Japan*. Princeton, NJ: Princeton University Press, 2005.

Brown, Philip C. *Central Authority and Local Autonomy in the Formation of Early Modern Japan: The Case of Kaga Domain*. Stanford, CA: Stanford University Press, 1993.

Burbank, Jane, and Frederick Cooper. *Empires in World History: Power and the Politics of Difference*. Princeton, NJ: Princeton University Press, 2010.

Cams, Mario. *Companions in Geography: East-West Collaboration in the Mapping of Qing China (c. 1685–1735)*. Leiden, Netherlands: Brill, 2017.

———. "Recent Additions to the New Qing History Debate." *Contemporary Chinese Thought* 47, no. 1 (2016): 1–4.

Cangšan 長善, ed. *Gazetteer for the Eight Banners Garrisoned in Canton* 駐粵八旗志, compiled 1884 (Guangzhou), reprinted Taipei: Wenhai chubanshe, 1997.

Cao Xueqin. *The Story of the Stone*. Vol. 1, "The Golden Days." Trans. David Hawkes. London: Penguin, 1973.

Cassel, Pär Kristoffer. *Grounds of Judgment: Extraterritoriality and Imperial Power in Nineteenth-Century China and Japan*. Oxford: Oxford University Press, 2012.

Chang, Michael G. *A Court on Horseback: Imperial Touring & the Construction of Qing Rule, 1680–1785*. Cambridge, MA: Harvard Asia Center, 2007.

Chen, Bijia, Cameron Campbell, and Hao Dong. "Interethnic Marriage in Northeast China, 1866–1913." *Demographic Research* 38, no. 34 (March 2018): 929–966.

Chen, Kaijun. 'The Rise of Technocratic Culture in High-Qing China: A Case Study of Bondservant (Booi) Tang Ying (1682–1756)." PhD dissertation, Columbia University, 2014.

Chen, Shuang. *State-Sponsored Inequality: The Banner System and Social Stratification in Northeast China*. Stanford, CA: Stanford University Press, 2017.

Chevaleyre, Claude. "Slavery in Late Ming China." In *The Palgrave Handbook of Global Slavery throughout History*, ed. Damian A. Pargas and Juliane Schiel, 297–317. Cham, Switzerland: Palgrave Macmillan, 2023.

Chia Ning. "Lifanyuan and Libu in Early Qing Empire Building." In *Managing Frontiers in Qing China: The Lifanyuan and Libu Revisited*, ed. Dittmar Schorkowitz and Chia Ning, 43–69. Leiden, Netherlands: Brill, 2017.

Chiu, Elena Suet-Ying. *Bannermen Tales (Zidishu): Manchu Storytelling and Cultural Hybridity in the Qing Dynasty*. Cambridge, MA: Harvard Asia Center, 2018.

Confino, Michael. "The 'Soslovie' (Estate) Paradigm: Reflections on Some Open Questions." *Cahiers du Monde russe* 49, no. 4 (October–December 2008): 681–699.

Constant, Frédéric. "The Legal Administration of Qing Mongolia." *Late Imperial China* 40, no. 1 (June 2019): 133–173.

Crossley, Pamela Kyle. "The Conquest Elite of the Ch'ing Empire." In *The Cambridge History of China*, vol. 9, part 1, ed. Willard J. Peterson, 310–359. Cambridge: Cambridge University Press, 2002.

——. *Hammer and Anvil: Nomad Rulers at the Forge of the Modern World*. Lanham, MD: Rowman & Littlefield, 2019.

——. *Orphan Warriors: Three Manchu Generations and the End of the Qing World*. Princeton, NJ: Princeton University Press, 1990.

——. "The Rulerships of China." *American Historical Review* 97, no. 5 (December 1992): 1468–1483.

——. "Thinking About Ethnicity in Early Modern China." *Late Imperial China* 11, no. 1 (June 1990): 1–35.

——. *A Translucent Mirror: History and Identity in Qing Imperial Ideology*. Berkeley: University of California Press, 1999.

Crummey, Robert O. *Aristocrats and Servitors: The Boyar Elite in Russia, 1613–1689*. Princeton, NJ: Princeton University Press, 1983.

Dai, Yingcong. *The White Lotus War: Rebellion & Suppression in Late Imperial China*. Seattle: University of Washington Press, 2019.

Dai Yinghua 戴迎华. *Research on the Living Conditions of Banner People in the Late Qing and Early Republic* 清末民初旗民生存状态研究. Beijing: Renmin chubanshe, 2010.

Da-li-zha-bu 达力扎布. "A Brief Examination of the Question of the Early Qing Establishment of the Chahar Banners" 清初察哈尔设旗问题考略. *Nei Menggu daxue xuebao* 31, no. 1 (January 1999): 38–44.

Darling, Linda T. "Historicizing the Ottoman *Timar* System: Identities of *Timar*-holders, Fourteenth to Seventeenth Centuries." *Turkish Historical Review* 8 (2017): 145–173.

——. "Nasihatnameler, İcmal Defterleri, and the Timar-Holding Ottoman Elite in the Late Sixteenth Century." *Journal of Ottoman Studies* 43 (2014): 193–226.

——. "The Sultan's Advisors and Their Opinions on the Identity of the Ottoman Elite, 1580–1633." In *Living in the Ottoman Realm: Empire and Identity, 13th to 20th Centuries*, ed. Christine Isom-Verhaaren and Kent F. Schull, 171–181. Bloomington: Indiana University Press, 2016.

Ding Yizhuang 定宜庄. "A Brief Discussion of the Garrison Hanjun Leaving the Banners in the Qianlong Period" 乾隆朝驻防汉军出旗浅议. *Qingshi yanjiu tongxun* 1990, no. 3: 11–17.

——. "A Brief Examination of Qing Judicial Subprefects" 清代理事同知考略. In *A Collection of Scholarly Essays Celebrating the Eightieth Birthday of Wang Zhonghan* 庆祝王钟翰先生八十寿辰学术论文集, ed. Wei Qingyuan 韦庆远, et al., 263–274. Shenyang, China: Liaoning daxue chubanshe, 1993.

——. *Research on the Lives of Women and the Marriage System of the Manchu People* 满族的妇女生活与婚姻制度研究. Beijing: Beijing daxue chubanshe, 1999.

Dittmer, C. G. "An Estimate of the Standard of Living in China." *Quarterly Journal of Economics* 33, no. 1 (1918): 107–128.

DQHD. *Administrative Code of the Qing Dynasty* 大清會典. Beijing: Wuying dian. Editions of 1818 (80 *juan*) and 1899 (100 *juan*).

Du, Fangqin, and Susan Mann. "Competing Claims on Womanly Virtue in Late Imperial China." In *Women and Confucian Cultures in Premodern China, Korea, and Japan*, ed. Dorothy Ko, JaHyun Kim Haboush, and Joan R. Piggott, 219–248. Berkeley: University of California Press, 2003.

Du, Yue. "Legal Justice in Eighteenth-Century Mongolia: Gender, Ethnicity, and Politics in the Manchu-Mongol Marriage Alliance." *Late Imperial China* 37, no. 2 (December 2016): 1–40.

Dzengšeo. *The Diary of a Manchu Soldier in Seventeenth Century China*. Trans. Nicola Di Cosmo. London: Routledge, 2006.

Ebrey, Patricia Buckley. "Introduction." In *Marriage and Inequality in Chinese Society*, ed. Rubie Watson and Patricia Ebrey, 1–23. Berkeley: University of California Press, 1991.

Ehlers, Maren A. *Give and Take: Poverty and the Status Order in Early Modern Japan*. Cambridge, MA: Harvard Asia Center, 2018.

Elliott, Mark C. "Bannerman and Townsman: Ethnic Tension in Nineteenth-Century Jiangnan." *Late Imperial China* 11, no. 1 (June 1990): 36–74.

——. "Ethnicity in the Qing Eight Banners." In *Empire at the Margins: Culture, Ethnicity, and Frontier in Early Modern China*, ed. Pamela Kyle Crossley, Helen F. Siu, and Donald S. Sutton, 27–57. Berkeley: University of California Press, 2006.

——. "Frontier Stories: Periphery as Center in Qing History." *Frontiers of History in China* 9, no. 3 (September 2014): 336–360.

——. *The Manchu Way: The Eight Banners and Ethnic Identity in Late Imperial China*. Stanford, CA: Stanford University Press, 2001.

——. "Manchu Widows and Ethnicity in Qing China." *Comparative Studies in Society and History* 41, no. 1 (January 1999): 33–71.

——. "Whose Empire Shall It Be? Manchu Figurations of Historical Process in the Early Seventeenth Century." In *Time, Temporality, and Imperial Transition: East Asia from Ming to Qing*, ed. Lynn A. Struve, 31–72. Honolulu: University of Hawai'i Press, 2005.

Elliott, Mark C., Cameron D. Campbell, and James Z. Lee. "A Demographic Estimate of the Population of the Qing Eight Banners." *Études chinoises* 35, no. 1 (2016): 9–39.

Elliott, Mark C., and Ning Chia, "The Qing Hunt at Mulan." In *New Qing Imperial History: The Making of Inner Asian Empire at Qing Chengde*, ed. James A. Millward, Ruth W. Dunnell, Mark C. Elliott, and Philippe Forêt, 66–83. London: Routledge Curzon, 2004.

Elman, Benjamin A. *A Cultural History of Civil Examinations in Late Imperial China*. Berkeley: University of California Press, 2000.

Esherick, Joseph W. "How the Qing Became China." In *Empire to Nation: Historical Perspectives on the Making of the Modern World*, ed. Joseph W. Esherick, Hasan Kayalı, and Eric Van Young, 229–259. Lanham, MD: Rowman & Littlefield, 2006.

Fei, Siyen. " 'We Must Be Taxed': A Case of Populist Urban Fiscal Reform in Ming Nanjing (1368–1644)." *Late Imperial China* 28, no. 2 (December 2007): 1–40.

Feng Erkang 冯尔康. *Biography of the Yongzheng Emperor* 雍正传. Beijing: Renmin chubanshe, 2014.

Finkel, Caroline. *Osman's Dream: The History of the Ottoman Empire*. New York: Basic Books, 2005.

Fitzgerald, Devin. "Manchu Language Pedagogical Practices: The Connections Between Manuscript and Printed Books." *Saksaha* 17 (2021): 1–31.

Fleischer, Cornell H. *Bureaucrat and Intellectual in the Ottoman Empire: The Historian Mustafa Ali (1541–1600)*. Princeton, NJ: Princeton University Press, 1986.

Freeze, Gregory L. *The Russian Levites: Parish Clergy in the Eighteenth Century*. Cambridge, MA: Harvard University Press, 1977.

———. "The Soslovie (Estate) Paradigm and Russian Social History." *American Historical Review* 91, no. 1 (February 1986): 11–36.

Fuma Susumu 夫馬進. *Research on the History of Charitable and Benevolent Organizations in China* 中国善会善堂史研究. Kyoto, Japan: Dōhōsha shuppan, 1997.

Giersch, C. Patterson. *Asian Borderlands: The Transformation of Qing China's Yunnan Frontier*. Cambridge, MA: Harvard University Press, 2006.

Goody, Jack. *The Oriental, the Ancient, and the Primitive: Systems of Marriage and the Family in the Pre-industrial Societies of Eurasia*. Cambridge: Cambridge University Press, 1990.

Grebenkin, I. N. "From War to Revolution: Political Aspects of the Mood of Russian Officers between 1914 and 1917." Trans. Kenneth Cargill. *Russian Studies in History* 56, no. 2 (January 2018): 145–158.

Groemer, Gerald. "The Creation of the Edo Outcaste Order." *Journal of Japanese Studies* 27, no. 1 (Summer 2001): 263–293.

Guo Taifeng 郭太风. "An Initial Survey of the Salary System of the Eight Banners and Green Standards" 八旗绿营俸饷制度初探. *Fudan xuebao (shehui kexue ban)* 1982, no. 4: 103–108.

Gustafsson, Harald. *Political Interaction in the Old Regime: Central Power and Local Society in the Eighteenth-Century Nordic States*. Trans. Alan Crozier. Lund, Sweden: Studentlitteratur, 1994.

Hall, John Whitney. "Feudalism in Japan—A Reassessment." *Comparative Studies in Society and History* 5, no. 1 (October 1962): 15–51.

———. "Rule by Status in Tokugawa Japan." *Journal of Japanese Studies* 1, no. 1 (Autumn 1974): 39–49.

Hang, Xing. *Conflict and Commerce in Maritime East Asia: The Zheng Family and the Shaping of the Modern World, c. 1620–1720*. Cambridge: Cambridge University Press, 2015.

Hansson, Anders. *Chinese Outcasts: Discrimination & Emancipation in Late Imperial China*. Leiden, Netherlands: Brill, 1996.

Harrison, Henrietta. "A Faithful Interpreter? Li Zibiao and the 1793 Macartney Embassy to China." *International History Review* 41, no. 5 (2019): 1076–1091.

Hata Hisako. "Servants of the Inner Quarters: The Women of the Shogun's Great Interior." Trans. Anne Walthall. In *Servants of the Dynasty: Palace Women in World History*, ed. Anne Walthall, 172–190. Berkeley: University of California Press, 2008.

He Changling 賀長齡, ed. *A Collection of Essays on Statecraft from Our Dynasty* 皇朝經世文編, compiled 1826. Reprinted Shanghai: Guangbaisong zhai, 1887.

Hellie, Richard. *Enserfment and Military Change in Muscovy*. Chicago: University of Chicago Press, 1971.

Herman, John E. "The Cant of Conquest: Tusi Offices and China's Political Incorporation of the Southwest Frontier." In *Empire at the Margins: Culture, Ethnicity, and Frontier in Early Modern China*, ed. Pamela Kyle Crossley, Helen F. Siu, and Donald S. Sutton, 135–168. Berkeley: University of California Press, 2006.

Heuschert, Dorothea. "Legal Pluralism in the Qing Empire: Manchu Legislation for the Mongols." *International History Review* 20, no. 2 (June 1998): 310–324.

Hongzhou 弘晝, ed. *Statutes and Regulations of the Great Qing Dynasty, Compiled at Imperial Order* (*Hesei toktobuha Daicing gurun i fafun i bithe kooli*). Beijing, 1741. Staatsbibliothek zu Berlin version available digitally at https://digital.staatsbibliothek-berlin.de/werkansicht/?PPN=PPN3346157741.

Hosoya Yoshio 細谷良夫. "The Transformation of Eight Banner Household Registration Law in the Mid-Qing: With a Focus on *Kaihu*" 清朝中期の八旗戸籍法の変革：開戸を中心にして. *Shūkan tōyōgaku* 15 (May 1966): 51–63.

Hostetler, Laura. *Qing Colonial Enterprise: Ethnography and Cartography in Early Modern China*. Chicago: University of Chicago Press, 2001.

Hou Ching-Lang 侯錦郎, and Michèle Pirazzoli, "Les chasses d'automne de l'empereur Qianlong à Mulan." *T'oung Pao* 65, nos. 1–3 (1979): 13–50.

Howell, David L. *Geographies of Identity in Nineteenth-Century Japan*. Berkeley: University of California Press, 2005.

Howland, Douglas R. "Samurai Status, Class, and Bureaucracy: A Historiographical Essay." *Journal of Asian Studies* 60, no. 2 (May 2001): 353–380.

Huang, Pei. *Autocracy at Work: A Study of the Yung-cheng Period, 1722–1735*. Bloomington: Indiana University Press, 1974.

Huang Yi-Long 黄一农. "Dutch Cannons and the Eight Banner Hanjun Established by Hong Taiji" 红夷大炮与皇太极创立的八旗汉军. *Lishi yanjiu* 2004, no. 4: 74–105.

Hughes, Lindsey. *Russia in the Age of Peter the Great*. New Haven, CT: Yale University Press, 1998.

Hung, Ho-fung. *Protest with Chinese Characteristics: Demonstrations, Riots, and Petitions in the Mid-Qing Dynasty*. New York: Columbia University Press, 2011.

Ikegami, Eiko. *The Taming of the Samurai: Honorific Individualism and the Making of Modern Japan*. Cambridge, MA: Harvard University Press, 1995.

İnalcık, Halil. "The Nature of Traditional Society: Turkey." In *Political Modernization in Japan and Turkey*, ed. Robert E. Ward and Dankwart A. Rostow, 42–63. Princeton, NJ: Princeton University Press, 1964.

——. *The Ottoman Empire: The Classical Age 1300–1600*. New York: Weidenfeld and Nicolson, 1973.

Isett, Christopher Mills. *State, Peasant, and Merchant in Qing Manchuria, 1644–1862*. Stanford, CA: Stanford University Press, 2007.

Itzkowitz, Norman. *Ottoman Empire and Islamic Tradition*. Chicago: University of Chicago Press, 1972.

Jami, Catherine. *The Emperor's New Mathematics: Western Learning and Imperial Authority during the Kangxi Reign (1662–1722)*. Oxford: Oxford University Press, 2012.

Jaundrill, Colin. *Samurai to Soldier: Remaking Military Service in Nineteenth-Century Japan*. Ithaca, NY: Cornell University Press, 2016.

Jenne, Jeremiah. "Making History." *The World of Chinese* (September–October 2017). http://www.theworldofchinese.com/2017/11/making-history/.

Jiang, Yonglin. *The Great Ming Code: Da Ming lü*. Seattle: University of Washington Press, 2005.

Jones, Robert E. *Emancipation of Russian Nobility, 1762–1785*. Princeton, NJ: Princeton University Press, 1973.

Kafadar, Cemal. "On the Purity and Corruption of the Janissaries." *Turkish Studies Association Bulletin* 15, no. 2 (September 1991): 273–280.

Kappeler, Andreas. *The Russian Empire: A Multiethnic History*. Trans. Alfred Clayton. Harlow, UK: Pearson Education Limited, 2001.

Katsu Kokichi. *Musui's Story: The Autobiography of a Tokugawa Samurai*. Trans. Teruko Craig. Tucson: University of Arizona Press, 1998.

Keliher, Macabe. *The Board of Rites and the Making of Qing China*. Oakland: University of California Press, 2019.

Kennelly, M. "China's Social and Economic Progress." *America: A Catholic Review of the Week* 1, no. 12 (July 3, 1909): 323.

Kicengge 承志. "On the Origins and Classification of Eight Banner Niru" 八旗ニルの根源とニル分類について. *Tōyōshi kenkyū* 65, no. 1 (2006): 202–169.

Kim, Kwangmin. "Saintly Brokers: Uyghur Muslims, Trade, and the Making of Qing Central Asia, 1696–1814." PhD dissertation, University of California at Berkeley, 2008.

Kim, Loretta E. *Ethnic Chrysalis: China's Orochen People and the Legacy of Qing Borderland Administration*. Cambridge, MA: Harvard Asia Center, 2019.

Kivelson, Valerie A. *Autocracy in the Provinces: The Muscovite Gentry and Political Culture in the Seventeenth Century*. Stanford, CA: Stanford University Press, 1996.

Kollman, Nancy Shields. " 'What's Love Got to Do with It?': Changing Models of Masculinity in Muscovite and Petrine Russia." In *Russian Masculinities in History and Culture*, ed. Barbara Evans Clements, Rebecca Friedman, and Dan Healey, 15–32. New York: Palgrave, 2002.

Kuhn, Philip A. *Soulstealers: The Chinese Sorcery Scare of 1768*. Cambridge, MA: Harvard University Press, 1990.

Kunt, I. Metin. *The Sultan's Servants: The Transformation of Ottoman Provincial Government, 1550–1650*. New York: Columbia University Press, 1983.

KXCMWZPZZ. *Complete Translation of the Kangxi-Period Manchu-Language Vermillion-Rescripted Palace Memorials* 康熙朝满文朱批奏折全译. Ed. Guan Xiaolian 关孝廉 and Qu Liusheng 屈六生. Beijing: Zhongguo shehui kexue chubanshe, 1996.

Lam, Tong. *A Passion for Facts: Social Surveys and the Construction of the Chinese Nation State, 1900–1949*. Berkeley: University of California Press, 2011.

Lao She. *Beneath the Red Banner*. Trans. Don J. Cohn. Beijing: Panda Books, 1982.

LeDonne, John P. *Absolutism and Ruling Class: The Formation of the Russian Political Order, 1700–1825*. Oxford: Oxford University Press, 1991.

Leibold, James. *Reconfiguring Chinese Nationalism: How the Qing Frontier and Its Indigenes Became Chinese*. New York: Palgrave Macmillan, 2007.

Lei Jin 雷瑨, ed. *Banner Affairs* 旗務. Vol. 38 of *A Topically Arranged Compilation of the Government Gazette* 政府公報分類彙編. Shanghai: Saoye shanfang, 1915.

Leping. *Muwa gisun*. Unpublished manuscript at HYL. Digital version available at https://iiif.lib.harvard.edu/manifests/view/drs:45806328$1i.

Lieven, Dominic. *Empire: The Russian Empire and Its Rivals*. New Haven, CT: Yale University Press, 2000.

Lincoln, W. Bruce. *In the Vanguard of Reform: Russia's Enlightened Bureaucrats, 1825–1861*. DeKalb: Northern Illinois University Press, 1982.

Lipman, Jonathan. " 'A Fierce and Brutal People': On Islam and Muslims in Qing Law." In *Empire at the Margins: Culture, Ethnicity, and Frontier in Early Modern China*, ed. Pamela Kyle Crossley, Helen F. Siu, and Donald S. Sutton, 83–110. Berkeley: University of California Press, 2006.

Liu Xiaomeng 刘小萌. *Banner Society in Qing Dynasty Beijing* 清代北京旗人社会. Beijing: Zhongguo shehui kexue chubanshe, 2008.

———. *Eight Banner People of the Qing Dynasty* 清代八旗子弟. Liaoyang: Liaoning minzu chubanshe, 2008.

Li Yanguang 李燕光. "Eight Banner Hanjun in the Qing" 清代的八旗汉军. *Manxue yanjiu* (1992): 91–103.

Lu Cheng-Heng 盧正恆. "Banner and Commoner: A Study of the Banner Zheng Clan and the Quanzhou Zheng Lineage of the Qing Dynasty" 旗與民：清代旗人鄭氏家族與泉州鄭氏宗族初探. *Jifeng Yazhou yanjiu* 2, no. 1 (April 2016): 115–151.

Luo Ergang 罗尔纲. *An Account of the Green Standards* 绿营兵志. Beijing: Shangwu yinshu guan, 2011. First published 1945 by Shangwu yinshu guan (Chongqing); revised ed. issued 1984 by Zhonghua shuju (Beijing).

Lu, Weijing. *True to Her Word: The Faithful Maiden Cult in Late Imperial China*. Stanford, CA: Stanford University Press, 2008.

Lu Zhijun 鹿智鈞. *Dynastic Basis and Hereditary Slaves: The Legal Status of Bannermen in Qing China* 根本與世僕：清朝旗人的法律地位. Taipei: Xiuwei zixun keji, 2017.

Madariaga, Isabel de. *Russia in the Age of Catherine the Great*. New Haven, CT: Yale University Press, 1981.

Man-Cheong, Iona D. *The Class of 1761: Examinations, State, and Elite in Eighteenth-Century China*. Stanford, CA: Stanford University Press, 2004.

Mann, Susan. *Precious Records: Women in China's Long Eighteenth Century*. Stanford, CA: Stanford University Press, 1997.

———. *The Talented Women of the Zhang Family*. Berkeley: University of California Press, 2007.

Martin, Russell E. *A Bride for the Tsar: Bride Shows and Marriage Politics in Early Modern Russia*. DeKalb: Northern Illinois University Press, 2012.

Ma Zimu 马子木. "On the Formation and Development of the Qing Translation Examinations (1723–1850)" 论清朝翻译科举的形成与发展 (1723–1850). *Qingshi yanjiu* 2014, no. 3 (August 2014): 23–47.

McClain, James L. *Kanazawa: A Seventeenth-Century Japanese Castle Town*. New Haven, CT: Yale University Press, 1982.

McCormick, Noah Y. *Japan's Outcaste Abolition: The Struggle for National Inclusion and the Making of the Modern State*. Oxford: Routledge, 2013.

Meehan-Waters, Brenda. *Autocracy and Aristocracy: The Russian Service Elite of 1730*. New Brunswick, NJ: Rutgers University Press, 1982.

Millward, James A. *Beyond the Pass: Economy, Ethnicity, and Empire in Qing Central Asia*. Stanford, CA: Stanford University Press, 1998.

———. *Eurasian Crossroads: A History of Xinjiang*. New York: Columbia University Press, 2007.

Mizubayashi Takeshi 水林彪. *The Restructuring of the Feudal System and the Formation of Japanese Society* 封建制の再編と日本的社会の確立. Tokyo: Yamakawa shuppansha, 1987.

Morishita Tōru 森下徹. *The Status of Warriors: The Daimyō Retainer Band of Castle Town Hagi* 武士という身分: 城下町萩の大名家臣団. Tokyo: Yoshikawa kōbunkan, 2012.

Mosca, Matthew W. "The Literati Rewriting of China in the Qianlong-Jiaqing Transition." *Late Imperial China* 32, no. 2 (December 2011): 89–132.

Mullaney, Thomas S. *Coming to Terms with the Nation: Ethnic Classification in Modern China.* Berkeley: University of California Press, 2011.

Naquin, Susan, and Evelyn S. Rawski. *Chinese Society in the Eighteenth Century.* New Haven, CT: Yale University Press, 1987.

Narakino Shimesu 楢木野宣. *Research on Important Officials in the Qing Dynasty: With Full Details on the Joint Usage of Manchus and Han* 清代重要職官の研究：滿漢併用の全貌. Tokyo: Kazama shobō, 1975.

Nenzi, Laura. *Excursions in Identity: Travel and the Intersection of Place, Gender, and Status in Edo Japan.* Honolulu: University of Hawai'i Press, 2008.

Newlin, Thomas. *The Voice in the Garden: Andrei Bolotov and the Anxieties of Russian Pastoral, 1738–1833.* Evanston, IL: Northwestern University Press, 2001.

Offord, Derek, Vladislav Rjéoutski, and Gesine Argent. *The French Language in Russia: A Social, Political, Cultural, and Literary History.* Amsterdam: Amsterdam University Press, 2018.

Oidtmann, Max. *Forging the Golden Urn: The Qing Empire and the Politics of Reincarnation in Tibet.* New York: Columbia University Press, 2018.

O'Neill, Kelly. "Rethinking Elite Integration: The Crimean Murzas and the Evolution of Russian Nobility." *Cahiers du Monde russe* 51, no. 2 (2010): 397–417.

Onuma Takahiro. "250 Years History of the Turkic-Muslim Camp in Beijing." *TIAS Central Eurasian Research Series* no. 2 (2009): 1–59.

Ostapchuk, Victor. "The Trouble with Timars: An Excursion into a Seventeenth-Century Documentary Landscape." In *Ottoman War and Peace: Studies in Honor of Virginia H. Aksan*, ed. Frank Castiglione, Ethan L. Menchinger, and Veysel Şimşek, 35–62. Leiden, Netherlands: Brill, 2019.

Pang, Tatiana A. "The 'Russian Company' in the Manchu Banner Organization." *Central Asiatic Journal* 43, no. 1 (1999): 132–139.

Peirce, Leslie P. "Beyond Harem Walls: Ottoman Royal Women and the Exercise of Power." In *Servants of the Dynasty: Palace Women in World History*, ed. Anne Walthall, 81–95. Berkeley: University of California Press, 2008.

Perdue, Peter C. *China Marches West: The Qing Conquest of Central Eurasia.* Cambridge, MA: Harvard University Press, 2005.

——. "Empire and Nation in Comparative Perspective: Frontier Administration in Eighteenth-Century China." *Journal of Early Modern History* 5, no. 4 (2001): 282–304.

Pflugfelder, Gregory M. "The Nation-State, the Age/Gender System, and the Reconstitution of Erotic Desire in Nineteenth-Century Japan." *Journal of Asian Studies* 71, no. 4 (November 2012): 963–974.

Platt, Stephen R. *Autumn in the Heavenly Kingdom: China, the West, and the Epic Story of the Taiping War.* New York: Vintage Books, 2012.

Poe, Marshall. "What Did Russians Mean When They Called Themselves 'Slaves of the Tsar'?" *Slavic Review* 57, no. 3 (Autumn 1998): 585–608.

Porter, David C. "Bannermen as Translators: Manchu Language Education in the Hanjun Banners." *Late Imperial China* 40, no. 2 (December 2019): 1–43.

———. "Ethnic and Status Identity in Qing China: The Hanjun Eight Banners." PhD dissertation, Harvard University, 2018.

———. "Manchu Racial Identity on the Qing Frontier: Donjina and Early Twentieth-Century Ili." *Modern China* 44, no. 1 (January 2018): 3–34.

Pratt, Edward E. *Japan's Proto-Industrial Elite: The Economic Foundations of the Gōnō.* Cambridge, MA: Harvard Asia Center, 1999.

QDBQTZ. *Imperially-Commissioned Comprehensive Gazetteer of the Eight Banners* 欽定八旗通志, 1796. Reprinted in 12 vols. Changchun, China: Jilin wenshi chubanshe, 2002.

Qu Cheng 屈成. "The Auditing of the 'Separate Registers' during the Yongzheng and Qianlong Reigns" 清雍乾时期的"另记档案"清查. *Qing shi yanjiu* 2018, no. 3 (August 2018): 16–32.

Qu Chunhai 屈春海. "Public Order and Defense Organizations in the Qing Capital: An Outline of the Office of the Gendarmerie" 清代京师治安防务机构：步军统领衙门述略. *Gong'an daxue xuebao* 1989, no. 2: 68–70.

Radushev, Evgeni. " 'Peasant' Janissaries?" *Journal of Social History* 42, no. 2 (Winter 2008): 447–467.

Ravina, Mark. *Land and Lordship in Early Modern Japan.* Stanford, CA: Stanford University Press, 1999.

———. *To Stand with the Nations of the World: Japan's Meiji Restoration in World History.* Oxford: Oxford University Press, 2017.

Rawski, Evelyn S. "Ch'ing Imperial Marriage and the Problems of Rulership." In *Marriage and Inequality in Chinese Society*, ed. Rubie S. Watson and Patricia Buckley Ebrey, 170–203. Berkeley: University of California Press, 1991.

———. "Economic and Social Foundations of Late Imperial Culture." In *Popular Culture in Late Imperial China*, ed. David Johnson, Andrew J. Nathan, and Evelyn S. Rawski, 3–33. Berkeley: University of California Press, 1985.

———. *The Last Emperors: A Social History of Qing Imperial Institutions.* Berkeley: University of California Press, 1998.

Reischauer, Edwin O. *Japan: The Story of a Nation.* New York: Knopf, 1970.

Rendle, Matthew. "Counter-Revolution and the Tsarist Elite." In *A Companion to the Russian Revolution*, ed. Daniel Orlovsky, 187–195. Hoboken, NJ: Wiley, 2020.

———. *Defenders of the Motherland: The Tsarist Elite in Revolutionary Russia.* Oxford: Oxford University Press, 2010.

Rhoads, Edward J. M. *Manchus & Han: Ethnic Relations and Political Power in Late Qing and Early Republican China, 1861–1928.* Seattle: University of Washington Press, 2000.

Roberts, Luke S. "Governing the Samurai Family in the Late Edo Period." In *What Is a Family? Answers from Early Modern Japan*, ed. Mary Elizabeth Berry and Marcia Yonemoto, 149–173. Oakland: University of California Press, 2019.

———. *Mercantilism in a Japanese Domain: The Merchant Origins of Economic Nationalism in 18th-Century Tosa*. Cambridge: Cambridge University Press, 1998.

———. *Performing the Great Peace: Political Space and Open Secrets in Tokugawa Japan*. Honolulu: University of Hawai'i Press, 2012.

Roth-Li, Gertraude. "State Building Before 1644." In *The Cambridge History of China*, vol. 9, part 1, ed. Willard J. Peterson, 9–72. Cambridge: Cambridge University Press, 2002.

Schillinger, Nicolas. *The Body and Military Masculinity in Late Qing and Early Republican China: The Art of Governing Soldiers*. Lanham, MD: Lexington Books, 2016.

Schlesinger, Jonathan. *A World Trimmed with Fur: Wild Things, Pristine Places, and the Natural Fringes of Qing Rule*. Stanford, CA: Stanford University Press, 2017.

Schluessel, Eric. *Land of Strangers: The Civilizing Project in Qing Central Asia*. New York: Columbia University Press, 2020.

Schoppa, R. Keith. *Revolution and Its Past: Identities and Change in Modern Chinese History*, 3rd ed. New York: Routledge, 2016.

Sen, Sudipta. "The New Frontiers of Manchu China and the Historiography of Asian Empires: A Review Essay." *Journal of Asian Studies* 61, no. 1 (February 2002): 165–177.

Shan, Patrick Fuliang. "Banner System (1601–1912)." In *China at War: An Encyclopedia*, ed. Xiaobing Li, 18–20. Santa Barbara, CA: ABC-CLIO, 2012.

Shao Dan. "Chinese by Definition: Nationality Law, Jus Sanguinis, and State Succession, 1909–1980." *Twentieth-Century China* 35, no. 1 (November 2009): 4–28.

———. *Remote Homeland, Recovered Borderland: Manchus, Manchoukuo, and Manchuria, 1907–1985*. Honolulu: University of Hawai'i Press, 2011.

Shenbao 申報, 1872–1949. Electronic Database. Changsha, China: Qing pingguo shuju zhongxin. http://www.huawenku.cn/html/huawenkuguihua/ruxuanbaokan-201303212453.html.

Sinju 新柱, ed. *Fuzhou Garrison Gazetteer* 福州駐防志, compiled 1744 (Fuzhou). Reprinted in *Fujian Province National Minority Ancient Book Series: Manchu Volume* 福建省少数民族古籍丛书:满族卷, 7–175. Beijing: Minzu chubanshe, 2004.

Smith, Alison K. *For the Common Good and Their Own Well-Being: Social Estates in Imperial Russia*. New York: Oxford University Press, 2014.

Smith, Richard J. *The Qing Dynasty and Traditional Chinese Culture*. Lanham, MD: Rowman & Littlefield, 2015.

Smits, Gregory. *Visions of Ryukyu: Identity and Ideology in Early-Modern Thought and Politics*. Honolulu: University of Hawai'i Press, 1999.

Söderblom Saarela, Mårten. "Linguistic Compartmentalization and the Palace Memorial System in the Eighteenth Century." *Late Imperial China* 41, no. 2 (December 2020): 131–179.

———. "Manchu and the Study of Language in China (1607–1911)." PhD dissertation, Princeton University, 2015.

Sommer, Matthew H. *Sex, Law, and Society in Late Imperial China*. Stanford, CA: Stanford University Press, 2000.

Sorensen, André. *The Making of Edo Japan: Cities and Planning from Edo to the Twenty First Century*. London: Routledge, 2002.

Soullière, Ellen. "The Imperial Marriages of the Ming Dynasty." *Papers on Far Eastern History* 37 (March 1988): 15–42.

Soyudoğan, Muhsin. "The Fall of Icarus: The Paradox of the Ottoman Centralization and the Abstraction of Timars." *Turkish Historical Review* 8 (2017): 174–200.

Spence, Jonathan D. *Treason by the Book*. New York: Viking Penguin, 2001.

———. *Ts'ao Yin and the K'ang-hsi Emperor: Bondservant and Master*. New Haven, CT: Yale University Press, 1966.

Stanley, Amy. "Adultery, Punishment, and Reconciliation in Tokugawa Japan." *Journal of Japanese Studies* 33, no. 2 (Summer 2007): 309–335.

———. *Stranger in the Shogun's City: A Japanese Woman and Her World*. New York: Scribner, 2020.

Steinwedel, Charles. "How Bashkiria Became Part of European Russian, 1762–1881." In *Russian Empire: Spaces, People, Power, 1700–1930*, ed. Jane Burbank, Mark von Hagen, and Anatolyi Remnev, 94–124. Bloomington: Indiana University Press, 2007.

Stewart, Daniel Robert. "Temporary Samurai: Status and Service in Early Modern Japan." PhD dissertation, University of California at Berkeley, 2003.

Strand, David. *Rickshaw Beijing: City People and Politics in the 1920s*. Berkeley: University of California Press, 1989.

Sunar, Mehmet Mert. "Cauldron of Dissent: A Study of the Janissary Corps, 1807–1826." PhD dissertation, SUNY Binghamton, 2006.

———. "'When Grocers, Porters, and Other Riff-raff Become Soldiers': Janissary Artisans and Laborers in the Nineteenth Century Istanbul and Edirne." *Kocaeli Üniversitesi Sosyal Bilimler Enstitüsü Dergisi* 17 (2009): 175–194.

Sun Jing 孙静. "A Discussion of the Change in Status of the Eight Banner Hanjun during the Qianlong Period" 乾隆朝八旗汉军身份变化述论. *Heilongjiang minzu congkan* 2005, no. 2: 59–64.

Sutton, Donald S. "Ethnicity and the Miao Frontier in the Eighteenth Century." In *Empire at the Margins: Culture, Ethnicity, and Frontier in Early Modern China*, ed. Pamela Kyle Crossley, Helen F. Siu, and Donald S. Sutton, 190–228. Berkeley: University of California Press, 2006.

Swope, Kenneth M. *The Military Collapse of China's Ming Dynasty, 1618–44*. London: Routledge, 2014.

Szonyi, Michael. *The Art of Being Governed: Everyday Politics in Late Imperial China*. Princeton, NJ: Princeton University Press, 2017.

SZZPYZ. Imperial Decrees in Vermillion Brush of Emperor Shizong [Electronic Resource] [360 juan] 世宗憲皇帝硃批諭旨 [電子資源] [360卷]. Hong Kong: Dizhi wenhua chuban youxian gongsi, 2006.

Tezcan, Baki. *The Second Ottoman Empire: Political and Social Transformation in the Early Modern World*. Cambridge: Cambridge University Press, 2010.

Toby, Ronald P. *Engaging the Other: "Japan" and Its Alter Egos*. Leiden, Netherlands: Brill, 2019.

Tolstoy, Leo. *Anna Karenina*. Trans. Richard Pevear and Larissa Volokhonsky. New York: Viking, 2000.

———. *War and Peace*. Trans. Richard Pevear and Larissa Volokhonsky. New York: Alfred A. Knopf, 2007.

Tong Jiajiang 佟佳江. "A New Opinion on When the Qing Eight Banner System Perished" 清代八旗制度消亡时间新议. *Minzu yanjiu* 1994, no. 5: 101–108.

Torbert, Preston M. *The Ch'ing Imperial Household Department: A Study of Its Organization and Principal Functions, 1662–1796*. Cambridge, MA: Harvard Asia Center, 1977.

Totman, Conrad. *Early Modern Japan*. Berkeley: University of California Press, 1993.

———. *Politics in the Tokugawa Bakufu, 1600–1843*. Berkeley: University of California Press, 1967.

Trott, Rosemary Gray. "The Politics of Famine in a Far-off Place: Nyūi Mitsugi and the Hōreki Crisis in Tsugaru." PhD dissertation, Australian National University, 2001.

Tsai, Wei-chieh. "Mongolization of Han Chinese and Manchu Settlers in Qing Mongolia, 1700–1911." PhD dissertation, Indiana University, 2017.

Ura Ren'ichi 浦廉一. "Regarding the Hanjun (Ujen Cooha)" 漢軍（烏真超哈）に就いて. In *Essay Collection on Oriental History in Honor of the Sixtieth Birthday of Dr. Kuwabara* 桑原博士還歷記念東洋史論叢, 815–849. Kyoto, Japan: Kōbundō Shōbō, 1931.

Vaporis, Constantine Nomikos. *Samurai: An Encyclopedia of Japan's Cultured Warriors*. Santa Barbara, CA: ABC-CLIO, 2019.

———. *Tour of Duty: Samurai, Military Service in Edo, and the Culture of Early Modern Japan*. Honolulu: University of Hawai'i Press, 2008.

Vollmer, John E. *Ruling from the Dragon Throne: Costume of the Qing Dynasty (1644–1911)*. Berkeley, CA: Ten Speed Press, 2002.

Wakeman, Frederic, Jr. *The Great Enterprise: The Manchu Reconstruction of Order in Seventeenth-Century China*. Berkeley: University of California Press, 1985.

Waley-Cohen, Joanna. "The New Qing History." *Radical History Review* 88 (Winter 2004): 193–206.

Walthall, Anne, and M.-P. Gaviano. "Fille de paysan, épouse de samouraï: Les lettres de Michi Yoshino." *Annales. Histoire, Sciences Sociales* 54, no. 1 (1999): 55–86.

Wang, Shuo. "Qing Imperial Women: Empresses, Concubines, and Aisin Gioro Daughters." In *Servants of the Dynasty: Palace Women in World History*, ed. Anne Walthall, 137–158. Berkeley: University of California Press, 2008.

———. "The Selection of Women for the Qing Imperial Harem." *Chinese Historical Review* 11, no. 2 (Fall 2004): 212–222.

Weber, Max. *Economy and Society: A New Translation*. Ed. and trans. Keith Tribe. Cambridge, MA: Harvard University Press, 2019.

———. *Economy and Society: An Outline of Interpretive Sociology*. Ed. Guenther Ross and Claus Wittich. Berkeley: University of California Press, 1978.

———. *Essays in Sociology*. Ed. and trans. H. H. Gerth and C. Wright Mills. New York: Routledge, 1948.

Werth, Paul W. "*Soslovie* and the 'Foreign' Clergies of Imperial Russia: Estate Rights or Service Rights?" *Cahiers du Monde russe* 51, nos. 2–3 (2010): 419–440.

Wheatcroft, Andrew. *The Ottomans*. London: Viking, 1993.

Wirtschafter, Elise Kimerling. "Power and the 18th-Century Nobility." *Kritika: Explorations in Russian and Eurasian History* 15, no. 3 (Summer 2014): 657–664.

———. "Social Categories in Russian Imperial History." *Cahiers du Monde russe* 50, no. 1 (January–March 2009): 231–250.

———. *Social Identity in Imperial Russia*. DeKalb: Northern Illinois University Press, 1997.

Wu, Yulian. *Luxurious Networks: Salt Merchants, Status, and Statecraft in Eighteenth-Century China*. Stanford, CA: Stanford University Press, 2017.

Yamamura, Kozo. "The Increasing Poverty of the Samurai in Tokugawa Japan, 1600–1868." *Journal of Economic History* 31, no. 2 (June 1971): 378–406.

Yang Zongjiong 楊宗炯. *Yang Charitable Hall Genealogy* 楊樂善堂族譜. Privately published, 2010.

Yi, Eunjeong. *Guild Dynamics in Seventeenth-Century Istanbul: Fluidity and Leverage*. Leiden, Netherlands: Brill, 2004.

Yılmaz, Gülay. "Becoming a *Devşirme*: The Training of Conscripted Children in the Ottoman Empire." In *Children in Slavery Through the Ages*, ed. Gwyn Campbell, Suzanne Miers, and Joseph C. Miller, 119–134. Athens: University of Ohio Press, 2009.

———. "The Devshirme System and the Levied Children of Bursa in 1603–4 A.D." *Belleten* 79, no. 286 (December 2015): 901–931.

———. "The Economic and Social Roles of Janissaries in a 17th Century Ottoman City: The Case of Istanbul." PhD dissertation, McGill University, 2011.

Yonemoto, Marcia. *The Problem of Women in Early Modern Japan*. Oakland: University of California Press, 2016.

YZCMWZPZZ. Complete Translation of the Yongzheng-period Manchu-Language Vermillion-Rescripted Palace Memorials 雍正朝满文朱批奏折全译. Ed. Guan Xiaolian 关孝廉 and Qu Liusheng 屈六生. 2 vols. Hefei: Huangshan shushe, 1998.

Zelin, Madeleine. *The Magistrate's Tael: Rationalizing Fiscal Reform in Eighteenth-Century Ch'ing China*. Berkeley: University of California Press, 1984.

Zhang, Lawrence. "Legacy of Success: Office Purchase and State-Elite Relations in Qing China." *Harvard Journal of Asiatic Studies* 73, no. 2 (December 2013): 259–297.

Zhang Yuxing 张玉兴. "A Brief Comment on Bondservants with Han Surnames and the Hanjun: A Historical Testimony on the Rise and Decline of the Eight Banner System" 包衣汉姓与汉军简论：八旗制度兴衰的一个历史见证. *Liaoning daxue xuebao (zhexue shehui kexue ban)* 31, no. 4 (July 2003): 37–45.

Zhao Bingzhong 赵秉忠 and Bai Xinliang 白新良. "An Investigation Regarding Qianlong-Era Eight Banner Policy" 关于乾隆时期八旗政策的考察. *Shixue yuekan* 1991, no. 2: 35–40, 7.

Zheng, Bingyu. "The Way of the Idle Men: Leisure and Daily Life of Bannermen in Qing Beijing, 1750–1900." PhD dissertation, Princeton University, 2018.

Zheng Zhenman. *Family Lineage Organization and Social Change in Ming and Qing Fujian*. Trans. Michael Szonyi. Honolulu: University of Hawai'i Press, 2001.

ZHMGSDAZL. Compilation of Archival Material on the History of the Republic of China 中华民国史档案资料汇编. Second Historical Archives of China 中国第二历史档案馆. Nanjing: Jiangsu guji chubanshe, 1991.

Zhu Taiwen 祝太文. "An Investigation and Discussion of the Establishment of Governor and Governor-General Posts in Qing Zhejiang" 清代浙江督抚设置考述. *Wenzhou daxue xuebao (shehui kexue ban)* 30, no. 5 (September 2017): 82–88.

Zito, Angela. *Of Body and Brush: Grand Sacrifice as Text/Performance in Eighteenth-Century China*. Chicago: University of Chicago Press, 1997.

Zou Rong. *The Revolutionary Army: A Chinese Nationalist Tract of 1903*. Trans. John Lust. The Hague: Mouton, 1968.

Index

Acengga, 61–62
administration/governance: frontier migration and, 36–37; in imperial Russia, 28; Qing status system and, 32–33; of Russian service nobility, 153; of samurai, 23, 159, 161–162; status and, 30; Tokugawa status system and, 23–24, 255n21. *See also* administration/governance of banner people
administration/governance of banner people: banner corporals and, 36; banner registers and, 36; company as identifier and, 34–35, 258–259n63, 259n66; company captain and, 35, 259n66; company captains and, 35, 259n66; marriage and, 35, 53, 135–140, *136*, 259n67, 285n45; rural banner people, 45
administrative service: banner people and, 6, 8, 80–81, 97–98, 271nn52–53, 274n6; Ottoman *askeri* elite and, 165–166; Russian service nobility and, 151, 152; samurai and, 157–158;

service elite commonalities and, 171; service elite definitions and, 14. *See also* banner service
adoption: banner status organization and, 47, 262n117, 263n122; Hanjun expulsion and, 182–183, 213–215; Qing status system and, 39, 40–41; Tokugawa status system and, 26
Afaqi Khwājas, 58
Ainu, 156
Aisin Gioro house: abdication, 231; banner ownership, 43–44; dynastic security and, 94–95; feudal authority and, 82–83; imperial brides and, 127; imperial tombs (Malan and Taining), 104; marriages and, 127, 128–129, 282n9, 282n11; meritocracy and, 81. *See also* banner people as slaves of emperor; Nurhaci; Qing administration; *specific emperors*
Alexander II (tsar of Russia), 229
Âli, Mustafa, 164, 169
ambans, 8
Ancestral Temple Party, 231

Anna Karenina (Tolstoy), 222
Argent, Gesine, 257n57
Arigūn, 66, 86, 90, 102–103, 275n20
Articles of Favorable Treatment, 231, 232
askeri elite (Ottoman empire). *See* Ottoman *askeri* elite
Atwood, Christopher, 280n78
Auspicious Incident (1826) (Ottoman Empire), 224

Bai Xinliang, 197
banner financial support, 6–7, 98–117; banner people as slaves of emperor and, 100, 118, 121, 279n67, 280n83; expansion of, 63, 107–108; Green Standard army job creation, 100–107, 108, 116–117, 186, 276n27, 276n33, 277n44; Guangzhou garrison case, 107–117, *115*, 278n63; Hanjun expulsion and, 108, 109–110, 184, 196, 203, 204, 206, 277n37, 277n39, 300n47; Household Selected Soldiers expulsion and, 188–189, 205, 298n30; investment schemes and, 113–115, 120; land grants, 4, 6, 98, 291n59; palace women draft and, 127, 282n5; postexpulsion era, 107–108, 117, 218; salaries, 6, 98–99
banner military service: banner status as reward for, 50, 51, 60–67, 68, 183, 186, 266n35, 267n47, 267n49, 298n35; Chahar banners and, 297n20; livelihood and, 39–40; military skills as status performance, 6, 87, 88–89, 90–91; official nature of, 71–74; postexpulsion era, 72, 268n10; service elite definitions and, 14
banner people: artistic professionals, 58; company as identifier for, 34–35, 258–259n63, 259n66; geography and, 34–35, 45–46, 258–259n63; Imperial Household Department bondservants, 44–45, 262n107; occupation/livelihood and, 38–40; rural vs. urban, 45–46. *See also* administration/governance of banner people; banner people as slaves of emperor; bannerwomen; marriages of banner people
banner people as slaves of emperor, 97, 118–122; banner financial support and, 100, 118, 121, 279n67, 280n83; banner slaves and, 118, 278–279n66; bannerwomen and, 126; imperial hunt and, 121–122, 281n88, 281n92; intimacy and, 118–119; loyalty and, 123, 133–134; palace women draft and, 133–134, 283n18; patrimonialism and, 122–123; protest tradition and, 212; terminology and, 119, 279nn70–71, 279–280nn74–76; Western perceptions of, 289n27. *See also* ruler household relationships
banner privilege, 96–123; administrative representation, 97–98, 274n6; banner slaves and, 96–97, 274n1, 274n3; legal/criminal justice systems and, 37–38, 45–46, 98, 260n78. *See also* banner financial support; banner people as slaves of emperor
banner service, 69–95; administrative service, 6, 8, 80–81, 97–98, 271nn52–53, 274n6; bureaucratization of, 12, 49, 71, 81–84, 123, 263n1, 268n4, 272n62; consolidation era changes, 70–71, 268n2; employment constraints and, 39, 69, 267–268n1; linguistic skills and, 6, 39, 74–78, 87–88, 91, 92,

[326] INDEX

270nn32–33, 270n37; masculinity and, 70, 84, 87; meritocracy and, 14, 81, 84; scientific and mathematical expertise, 79–80; technical expertise, 78–80. *See also* banner military service; banner status performance; linguistic skills

banner slaves: banner people as slaves of emperor and, 118, 278–279n66; banner privilege and, 96–97, 274n1, 274n3; Han commoners as, 5, 264n10, 267n47; number of, 262n118; status organization and, 43, 46–47, 63–64, 263n120. *See also* banner people as slaves of emperor; former slave status

banner status. *See* banner privilege; banner status acquisition; banner status organization; banner status performance

banner status acquisition, 49–68; Cossack soldiers and, 265n30; early Qing familial connections and, 50, 51–54, 263n3, 264n9; foreigners and, 59; loyalty and, 50, 51, 53, 57, 58, 156; as reward for military service, 50, 51, 60–67, 68, 183, 186, 266n35, 267n47, 267n49, 298n35; subject population management and, 41–42, 50–51, 54–59, 67–68, 265nn21–22, 265n25, 265n31

banner status organization, 42–47; adoption and, 47, 262n117, 263n122; banner slaves and, 43, 46–47, 63–64, 263n120; bondservant banner people and, 44–45, 262n107; ethnicity and, 44, 261n104; former slaves and, 46, 47, 63–64, 263n121; Hanjun expulsion and, 198–199, 301n10, 302n11; imperial ownership, 43–44; secondary status, 46–47,

207, 213, 262n117, 263n121, 301n10, 302n11; Upper Three vs. Lower Five Banners, 43–44, 203, 261n107

banner status performance, 69–70, 84–94; bannerwomen and, 84, 124, 126, 130–133, 283n21, 283n24, 284n27; behavior and, 91–92, 275n8; dynastic security and, 93; ethnicity and, 85–86, 89, 92–94, 272n65, 273n94; Green Standard army job creation and, 102; Hanjun expulsion and, 92–93; legal/criminal justice systems and, 275n8; linguistic skills and, 87–88, 91; masculinity and, 84, 87, 93, 124; military skills and, 6, 87, 88–89, 90–91; postexpulsion era, 93

"banner way," 90, 91, 102, 273n93. *See also* banner status performance

bannerwomen, 124–135; chastity cult and, 140–141, 285n51; dynastic reproduction and, 127–128, 133–134; household subordination and, 134–135, 284n29; marriage of, 135, *136*, 137–138, 140–146, *142*, *143*, 285nn45–46, 286n56; status performance and, 84, 124, 126, 130–133, 283n21, 283n24, 284n27. *See also* palace women (*xiunü*) draft

baojia surveillance system, 36, 180, 194

Barkey, Karen, 164, 293n87

Bartlett, Beatrice, 300n50

begs, 58

Beijing, 5, 45, 171

Bello, David, 298n23

bondservant banner people, 44–45, 262n107

boundaries. *See* status mobility

Buhi, 184, 186–187, 188–189, 196–197, 300n50

burakumin, 32, 258n59

bureaucracy. *See* administrative service
bureaucratization: of banner service,
  12, 49, 71, 81–84, 123, 263n1, 268n4,
  272n62; of Ottoman *askeri* elite,
  166; of Russian service nobility,
  151–153, 220; of samurai, 158–159;
  service elite commonalities and,
  173

Campbell, Cameron, 215
Cangšan, 73–74, 78
cangue, 37, 260–261n76
Cao Xueqin, 282n9
Cao Yin, 45, 79
caste, 32
Catherine II (the Great) (tsar of
  Russia), 27, 150, 152, 177, 220–221,
  222, 289n26
Chahar banners: Chahar banner status
  acquisition and, 54–55; ethnicity
  and, 261n104; Household Selected
  Soldiers transfer proposal, 184–186,
  191–192, 197, 205, 297n19–21,
  299n39
Chang, Michael, 122–123
Charter to the Nobility (1785) (Russia),
  221, 222
Chen, Kaijun, 78–79
Cheng Yuanzhang, 103–104, 106,
  275n20
citizenship, 234–235
civil service examinations: abolition
  of, 237; banner status performance
  and, 86, 87; gentry-literati elite and,
  7, 81, 238–239; Hanjun expulsion
  and, 194, 195; loyalty and, 94; subject
  population management and, 67; in
  Tokugawa Japan, 157
Cixi (dowager empress), 135, 230,
  307n16
class, 258n58

clothing. *See* sumptuary/tonsorial
  practice
commoner status, 21, 23;
  administration/governance and,
  36; frontier migration and, 36–37;
  imperial marriage and, 128–129,
  282n11; legal/criminal justice
  systems and, 36; marriages of banner
  people and, 135–140, *136*, 285n45;
  occupation and, 39; palace women
  draft and, 130; Sino-Muslims and,
  138, 284n40; sumptuary/tonsorial
  practice and, 131, 133, 283n24; in
  Tokugawa Japan, 23, 25. *See also*
  Han commoners; Hanjun expulsion;
  Household Selected Soldiers
  expulsion; Qing status system; status
  mobility
compliance capacity, 236
Confino, Michael, 27
Confucianism, 22–23, 254n13, 280n78
consolidation era, 12; banner service
  changes during, 70–71, 268n2; banner
  status acquisition during, 49, 57
coordination capacity, 236, 308n37
criminal justice systems. *See* legal/
  criminal justice systems
Crossley, Pamela, 9–10, 14, 16, 118–119,
  251n25, 251n30, 251–252n32,
  252n40
culture as marker of status, 31, 257n57

Danzaemon, 23
Daoguang emperor, 116, 120
Darling, Linda, 165
devşirme (Ottoman empire), 163–164,
  165
Ding Yizhuang, 136, 139–140
Dittmer, C. G., 233
Donjina, 73, 219
Dorgon, 1, 82

Dream of the Red Chamber, The (Cao Xueqin), 282n9
Du, Yue, 125
Duanfang, 231
dvorianstvo. *See* Russian service nobility
dynastic security, 93, 94–95. *See also* loyalty

economic privileges, 15–16; of Ottoman *askeri* elite, 167–168; of Russian service nobility, 153–154, 288–289n23; of samurai, 159–160, 291n59. *See also* banner financial support
Edo Japan. *See* samurai; Tokugawa status system
Eight Banners. *See* Qing banner system
Ejei Khan, 54, 55
Elliott, Mark, 9, 85, 92, 141, 144, 215, 251n30, 251–252n32, 263n121, 266n35, 272n65, 286n57, 286–287n60, 294–295n3, 295n6
Elman, Benjamin, 237
emperor's household. *See* banner people as slaves of emperor
Encungge, 90
entailed households (*kaihu*), 47, 207, 263n121, 266n35. *See also* secondary-status banner people
estates (*soslovie*) (imperial Russia), 26–30, 149, 257n44, 257n46, 257n49
ethnic hierarchy within banner system, 44, 286n57; chastity awards and, 144; Hanjun expulsion and, 92–93, 108, 176, 179, 196; Hanjun Green Standard army job creation and, 100, 101; marriages of banner people and, 126, 130, 135, 140, 142, 143–146, 287n64; status performance and, 92–93
ethnicity: banner financial support and, 101, 105, 108, 116, 280n83; banner service and, 70; banner status organization and, 44, 261n104; banner status performance and, 85–86, 89, 92–94, 272n65, 273n94; as basis of Hanjun expulsion, 183, 196, 197–198, 206, 208, 210; Household Selected Soldiers expulsion and, 187, 191, 298n34; imperial hunt and, 121–122, 281n88, 281n92; marriage and, 285n43; marriages of banner people and, 139, 141–143, *142*, *143*, 285n46, 286n54, 286n56, 286–287nn58–60; masculinity and, 87; Ottoman *askeri* elite and, 163–164, 292n71; persistence across system change, 32, 258n58; physical spaces and, 198, 300–301n57; Qianlong emperor and, 197–198, 206, 301n58; in Qing banner system population, 4–5, 43, 217, 250n12, 303–304nn34–36; Qing importance of, 21; scholarly emphasis on, 10, 173, 251n30, 251–252n32; service elite commonalities and, 15, 173; vs. status, 10, 20, 32, 41, 253n4, 261n95; status as reward for military service and, 63, 267n47, 298n35; sumptuary/tonsorial practice and, 130–131, 133, 283n21, 284n27. *See also* ethnic hierarchy within banner system
European incursions: banner linguistic skills and, 70, 77–78, 270n37; banner military service and, 72; technical expertise and, 78, 80
examinations: translation, 39, 75, 77, 98. *See also* civil service examinations
expulsion of banner people. *See* Hanjun expulsion; Household Selected Soldiers expulsion

Fan Yubin, 62
Feng Guozhang, 233

feudalism: banner system origins and, 70–71, 81–83; bureaucratization of service elites as departure from, 123, 159, 162, 166, 171–172, 239; Ottoman *askeri* elite and, 166; service elite commonalities and, 171; Tokugawa Japan and, 22, 158, 159, 162. *See also* hereditary status

Finkel, Caroline, 293n86

foot-binding, 131, 133, 283n21, 284n27

former slave status: adoption and, 47, 262n117; banner status as reward for military service and, 60–67, 68, 183, 186, 266n35, 267n47, 267n49, 298n35; banner status organization and, 46, 47, 63–64, 263n121; Hanjun expulsion and, 207; Household Selected Soldiers expulsion and, 191, 299n38; secondary status and, 46; status mobility and, 47, 263n20

freed slaves. *See* former slave status

Fuk'anggan, 65

Fuzhou garrison: banner status performance and, 85, 86, 88–89; ethnic populations at, 6, 108; Green Standard army banner job creation and, 101, 102, 104, 107; Hanjun expulsion and, 177, 183, 193–196, 201, 205, 208, 210–213, *216*, 284n34, 296n12, 299n43, 300n45, 301n10, 301n59; subject population management and, 56, 57

Gao Bin, 96–97, 98, 100, 274n1

Geng Jingzhong, 55–56, 57, 264n15, 265n22

Geng Zhongming, 55, 264n15

gentry-literati elite, 7, 81, 238–239

geography: banner people and, 34–35, 45–46, 258–259n63; Qing status system and, 34, 258–259n63; status and, 31

ginseng picking, 79

Ginšun, 73

governance. *See* administration/governance

Green Standard army: commoner status and, 60, 63, 80, 90; Hanjun expulsion and, 175, 193–195, 199, 209, 215–217, *216*, 300n45, 302n17; Hanjun job creation in, 100–107, 108, 116–117, 186, 276n27, 276n33, 277n44; hereditary status and, 299n44; Household Selected Soldiers transfer, 187–191, 195, 300n45; military skills and, 87; subject population management and, 59

Guangxu emperor, 230

Guangzhou garrison: abandonment of Hanjun expulsion and, 218, 304n38; adoption and, 213–215; banner financial support and, 107–117, *115*, 277n37, 277n39, 277n44, 278n63; banner status performance and, 85–86; ethnic hierarchy in, 144–146; ethnic populations at, 72, 277n37; Green Standard army banner job creation and, 102, 104, 107; Hanjun expulsion and, 109–110, 175, 195, 196, 197, 208, 210, 211, *216*, 277n37, 277n39, 277n44, 284n34; investment schemes and, 120; military service and, 73–74; official resistance to Hanjun expulsion at, 200, 201–207, 301n8; subject population management and, 56, 57

hairstyle. *See* sumptuary/tonsorial practice

Hall, John W., 22

Han commoners: as banner slaves, 5, 264n10, 267n47; frontier migration of, 36; Green Standard army banner job creation and, 100–101; number of, 21; occupation and, 39, 260n84

Hangzhou garrison: banner status as reward for military service and, 65–67, 86; banner status performance and, 86, 90; Green Standard army banner job creation and, 102–104, 106; Hanjun expulsion and, 195, 196, 207, 208, *216*, 284n34; imperial hunt and, 122; military service and, 72–73

Hanjun banner people: banner military service and, 72, 250n8; banner people as slaves of emperor and, 279n71, 279n74; banner status organization and, 44; banner status performance and, 85–86, 88–90, 92–93; early Qing familial connections and, 53; garrisons and, 6; Green Standard army job creation, 100–107, 108, 116–117, 186, 276n27, 276n33, 277n44; Han ethnicity and, 9, 179–180, 251n25; Hanjun origins, 4–5, 250n8, 296nn10–11; as imperial brides, 128; imperial hunt and, 122, 281n88, 281n92; linguistic skills and, 75, 88; loyalty as suspect, 9–10; marriage and, 137, 139–140; number of, 10, 12–13; palace women draft and, 129–130, 283n17; Revolt of the Three Feudatories and, 56, 57. *See also* banner financial support; ethnic hierarchy within banner system; ethnicity; Hanjun expulsion

Hanjun expulsion, 9, 12, 175–183, 192–199; abandonment of, 217–219, 303–304n34, 304n35, 304n38; adoption and, 182–183, 213–215; alternate explanations for, 218, 304n40; banner financial support and, 108, 109–110, 184, 196, 203, 204, 206, 277n37, 277n39, 300n47; banner status organization and, 198–199, 301n10, 302n11; commoner customs and, 193, 299n41; competing ideological priorities and, 177; dynastic precedent and, 175–176, 192–193, 294n2; ethnic hierarchy within banner system and, 92–93, 108, 176, 179, 196; ethnicity as basis of, 183, 196, 197–198, 206, 208, 210; failure of, 200; final wave of, 209–210, 302n17; former slave status and, 207; Green Standard army transfer and, 175, 193–195, 199, 209, 215–217, *216*, 300n45, 302n17; Hanjun responses to, 201, 210–217, *216*, 303n31; Household Selected Soldiers expulsion as precedent for, 183, 195, 205–206, 209; imperial edict on, 175, 192–193, 294n1, 296nn10–12; livelihood and, 39, 178–179, 193, 260n84, 295nn7–8; Manchus as beneficiaries of, 12, 176, 193, 209–210, 300n47; marriage and, 137, 143–144, 194, 284n34, 299n43; military service and, 65, 208; official resistance to, 197, 200, 201–207, 301n8; precursor edict (1742), 178, 179–183, 203, 294–295nn3–4; preservation of service elite framework and, 198–199; second wave of, 207–209; secondary-status banner people and, 207, 213, 301n10, 302n11; status performance and, 92–93; Sun Jiagan memorials and, 178–179, 180, 295n4, 295nn6–8; Zunghar campaigns and, 208, 220

Hellie, Richard, 288n8

hereditary banner status: adoption and, 41; banner service and, 70–71, 268n2; banner status as reward for military service and, 67; familial connections and, 51; feudal authority and, 82–83, 271n58; garrison assignments and, 46; Hanjun expulsion and, 174, 175–176, 182; loyalty and, 175; postexpulsion era, 218

hereditary status: definitions of status and, 31–32; Green Standard army and, 299n44; in imperial Russia, 27; modern citizenship and, 234–235; Ottoman *askeri* elite and, 163; of Russian service nobility, 149, 153; of samurai, 156, 157, 162; servile/mean status, 20–21; state capacity and, 236; in Tokugawa Japan, 23

Hešen, 20, 42, 50

Hong Taiji: banner military service and, 72; banner origins and, 1, 4, 67, 263n1; dynastic security and, 93; familial connections and, 52; succession after death of, 82; sumptuary/tonsorial practice and, 132

Hongwu emperor (Ming), 283n18

Hooge, 82

Hosoya Yoshio, 266n35

Household Selected Soldiers: banner status as reward for military service and, 60–64, 186, 267n47, 298n35. *See also* Household Selected Soldiers expulsion

Household Selected Soldiers expulsion, 65, 183–192; banner financial support and, 188–189, 205, 298n30; Buhi memorial, 184, 186–187, 188–189, 196–197, 300n50; Chahar banner transfer proposal, 184–186, 191–192, 197, 205, 297n19–21, 299n39; ethnicity and, 187, 191, 298n34; former slave status and, 191, 299n38; Green Standard army transfer, 187–191, 195, 300n45; as policy innovation, 183, 191–192, 197; as precedent for Hanjun expulsion, 183, 195, 205–206, 209

households: banner status organization and, 47, 182; entailed, 47, 207, 263n121, 266n35; Hanjun expulsion and, 182; Qing status system and, 33–34, 47; standard vs. detached, 62, 266–267n43; Tokugawa status system and, 26, 256n32

Howell, David, 25, 29, 256n31

Huang, Pei, 71, 263n1

Hughes, Lindsey, 151

Hui (Sino-Muslims), 138–139, 284n40

Hundred Days' Reform (1898), 230, 307n16

Hung, Ho-fung, 212

ideological challenges to service elite framework, 219–226; Ottoman *askeri* elite and, 224–226; Russian service nobility and, 177, 219–222, 305n43; samurai and, 222–224, 306n58, 306n60. *See also* Hanjun expulsion

Imperial Household Department: banner service and, 268n2; bondservant banner people in, 44–45, 262n107; linguistic skills and, 76, 270n32; palace maid draft, 127; Qianlong emperor and, 58; technical expertise and, 78–79, 80

imperial hunt, 121–122, 281n88, 281n92

Imperial Porcelain Manufactory, 78–79

imperial Russia: Duma, 229, 237; emancipation of the serfs (1861), 229; status in, 26–30, 39, 257n44,

257n46, 257n49, 257n57. *See also* Russian-Qing relations; Russian service nobility
India, 15
Inner Asian territories: banner administrative service in, 6, 80–81, 271nn52–53; banner military service and, 71; imperial hunt and, 121; Lifan yuan and, 54, 58, 75, 76, 80, 92, 264n13, 270n32; linguistic skills and, 74. *See also* Mongols; subject population management
Iran, 15
Ivan IV (the Terrible) (tsar of Russia), 155

janissaries: economic privileges of, 167–168; elimination of, 177, 224–225; origins of, 16; recruitment of, 162–164, 165; uprisings of, 169, 237; urbanization and, 171. *See also* Ottoman *askeri* elite
Japan: Meiji Restoration, 31, 32, 159, 227–229, 237. *See also* samurai; Tokugawa status system
jasagh system, 37, 38, 54, 239–240
Jesuits, 79, 80
Jiaqing emperor: banner financial support and, 111–112; banner status acquisition and, 42; Empress Xiaoshurui and, 282n6; palace women draft and, 129; subject population management and, 59; sumptuary/tonsorial practice and, 131–132
Jinchuan campaigns, 65
Jingkou garrison: banner status performance and, 91, 92–93; Green Standard army banner job creation and, 102, 107; Hanjun expulsion and, 175, 195, 196, 207, 208, *216*; military service and, 72

Jirgalang, 82
jus sanguinis, 234

Kangxi emperor: banner bureaucratization and, 83; banner status organization and, 43; Green Standard army banner job creation and, 101; Imperial Household Department and, 45; subject population management and, 57, 265n25
Kargišan, 175, 193–195, 202, 294n1
Katsu Kaishū, 29, 159
Katsu Kokichi, 29, 159
Khalka Mongols, 55
Kong Youde, 56, 265n25
Kornilov, L. G., 230
Križanić, Juraj, 154
Kuhn, Philip, 197
Kunt, I. Metin, 292n71

land grants: banner people and, 4, 6, 98, 291n59; samurai and, 160, 291n59
language. *See* linguistic skills
Lao She, 99, 230
Laws for the Military Houses (*buke shohattō*) (Japan), 161
Lê Duy Kỳ, 59
Lee, James, 215
legal/criminal justice systems: banner privilege and, 37–38, 45–46, 98, 260n78; banner status organization and, 45–46; banner status performance and, 275n8; cangue, 37, 260–261n76; commoner status and, 36
Leibold, James, 295n4
Li Shiyao, 204, 206, 218, 301n8
Li Yanguang, 265n21
Li Yuanhong, 231
Lifan yuan, 54, 58, 75, 76, 80, 92, 264n13, 270n32

lijia system, 190, 298n32

Lin family case, 19–20, 32, 33–34, 40

Lin Shuangwen rebellion (1787–88), 65, 73, 110

linguistic skills, 6, 74–78; banner employment constraints and, 39; banner status performance and, 87–88, 91, 92; education for, 75, 76–77, 270n37; Lifan yuan and, 76, 92, 270n32; Russian-Qing relations and, 76–77, 270n33

livelihood: Hanjun expulsion and, 39, 178–179, 193, 260n84, 295nn7–8; vs. occupation, 25, 29, 39–40, 255n29. *See also* banner financial support

local elites, 7, 238–240

Lower Five Banners, 43–44, 203, 261n107

loyalty: banner people as slaves of emperor and, 123, 133–134; banner status acquisition and, 50, 51, 53, 57, 58, 156; Hanjun banner people as suspect, 9–10; Hanjun expulsion and, 194; hereditary banner status and, 175; imperial hunt and, 121; Manchus and, 8–9; Ottoman *askeri* elite and, 164, 168; Ottoman imperial harem and, 170; palace women draft and, 133–134; service elite population size and, 236–237; state capacity and, 236; subject population management and, 57, 58; sumptuary/tonsorial practice and, 132

Lu, Weijing, 285n51

Lu Zhijun, 252n35, 275n8

Ma Guangyuan, 5

Mahmud II (Ottoman sultan), 177, 225, 226

Manchu banner people: banner military service and, 72; banner people as slaves of emperor and, 279–280n75; banner status organization and, 44; as beneficiaries of Hanjun expulsion, 12, 176, 193, 209–210, 300n47; financial support of, 108–109, 110, 111, 115–116, *115*, 277n39; Green Standard army and, 276n33; Hanjun expulsion and, 109; linguistic skills and, 75. *See also* ethnic hierarchy within banner system

Manchu language. *See* linguistic skills

Manchu way, 85, 272n65. *See also* banner status performance

Manchu Way, The (Elliott), 85

Manchus: decrease in population, 264n10; ethnicity and, 94; loyalty and, 8–9; "new Manchu" groups, 20, 253n4; physical spaces and, 198, 300–301n57; as synonymous with banner people, 5, 10. *See also* ethnic hierarchy within banner system; ethnicity

"Manifesto on the Liberty of the Nobility" (Peter III), 219–220, 221, 305n43

mapmaking, 80

marriage: adopted-in son-in-laws and, 138, 285n41; ethnicity and, 285n43; female hypergamy, 140; female subordination and, 134, 284n29; Hanjun expulsion and, 137, 143–144, 194, 284n34, 299n43; imperial, 127, 128–129, 282n9, 282n11; Qing status system and, 40; samurai and, 161–162, 224, 291n68; in Tokugawa Japan, 26. *See also* marriages of banner people

marriages of banner people, 135–146; administration/governance of, 35, 53, 135–140, *136*, 259n67, 285n45; ethnic hierarchy within banner system and, 126, 130, 135, 140, 142, 143–146, 287n64; ethnicity and, 139, 141–143, *142*, *143*, 285n46, 286–287n54, 56, 58–60; Hanjun expulsion and, 137, 143–144, 284n34; within banners, 140–146, *142*, *143*, 286n56

Martin, Russell E., 289n27

masculinity: banner service and, 70, 84, 87; banner status performance and, 84, 87, 93, 124; dynastic security and, 93; Ottoman *askeri* elite and, 167; Russian service nobility and, 153; samurai and, 159, 291n57; service elite commonalities and, 172

mature era, 12, 49

Meehan-Waters, Brenda, 14, 252n36

Mehmed II (the Conqueror) (Ottoman sultan), 166

Meiji Restoration (Japan), 31, 32, 159, 227–229, 237

mercantilism, 177, 222–223, 305n56

meritocracy: banner service and, 14, 81, 84; Ottoman *askeri* elite and, 166, 293n87; Russian service nobility and, 153, 220; samurai and, 158–159

mibun. *See* Tokugawa status system

military service: Ottoman *askeri* elite and, 165, 168; Republic of China and, 233; Russian service nobility and, 151, 220, 288n9; service elite definitions and, 14; urbanization and, 172. *See also* banner military service

Ming period: households during, 33; *lijia* system, 298n32; occupations during, 39; palace women draft during, 130, 283n18; Single Whip Reform, 260n85; slavery during, 279n67

Mizubayashi Takeshi, 160

Mōnai Giō, 223

Mongol banner people: banner military service and, 72; banner status organization and, 44, 261n104; linguistic skills and, 75–76, 92; Mongol way and, 92. *See also* Chahar banners

Mongols, 16; administration/governance and, 37; as imperial brides, 127; *jasagh* system and, 37, 38, 54, 239–240; legal/criminal justice systems and, 38; Lifan yuan and, 75, 76, 92, 264n13; occupation and, 295n7, 298n23; Qing status system and, 260n63. *See also* Chahar banners; Mongol banner people

Montesquieu, 221, 222

Mughal India, 15

national identity, 229

Necin, 184–185, 186, 188, 191–192, 205, 297n21, 299n39

New Qing History, 249n3, 251–252n32

Nguyễn Quang Bình, 59

Nozoki Yoshimasa, 223

Nurhaci, 1, 3–4, 54, 67, 81–82

occupation: in imperial Russia, 29; vs. livelihood, 25, 29, 39–40, 255n29; Qing status system and, 38–40, 260n84; status and, 30; Tokugawa status system and, 24–25, 223, 255nn28–29. *See also* livelihood

Offord, Derek, 257n57

Oirat Mongols, 55, 76–77

Onuma Takahiro, 58

Opium Wars, 73, 268n10

Orochen, 253n5

Ortai, 280n76

Osman II (Ottoman sultan), 169

Ottoman *askeri* elite, 13, 15, 162–170, 252n40; administrative service and, 165–166; bureaucratization of, 166; economic privileges of, 167–168; entry as reward for service, 164–165; ethnic heterogeneity and, 163–164, 292n71; ideological challenges and, 224–226; janissary elimination, 177, 224–225; janissary uprisings, 169, 237; masculinity and, 167; meritocracy in, 166, 293n87; military service and, 165, 168; non-service elite political authorities and, 240; origins of, 16, 166, 293n86; ruler household relationships and, 162–163, 168–169; status performance and, 166–167; *timar*-holders, 163, 164, 165–166, 168, 292n75; urbanization and, 171

outcaste status: persistence across system change, 32, 258n59; in Tokugawa Japan, 23, 24–25, 32, 255n23, 256n31

palace women (*xiunü*) draft, 127–130, 133–135; banner people as slaves of emperor and, 133–134, 283n18; compensation and, 127, 282n5; eligibility for, 129, 283–284n16; Hanjun bannerwomen and, 129–130, 283n17; imperial brides and, 127, 128, 282n9; importance of, 125; marriage governance and, 259n67; terms for, 127, 281n4; under Ming empire, 130, 283n18

patrimonialism, 122–123, 236

pearl harvesting, 79

Peirce, Leslie, 170

Perdue, Peter, 14–15

Perry, Matthew, 227

Peter I (the Great) (tsar of Russia), 27, 149, 151, 152, 153, 155, 220, 288n8

Peter III (tsar of Russia), 177, 219, 220, 221

Poe, Marshall, 154

postexpulsion era, 12–13; banner financial support during, 107–108, 117, 218; banner military service during, 72, 268n10; banner status as reward for military service during, 65; banner status performance during, 93

postnomadic world, 16

Qianlong emperor: banner financial support and, 111, 121, 280n83; banner people as slaves of emperor and, 119–120, 121; banner slaves and, 96–97, 274n1; banner status as reward for military service and, 63, 65; banner status performance and, 85–86, 88; dynastic precedents and, 294n2; Empress Xiaoyichun and, 282n6; ethnicity and, 197–198, 206, 301n58; Hanjun expulsion edict (1754), 175, 192–193, 294n1, 296nn10–12; Hanjun expulsion implementation and, 176, 195, 196, 202, 203–205; Hanjun expulsion precursor edict (1742), 178, 179–183, 203, 294–295nn3–4; Hešen and, 20, 42, 50; Household Selected Soldiers expulsion and, 183, 186, 197, 300n50; Imperial Household Department and, 58; Manchus as beneficiaries of Hanjun expulsion and, 12, 176; palace women draft and, 133–134; subject population management and, 59; sumptuary/tonsorial practice and, 132

Qing administration: *baojia* surveillance system, 36, 180, 194; Board of Revenue, 19, 253n1; governors-general, 275n20; Lifan yuan, 54, 58, 75, 76, 80, 92, 264n13, 270n32; *lijia* system, 190, 298n32; mapmaking and, 80; reforms, 230, 237–238, 307n16; Six Boards, 8, 251n8. *See also* administration/governance of banner people; civil service examinations

Qing banner system: chronology of, 11–13; as conquest elite, 14; elimination of, 230–233; ethnic composition of, 4–5, 43, 217, 250n12, 303–304nn34–36; garrison locations, 2, 5–6, 171; importance of, 1, 3, 7–8, 241; nonbanner elites and, 238–241; origins of, 3–4; scholarly treatment of, 3, 249n2; urbanization and, 171. *See also entries beginning with* banner

Qing conquest of China (1644), 5–6

Qing imperial tombs (Malan and Taining), 104

Qing status system, 32–42; administration/governance and, 32–33; adoption and, 39, 40–41; banner status acquisition and, 41–42; geography and, 34, 258–259n63; household as basis of, 33–34, 47; occupation and, 38–40, 260n84; political system dependency, 41; status mobility and, 20, 39, 40–41. *See also* commoner status; status mobility

Qu Cheng, 299n38

Ravina, Mark, 224
Republic of China, 231–233, 235

Retribution-Bringing Soldiers, 61
Revolt of the Three Feudatories (1673–81), 55–57, 71–72, 264n15, 265nn21–22, 265n25, 265n31
Rhoads, Edward, 10, 12
Rjéoutski, Vladislav, 257n57
Roberts, Luke, 222, 224
Roth-Li, Gertraude, 82
ruler household relationships: Ottoman *askeri* elite and, 162–163, 168–169; Russian service nobility and, 154, 289n26; samurai and, 160–161; service elite commonalities and, 148, 172. *See also* banner people as slaves of emperor
Russia. *See* imperial Russia; Russian service nobility
Russian-Qing relations: banner military service and, 72; Lifan yuan and, 54; linguistic skills and, 76–77, 270n33
Russian Revolution (1917), 31, 229, 230
Russian service nobility (*dvorianstvo*), 13, 149–155; administrative service and, 151, 152; bureaucratization of, 151–153, 220; economic privileges of, 153–154, 288–289n23; elimination of, 229–230; emancipation of the nobility and, 177, 219–222, 305n43; meritocracy and, 153, 220; military service and, 151, 220, 288n9; non-service elite political authorities and, 240; origins of, 16, 151, 288n8; as slaves of tsar, 154, 289n26; status performance and, 153, 220; subject population management and, 149–150; urbanization and, 172; women and, 154–155, 289n27
Ryukyuans, 156, 289n31

INDEX [337]

Safavid Iran, 15
Saigō Takamori, 228
salt administrators, 79
samurai (Tokugawa Japan), 13, 156–162; administration/governance of, 23, 24–25, 159, 161–162; administrative service and, 157–158; bureaucratization of, 158–159; economic privileges of, 159–160, 291n59; hereditary status of, 156, 157, 162; ideological challenges and, 222–224, 306n58, 306n60; marriage and, 161–162, 224, 291n68; masculinity and, 159, 291n57; Meiji Restoration and, 227–229, 237; mercantilism and, 177, 222–223, 305n56; meritocracy and, 158–159; origins of, 16, 156, 158; ruler household relationships and, 160–161; status acquisition and, 156–157; status organization and, 29; status performance and, 159, 291n57; subject population management and, 156, 289n31; urbanization and, 171–172; women and, 161, 291n67
Satsuma Rebellion (1877) (Japan), 228–229
Schillinger, Nicolas, 87
secondary-status banner people, 46–47, 207, 213, 262n117, 263n121, 301n10, 302n11
Selim III (Ottoman sultan), 225
Sen, Sudipta, 15
service elite elimination: banner system, 230–233; janissaries, 177, 224–225; Russian service nobility, 229–230; samurai, 227–229, 237
service elites: comparative framework for, 13, 14–15, 147–149, 170–173, 177, 252n40; definitions of, 14, 252nn35–36; elimination of, 177; emergence of, 16–17; entry as reward for service, 60–67, 68, 164–165, 171, 183, 186, 266n35, 267n47, 267n49, 298n35; ideological challenges and, 219–226; importance of, 235–238; non-service elite political authorities and, 238–241; patrimonialism and, 122–123; political system dependency, 233–234; population sizes, 236–237; state capacity and, 236, 308n37; terminology, 13–14; urbanization and, 171–172; value of, 14. *See also* Ottoman *askeri* elite; Russian service nobility; samurai
Seven Years' War, 220
sexual misbehavior, 23–24, 255n21
Shang Kexi, 55, 264n15, 265n25
Shang Zhixin, 55–56, 57, 264n15, 265n22, 265n25
Shao Dan, 234–235
Shi Lang, 41, 50
Shi Tingzhu, 5
Shunzhi emperor, 82
Sinicization, 11
Sinju, 175, 193–195, 202, 210–213
Sino-Muslims, 138–139, 284n40
Sitku, 85–86, 197, 201–206, 210, 211, 301n8
Six Boards, 8, 251n8
slavery metaphors. *See* banner people as slaves of emperor; ruler household relationships
slaves. *See* banner slaves; former slave status
Smith, Alison, 29
soslovie (estates) (imperial Russia), 26–30, 149, 257n44, 257n46, 257n49
Spence, Jonathan, 79
status: administration/governance and, 30; vs. caste, 32; characteristics of, 30–31; vs. class, 31–32; Confucian

four-class paradigm, 22–23, 254n13; culture as marker of, 31, 257n57; definitions of, 11; vs. ethnicity, 10, 20, 32, 41, 253n4, 261n95; geography and, 31; ideological categories, 20–21; in imperial Russia, 26–30, 39, 257n44, 257n46, 257n49, 257n57; as irrelevant to Ottoman *askeri* elite, 163; legal nature of, 30, 31; occupation and, 30; political system dependency, 31, 32, 41. *See also* Qing status system; Tokugawa status system

status mobility: banner slaves and, 47; banner status acquisition and, 68; banner status organization and, 47; characteristics of status and, 31; former slaves and, 47, 263n20; Qing status system and, 20, 39, 40–41; Tokugawa status system and, 23, 26, 27

status performance: Ottoman *askeri* elite and, 166–167; Russian service nobility and, 153, 220; samurai and, 159, 291n57. *See also* banner status performance

subject population management: banner system and, 41–42, 50–51, 54–59, 67–68, 265nn21–22, 265n25, 265n31; Ottoman *askeri* elite and, 162–164, 292n71; Russian service nobility and, 149–150; samurai and, 156, 289n31

Suiyuan garrison: ethnic populations at, 298n34; Hanjun expulsion and, 207, 208, 209, 215–216, *216*, 217; Household Selected Soldiers placement at, 62, 63, 184. *See also* Household Selected Soldiers expulsion

Süleyman I (Ottoman sultan), 163

sumptuary/tonsorial practice: bannerwomen and, 130–133, 283n21, 283n24, 284n27; Russian service nobility and, 153; Tokugawa status system and, 24, 255n23

Sun Jiagan, 178–179, 180, 295n4, 295nn6–8

Sun Jing, 218

Sun Shiyi, 42, 49–50

Sweden, 152, 155

Table of Ranks (Russia), 149, 151

Taiping Rebellion, 72–73, 268n10

Taiwan: Lin Shuangwen rebellion (1787–88), 65, 73, 110; Qing conquest of, 41–42, 50

Tarim Basin Muslims, 58

Three Feudatories, Revolt of (1673–81), 55–57, 71–72, 264n15, 265nn21–22, 265n25, 265n31

timar-holders (Ottoman empire), 163, 164, 165–166, 168, 292n75

Tokugawa Ieyasu (shogun of Japan), 156, 171

Tokugawa status system (*mibun*) (Japan), 22–26; administration/governance and, 23–24, 255n21; caste and, 32; Confucian four-class paradigm and, 22–23, 254n13; households and, 26, 256n32; imperial Russian status system and, 28–29; legal nature of, 30; occupation and, 24–25, 30, 255nn28–29; outcaste status in, 23, 24–25, 32, 255n23, 256n31; status mobility and, 23, 26, 27, 254n16; sumptuary/tonsorial practice and, 24, 255n23

Tolstoy, Leo, 221, 222

Tongwen Guan, 77–78, 270n37

translation services. *See* linguistic skills

Tusi (native officials), 20, 138–139, 238–241

Ulozhenie (Russia), 153
Upper Three Banners, 43–44, 203, 261n107

Vietnam, 59

Wang, Shuo, 125
War and Peace (Tolstoy), 221
Warashina Ryūen, 223
Weber, Max, 22, 123, 171, 236
women: Ottoman *askeri* elite and, 163; Ottoman imperial harem and, 169–170; Russian service nobility and, 154–155, 289n27; in samurai system, 161, 291n67; service elite commonalities and, 172; in Tokugawa Japan, 24, 254n16. *See also* bannerwomen; palace women (*xiunü*) draft
World War I, 229, 237
Wu Sangui, 55–56, 57, 264n15
Wuchang Uprising, 237

Xi'an garrison: administration/governance of banner people and, 34, 258n63; Articles of Favorable Treatment and, 231–232; ethnic populations at, 6; Hanjun expulsion and, 175, 209–210, 301n59, 302n17
Xianfeng emperor, 129
Xiaoshurui (empress), 282n6
Xiaoyichun (empress), 282n6
Xinhai Revolution (1911), 231
Xinjiang: conquest of, 58, 72, 208–209; exile to, 213–214, 279n67; nineteenth century reconquest of, 73, 271n52; undesirability of service in, 301n8
xiunü selection. *See* palace women (*xiunü*) draft

Yongzheng emperor: banner bureaucratization and, 83, 263n1; banner status as reward for military service and, 60–61, 62, 63, 183; banner status organization and, 43; banner status performance and, 88–89; ethnicity and, 198; Green Standard army banner job creation and, 101–102; hereditary status and, 20; linguistic skills and, 75, 88
Youwei garrison, Hanjun expulsion and, 207, 208, 209, *216*, 217
Yuan Shikai, 232, 233
Yue Zhongqi, 266n36

Zaifeng, 119
Zaixun, 119
Zeng Guofan, 73
Zeng Jing case, 198
Zhang Tingyu, 105
Zhao Bingzhong, 197
Zheng Keshuang, 41–42
Zhun-tai, 88, 139–140, 285n46
Zou Rong, 8
Zunghar campaigns: banner importance and, 1; banner status as reward for military service and, 61–62, 63, 64, 266n36, 267n49; Chahar banners and, 55; Hanjun expulsion and, 208, 220; subject population management and, 58
Zuo Zongtang, 73

GPSR Authorized Representative: Easy Access System Europe, Mustamäe tee 50, 10621 Tallinn, Estonia, gpsr.requests@easproject.com

www.ingramcontent.com/pod-product-compliance
Lightning Source LLC
Chambersburg PA
CBHW032334300426
44109CB00041B/799